$52.00

Juvenile-Onset Schizophrenia

Juvenile-Onset Schizophrenia

Assessment, Neurobiology, and Treatment

Edited by

Robert L. Findling, M.D.
Professor of Psychiatry and Pediatrics
Case Western Reserve University
Cleveland, Ohio

and

S. Charles Schulz, M.D.
Professor and Chair
Department of Psychiatry
University of Minnesota Medical School
Minneapolis, Minnesota

The Johns Hopkins University Press
Baltimore and London

The Johns Hopkins University Press
2715 North Charles Street
Baltimore, Maryland 21218-4363
www.press.jhu.edu

Library of Congress Cataloging-in-Publication Data

Juvenile-onset schizophrenia : assessment, neurobiology, and
treatment / edited by Robert L. Findling and S. Charles Schulz.
    p. ; cm.
  Includes bibliographical references and index.
  ISBN 0-8018-8018-1 (hardcover : alk. paper)
  1. Schizophrenia in children.   2. Schizophrenia in
adolescence.   3. Psychoses in children.   4. Psychoses in
adolescence.
    [DNLM: 1. Schizophrenia—physiopathology—Adolescent.
2. Schizophrenia—physiopathology—Child.   3. Schizophrenia
—therapy—Adolescent.   4. Schizophrenia—therapy—Child.
WM 203 J97 2004]   I. Findling, Robert L.   II. Schulz, S.
Charles.
    RJ506.S3J88 2004
    618.92′898—dc22   2004008934

A catalog record for this book is available from the British
Library.

Contents

Contributors

G. Paul Amminger, M.D., Klinik für Neuropsychiatrie des Kindes und Jugendalters, Vienna University, Vienna, Austria

Annie M. Bollini, M.A., Ph.D. candidate, Department of Psychology, Emory University, Atlanta, Georgia

Evelyn J. Bromet, Ph.D., professor, Division of Child and Adolescent Psychiatry, Department of Psychiatry and Behavioral Science, State University of New York at Stony Brook, Stony Brook, New York

Gabrielle A. Carlson, M.D., professor, Division of Child and Adolescent Psychiatry, Department of Psychiatry and Behavioral Science, State University of New York at Stony Brook, Stony Brook, New York

Shermeil Dass, M.D., psychiatrist, County of Santa Cruz, California

Elizabeth DeOreo, M.D., Medical House Staff, Emory University, School of Medicine, Atlanta, Georgia

Shona Francey, Ph.D., PACE Clinic, ORYGEN Research Centre, Parkville, Victoria, Australia

Sophia Frangou, M.D., Section of Neurobiology of Psychosis, Institute of Psychiatry, King's College, University of London, London, England

Nitin Gogtay, M.D., staff clinician, Child Psychiatry Branch, National Institute of Mental Health, Bethesda, Maryland

Michael Hadjulis, M.D., Section of Neurobiology of Psychosis, Institute of Psychiatry, King's College, University of London, London, England

James M. Harle, M.D., private practice, Bellingham, Washington

Karen M. Hochman, M.D., assistant professor, Department of Psychiatry and Behavioral Sciences, School of Medicine, Emory University, Atlanta, Georgia

Matcheri S. Keshavan, M.D., professor of psychiatry, Western Psychiatric Institute and Clinic, University of Pittsburgh, Pittsburgh, Pennsylvania

Lisa P. Kestler, M.A., Ph.D. candidate, Department of Psychology, Emory University, Atlanta, Georgia

Michael A. Kisley, Ph.D., assistant professor, Department of Psychology, University of Colorado, Colorado Springs, Colorado

Johanna Lamm, Psy.D., private practice, Brooklyn Center, Minnesota

Steven Leicester, M.Psych., research fellow, ORYGEN Youth Health, Parkville, Victoria, Australia

Jon M. McClellan, M.D., associate professor, Department of Psychiatry and Behavioral Sciences, University of Washington School of Medicine, Seattle, Washington

Patrick D. McGorry, M.D., Ph.D., professor, Department of Psychiatry, University of Melbourne, Parkville, Victoria, Australia

Nora K. McNamara, M.D., senior instructor, Division of Child and Adolescent Psychiatry, Case Western Reserve University, Cleveland, Ohio

Robin M. Murray, M.D., Institute of Psychiatry, King's College, University of London, London, England

Bushra Naz, M.D., Division of Child and Adolescent Psychiatry, Department of Psychiatry and Behavioral Science, State University of New York at Stony Brook, Stony Brook, New York

Charles A. Nelson, M.D., Distinguished McKnight University Professor of Child Psychology, Division of Child and Adolescent Psychiatry, Department of Psychiatry, University of Minnesota, Minneapolis, Minnesota

Judith L. Rapoport, M.D., chief, Child Psychiatry Branch, National Institute of Mental Health, Bethesda, Maryland

Randal G. Ross, M.D., associate professor, Department of Psychiatry, University of Colorado Health Sciences Center, Denver, Colorado

Linmarie Sikich, M.D., associate professor, Division of Child and Adolescent Psychiatry, Department of Psychiatry, University of North Carolina, Chapel Hill, North Carolina

Jason R. Tregellas, Ph.D., postdoctoral fellow, Department of Psychiatry, University of Colorado Health Sciences Center, Denver, Colorado

Elaine F. Walker, Ph.D., Samuel Candler Dobbs Professor and chair, Department of Psychology, Emory University, Atlanta, Georgia

Tonya White, M.D., assistant professor, Division of Child and Adolescent Psychiatry, Department of Psychiatry, University of Minnesota, Minneapolis, Minnesota

Jeffrey R. Wozniak, Ph.D., assistant professor, Division of Child and Adolescent Psychiatry, Department of Psychiatry, University of Minnesota, Minneapolis, Minnesota

Preface

Schizophrenia is currently considered to be a disorder that occurs, at least in part, as a result of aberrant brain development. Despite this construct, most patients do not develop the full syndromal expression of schizophrenia until they are in their twenties. Although juvenile-onset schizophrenia has accordingly been regarded as a rare phenomenon, this is to some extent a misconception. While it is indeed extremely uncommon for the illness to develop before the age of puberty, it has been estimated that almost one-third of persons with schizophrenia first develop psychotic symptomatology during adolescence. At present, the etiological factors underlying an earlier age at onset have yet to be fully elucidated.

Nonetheless, over the past decade, much has been learned about the phenomenology, epidemiology, pathophysiology, and treatment of schizophrenia as it appears in adolescents and children. From a research standpoint, an understanding of the neurobiology of juvenile-onset schizophrenia is vital, in part because, as some findings have suggested, youths with this condition may suffer a more debilitating form of the disorder than persons who develop schizophrenia during adulthood. Young patients may therefore be ideally suited to inform investigators about the genetic and neurodevelopmental underpinnings of this severe, potentially devastating illness.

The volume opens with a consideration of diagnostic issues. In chapter 1, Dr. Carlson and colleagues review the study of first-episode schizophrenia carried out in Suffolk County, Long Island, between 1989 and 1995. As this study demonstrated, a thorough clinical assessment of patients at intake can lead to a stable diagnosis of early-onset schizophrenia, which can in turn be counted on with substantial certainty for purposes of research and treatment. In order to clarify the physiological context of adolescent schizophrenia, the following two chapters focus on brain development—a key element in the neurodevelopmental hypothesis of the illness. Dr. Keshavan reviews this hypothesis in chapter 2 and calls attention to the need for a theory capable of unifying the

three major pathophysiological models of schizophrenia that have been proposed to date. As his discussion of glutamatergic dysfunction demonstrates,
disparate biology may in fact be implicated in a juvenile onset of the illness.
This theory in turn provides a heuristic model that researchers can test and
clinicians can relate to practice. Drs. White and Nelson then offer a helpful
overview of the specific neurobiological processes at work in brain development, particularly in the central nervous system and the prefrontal cortex. The
developmental theme is extended by Dr. Frangou and colleagues in their evaluation of the genetic risk factors for schizophrenia and the role of birth events
and environmental factors in the etiology of the disorder.

Chapters 5 to 7—on neuroimaging and neurophysiology—outline specific
approaches that researchers have adopted in an effort to answer questions regarding the illness. Besides yielding valuable insights into adult patients, imaging studies and neurophysiological testing have identified certain similarities
of biology between adolescents and adults, while also pointing to some tanta-
lizing differences. In particular, data obtained through imaging studies suggest
the existence of structural changes in the brain that are specific to adolescents,
which puts an interesting twist on the developmental versus progressive de-
bate concerning schizophrenia that continued throughout much of the twen-
tieth century.

In chapter 8, Dr. Walker and colleagues survey the indicators of risk that can
signal the possible onset of schizophrenia in teenagers. Their review, in tandem with their own work, provides clear evidence that both biological and psychological antecedents are operative in the evolution of the disease. Their integrative approach is satisfying to those working with young patients, who
must confront the complexity of the illness on a daily basis.

Related to the Suffolk County first-episode study is the valuable work on the
schizophrenic prodrome that has emerged from the Personal Assistance and
Crisis Evaluation Clinic in Melbourne, Australia, a service for adolescents and
young adults who are experiencing signs of a mental disorder. In chapter 9, Dr.
Amminger and colleagues describe the symptoms characteristic of the prodromal period as well as the methods by which these symptoms can be evaluated.
Their report that the prodrome can be reliably assessed should encourage further explorations into this phase of the illness as it occurs in adolescents. Attention is then turned to the NIMH study of patients with childhood-onset
psychoses that has been underway since 1990. In addition to illustrating the
fact that not all psychoses are schizophrenia, this study has introduced the im-

portant diagnostic concept of a "multidimensionally impaired" youngster, which Drs. Gogtay and Rapoport examine in chapter 9. They go on to compare the patients so designated in the NIMH study to those with childhood-onset schizophrenia, thereby enriching the research on the illness by describing its near neighbors.

The treatment of child or adolescent patients with schizophrenia must necessarily take into account multiple factors—not only the medical management of the condition but also the patient's family environment and schooling, along with problems of social adjustment. In chapter 11, Dr. Dass and colleagues describe the array of psychopharmacological medications that can be employed in the treatment of young people with psychotic disease—an area of interest and challenge. Although the newer, atypical antipsychotics offer much promise and have to some extent already displaced traditional neuroleptics, difficult issues still face investigators trying to sort out questions of efficacy and the various age-specific considerations that surround the use of antipsychotic medications in the treatment of patients who are not yet physically mature. From a clinical perspective, it is essential to appreciate that the pharmacological treatment of young people with schizophrenia differs from that of adults, as do the respective outcomes. The fact that adolescent-onset schizophrenia is often associated with a poorer outcome than that reported for adults no doubt reflects a combination of biological, psychological, and environmental circumstances that interact in ways yet to be adequately untangled. Furthermore, because their age limits their ability to function independently, youths with schizophrenia are generally considered more vulnerable than their adult counterparts. For this reason, the psychosocial interventions that are provided as adjuncts to medications must be tailored to meet the needs of these patients in a developmentally informed fashion. Appropriately, then, the final two chapters are devoted to psychosocial methods and concerns and serve to point up the complexity of the therapeutic program required for successful outcome. Dr. Sikich's contribution evaluates a number of specific psychotherapeutic methods, including psychoeducation and school interventions, and so draws attention to vital issues that bear on the clinical management of the individual patient. Drs. Harle and McClellan then take up the question of how best to involve family members in the treatment of young people with schizophrenia, with the goal of helping both patients and families cope with the symptoms and consequences of the disorder.

Given the well-worn observation that schizophrenia is an illness with its onset in the late teenage or early adult years, studies that specifically target the adolescent population have been undertaken all too infrequently. This book offers a review of both the state-of-the-art clinical care and the cutting-edge science pertaining to adolescent and childhood schizophrenia. In so doing, it brings forward a substantial breadth of material on an area of clinical research and practice that has long been underappreciated. It is our hope that the information it provides will be of considerable benefit to clinicians currently working with young people and that it will serve as a springboard for those pushing forward the boundaries of research.

Juvenile-Onset Schizophrenia

CHAPTER ONE

The Phenomenology and Assessment of Adolescent-Onset Psychosis

Observations from a First-Admission Psychosis Project

Gabrielle A. Carlson, M.D., Bushra Naz, M.D., and Evelyn J. Bromet, Ph.D.

Whether the result of genetically programmed changes in the central nervous system (CNS), puberty, increased exposure to mind-altering drugs (including alcohol), factors as yet undiscovered, or all of these, the increased incidence of psychotic disorders in midadolescence is well known (Remschmidt et al. 1994). Although research into the onset of psychosis in adolescence has most often focused on schizophrenia (DeLisi 1992; Galdos and van Os 1995), the emergence of mood disorder with psychosis is also seen by virtue of increased rates of mania (Loranger and Levine 1978) and depression (Angold, Costello, and Worthman 1998) at puberty. Even though we have been able, using operational criteria, to distinguish between these conditions in research settings, the ultimate diagnostic resolution of psychotic symptoms may not be obvious at the outset (Werry, McClellan, and Chard 1991; Carlson, Fennig, and Bromet 1994). This chapter will therefore address psychotic disorders in general rather than schizophrenia only. The complexities of psychosis in children have been reviewed elsewhere (e.g., Volkmar 1996); we will thus concentrate on adolescents, drawing on data from the Suffolk County Mental Health Project (SCMHP; Bromet et al. 1992). This study aimed to recruit every patient aged

15 to 60 admitted with a first episode of psychosis to any one of twelve hospitals in a Long Island county (population roughly 1.2 million people) between 1989 and 1995. Of 695 consenting subjects, 58 (8.3%) were between the ages of 15 and 18.

Because we will primarily address phenomenology and assessment, it is important to review our current definitions of the symptoms of psychosis. The term *psychosis* is by no means fixed. As the *DSM-IV-TR* (American Psychiatric Association 2000, p. 827) notes, the scope of the concept varies from the most stringent definition of "delusions or prominent hallucinations, with the hallucinations occurring in the absence of insight into their pathologic nature," to the symptoms of schizophrenia (prominent hallucinations and delusions, disorganized speech, grossly disorganized or catatonic behavior), to a conceptual definition of "loss of ego boundaries or a gross impairment in reality testing." Even though symptoms are viewed categorically by the *DSM*, however, the dimensional nature of psychotic phenomena has in fact been recognized for many years (see van Os et al. 1999 for a review).

Definitions

Hallucinations have been defined as "a sensory perception that has the compelling sense of reality of a true perception but that occurs without external stimulation of the relevant sensory organ" (American Psychiatric Association 2000, p. 823). The person may or may not know that he or she is having a hallucination. Hallucinations may be auditory, visual, somatic, tactile, or gustatory. Auditory hallucinations are the most common and may come from either within or outside the head. There is a spectrum of sensory phenomena from a single word uncertainly heard, to a few words, to words or phrases that the subject thinks may be his or her own thoughts, only a little louder than usual (but not to the point of thought broadcasting). Deciding whether these phenomena cross the hallucinatory threshold depends on a variety of criteria, including the patient's state of alertness, age and level of cognitive development, ability to express his or her internal state, and the biases and convictions of the interviewer. People who hear actual commands, voices making comments, or conversations between voices have crossed the threshold and have prominent hallucinations.

Delusions are false beliefs that, while not culturally accepted, are firmly held despite incontrovertible evidence to the contrary. Again, a spectrum exists between overvalued ideas and actual delusions (American Psychiatric Association 2000, p. 821), with developmental factors playing an inherent role in defining what qualifies as a delusion. For example, the conviction that there are monsters under the bed is not considered delusional in young children but would be so considered in someone older. Finally, the boundary between an obsession and a delusion is not always clear. Persecutory delusions (that one is being "attacked, harassed, cheated, persecuted, or conspired against"), delusions of reference ("events, objects or other persons in one's immediate environment have a particular and unusual significance"), and grandiose delusions ("delusion of inflated worth, power, knowledge, identity or special relationship to a deity or famous person") are the more common and are not diagnostically specific. Delusions of being controlled ("feelings, impulses, thoughts or actions . . . are under the control of some external force"), thought broadcasting ("one's thoughts are being broadcast out loud so that they can be perceived by others"), thought insertion ("one's thoughts are not one's own, but rather are inserted into one's mind"), and bizarre delusions (other delusions that are totally implausible) have been considered first-rank symptoms of schizophrenia as originally delineated by Schneider (American Psychiatric Association 2000, pp. 821–22; see Tanenberg-Karant et al. 1995 for a review), although they occasionally occur in other conditions. Somatic delusions, centering around the subject's appearance or the belief that abnormal things are happening to his or her body, and the delusion that someone is in love with the subject are also described.

Psychotic symptoms have been categorized as either mood congruent or mood incongruent. Mood-congruent delusions and hallucinations can focus on themes of nihilism, guilt, deserved punishment, or personal failures that are consistent with depression; those that involve an inflated sense of self-worth, as well as the belief that the subject has access to extraordinary powers or knowledge or stands in a special relationship to a deity or famous person, are consistent with mania. Persecutory delusions or paranoia may be mood congruent either with severe depression or with mania: one is being hounded because of terrible failings or instead because one possesses some very valuable power. Mood-incongruent delusions include those considered first-rank symptoms as well as delusions of persecution or reference that do not fit the mood in question.

Thought or speech disorder and negative symptoms, while usually associated with schizophrenia, are more difficult both to measure reliably and to distinguish from developmental disorders that affect pragmatic language, most notably, pervasive developmental disorders and attention deficit hyperactivity disorder (ADHD). Speech accomplishes a given purpose, and under normal circumstances the speaker regulates speech style and content to suit the situation and the listener. Rules of language define quantity (information is imparted without being verbose; the speaker is attentive to listener boredom), as well as truthfulness, relevance (the information conveyed pertains to the topic at hand), and clarity (the information conveyed is clear and understandable to the listener rather than emanating from the middle of a thought to which the listener has no access).

"Formal thought disorder" is known in the *DSM-IV* as disorganized speech. This resolves the concern about whether it is a subject's thoughts or his or her language that is disordered. Andreasen's summary of positive formal thought disorder, as operationalized in the Scale for the Assessment of Positive Symptoms (SAPS), reads as follows: "Positive formal thought disorder is fluent speech that tends to communicate poorly for a variety of reasons. The subject tends to skip from topic to topic without warning, to be distracted by events in the nearby environment, to join words together because they are semantically or phonologically alike, even though they make no sense, or to ignore the question and ask another. This type of speech may be rapid, and it frequently seems quite disjointed. Unlike alogia (negative formal thought disorder), a wealth of detail is provided, and the flow of speech tends to have an energetic, rather than an apathetic quality to it" (Andreasen 1984).

Disorganized speech is categorized according to whether the connections that go awry are *between* sentences or clauses (loose associations or derailment), because of unclear pronoun references or a slight or blatant lack of cohesion, or *within* the sentence or clause (incoherence or word salad). The former is much more common than the latter. When answers to questions are off the mark, they are called tangential. Circumstantiality is a pattern of speech in which extraneous and pedantic details keep the individual from reaching the goal of an idea within a reasonable time frame. These speech abnormalities are also seen in children and adolescents who suffer from autism spectrum disorders (Klin et al. 2000). Illogicality, which occurs when conclusions are reached that do not follow logically, is characteristic of schizophrenia, although it is sometimes seen in normal preschool children and referred to as "preoperational thinking." It diminishes in frequency after age 7 (Caplan et al. 2000). Disorder of rate and quantity of speech includes pressured speech, which may be rapid, voluminous, loud, and uninterruptible, and is often associated with distractible speech, in which the speaker stops in the middle of a thought and changes subjects because he or she is distracted by something in the environment and is unable to disinhibit the need to respond to it. The latter abnormality is seen in mania and is also called "esophoria" by speech pathologists because it sometimes characterizes the speech of children (and presumably adults) with ADHD (Caplan et al. 2001).

Negative symptoms, such as affective flattening, alogia, avolition, and anhedonia, are responsible for much of the morbidity of schizophrenia. Affective flattening is common and is characterized by a wooden or immobile facial expression, poor eye contact, reduced body gestures, and an overall diminished emotional expressiveness most of the time. Alogia is characterized by brief, empty speech and by decreased fluency and productivity of speech. Avolition is the inability to initiate and persist in goal-directed activities. A person may, for example, sit for long hours rather than participate in work and social activities. Anhedonia or asociality manifests itself as a paucity of interests or activities, a disinterest in relationships with others, or an inability to form close, intimate relationships. Although not listed in the *DSM* as a negative symptom, the attention problems that occur in schizophrenia, which are not listed in the *DSM* as negative symptoms but are included in the Scale for the Assessment of Negative Symptoms, or SANS, are especially troublesome in the case of school-aged children; such problems are among the most frequently studied neuropsychological characteristics of the disorder (Asarnow et al. 1994). Specific negative symptoms are not unique to schizophrenia, however. The extrapyramidal side effects of antipsychotic drugs can produce such symptoms. Similarly, a person with a psychomotor-retarded depression will appear to have subdued affect, reduced speech, and little to no interest or energy. Children and adolescents with pervasive developmental disorders also present with poor eye contact and inadequate nonverbal communication. Attention problems thus characterize mood, developmental, and schizophrenic disorders (Cornblatt et al. 1999).

The criteria for psychiatric disorders in which psychosis is a major element are summarized in Tables 1.1 through 1.3.

Table 1.1. Psychotic disorders in adolescents

	Schizophrenia	Schizophreniform disorder	Brief psychotic disorder	Psychosis not otherwise specified
Frequency of symptoms	Two or more per month during active phase	As in schizophrenia	Sudden onset of positive symptoms that may or may not be associated with specific stressor	
Positive symptoms	Delusions, especially bizarre ones. Hallucinations with clear sensorium, especially conversing voices or running commentary. Disorganized thinking (formal thought disorder), loose associations, tangentiality, incoherence. Disorganized behavior (sometimes including periods of catatonia)	As in schizophrenia	As in schizophrenia	Positive symptoms with or without negative symptoms. Symptoms do not fit criteria for other psychotic disorders; e.g., not clear whether psychosis antedated mood symptoms or whether caused by drugs or prior medical condition; unclear how marked the hallucinations or delusions are; difficult to distinguish negative symptoms from developmental disorder

Negative symptoms	Affective flattening Avolition and/or anhedonia	No affective flattening; confusion or perplexity at height of psychosis; good premorbid adjustment Good prognosis		
Duration of signs and symptoms	Apparent in some degree for at least 6 months during residual phase	Continuing for at least a month but less than 6 months, followed by full return to premorbid functioning	At least a day, but less than a month, followed by full return to premorbid functioning	Duration unclear, but less than a month
Prodromal or residual symptoms	Odd beliefs and/or referential ideas Suspicious or paranoid ideation Odd thinking and/or speech Eccentric behavior Constricted affect and/or lack of close friends			
Rule-outs	Mood disorder with psychosis Substance abuse or medical condition Pervasive developmental disorder (negative symptoms)			

Table 1.2. Psychotic symptoms accompanying mood disorders

	Schizoaffective disorder		Mania with psychotic features	Major depression with psychotic features
	Manic	Depressed		
Symptoms	Concurrent symptoms that meet schizophrenia criteria, including:	Concurrent symptoms that meet schizophrenia criteria including:	Distinct period of abnormally and persistently elevated, expansive, or irritable mood including:	Patient reports or looks sad or irritable for most of day and/or displays a marked loss of interest in surroundings (daily or almost daily for at least 2 weeks)
	Delusions	Delusions	Delusions or hallucinations of grandeur, special powers, beatific experiences	Significant appetite or weight change
	Hallucinations with clear sensorium	Hallucinations with clear sensorium	Decreased need for sleep	Insomnia or hypersomnia
	Disorganized thinking (FTD)*	Disorganized thinking (FTD)	More talkative or feeling pressured to keep talking	Psychomotor agitation or retardation
	Disorganized behavior (sometimes including periods of catatonia)	Disorganized behavior (sometimes including periods of catatonia)	Distractability	Fatigue or loss of energy
	Negative symptoms and manic or mixed episode symptoms	Negative symptoms and depressed episode (including depressed mood)	Increase in goal-directed activity	Delusions or hallucinations of guilt, nihilism, poverty, or disease, or a sense of deserving
			Excessive involvement in	

	pleasurable activities that have a high potential for painful consequences	punishment Diminished ability to think or concentrate Recurrent thoughts of death or suicide
	At least a week (or of any duration at all if hospitalization necessary), but psychosis must occur within the mood episode	At least 2 weeks with impairment, but psychosis must occur within the mood episode
	Mood *incongruent* delusions, including persecutory delusions not related to grandiosity, bizarre delusions or hallucinations	Mood *incongruent* delusions or hallucinations that lack depressive content and can include bizarre delusions or hallucinations
Duration	Delusions and hallucinations have been present for at least 2 weeks *without* mood symptoms	Delusions and hallucinations have been present for at least 2 weeks *without* mood symptoms
	Mood episode symptoms have been present for a significant proportion of the psychotic episode	Mood episode symptoms have been present for a significant proportion of the psychotic episode

Mixed episode: criteria for both mania and depression

*FTD, formal thought disorder

Table 1.3. Psychosis associated with medical conditions or drugs

	Psychosis due to medical condition	Substance-induced psychosis
Etiology	Evidence that disturbance is the direct physiological consequence of a general medical condition	Evidence that disturbance is the direct physiological consequence of drug abuse, medication, or exposure to a toxin
Symptoms	Prominent delusions (persecutory, distortions of body image), hallucinations—most often auditory, with nonauditory usually due to substance-induced psychosis or general medical condition	Prominent delusions (persecutory, distortions of body image), hallucinations—most often auditory, with nonauditory usually due to substance-induced psychosis or general medical condition
Specific medical conditions	Epilepsy, especially temporal lobe Migrane, CNS infections (e.g., Lyme disease) Traumatic brain injury Endocrine conditions (thyroid, Cushing disease, congenital adrenal hyperplasia) Metabolic conditions (porphyria, autoimmune disorders [SLE])*	Substance intoxication (alcohol, cannabis, cocaine, hallucinogens, amphetamines, phencyclidine, sedatives, hypnotics, anxiolytics) Withdrawal from alcohol, sedatives, hypnotics, or anxiolytics Arise within the context of intoxication or withdrawal but may persist for weeks, although no longer considered substance-induced if continuing over a month

*SLE, systemic lupus erythematosus

Epidemiology

Rates of psychosis in general depend on how broadly or narrowly the concept is defined, how it is ascertained (whether clinically or by means of a computer algorithm based on structured interviews), and where it is ascertained (community, clinic, urban versus rural setting, etc.). For instance, in the National Comorbidity Survey (NCS), lifetime rates of nonaffective psychosis broadly defined and generated by computer algorithm were 2.2 percent, whereas ratings by clinicians yielded a figure of 0.7 percent (Kendler et al. 1996). The Netherlands Mental Health Survey and Incidence Study (van Os et al. 2001), which used the same interview as the NCS, subsequently reported lifetime rates of schizophrenia spectrum disorders at 0.37 percent, affective psychosis at 1.51 percent, and any psychotic symptom at 17.5 percent, but psychotic symptoms specifically stemming from a psychiatric condition at 4.4 percent. The patient's level of urbanicity, interestingly, was significantly associated with psychosis (OR = 1.47, CI = 1.25–1.72).

A recent examination of more than 2,000 children and adolescents seen in a mood and anxiety disorders clinic and systematically interviewed with the original version of the K-Schedule for Affective Disorders and Schizophrenia for Children (Kiddie-SADS or K-SADS) (Chambers et al. 1985) revealed that 91 (4.5%) had definite psychotic symptoms as defined by computer algorithm, and 95 (4.5%) had possible psychotic symptoms (Ulloa et al. 2000). Because the study took place at a mood disorders clinic, the diagnostic spectrum was skewed toward affective disorders. The investigators found that 41 percent of subjects had a major depressive disorder (MDD), 24 percent had bipolar disorder (BD), 21 percent had depressive symptoms but did not meet MDD criteria, and 14 percent had a schizophrenia spectrum disorder. When these patients were compared with the nonpsychotic majority, the odds ratios and 95 percent confidence intervals for psychotic youth were, for bipolar disorder, 4.9 (2.8–8.3); for panic disorder, 4.8 (2.0–11.3); for generalized anxiety disorder 2.0 (1.2–3.4); and for MDD 1.8 (1.2–3.0). Schizophrenia spectrum disorders could not be compared by definition, there being no nonpsychotic schizophrenia spectrum disorders. Of psychotic symptoms, 80 percent were hallucinations (73.6% auditory, 38.5% visual, 26.2% olfactory), 22 percent were delusions (most commonly delusions of reference, mind reading, and the conviction that others can "hear my thoughts," at rates of 6% each). Thought disorder was uncommon (2%).

Gillberg and colleagues (1993) conducted one of the only studies to extrapolate rates of psychosis from hospital records. They defined adolescent psychosis as follows: the presence of hallucinations, formal thought disorder of the schizophrenic kind, delusions, disorientation, and mania or major depression with mood-congruent psychotic features. After systematically reviewing the clinical records of 401 subjects aged 13 to 19 in Goteborg, Sweden (population 450,000), they estimated that 0.5 percent of all youngsters developed "clear-cut psychotic symptoms" sometime during their teenage years. Of the 61 cases (32 boys, 29 girls) that met the above criteria, the mean yearly prevalence for psychosis requiring hospitalization ranged from 0.9 per 10,000 at age 13 to a peak of 17.6 per 10,000 at age 18, for a cumulative prevalence of 53.8 per 10,000. In Gillberg's population, schizophrenia was the most common diagnosis, followed by substance-induced psychosis, psychotic depression, and mania. The diagnostic distribution by gender is presented in Table 1.4.

In the SCMHP, respondents were identified at the time of their first admission to a hospital. Interviews were conducted after the psychosis had cleared, primarily to enhance understanding of the informed-consent process. This was especially necessary because the research team was not part of the standard program of care. Potential respondents were identified by the head nurse or by a social worker from that facility, or by project staff. Inclusion criteria were as follows: age between 15 and 60; residency in Suffolk County; presence of psychotic symptoms or behavior indicative of psychosis and/or the prescription of antipsychotic medication; no psychiatric hospitalization more than six months before the current one; and the ability to understand English with respect to language and cognitive functioning. Initial diagnoses, made at the

Table 1.4. *Sex-specific distribution of disorders in a Swedish sample of 13- to 19-year-olds with psychotic symptoms*

Disorder	Total (N = 61) n (%)	Males (N = 32) n (%)	Females (N = 29) n (%)
Schizophrenia	25 (41.0)	16 (50.0)	9 (31.0)
Psychotic depression	8 (13.1)	3 (9.4)	5 (17.4)
Bipolar disorder	7 (11.5)	3 (9.4)	4 (13.8)
Schizoaffective disorder	2 (3.3)	1 (3.1)	1 (3.4)
Substance-induced psychosis	13 (21.3)	7 (21.9)	6 (20.7)
Atypical psychosis	6 (9.8)	2 (6.3)	4 (13.8)*

*Two cases not clearly described

time subjects were recruited to the study, were based primarily on the Structured Clinical Interview for *DSM-IV* (SCID; Spitzer et al. 1992), amplified by material gleaned from a close friend or relative of the patient, such as a parent, together with information currently available in the medical record at the time of the SCID and a brief interview with the treating doctor. Additional information was gathered at a 6-month follow-up on hospital course, treatment, prior schooling, and the patient's own recollection of premorbid functioning. Because clinicians may be unable to benefit from the hindsight afforded by such supplementary material, however, our chapter focuses primarily on the baseline information.

Table 1.5 displays the diagnostic distribution of the SCMHP teen cohort according to gender. Of the 58 respondents aged 15 to 18 at admission, schizophrenia (including schizophreniform and schizoaffective disorders) occurred in 31 percent, while acute mania accounted for 22.4 percent of admissions. Roughly 31 percent had a severe depression, although three patients were actually in the depressive phase of a bipolar illness, so that the true rate of bipolar disorder was 27.6 percent. Nine subjects (15.5%) did not fit the criteria for a well-defined condition. Only one subject was diagnosed with substance-induced psychosis, but in fact 27 out of the 58 subjects (46.7%) were heavily involved in alcohol, cannabis, and/or other psychoactive substances at the time of admission, rates that were virtually identical across diagnoses. Males predominated in every category except major depression with psychosis.

In the SCMHP sample, 43 percent of the subjects had been hospitalized in community hospitals, 20 percent in state hospitals (including the children's

Table 1.5. *Diagnostic distribution of Suffolk County Mental Health Project cohort stratified by gender*

Disorder	Total (N = 58) n (%)	Males (N = 40) n (%)	Females (N = 18) n (%)
Schizophrenia spectrum disorders*	18 (31.0)	12 (30.0)	6 (33.3)
Psychotic depression	12 (20.7)	6 (15.0)	6 (33.3)
Bipolar disorder	16 (27.6)	12 (30.0)	4 (22.2)
Unclear diagnosis	9 (15.5)	7 (77.8)	2 (22.2)
Other†	3 (5.2)	3 (7.5)	

*Includes schizoaffective and schizophreniform disorders
†Conduct disorder, substance-induced psychosis, no agreement among diagnosticians

Table 1.6. Reasons for referral or admission

Reason	Schizophrenia (N = 18) n (%)	Bipolar disorder (N = 16) n (%)	Major depressive disorder (N = 12) n (%)	Other (N = 12) n (%)	Total (N = 58) n (%)
Aggression	6 (33.3)	4 (25.0)	0 (0)	4 (33.3)	14 (24.1)
Suicidal behavior	2 (11.1)	0 (0)	8 (66.7)	3 (25.0)	13 (22.4)
Psychotic behavior	9 (50.0)	8 (50.0)	2 (16.7)	5 (41.7)	24 (41.4)
Other*	1 (5.6)	4 (25.0)	2 (16.7)	0	7 (12.1)

*All other diagnostic categories

state hospital), and 37 percent at the university hospital. At the time, the median length of stay was about 3 weeks, although the mean length of stay was 40 days. Reasons for admission were predictable. As Table 1.6 illustrates, psychotic or bizarre behavior, followed by aggressive behavior, was commonplace in schizophrenia and mania, while suicidal behavior was most evident in psychotically depressed subjects. The problems presented by the subjects whose psychosis remained undiagnosed were evenly distributed.

The twelve undiagnosed subjects at baseline either had psychosis not otherwise specified (NOS) ($n = 3$), were completely undiagnosable ($n = 6$), or had severe behavior disorders with questionable enduring psychosis ($n = 3$). At the 24-month point, on the basis of interval data these cases had been reformulated as mood disorder ($n = 3$), schizophrenia ($n = 3$), psychosis NOS or brief psychosis ($n = 2$), and substance-induced psychosis ($n = 2$), while two subjects were dropped from the study as not having been truly psychotic.

The precise age of onset of psychotic conditions is not always easy to ascertain. Other psychopathology and/or prodromal symptoms may antedate the actual psychosis by many months or years (Beiser et al. 1993). Maziade et al. demonstrated this most clearly in their long-term follow-up of young onset patients with schizophrenia. Almost two-thirds had antecedent behavior problems, dating from about 7 years of age, but psychotic symptoms did not appear until about 14 years of age, and age at first hospitalization was about 15 (Maziade, Bouchard, et al. 1996; Maziade, Gingras, et al. 1996). Because the lower age limit of the SCMHP sample was 15, age-of-onset figures may not be helpful to an understanding of the age distribution of psychosis overall. When the sample's diagnostic groups of schizophrenia, mood disorder, and other psy-

Table 1.7. *Ages of onset of mood disorder, psychosis, and substance abuse*

	Schizophrenia	Bipolar disorder and major depressive disorder	Other
	Mean (SD)	Mean (SD)	Mean (SD)
Age of onset of mood disorder		15.9 (2.6)	
Age of onset of psychosis	15.7 (4)	16.6 (1.7)	16.3 (1.3)
Age at admission	17.1 (1)	16.8 (1.2)	16.9 (1)
Age of onset of alcohol or drug abuse (*n* = 26)	13.4 (2.5)	15.3 (1.8)	13.0 (1.5)

choses were themselves compared, however, no differences in age of onset were found. As Table 1.7 shows, an earlier onset of substance abuse was more associated with schizophrenia than with mood disorder, although even in the latter case substance abuse usually preceded the onset of the mood disorder or schizophrenia.

Premorbid Characteristics

Childhood predictors of adult schizophrenia have frequently been the object of study and usually include social class at birth, obstetrical complications, viral infection in childhood, motor and language delay, lower intelligence, and personality characteristics such as odd behavior or social withdrawal (see Isohanni et al. 2001 for a recent review). However, the antecedents of affective psychosis have seldom been evaluated. Cannon et al. (1997) examined putative preschizophrenic and affective variables from the "childhood" (mean age 14 years) records of 56 late-adolescent or young-adult patients suffering from ICD-10 schizophrenia, along with another 24 subjects with ICD-10 affective psychosis (either bipolar disorder or MDD with psychosis). The sample was from Maudsley Hospital, in London, and was compared with childhood attendees without these adult conditions. Among teens destined to become schizophrenic, as compared with those who were not, odds ratios were significantly higher for abnormal suspiciousness or sensitivity, social withdrawal, severe tantrums, relationship problems, disturbed sleeping, "morbid depression," family psychiatric history, prior evaluation, out-of-home placement, and Caribbean or African ancestry. Among those who ultimately developed affective psychosis, "hysterical symptoms," gross overactivity, morbid depression, disturbances of eating and hypochondriasis, and parent or sibling psychiatric history were significant. Rather than comparing these variables between the subjects destined for schizophrenia and those destined for affective disorders, the study focused on the comparison of adolescent psychopathology with young-adult outcome.

One major question is whether antecedent behavior problems and earlier developmental disorders represent early symptoms of the psychosis, as opposed to risk factors, comorbid disorders, or red herrings. Table 1.8 summarizes the multiple background difficulties experienced by the SCMHP sample. According to information drawn from parents, the subjects themselves, and school records, 53 percent of those with schizophrenia, 25 percent of those with mood disorders, and 75 percent of those with nonspecific psychoses had prior diagnoses of significant behavior disorders—either ADHD or conduct disorder, or both (Carlson, Bromet, and Jandorf 1998). Interviews specifically designed to ascertain prior traumatic events revealed that one-third of the sample had been seriously abused, physically or sexually, in childhood. Some 33 percent had been placed in special education classes, and 28 percent had either been retained in a grade, had IQs below 80, or had dropped out of school before graduation and probably should have been in special education. Subjects with schizophrenia were twice as likely to have experienced such educational difficulties as those with mood disorders. Premorbid adjustment, as measured by the Cannon-Spoor index obtained from subjects, was no different among these groups. Only five of the patients (8.6%) had no history of behavioral, emotional, or educational problems prior to the onset of their psychosis. As these figures indicate, adolescent-onset psychosis requiring psychiatric hospitalization is associated with considerable impairment before the onset of the actual psychosis.

Substance misuse not only is common but also appears to influence the age of onset of psychosis. For example, in one study, patients who abused drugs had an earlier onset of psychosis than those who did not (Addington and Addington 1998). As we noted above, heavy substance use occurred in 48 percent of the SCMHP population of older adolescents and young adults. Of those who had either a lifetime or a current record of substance abuse or dependence, 26 percent abused marijuana, the majority of whom had alcohol problems as well. Another 19 percent abused other drugs that could include marijuana. Only three subjects (5.6%) abused alcohol alone. More than one-third of the sample was using marijuana or alcohol regularly by the age of 13 (see Table

Table 1.8. Rates of prepsychotic psychopathology, stress, and behavior problems

	Schizophrenia (N = 18)	Bipolar disorder (N = 16)	Major depressive disorder (N = 12)	Other (N = 12)	Total (N = 58)
	n (%)	n (%)	n (%)	n (%)	n (%)
Childhood psychopathology (n = 55)					
Externalizing disorder	9 (52.9)	5 (31.2)	2 (16.7)	9 (75)	25 (43.9)
Other/internalizing symptoms	6 (35.3)	9 (56.3)	8 (66.7)	2 (16.7)	25 (43.9)
No prior psychopathology	1 (5.9)	2 (12.5)	2 (16.7)	0	5 (8.8)
Raped, molested, neglected, or abused before the age of 16	7 (38.9)	7 (43.8)	4 (33.3)	2 (16.7)	20 (34.5)
Lifetime substance abuse	8 (44.4)	8 (50)	5 (41.67)	6 (50)	27 (46.7)
Educational status (n = 57)					
No major academic problems	4 (22.2)	8 (50.7)	8 (46.7)	2 (16.7)	22 (37.9)
In special education	9 (50)	4 (25)	3 (25)	3 (25)	19 (33.3)
Patient dropped out early or was held back and/or has a below-average IQ	5 (27.8)	4 (25)	1 (8.3)	6 (50)	16 (28.1)

1.8). It is worth pointing out, however, that in a sample of relatively young people, "lifetime" is usually synonymous with "current," simply because their life has as yet been short.

Two other studies examined rates of psychiatric comorbidity in adolescent psychosis. McClellan and colleagues (2003) found even higher rates of co-morbidity in their sample of patients from a state hospital in Washington State. Almost 69 percent of those with schizophrenia, 73 percent of those with bipolar disorders, and 85 percent of those with psychosis NOS had comorbid behavior disorders, and within these three groups 22 percent, 41 percent, and 35 percent, respectively, had a history of substance abuse. Anxiety disorders were not quite as prominent, occurring at rates of 15 to 25 percent. Post-traumatic stress disorder (probably the result of physical abuse) occurred in 11 percent of the patients with schizophrenia, 27 percent of the bipolar patients, and 55 percent of psychosis-NOS patients. Finally, evidence of pervasive developmental disorders was found in 11 percent of those with schizophrenia and 18 percent of those with psychosis NOS but not at all in bipolar subjects. Their sample was about two years younger than ours, as it included subjects between the ages of 12 and 18, and the data was gathered by child psychiatrists. An earlier study comparing a Washington State and a New Zealand sample found that "disruptive" personalities occurred in 6 percent of the latter group as opposed to 38 percent of the former (Werry et al. 1994).

Schizophrenia, especially early-onset schizophrenia, is believed to be a neurodevelopmental disorder (Murray 1991; see Marenco and Weinberger 2000 for a review), and according to some this theory accounts for the preponderance of males, poor premorbid adjustment, negative symptoms, and poor outcome (Murray 1991). Perinatal distress and birth difficulties are part of the neurodevelopmental risk traditionally associated with schizophrenia (Geddes et al. 1999; Isohanni et al. 2001), although certain data suggest that these risk factors may also be found in some subjects with bipolar disorder (Kinney et al. 1993; Marcelis et al. 1998). Pregnancy and perinatal data were available for 38 of the 46 SCMHP subjects who had a definable disorder at baseline. Only 18 percent of the sample was without any developmental risk factors. Schizophrenia and major depressive subjects had fewer developmental risk factors on average (1.08 ± 0.86) than bipolar subjects (2.00 ± 1.15) ($F = 3.744, p = .034$). This suggests again that neurodevelopmental risk factors may underpin psychosis in general rather than just schizophrenia.

Significantly lower IQ scores are also associated with early-onset schizophrenia (Aylward, Walker, and Bettes 1984). The Quick Test (Ammons and Ammons 1962), which correlates highly with the WAIS verbal IQ (Vance, Hankins, and Reynolds 1988), was administered at baseline and at the 6- and 24-month follow-ups in the SCMHP. Those with schizophrenia, whether the diagnosis was made at baseline or at 24 months, proved to have substantially lower IQs. There were no significant gender effects. An examination of the entire sample of SCMHP schizophrenic subjects for whom Quick Test IQ data were available ($N = 205$) revealed a significant positive correlation of $r = 0.222$ ($p < .001$) with age: young-onset schizophrenic patients generally had lower IQs. (Subjects for whom IQ data were missing had the same mean age as the rest of the sample.) Age was not a significant predictor of IQ for other psychoses. Moreover, because the overall IQ of schizophrenic patients was significantly lower than that of patients with other psychoses (a mean of 82 versus 94), performance on virtually all of the neuropsychological tests administered as part of the 24-month follow-up assessment was also significantly poorer (Mojtabai et al. 2000). Table 1.9 summarizes the IQ data gathered at 24 months, when the diagnoses were finalized. Schizophrenic patients were clearly weaker on verbal items than on performance items. The degree of scholastic difficulties antedating the onset of psychosis strongly suggested that the lower IQ preceded the onset of schizophrenia rather than resulting from the illness (Russell et al. 1997), although we were unable to document this from the hospital records we studied.

Other factors pertinent to the study of early-onset schizophrenia include the type of onset of the psychosis and the presence of less well-formed psychotic symptoms (Werry et al. 1994). For instance, insidious onset has proved characteristic of schizophrenia, whereas acute onset appears to be typical of mood disorders. In the SCMHP study, insidious onset was most common in schizophrenic patients (50%), subacute onset in MDD subjects (66.6%), and acute onset in manic and bipolar patients (50%) ($\chi^2 = 18.268$, df = 6, $p = .006$). It was possible to calculate the number of days from the first appearance of symptoms to index hospitalization in 52 subjects, and, as Table 1.10 shows, this variable also differed significantly by diagnosis.

Ascertaining psychotic symptoms has been made easier through the use of various structured interviews. However, as we noted earlier, a range of psychotic symptoms is present in both the general and the clinical population. For instance, in a study of childhood-onset schizophrenia conducted by the National Institute of Mental Health (NIMH), 80 percent of the subjects referred

Table 1.9. IQ and subtest scores in Suffolk County Mental Health Project young sample

	Schizophrenia	Bipolar disorder	Major depressive disorder	Other	Significance
	Mean (SD)	Mean (SD)	Mean (SD)	Mean (SD)	F (p)
Quick test	n = 16	n = 11	n = 12	n = 10	
	81.75 (13.35)	93.54 (11.11)	93.08 (9.90)	94.60 (17.04)	3.059 (0.038)
WAIS scaled score	n = 12	n = 9	n = 12	n = 8	
Vocabulary information	7.00 (1.70)	9.11 (2.02)	9.83 (2.12)	9.50 (4.0)	3.074 (0.039)
	4.92 (2.68)	8.55 (2.70)	9.75 (4.20)	8.75 (3.57)	4.615 (0.008)
Picture completion	6.58 (2.54)	7.00 (2.83)	9.67 (2.93)	8.88 (3.40)	2.881 (0.049)
Digit symbol	6.83 (1.6)	8.37 (2.56)	10.50 (3.31)	8.75 (5.25)	2.502 (0.079)

Note: Scores throughout are based on a 24-month consensus diagnosis.

Table 1.10. Type of onset as rated on the World Health Organization (WHO) onset scale

	Schizophrenia	Bipolar disorder	Major depressive disorder	Other
	N (%)	N (%)	N (%)	N (%)
Acute without prodrome	4 (22.0)	1 (6.23)	0	5 (10.9)
Acute with prodrome	1 (5.6)	7 (43.8)	2 (16.7)	10 (21.7)
Subacute	2 (22.2)	6 (37.5)	8 (66.7)	18 (39.1)
Insidious	9 (50.0)	12 (12.5)	2 (16.7)	13 (28.3)
30 days or less	2 (11.8)	13 (81.3)	5 (45.5)	4 (50.0)
31 to 90 days	8 (47.1)	3 (18.8)	3 (27.3)	3 (37.5)
Over 90 days	7 (41.2)	0	3 (27.3)	1 (12.5)

did *not* have schizophrenia (although presumably they displayed some sort of psychotic or bizarre behavior). As Nicolson and colleagues recently described in a follow-up study (2001), 13 percent of the nonschizophrenic subjects had transient psychotic symptoms in association with other risk factors for schizophrenia, including family psychopathology, eye-tracking dysfunction, and/or severe attention problems, although these subjects were also characterized by severe mood swings and an interest in, if not the ability to manage successfully, social interaction. Among the relatively young patients in the NIMH sample, psychotic symptoms proved to be relatively transient (they were not apparent at a 2- to 8-year follow-up), whereas the other aspects of their psychopathology, such as mood swings, aggressive behavior, and problems with attention, remained stable. In a community sample, however, self-reported psychotic symptoms at age 11 predicted schizophreniform symptoms that emerged in the subjects' mid-20s, suggesting a considerable stability of such symptoms (Poulton et al. 2000).

Deciding whether a subject suffers from a thought or language disorder, overideation, or psychosis is not always simple, even though operational criteria exist for all three. Although in most patients delusions and hallucinations were easy to identify, certain symptoms were designated only as "possibly present"—delusions of reference in almost 20 percent of subjects, for example, and persecutory delusions in 14 percent, using the SCID's subthreshold designation. For instance, one 15-year-old male was hospitalized because of increased irritability and a violent argument with his mother, which was out of character for him. This was superimposed on several months of frightening nightmares, following the death of a classmate, suicidal feelings, and the sense that classmates were talking behind his back, knew what was wrong with him, and were aware that he was the "scapegoat of the world." As a preschooler, he had been in a special program for language-impaired youngsters because of "slow processing" and what was probably a receptive language disorder (although his IQ was normal). Although he was subsequently mainstreamed and earned reasonable grades, he was overanxious, had a phobia about school, and was on the whole miserable as a child. He dated the onset of his depression to age 8. He was diagnosed at baseline with MDD with psychotic features, although his psychiatrist treating him did not feel his ideation was truly psychotic. At the 6- and 24-month interviews, he continued to describe vague feelings of being controlled by God and of thinking that he heard his mother yelling at him or that Elton John was writing songs especially for him. His communication style was chronically circumstantial and mildly tangential. Within the structure of a day-treatment program, the subject functioned better than he had before, but once out of school he was not employed or doing much socially.

Bettes and Walker (1987) studied a large series of patients with psychotic symptoms ($N = 1,085$, ages 5 to 18). They found that the number of positive psychotic symptoms increased linearly with age, the biggest increase beginning at about age 12 to 13 and increasing steadily through age 18. Differences between the sexes were more prominent among older children, evidently owing to higher rates of positive symptoms in 17- to 18-year-old males. Negative symptoms, however, were more prevalent from an early age. Symptoms such as inappropriate affect, incoherence, and disorientation were present at all ages. Although 87 percent of the sample was diagnosed as having schizophrenia, the quality of the diagnostic data, which were drawn from intake and discharge records at the New York State Department of Mental Hygiene during the *DSM-II* era, makes it difficult to draw very reliable diagnostic conclusions.

Among the young patients surveyed in the SCMHP sample, no age or sex differences were observed with regard to positive or negative symptoms. Frank positive symptoms were the most apparent. Schizophrenic youth had the highest incidence of delusions (3.8 ± 2.4), followed by bipolar patients (2.8 ± 1.9), and patients suffering from depression or some other disorder (1.5 ± 1.5). Because bizarre delusions, mind reading, the sense of being controlled, and thought broadcasting are defining symptoms of schizophrenia, they too oc-

curred more often in schizophrenic youth, although they occasionally occurred in manic teens as well. Paranoid, referential, grandiose, and somatic
delusions and/or delusional jealousy were more common in bipolar teens, although this could be because grandiosity is one of the criteria of mania. In fact,
delusions were more often the psychotic manifestation in bipolar disorder,
whereas auditory hallucinations were more common in psychotic depression
(see Table 1.11). Mood congruence occurred in one-third of the bipolar patients
and one-half of the patients with psychotic depression.

Positive formal thought disorder as measured by the SAPS (Andreasen 1984)
was also relatively rare and did not distinguish types of psychosis. Tangential
responses to questions were the most common symptom (n = 15, 26%), followed by pressured speech (n = 10, 17.2%), loose associations (n = 8, 13.8%),
distracted speech (n = 7, 12%), and incoherence (n = 7, 12%). Circumstantiality and illogicality were present in fewer than 10 percent of the patients.

Because negative symptoms are viewed as characteristic of schizophrenia, it
should be no surprise they were more common in schizophrenic patients, at
least as rated on the SANS (Andreasen 1984), than in patients suffering from
other disorders, as the data presented in Table 1.12 demonstrate. That is, 61
percent of those with schizophrenia, 38 percent of the manic patients, and 25
percent of the undiagnosed patients had negative symptom scores greater than
2 (scores greater than 1 are clinically meaningful). However, scores were significantly worse among schizophrenic patients only for alogia and inattention,
and they remained so at the 48-month interview as well. There was, however,
a high and significant (p = .001) negative correlation between IQ and those
two traits ($-$.535 for alogia and $-$.504 for inattention), so it is unclear whether
these were indicative of schizophrenia or simply the result of intellectual limitations.

In general, diagnostic stability within research diagnoses over the 24-month
period was good. There was consistency between the baseline and the 6- and
24-month diagnoses in 83 percent of the patients with schizophrenic or schizophrenic spectrum disorders, 75 percent of those with bipolar disorder, and 100
percent of the subjects with psychotic depression. Discharge diagnoses from
the referring facility agreed with the research diagnosis 33 percent of the time
for schizophrenic patients, 50 percent of the time for bipolar patients and 30
percent of the time for patients with MDD with psychosis. Psychosis NOS was
the most frequent misdiagnosis.

Table 1.11. Frequency of psychotic symptoms by diagnostic group

	Schizophrenia	Bipolar disorder	Major depressive disorder	Other	Total	Chi square	df	p
	N (%)	N (%)	N (%)	N (%)	N (%)			
Any delusions	16 (88.9)	14 (87.5)	5 (41.7)	9 (75.0)	44 (75.9)	10.519	3	0.015
Any hallucinations	14 (78.8)	14 (25.0)	8 (66.7)	5 (41.7)	31 (46.6)	10.999	3	0.012
Delusions of reference	11 (64.7)	10 (62.5)	5 (41.7)	2 (20.0)	28 (50.9)	6.39	3	0.094
Grandiose delusions	5 (29.4)	10 (62.5)	1 (8.3)	4 (40.0)	2 (36.4)	9.21	3	0.027
Persecutory delusions	5 (29.4)	6 (37.5)	4 (40.0)	4 (40.0)	19 (35.9)	NS*	3	
Mind-reading delusions	9 (52.9)	3 (20.0)	2 (18.2)	2 (18.2)	16 (29.6)	6.48	3	0.090
Feeling of being controlled	9 (64.3)	3 (18.8)	2 (16.7)	1 (8.3)	15 (27.8)	12.95	3	0.005
Thought broadcasting	4 (25.0)	0	0	1 (9.1)	5 (9.4)	—	3	
Bizarre delusions	11 (64.7)	3 (20.0)	2 (16.7)	2 (20.0)	18 (33.3)	11.03	3	0.012
First-rank symptoms	14 (77.8)	6 (37.5)	3 (25.0)	4 (33.3)	27 (6.6)	10.66	3	0.014
Auditory hallucinations	14 (87.5)	4 (26.7)	8 (63.6)	5 (45.5)	31 (56.6)	12.47	3	0.006
General	8 (44.4)	3 (18.8)	6 (50.0)	4 (33.3)	21 (36.21)			
Mood incongruent	6 (3.3)	1 (6.25)	2 (16.7)	1 (8.3)	10 (17.2)			
Visual hallucinations	5 (29.41)	3 (20.00)	1 (8.33)	2 (16.67)	11 (19.64)	NS		

*Not significant

Table 1.12. Comparative distribution of negative symptoms on the Scale for the Assessment of Negative Symptoms (scores of 2+)

	Schizophrenia		Bipolar disorder		Major depressive disorder		Other		Significance	
	Baseline	24 months	Baseline	24 months	Baseline	24 months	Baseline	24 months	Baseline	24 months
	N (%)	N (%)	N (%)	N (%)	N (%)	N (%)	N (%)	N (%)	p	p
Flat affect	13 (72.2)	6 (46.2)	7 (43.8)	2 (16.7)	9 (75.0)	1 (9.1)	7 (58.3)	4 (57.0)	NS*	NS
Poverty of thought	13 (72.2)	7 (53.9)	5 (31.3)	2 (16.7)	0	0	5 (41.7)	4 (57.1)	0.001	0.009
Amotivation	9 (50.0)	8 (61.5)	6 (37.5)	8 (66.7)	10 (83.3)	6 (54.5)	6 (50.0)	4 (57.1)	NS	NS
Inattention	13 (72.2)	5 (38.5)	5 (31.3)	1 (8.3)	0	0	4 (33.3)	4 (57.1)	0.001	0.011
Avolition	12 (66.7)	8 (61.5)	8 (50.0)	6 (50.0)	4 (33.3)	2 (18.2)	6 (50.0)	2 (18.2)	NS	NS

*Not significant

Outcome

It is customary to think of early-onset schizophrenia as having a grim outcome, with good outcomes usually occurring in less than 26 percent of the cases (Maziade, Bouchard, et al. 1996; Maziade, Gingras, et al. 1996; Eggers and Bunk 1997). However, Gillberg, Hellgren, and Gillberg (1993) examined the broader concept of adolescent psychosis (this included schizophrenia, major affective disorders, substance-induced disorder, and atypical psychosis) thirty years after hospitalization and found an extremely poor outcome almost irrespective of diagnosis. A good outcome was reported in 13 percent of the patients diagnosed with schizophrenia, an intermediate outcome in 8.7 percent, and a poor outcome in 78.2 percent. Among the bipolar subjects, none had a good outcome and 75 percent had a poor outcome. Those with unipolar depression fared the best, with 75 percent having a good outcome. Gillberg based his assessment of outcome on a variety of psychosocial markers. For instance, more than half of his sample received a full pension, and only a few in the sample were married. Twenty-two percent of the sample had committed serious crimes. All but one of the bipolar patients and more than half of those with schizophrenia received psychiatric inpatient treatment during the follow-up, whereas none of the patients with psychotic depression had been readmitted. Nor was this a selected sample: it represented all the cases of psychosis hospitalized in Goteborg at the time. Although patients with psychotic depression functioned slightly better than those with manic-depression or schizophrenia, in comparison with their nonpsychotic counterparts all had a relatively poor outcome.

Besides noting that bipolar youth were often initially misdiagnosed, Werry and colleagues (1991) found that those with child- or adolescent-onset schizophrenia suffered from a chronic, relapsing disorder with considerable disability and deterioration in adaptive functioning. They also found a 15 percent mortality rate from suicide within the first ten years of illness. Youths with bipolar disorder experienced less disability and fewer episodes of the illness. A quarter of them were entirely symptom free, and half either were employed full time or were in school; half of those who were employed full time or were in school still suffered significant active symptoms or impaired functioning.

Most studies examining predictive factors address schizophrenia only. There is some consistency in the findings. Demographic variables related to poor outcome include a younger age of onset (Eggers and Bunk 1997) and male gender (Gillberg, Hellgren, and Gillberg 1993). Certain characteristics of the illness, such as insidious onset (Eggers and Bunk 1997), severity of positive symptoms (McGlashan 1986; Werry and McClellan 1992; Maziade, Bouchard, et al. 1996; Maziade, Gingras, et al. 1996), and flat affect (Werry and McClellan 1992), appear to be associated with poor outcome. A lower degree of recovery (the degree of impairment following the first admission, for example) (Werry and McClellan 1992; Eggers and Bunk 1997) and a greater number of subsequent episodes of the illness predict a poorer outcome.

Poor premorbid adjustment (McGlashan 1986; Werry and McClellan 1992; Maziade, Bouchard, et al. 1996; Maziade, Gingras, et al. 1996; Eggers and Bunk 1997) also predicts a poor outcome, although the exact nature of the premorbid adjustment seems to vary. For instance, a developmental disorder that Gillberg and colleagues (1993) referred to as "DAMP" (deficit in attention, motor control, and perception) may be an important predictor for long-term psychosocial outcome, regardless of whether the disorder is associated with psychosis. Although Maziade et al. found that 75 percent of their schizophrenic patients had had prior behavior or developmental problems, these apparently were not related to the long-term outcome (Maziade, Bouchard, et al. 1996; Maziade, Gingras, et al. 1996). In the Chestnut Lodge study, McGlashan (1986) showed that premorbid functioning correlated with the short-term outcome, family overinvolvement and positive psychotic symptoms affected the midterm outcome, and a family history of schizophrenia and premorbid social functioning influenced the long-term outcome.

In summary, those working in the field have largely defined schizophrenia by the presence of chronic positive and negative symptoms and bipolar disorder by episodes of mood disorder with or without psychosis and with or without a complete remission of mood symptoms in the interim. Major depression is also frequently recurrent, often with milder symptoms persisting between fulminant episodes. While a thorough discussion of outcome is beyond the scope of this chapter, it is impossible to disentangle phenomenology from long-term course, in view of the relationship between the two. In the SCMHP sample, given the diagnostic stability of the diagnoses, GAF (Global Assessment of Functioning) scores were predictable, as is evident in Table 1.13. While there were no differences at baseline, by the 6-month point group differences had emerged. Subjects with psychotic depression were functioning the best, while schizophrenic patients and those with an undiagnosed psychosis at baseline were in the worst condition, with bipolar subjects falling somewhere in between.

With regard to course of the disorder, four of the patients with a baseline diagnosis of schizophrenia or a schizophrenia spectrum disorder in fact recovered from their psychosis. At the 24-month follow-up, one of these patients was given the diagnosis of schizoaffective bipolar, and two were considered schizophreniform. Rates of recovery and of partial recovery were similar for all of the psychotic groups, as Table 1.14 illustrates. However, of the five people who went on to become chronically psychotic, four were initially diagnosed with schizophrenia. Two of the subjects with an undiagnosed psychosis at baseline were not felt to be psychotic at the 6-month point and were dropped from the study. Three subjects were lost to follow-up.

More than 50 percent of the young bipolar subjects had recurrent episodes that never completely remitted. Subjects suffering from major depression with psychosis also followed an episodic course but were more likely to achieve intermorbid recovery. Patients who had only a single episode or had multiple episodes with intermorbid recovery basically returned to their premorbid level of functioning, not that this was necessarily a very high level. Of those with chronic psychosis or multiple episodes with incomplete recovery, 100 percent and 53 percent, respectively, showed significant deterioration.

Predictive validity of symptoms traditionally felt to be characteristic of schizophrenia (bizarre delusions, thought insertion, thought broadcasting, commenting or conversing voices) occurred in 80 percent of patients with chronic psychosis but also in 57 percent of patients who had a single episode of psychosis. Insidious onset was present in 100 percent of patients with chronic psychosis but in only 64 percent of the patients who suffered a single psychotic episode and 43 percent of those who had multiple episodes with remission.

Regarding mood symptoms, prominent depressed mood occurred in fewer than half of patients who had a single or multiple episodes of illness and in none of the chronically psychotic subjects. Elated mood was observed in 15 percent of the patients with a single episode of psychosis, in 40 percent of those with episodic disorders, and in 20 percent of those with chronic psychosis.

The observation that premorbid function is one of the best predictors of

Table 1.13. Global assessment of functioning scores through 48 months

	Schizophrenia		Bipolar disorder		Major depressive disorder		Other		Significance F (p)	
	Low	High	Low	High	Low	High	Low	High	Low	High
Baseline	27.4	54.7	25.8	64.3	28.9	61.2	24.9	56.7	NS*	NS
6 months	38.5	51.0	48.4	58.7	57.7	65.0	55.1	65.6	5.61 (0.002)	4.21 (0.011)
24 months	40.2	51.6	55.6	63.8	58.2	67.9	52.0	61.2	3.61 (0.021)	5.42 (0.003)
48 months	42.5	52.8	51.9	67.3	63.5	74.3	53.7	66.2	4.21 (0.011)	6.96 (0.001)

*Not significant

Table 1.14. Episode recurrence according to baseline diagnosis

	Schizophrenia (N = 17)	Bipolar disorder (N = 15)	Major depressive disorder (N = 12)	Other (N = 9)	Total (N = 53)
	n (%)	n (%)	n (%)	n (%)	n (%)
Single episode, complete remission	4 (23.5)	3 (20.0)	4 (33.3)	3 (33.3)	14 (26.4)
Multiple episodes, complete remission	3 (17.6)	3 (20.0)	3 (25.0)	2 (22.2)	11 (20.8)
Multiple episodes, incomplete remission	6 (35.3)	8 (53.3)	4 (33.3)	3 (33.3)	21 (39.6)
Chronic psychosis	4 (23.5)	0	0	1 (11.1)	5 (9.4)
Chronic nonpsychosis	0	1 (6.7)	1 (8.3)	0	2 (3.8)

outcome (Werry and McClellan 1992; Eggers and Bunk 1997) is true for all psychoses, not just schizophrenia. The following example demonstrates the relationship between premorbid function and outcome. A 17-year-old male was given a research diagnosis of schizophrenia, specifically schizoaffective-bipolar. As an elementary school student, he had had multiple fears (including the fear of not being able to get to the bathroom on time) and had been a "loner" who was chronically absent from school for anywhere from 28 to 55 days per year. This pattern continued through middle school. At age 17 he became increasingly delusional. He inferred from the way certain signs were arranged that Christ was returning, and he also feared that evil forces were inserting thoughts into his head. Some months later he became euphoric and expansive, with increased speech and decreased sleep but without increased energy or racing thoughts. When he started hearing the voice of the "evil caretaker," he was hospitalized. He was treated with lithium and stelazine, became depressed, and when seen at the 6-month point, was still delusional but without mood symptoms. At the 24-month point, while on medication he was neither psychotic nor thought- or mood-disordered. He had returned to school and was attending special education classes when he was threatened with dismissal. Once he left school, he was supposedly actively seeking employment, but in fact he mostly sat around and watched television. Things had not changed at the 48-month point. However, there was no evidence of psychosis or negative symptoms. His mother had been diagnosed with bipolar disorder, and his father suffered from paranoia without mood disorder. This young man blended relatively poor premorbid adjustment with symptoms of both schizophrenia and bipolar disorder and ultimately returned to his premorbid state of relatively poor functioning (now in an occupational rather than an academic setting), although not without some modest social contact. Thus, even though he returned to his premorbid level of function, his outcome, as measured against productivity, was at best fair.

Assessment

One usually undertakes an assessment for psychosis for one of three reasons, the most common of which is clinical. The practice parameters formulated by the American Academy of Child and Adolescent Psychiatry (2001) do a good job of covering the areas in need of systematic assessment in cases of psychosis. If one is trying to understand the patient, as opposed to merely deriving a diagnosis, a comprehensive clinical assessment is necessary. This includes a thorough clinical interview with the parent(s) and the child or adolescent, designed to determine the presence or absence of specific *DSM* symptoms. The interview needs to include a period of at least five minutes during which the subject is permitted to talk at length on some topic unrelated to his or her psychopathology; this part of the interview is intended to assess affect, thought and language ability, motivation, curiosity, and interest. Such an assessment is necessary in cases of psychosis so that negative symptoms and developmental difficulties can subsequently be evaluated.

An interview with the family or with a significant other is imperative because it can furnish important information about the onset of symptoms. A review of medical records or prior clinical contact is also needed to determine the clinical course of the illness before the time of assessment. When the subject is a child, it is useful to conduct several interview sessions assessing mental status both to help the child feel comfortable and to specifically inquire about psychotic symptoms. A high rate of cognitive and educational impairment necessitates psychoeducational testing. In the case of school-aged youth, this should include a review of school records, a comprehensive IQ test, achievement testing, and, if possible, an assessment of language skills on the basis of a language sample.

The second reason to undertake an assessment for psychosis is simply to determine whether a specific condition is present or absent—that is, to fit the subject into a diagnostic category. If that is all one is trying to do, a semistructured interview may be more helpful than a structured one. Structured interviews can lead to the overreporting of so-called unusual phenomena, such as manic or psychotic symptoms, probably because the respondent has misunderstood a question or the concept being described (McClellan and Werry 2000) or lacks the verbal skills necessary to understand the concepts and questions in the first place (Valla et al. 1994).

Third, an assessment for psychosis might be carried out in an effort to understand the phenomenology of a given disorder or comorbid conditions related to the disorder of interest. If that is one's goal, *DSM*-based structured interviews, most of which were designed to be "lean and mean" rather than comprehensive and detailed, may prove too limited in scope. For instance, given the high rates of comorbidity in the case of childhood disorders, in our opinion a comprehensive (semistructured) interview should be able to identify childhood as well as adult disorders. Although psychiatric interviews of children are designed to encompass most childhood disorders, they do not include pervasive developmental disorders. Given the overlap in the phenomenology of language and thought disorder, odd-relatedness, and negative symptoms, however, this is an important oversight. Structured interviews of adults cover neither developmental nor childhood behavior disorders. The latter may not be adequately ascertained from the subject, with the result that clinicians must rely on a parent or childhood caregiver to provide such early information (Barkley 1997).

Several rating scales have been developed to systematically rate the mental status and aspects of psychosis in adults and children. The Child Psychiatric Rating Scale (Anonymous 1985) and the Brief Psychiatric Rating Scale for Children (Hughes et al. 2001) are the most comprehensive and are meant to be carried out at the completion of the psychiatric interview. Specific instruments for evaluating positive and negative symptoms include the scales for the assessment of positive and negative symptoms (SAPS and SANS) (Andreasen 1984), which were developed for research purposes (as opposed to clinical care). They require considerable training to administer and take about half an hour each. The Positive and Negative Syndrome Scale (PANSS) (Kay, Fiszbein, and Opler 1987) adapted items from other rating scales and then added to them to produce an instrument more focused on psychosis. A childhood version of the adult PANSS, the kiddie-PANSS (Fields et al. 1994), was modified through successive field trials to encompass developmental characteristics of both children and adolescents. It appeared to show adequate reliability and validity in the case of the inpatient sample that was tested, but it does not seem to have been used beyond its initial publication.

Finally, although this chapter has focused on psychosis resulting from psychiatric disorders, organic causes should also be kept in mind. The physical conditions that most often cause psychosis are:

1. Acute intoxication (both drug and alcohol)
2. CNS lesions (seizure disorder, infections—especially Lyme disease, head trauma, tumors)
3. Endocrine disorders (Cushing's disease, congenital adrenal hyperplasia, hyper- or hypothyroidism)
4. Metabolic disorders (Wilson's disease and in rare cases porphyria)

A thorough physical and neurological examination may be needed, and appropriate tests should be performed, as indicated by the patient's history and by clinical examination, including toxicology screens, laboratory tests, electroencephalogram, and neuroimaging (see Table 1.1).

Conclusions

Psychosis in adolescence is a serious condition regardless of the specific diagnosis. Poor premorbid functioning, which has been considered a robust predictor of outcome, appears to be a mixture of poor cognitive functioning and an early psychiatric comorbidity (including early substance abuse) that persists regardless of the status of the psychotic and affective symptoms, although clearly those symptoms and behaviors further compromise functioning. We do not yet understand the relationship between early comorbidity and the onset of schizophrenic or affective psychosis. From a practical standpoint, however, assessment and treatment need to focus not only on the typical symptoms of psychosis, depression, and mania but also on the educational, psychosocial, and child psychiatric comorbidities that appear to underpin all instances of psychosis in young people.

ACKNOWLEDGMENTS

This work was supported by a grant from the National Institute of Mental Health (MH44801). We are indebted to Janet Lavelle, to the project psychiatrists, interviewers, and data team, and to the mental health professionals in Suffolk County, Long Island, for their continued support. We are particularly grateful to the people who participated in this study for graciously giving us their time and their valuable input.

REFERENCES

Addington, J., and Addington, D. (1998). Effect of substance misuse in early psychosis. *British Journal of Psychiatry* 172:134–36.
American Academy of Child and Adolescent Psychiatry. (2001). Summary of the practice parameters for the assessment and treatment of children and adolescents with schizophrenia. *Journal of the American Academy of Child and Adolescent Psychiatry* 40(7):S4–S23.

American Psychiatric Association. (2000). *Diagnostic and Statistical Manual of Psychiatric Disorders IV-TR.* Washington, D.C.: APA Press.

Ammons, R. B., and Ammons, C. H. (1962). The Quick Test: Provisional manual. *Psychological Reports* 11:111–61.

Andreasen, N. C. (1983). *Scale for the Assessment of Negative Symptoms (SANS).* Iowa City: University of Iowa Press.

Andreasen, N. C. (1984). *Scale for the Assessment of Positive Symptoms (SAPS).* Iowa City: University of Iowa Press.

Angold, A., and Costello, E. J. (1993). Depressive comorbidity in children and adolescents: Empirical, theoretical, and methodological issues. *American Journal of Psychiatry* 50:1779–91.

Angold, A., Costello, E. J., and Worthman, C. M. (1998). Puberty and depression: The roles of age, pubertal status, and pubertal timing. *Psychological Medicine* 28:51–61.

Anonymous. (1985). Rating scales and assessment instruments for use in pediatric psychopharmacology research. *Psychopharmacology Bulletin* 21:714–1124.

Asarnow, R. F., Asamen, J., Granholm, E., Sherman, T., Watkins, J. M., and Williams, M. E. (1994). Cognitive/neuropsychological studies of children with a schizophrenic disorder. *Schizophrenia Bulletin* 20:647–69.

Aylward, E., Walker, E., and Bettes, B. (1984). Intelligence in schizophrenia: Meta-analysis of the research. *Schizophrenia Bulletin* 10:430–59.

Barkley, R. A. (1997). Advancing age, declining ADHD. *American Journal of Psychiatry* 154:1323–25.

Beiser, M., Erickson, D., Fleming, J. A., and Iacono, W. G. (1993). Establishing the onset of psychotic illness. *American Journal of Psychiatry* 150:1349–54.

Bell, R. C., Dudgeon, P., McGorry, P. D., and Jackson, H. J. (1998). The dimensionality of schizophrenia concepts in first-episode psychosis. *Acta Psychiatrica Scandinavica* 97:334–42.

Bettes, B. A., and Walker, E. (1987). Positive and negative symptoms in psychotic and other psychiatrically disturbed children. *Journal of Child Psychology and Psychiatry* 28:555–68.

Bromet, E. J., Schwartz, J. E., Fennig, S., Geller, L., Jandorf, L., Kovasznay, B., et al. (1992). The epidemiology of psychoses: The Suffolk County Mental Health Project. *Schizophrenia Bulletin* 18:243–55.

Cannon, M., Jones, P., Gilvarry, C., Rifkin, L., McKenzie, K., Foerster, A., et al. (1997). Premorbid social functioning in schizophrenia and bipolar disorder: Similarities and differences. *American Journal of Psychiatry* 154:1544–50.

Caplan, R., Guthrie, D., Tang, B., Komo, S., and Asarnow, R. F. (2000). Thought disorder in childhood schizophrenia: Replication and update of concept. *Journal of the American Academy of Child and Adolescent Psychiatry* 39:771–78.

Caplan, R., Guthrie, D., Tang, B., Nuechterlein, K. H., and Asarnow, R. F. (2001). Thought disorder in attention-deficit hyperactivity disorder. *Journal of the American Academy of Child and Adolescent Psychiatry* 40:965–72.

Carlson, G. A., Bromet, E. J., and Jandorf, L. (1998). Conduct disorder and mania: What does it mean in adults? *Journal of Affective Disorders* 148:199–205.

Carlson, G. A., Bromet, E. J., and Sievers, S. B. (2000). Phenomenology and outcome of youth and adult onset subjects with psychotic mania. *American Journal of Psychiatry* 157:213–19.

Carlson, G. A., Fennig, S., and Bromet, E. T. (1994). The confusion between bipolar disorder and schizophrenia in youth: Where does it stand in the 1990's? *Journal of the American Academy of Child and Adolescent Psychiatry* 33:453–60.

Chambers, W. J., Puig-Antich, J., Hirsch, M., Paez, P., Ambrosini, P. J., Tabrizi, M. A., et al. (1985). The assessment of affective disorders in children and adolescents by semi-structured interview: Test-retest reliability of the schedule for affective disorders and schizophrenia for school-age children, present episode version. *Archives of General Psychiatry* 42:696–702.

Cornblatt, B., Obuchowski, M., Roberts, S., Pollack, S., and Erlenmeyer-Kimling, L. (1999). Cognitive and behavioral precursors of schizophrenia. *Development and Psychopathology* 11:487–508.

DeLisi, L. E. (1992).The significance of age of onset for schizophrenia. *Schizophrenia Bulletin* 18:209–15.

Eggers, C., and Bunk, D. (1997).The long term course of childhood-onset schizophrenia: A 42-year follow-up. *Schizophrenia Bulletin* 23:105–17.

Fields, J. H., Grochowski, S., Lindenmayer, J. P., Kay, S. R., Grosz, D., Hyman, R. B., et al. (1994). Assessing positive and negative symptoms in children and adolescents. *American Journal of Psychiatry* 151:249–53.

Galdos, P., and van Os, J. (1995). Gender, psychopathology, and development: From puberty to early adulthood. *Schizophrenia Research* 14:105–12.

Geddes, J. R., Verdoux, H., Takei, N., Lawrie, S. M., Bovet, P., Eagles, J. M., et al. (1999). Schizophrenia and complications of pregnancy and labor: An individual patient data meta-analysis. *Schizophrenia Bulletin* 25:413–23.

Gillberg, D., Hellgren, L., and Gillberg, C. (1993). Psychotic disorders diagnosed in adolescence: Outcome at age 30 years. *Journal of Child Psychology and Psychiatry* 34:1173–85.

Hughes, C. W., Rintelmann, J., Emslie, G. J., Lopez, M., and MacCabe, N. (2001). A revised anchored version of the BPRS-C for childhood psychiatric disorders. *Journal of Child and Adolescent Psychopharmacology* 11:77–93.

Isohanni, M., Jones, P. B., Moilanen, K., Rantakallio, P., Veijola, J., Oja, H., et al. (2001). Early developmental milestones in adult schizophrenia and other psychoses: A 31-year follow-up of the Northern Finland 1966 birth cohort. *Schizophrenia Research* 52:1–19.

Kay, S. R., Fiszbein, A., and Opler, L. A. (1987). The Positive and Negative Syndrome Scale (PANSS) for schizophrenia. *Schizophrenia Bulletin* 13:261–76.

Kendler, K. S., Gallagher, T. J., Abelson, J. M., and Kessler, R. C. (1996). Lifetime prevalence, demographic risk factors, and diagnostic validity of nonaffective psychosis as assessed in a U.S. community sample: The National Comorbidity Survey. *Archives of General Psychiatry* 53:1022–31.

Kinney, D. K., Yurgelun-Todd, D. A., Levy, D. L., Medoff, D., Lajonchere, C. M., and Radford-Paregol, M. (1993). Obstetrical complications in patients with bipolar disorder and their siblings. *Psychiatry Research* 48:47–56.

Klin, A., Sparrow, S. S., Marans, W. D., Carter, A., and Volkmar, F. R. (2000). Assessment issues in children and adolescents with Asperger Syndrome. In *Asperger Syndrome*, ed. A. Klin, F. R. Volkmar, and S. S. Sparrow, 309–39. New York: Guilford Press.

Lachar, D., Randle, S. L., Harper, R. A., Scott-Gurnell, K. C., Lewis, K. R., Santos, C. W., et al. (2001). The brief psychiatric rating scale for children (BPRS-C): Validity and reliability of an anchored version. *Journal of the American Academy of Child and Adolescent Psychiatry* 40:333–40.

Loranger, A. W., and Levine, P. M. (1978). Age at onset of bipolar affective illness. *Archives of General Psychiatry* 35:1345–48.

Marcelis, M., van Os, J., Sham, P., Jones, P., Gilvarry, C., Cannon, M., et al. (1998). Obstetric complications and familial morbid risk of psychiatric disorders. *American Journal of Medical Genetics* 81:29–36.

Marenco, S., and Weinberger, D. R. (2000). The neurodevelopmental hypothesis of schizophrenia: Following a trail of evidence from cradle to grave. *Developmental Psychopathology* 12:501–27.

Maziade, M., Bouchard, S., Gingras, N., Charron, L., Cardinal, A., Gauthier, B., et al. (1996). Long-term stability of diagnosis and symptom dimensions in a systematic sample of patients with outset of schizophrenia in childhood and early adolescence, Pt. 2: Positive/negative distinction and childhood predictors of outcome. *British Journal of Psychiatry* 169:371–78.

Maziade, M., Gingras, N., Rodrigue, C., Bouchard, S., Cardinal, A., Gauthier, B., et al. (1996). Long-term stability of diagnosis and symptom dimensions in a systematic sample of patients with outset of schizophrenia in childhood and early adolescence, Pt. 1: Nosology, sex and age of onset. *British Journal of Psychiatry* 169:361–70.

McClellan, J., Breiger, D., McCurry, C., and Hlastala, S. A. (2003). Premorbid functioning in early-onset psychotic disorders. *Journal of the American Academy of Child and Adolescent Psychiatry* 42(6):666–72.

McClellan, J. M., and Werry, J. S. (2000). Introduction: Research psychiatric diagnostic interviews for children and adolescents. *Journal of the American Academy of Child and Adolescent Psychiatry* 39:19–27.

McGlashan, T. H. (1986). Predictors of shorter-, medium-, and longer-term outcome in schizophrenia. *American Journal of Psychiatry* 143:50–55.

Mojtabai, R., Bromet, E., Harvey, P., Carlson, G., Fennig, S., and Craig, T. (2000). Are there neuropsychological differences between first-admission schizophrenia and psychotic affective disorders? *American Journal of Psychiatry* 157:1453–60.

Murray, R. M. (1991). The neurodevelopmental basis of sex differences in schizophrenia. *Psychological Medicine* 21:565–75.

Nicolson, R., Lenane, M., Brookner, F., Gochman, P., Kumra, S., Spechler, L., et al. (2001). Children and adolescents with psychotic disorder not otherwise specified: A 2- to 8-year follow-up study. *Comprehensive Psychiatry* 42:319–25.

Peralta, V., and Cuesta, M. J. (1999). Diagnostic significance of Schneider's first-rank symptoms in schizophrenia: Comparative study between schizophrenic and non-schizophrenic psychotic disorders. *British Journal of Psychiatry* 174:243–48.

Poulton, R., Caspi, A., Moffitt, T. E., Cannon, M., Murray, R., and Harrington, H. (2000). Children's self-reported psychotic symptoms and adult schizophreniform disorder: A 15-year longitudinal study. *Archives of General Psychiatry* 57:1053–58.

Remschmidt, H. E., Schulz, E., Matthias, M., Warnke, A., and Trott, G. E. (1994). Childhood-onset schizophrenia: History of the concept and recent studies. *Schizophrenia Bulletin* 20:727–745.

Rosen, L. N., Rosenthal, N. E., van Dusen, P. H., Dunner, D. L., and Fieve, R. R. (1983). Age at onset and number of psychotic symptoms in bipolar I and schizoaffective disorder. *American Journal of Psychiatry* 140:1523–24.

Russell, A. J., Munro, J. C., Jones, P. B., Hemsley, D. R., and Murray, R. M. (1997). Schizophrenia and the myth of intellectual decline. *American Journal of Psychiatry* 154:635–39.

Sigurdsson, E., Fombonne, E., Sayal, K., and Checkley, S. (1999). Neurodevelopmental antecedents of early-onset bipolar affective disorder. *British Journal of Psychiatry* 174:121–27.

Spitzer, R., Williams, J., Gibbon, M., and First, M. (1992). The Structured Clinical Interview for *DSM-III-R* (SCID), Pt. 1: History, rationale, and description. *Archives of General Psychiatry* 49:624–29.

Tamminga, C. A., Buchanan, R. W., and Gold, J. M. (1998). The role of negative symptoms and cognitive dysfunction in schizophrenia outcome. *International Clinical Psychopharmacology* 13(Suppl. 3):21–26.

Tanenberg-Karant, M., Fennig, S., Ram, R., Krishna, J., Jandorf, L., and Bromet, E. (1995). Bizarre delusions and first-rank symptoms in a first-admission sample: A preliminary analysis of prevalence and correlates. *Comprehensive Psychiatry* 36:428–34.

Ulloa, R. E., Birmaher, B., Axelson, D., Williamson, D. E., Brent, D. A., Ryan, N. D., et al. (2000). Psychosis in a pediatric mood and anxiety disorders clinic: Phenomenology and correlates. *Journal of the American Academy of Child and Adolescent Psychiatry* 39:337–45.

Valla, J. P., Bergeron, L., Berube, H., Gaudet, N., and St.-Georges, M. (1994). A structured pictorial questionnaire to assess *DSM-III-R*–based diagnoses in children (6–11 years): Development, validity, and reliability. *Journal of Abnormal Child Psychology* 22:403–23.

van Os, J., Hanssen, M., Bijl, R. V., and Vollebergh, W. (2001). Prevalence of psychotic disorder and community level of psychotic symptoms: An urban-rural comparison. *Archives of General Psychiatry* 58:663–68.

van Os, J., Takei, N., Castle, D. J., Wessely, S., Der, G., and Murray, R. M. (1995). Premorbid abnormalities in mania, schizomania, acute schizophrenia, and chronic schizophrenia. *Social Psychiatry and Psychiatric Epidemiology* 30:274–78.

van Os, J., Verdoux, H., Maurice-Tison, S., Gay, B., Liraud, F., Salamon, R., and Bourgeois, M. (1999). Self-reported psychosis-like symptoms and the continuum of psychosis. *Social Psychiatry and Psychiatric Epidemiology* 34:459–63.

Vance, B., Hankins, N., and Reynolds, F. (1988). Prediction of Wechsler Intelligence Scale for Children—Revised Full Scale IQ from the Quick Test of Intelligence and the Test of Nonverbal Intelligence for a referred sample of children and youth. *Journal of Clinical Psychology* 44:793–94.

Volkmar, F. R. (1996). Child and adolescent psychosis: A review of the past 10 years. *Journal of the American Academy of Child and Adolescent Psychiatry* 35:843–51.

Werry, J. S. (1996). Pervasive developmental, psychotic, and allied disorders. In L. Hectman (Ed.), *Do They Grow Out of It? Long-Term Outcomes of Childhood Disorders* (pp. 195–224). Washington, D.C.: American Psychiatric Press.

Werry, J. S., and McClellan, J. M. (1992). Predicting outcome in child and adolescent (early onset) schizophrenia and bipolar disorder. *Journal of the American Academy of Child and Adolescent Psychiatry* 31:147–50.

Werry, J. S., McClellan, J. M., Andrews, L. K., and Ham, M. (1994). Clinical features and outcome of child and adolescent schizophrenia. *Schizophrenia Bulletin* 20:619–30.

Werry, J. S., McClellan, J. M., and Chard, L. (1991). Childhood and adolescent schizophrenic, bipolar, and schizoaffective disorders: A clinical and outcome study. *Journal of the American Academy of Child and Adolescent Psychiatry* 30:457–65.

CHAPTER TWO

Toward a Unitary Developmental Hypothesis of Schizophrenia

Matcheri S. Keshavan, M.D.

Over the past several decades, it has become increasingly clear that schizophrenia is a brain disease, as was originally conceptualized by Emil Kraepelin more than a century ago. However, the precise pathophysiology of schizophrenia is still elusive. During recent years, at least three types of pathophysiological models have been proposed: those that posit altered pre- or perinatal brain development, those proposing periadolescent developmental abnormalities, and those that argue for neuronal degenerative processes after the onset of illness. There is clearly a need for a unifying hypothesis. In what follows, I will attempt to integrate clinical facts concerning schizophrenic illness with insights emerging from basic neuroscience and developmental neurobiology. We will review the three competing models of schizophrenia and suggest that alterations in the glutamatergic system can potentially serve as an integrative model of this illness.

Essential Facts of Schizophrenia and the Neurodevelopmental Models

An understanding of both the clinical facts of schizophrenic illness and the process of human brain development is critical to efforts to clarify the pathophysiology of this illness (Wyatt et al. 1988). Certain clinical observations consistently characterize the course of schizophrenia: (1) clinical and epidemiological studies show premorbid cognitive deficits, in many cases dating back to early development (Done et al. 1994; Jones and Cannon 1998); (2) schizophrenia has a characteristic onset in adolescence (Häfner et al. 1993); and (3) there appears to be some deterioration during the early course of schizophrenia, at least in a subgroup of patients (McGlashan and Fenton 1993). Other central features in this illness involve relatively continual disturbances in working memory and executive functions that may precede and then persist during the illness (Elvevag and Goldberg 2000), the likely involvement of cortical and subcortical dopamine (DA) neurotransmission (Weinberger 1987), and the importance of genetic and environmental factors in pathogenesis.

Brain development, beginning at conception, continues well into adolescence and young adulthood. The developmental processes of neurogenesis, neuronal proliferation, neural differentiation, and migration characterize the prenatal and perinatal periods of human development. More neurons are generated than survive, and a process of programmed neuron loss, or apoptosis, occurs, mostly prenatally. Postnatally, the process of synaptic proliferation continues through middle childhood and is followed by a programmed elimination of synapses. Substantial refinement of brain structure and function therefore occurs during adolescence.

The Early Developmental Model

The well-known premorbid abnormalities in schizophrenia (for a review, see Haas and Sweeney 1992) have suggested that this illness may have its roots very early in development. The observed brain abnormalities in schizophrenia have been thought to stem primarily from one or another causal factors, both intrauterine and perinatal, perhaps during the second half of the gestation period. In these early neurodevelopmental models (Murray and Lewis 1987; Weinberger 1987), a fixed lesion traceable to early life interacts with normal brain maturation later on. The following observations have been advanced as evidence in favor of this view:

1. Neuropathological observations suggest altered cytoarchitecture indicative of possible errors in the early developmental phenomena of neural genesis or migration in schizophrenia (Kovelman and Scheibel 1984; Akbarian et al. 1993; Weinberger 1995).

2. Epidemiological data suggest associations between intrauterine or perinatal brain insult (Cannon 1997), exposure to viral infection (Mednick et al. 1988), and malnutrition (Susser and Lin 1992), and the subsequent emergence of schizophrenia. (For a review, see Jones and Cannon 1998.)

3. High-risk studies have revealed neurointegrative and cognitive deficits in preschizophrenic children that date back to early childhood (Fish 1987; Erlenmeyer-Kimling and Cornblatt 1992). Additionally, birth-cohort studies have found that children and adolescents who developed schizophrenia at a later date exhibited several characteristic abnormalities such as poorer intellectual and social functioning and language deficits (Done et al. 1994).

4. Magnetic resonance spectroscopy (MRS) studies have identified regional brain structural (Cannon and Marco 1994; Keshavan et al. 1997; Seidman et al. 1997; Lawrie et al.) and metabolic abnormalities in young relatives of schizophrenic patients (Keshavan et al. 1997).

It is unlikely that the early developmental dysmaturation involves the first steps of neurogenesis, because defects of neural tube formation (e.g., midline cysts, spina bifida) are not associated with an increased incidence of schizophrenia. Cell death by necrosis is also unlikely, because necrosis is typically followed by glial proliferation, and reactive gliosis is not seen in schizophrenia (Kotrla, Sater, and Weinberger 1997). Reactive gliosis typically occurs following lesions after 16 to 20 weeks of gestation (Norman 1996), which again supports the view that the pathological processes of schizophrenia could have set in before this stage of development. The processes of programmed cell death, neural migration, and/or synaptic proliferation, which begin during the second trimester of pregnancy, are more likely to be implicated. Regardless of the process involved, however, these abnormalities tend to be clinically manifest as premorbid behavioral precursors of schizophrenia (Watt 1978; Fish 1987).

The Late Developmental Model

Based on the typical adolescent onset of schizophrenic illness, an alternative view has been proposed that the pathophysiology of this disorder has its onset in postnatal life. Drawing on data that indicate substantial changes in brain biology during adolescence, Feinberg initially proposed that schizophrenia may result from an abnormality in periadolescent synaptic pruning

(Feinberg 1982–83, 1990), although this model did not clarify whether too many, too few, or simply the wrong synapses were being pruned.

Adolescence is characterized by substantive changes in several in vivo neurobiological measures that may indirectly reflect changes in synapse density. Delta sleep, which represents the summed postsynaptic potentials in large assemblies of cortical and subcortical axons and dendrites, dramatically decreases during adolescence (Feinberg 1982–83). Periadolescent reductions are also seen in the synthesis of membrane phospholipids as measured by phosphorus MRS (Pettegrew and Keshavan 1991) and cortical gray matter volume (Jernigan and Tallal 1990). Regional prefrontal metabolism also decreases (Chugani, Phelps, and Mazziotta 1987). In schizophrenia, similar, but more pronounced, decrements are seen, relative to healthy controls, in delta sleep (Keshavan, Reynolds, et al. 1998), membrane synthesis (Pettegrew and Keshavan 1991), gray matter volume (Zipursky 1992; Keshavan et al. 1994), and prefrontal metabolism (Andreasen et al. 1992). These observations indirectly suggest the possibility, in schizophrenia, of an exaggeration of the normative process of synaptic pruning in certain brain regions such as the prefrontal cortex (Keshavan, Anderson, and Pettegrew 1994; Pettegrew et al. 1997). Neural network modeling studies also support the view that schizophrenia may be associated with synaptic, or axonal, pruning, but not with neuronal cell death (Hoffman and McGlashan 1997; McGlashan and Hoffman 2000). Neuropathological studies point to a reduction in the synapse-rich neuropil and a consequent increase in cortical neuron density (Selemon, Rajkowska, and Goldman-Rakic 1995); reductions have also been reported in the expression of synaptophysin, a synaptic marker (Eastwood and Harrison 1995; Glantz and Lewis 1997), and in the density of dendritic spines (Garey, Patel, and Ong 1994). These observations suggest an overall reduction of cortical synapse-rich neuropil in schizophrenia, which could in turn lead to reduced neuronal plasticity. The net effect may be a reduction of the neuronal modulatory capacity to handle the normative academic, familial, and interpersonal demands of adolescence. When a critical threshold of such neuropil loss is exceeded, symptoms and signs of schizophrenia may appear.

The Neurodegenerative Model

Kraepelin (1919) suggested that schizophrenia may be associated with acquired neurodegenerative changes beginning in early adulthood, a view that led to the term *dementia praecox*. This view continues to receive support from several lines of clinical evidence:

1. Some, though not all, patients with schizophrenia may follow a deteriorating rather than static course, at least during the first few years of their illness (Loebel, Liberman, and Alvir 1992; McGlashan and Fenton 1993); such patients appear to take longer to recover and show less complete recovery over successive episodes of the illness (Lieberman et al. 1996).

2. Early treatment with antipsychotic drugs appears to arrest the progression of the disease in some schizophrenic patients (Wyatt 1991).

3. Prolonged untreated illness predicts a poorer outcome, suggesting a possible neurotoxic effect of psychosis (Lieberman 1993).

4. Some studies reveal progressive structural alterations in the brains of some schizophrenic patients (DeLisi 1995; Keshavan, Haas, et al. 1998; Thompson et al. 2001), although other studies show no change (Jaskiw et al. 1994) and yet others show increases in temporal lobe structures (Keshavan, Haas, et al. 1998; Lieberman et al. 2001). Alterations in neurophysiological (P300) indices are also consistent with ongoing cerebral degeneration in a significant subgroup of schizophrenic patients (Mathalon et al. 2000).

These lines of evidence converge in the view that at least a subgroup of patients with schizophrenia may suffer progressive brain degeneration. Proposed mechanisms for such neurodegeneration include oxidative stress (Coyle 1996) and neurochemical sensitization from repeated exposure to neurochemical stressors (Lieberman, Sheitman, and Kinon 1997). Nevertheless, one needs also to entertain the possibility that the observed neurobiological changes over the course of the illness may simply be plastic adaptations of the nervous system to the experience of being psychotic or cognitively impoverished (Weinberger and McClure 2002).

Glutamatergic Dysfunction as a Potential Integrative Model

Although the above models may seem to conflict on the surface, they can be reconciled. Studies of neurochemical and molecular mechanisms that regulate early brain development, postnatal brain plasticity, and brain degeneration can potentially help in understanding a complex disease, such as schizophrenia, that may be characterized by multiple pathophysiological processes.

Excitatory amino acid neurotransmitters such as the glutamatergic system are good candidates for examination in this context. The glutamatergic hypothesis of schizophrenia arose from the observation of similarities between the clinical manifestations of schizophrenia and psychosis caused by phencyclidine (PCP), an N-methyl-D-aspartate (NMDA) receptor antagonist (Javitt and Zukin 1991; Coyle 1996; Tamminga 1998), and reductions in cerebrospinal fluid glutamate levels (Kim et al. 1980), altered glutamate metabolism in schizophrenia (Tsai et al. 1995), and altered gene expression for NMDA receptor subunits (Akbarian et al. 1996). The glutamatergic hypothesis, which has received much attention in recent years, can be formulated in a "three-hit" model in order to provide a collective conceptualization of the early and late developmental and neurodegenerative processes (the three "hits") that may occur in this illness.

Glutamate, the predominant excitatory neurotransmitter in the mammalian brain, is critical to neuronal migration and neuronal survival during early development, for neuronal plasticity during adolescence, and for neuronal excitability and viability throughout life. Glutamate's effects are mediated by two types of receptors: those forming ion channels (ionotropic) and those linked to G-proteins (metabotropic). At least three types of ionotropic receptors—based on the ligand preference kainate; amino-3-hydroxy-5-methyl-4-isoxazole propionic acid (AMPA); or NMDA—and three types of metabotropic receptors have been identified (for a review, see Michaelis 1998). NMDA receptors are believed to be involved in learning, memory, and plasticity (McDonald and Johnstone 1990), while non-NMDA receptors may mediate much of fast excitatory neurotransmission in the brain. Metabotropic receptors, linked to second-messenger systems, may also serve as neuromodulators. Glutamate is therefore well positioned as a potential candidate for a pathophysiological role in a disorder like schizophrenia, in which processes of development, neuronal regulation, and neurotoxicity may all be involved.

Reduced Glutamate and Premorbid Neurocognitive Deficits

Glutamate is critically important to the early developmental processes of neurite outgrowth and neuronal migration (Komuro and Rakic 1993; Herkert, Rottger, and Becker 1998). The developing brain undergoes a period during which the stimulation of NMDA receptor channel complexes increases (McDonald, Silverstein, and Johnston 1988). This may be a critical period of vulnerability in the developing brain. Marked neuronal loss can be caused by nanomolar quantities of NMDA in the neonatal (day 7) rat; hypoxia during this period produces a similar kind of damage and can be prevented by NMDA antagonists (Johnston 1994). The net result of such excitotoxic damage may be a loss of neurons carrying glutamatergic receptors, or such damage may lead to a hypofunction of the NMDA receptors (Olney and Farber 1995). Continued activation of the glutamatergic system may be necessary for the survival of many neurons early in mammalian brain development; the absence of such activation can lead to programmed cell death (Ikonomidou et al. 1999). Exposure of the brain to a genetically or environmentally mediated brain insult (e.g., viruses, malnutrition) during a critical window of development such as the second or third trimester of pregnancy can therefore harm certain neuronal networks and cause a state of glutamatergic neuron loss. Such cell loss can underlie dysplastic neural networks manifest as structural and functional brain abnormalities in preschizophrenia individuals.

Reduced Tonic Glutamate During Adolescence and Premorbid Cognitive Deficits

Adolescence is a critical period of vulnerability in the developing brain. Synaptic proliferation proceeds throughout early childhood, followed by a programmed elimination of these synapses during late childhood and adolescence. The synaptic structural changes that occur in adolescence primarily involve asymmetric glutamatergic synapses (Zecevic, Bourgeois, and Rakic 1989). Synaptic survival is dependent on correlated neuronal activity and the principle that neurons that fire together wire together (Rabacchi et al. 1992; Constantine-Paton 1994; Hofer and Constantine-Paton 1994). During this period, the receptors for glutamate change their characteristics to enable participation in neuronal activity dependent on synaptic plasticity (Johnston 1995). Sustained activity of NMDA receptors is needed for synaptic survival (Constantine-Paton 1994). Silent NMDA receptors are converted to functional NMDA (hebbianlike) receptors by an activity-dependent mechanism. Excitatory postsynaptic potentials in these neurons lead to morphological changes (in length and/or cross-sectional size) in dendritic spines. The absence of such activity-dependent synaptic change that could result from the hypofunction of NMDA receptors could lead to a scenario in which too few functional synapses survive. A dysfunction of the glutamatergic system is therefore likely to be a key mechanism in setting the stage for the adolescent onset of schizophrenia.

The Role of Glutamate in Learning, Memory, and Other Cognitive Functions

Consolidation of memory is mediated by NMDA receptors through the process of long-term potentiation (LTP). Because this neurotransmitter system may play a critical part in working memory mechanisms, NMDA receptor dysfunction has been linked to the impairment of working memory characteristic of schizophrenia (Javitt et al. 1996). Moreover, deficits in NMDA receptor expression have recently been found to be associated with neuropsychological deficits in schizophrenia (Hirsch et al. 1997). It is therefore possible that a glutamatergic dysfunction underlies the cognitive deficits that appear to precede, and may be persistent aspects of, the schizophrenic illness.

Increased Phasic Glutamate Release and the Emergence of Psychotic Symptoms

The dopamine neurons leading from the striatum to the prefrontal cortex are under tonic excitatory control of both NMDA and non-NMDA (e.g., AMPA or kainate mediated) glutamatergic neurons (Whitton 1997; Takahata and Moghaddam 1998, 2000). On the one hand, both ionotropic as well as metabotropic receptors may be involved in such regulation (Cheramy et al. 1990; Ohno and Watanabe 1995). On the other hand, the mesolimbic dopamine neurons are under tonic inhibitory regulation by glutamatergic neurons (Floresco, Todd, and Grace 2001). Such inhibition may be mediated by gamma-aminobutyric acid (GABA) inhibitory neurons, which in turn inhibit major excitatory pathways, including the glutamatergic, cholinergic, and dopaminergic (Olney, Newcomer, and Farber 2002). Defective functioning of the corticostriatal glutamatergic systems could therefore lead to reduced tonic DA release in the prefrontal cortex and in turn increase phasic stress-induced DA release in mesolimbic circuits (Goff and Coyle 2001; Moghaddam 2002). The administration of ketamine, an NMDA receptor antagonist, produces psychotic symptoms in healthy volunteers; this effect, which might be related to a transient hyperglutamatergic state, is blocked by the glutamate-release inhibitor lamotrigene (Anand et al. 2000). A dysregulation of the tonic-phasic DA system has been considered to account for both the positive and negative symptoms of schizophrenia that emerge during adolescence (Grace 1993). An alteration of corticostriatal glutamatergic neurotransmission could therefore set the stage for a dysregulation in the tonic-phasic DA neurotransmission, thereby leading to the characteristic positive and negative symptoms of schizophrenia.

Increased Phasic Glutamate Release, Neurotoxicity, and Illness Progression

Another window of vulnerability may exist during the early course of the schizophrenic illness, especially if untreated. Excitotoxicity owing to excessive activation of the glutamate receptors has been implicated in the pathophysiology of ischemic stroke, hypoglycemic brain damage, and Huntington disease. A dysfunction in the glutamatergic system can potentially account for the neurodegenerative changes that may occur in some patients with untreated schizophrenic illness. Thus, reduced-tonic glutamatergic function could predispose a patient to excess phasic release of mesolimbic DA during recurrent psychotic exacerbations, which can in turn enhance glutamate release (Finlay and Zigmond 1997; Reid, Hsu, and Berger 1997). The enhanced glutamate release may provoke excitotoxic cell or dendrite loss via NMDA-receptor-mediated calcium influx into cells. The mechanisms underlying glutamate-induced excitotoxicity are complex and may be mediated by non-NMDA (e.g., AMPA) receptors (Deutsch et al. 2001) or by the stimulation of cholinergic, alpha-adrenergic, or dopamine D2 receptors (Garside, Furtado, and Mazurek 1996; Farber et al. 2002). The adolescent brain may be particularly vulnerable to such neurotoxicity. Farber et al. (1995) showed that while fetal rats younger than 6 weeks of age are insensitive to the neurotoxic action of NMDA antagonists, postpubertal rats (aged 3 to 4 months) become fully sensitive to this toxicity and remain so until young adulthood (10 months of age). Interestingly, the psychotogenic effects of glutamate antagonists such as phencyclidine (PCP) are very uncommon in children but are more commonly observed in adolescents and young adults. Such glutamatergic excess could also increase oxidative stress by the increased release of free radicals, thereby causing further neuronal damage (Coyle 1996). This effect appears to occur in all three classes of ionotropic glutamate receptors (Bondy and Lee 1993). Glutamatergic input to the mesolimbic DA tracts may also underlie the development of neurochemical sensitization (Karler, Calder, and Turkanis 1991; Itzhak and Martin 2000), although the development of sensitization to repeated stimulant administration can be blocked by NMDA antagonists (Karler, Calder, and Turkanis 1991; Kalivas 1993).

Genes, Environment, and the Glutamatergic Model

Among the best-established etiological factors in schizophrenia are genetic. While the precise gene(s) responsible remain undetermined, a multifactorial, polygenic etiology is considered most likely. Genes involved in brain development and plasticity are prime candidates for investigation (DeLisi 1997); genes involved in the regulation of glutamatergic transmission, such as glutamate receptor subunits, and receptor-associated proteins are also worthy of further investigation (Michaelis 1998). Partial deletion of the gene encoding a form of the NMDA receptor causes the same behavioral abnormalities as phencyclidine (Mohn et al. 1999). A possible linkage between schizophrenia in an African population and genetic loci for NMDA receptor subunits has also been described (Riley et al. 1997). Other recent studies, however, have failed to confirm an association between NMDA receptor subunits and the genetic transmission of schizophrenia (Rice et al. 2001).

The pathogenesis of schizophrenia may be determined by genes interacting with environmental factors such as perinatal hypoxia and intrauterine infections. It has been demonstrated that excessive glutamatergic activity may mediate some of the adverse effects of ischemia (Collins 1986). Cerebral ischemia caused by perinatal complications or viral infection may interact with genetic factors: inbred strains of mice with heritable differences in hippocampal anatomy show different susceptibility to anoxia, which lends support to the gene-environmental model of schizophrenia (Cruzio 1991). A genetically mediated glutamatergic defect may thus increase the risk of neuronal loss following early brain developmental insults.

Toward a Unitary Model of Schizophrenia Pathophysiology

As the above discussion indicates, glutamate may play a role in each of the characteristic components of schizophrenic illness: premorbid cognitive deficits, an adolescent onset of the illness, and early deterioration. Glutamatergic dysfunction could thus serve as a unitary explanation that ties these observations together. The schizophrenic syndrome may result from the cumulative effect of a possibly genetically mediated hypoplasia in the early and late maturational processes of brain development interacting with two factors: an adverse psychosocial environment during adolescence and early adulthood, and possible neurotoxic effects of untreated psychosis early in the schizophrenic illness. The premorbid vulnerability to schizophrenia may be caused by multiple genetic and environmental factors that interact to adversely affect early brain development. The adolescent onset of the disorder might therefore be determined by late brain maturational processes, as well as the stresses unique to adolescence. It is likely that early brain developmental defects (e.g., neuromigrational errors or defective neuronal proliferation) may create a predisposition to excessive postnatal synaptic pruning and/or neuronal apoptosis leading to the schizophrenic endophenotype. The development of a deficit state and of persistent psychopathology after the onset of illness may be determined by the possible neurotoxic effect of continuing psychotic illness.

Excitotoxic neuronal loss, interacting with genetic factors, may result from early brain adversity (viruses, malnutrition, perinatal trauma) leading to a selective loss of NMDA-receptor-bearing glutamatergic neurons in cortical and subcortical structures. This would account for the premorbid neurocognitive abnormalities seen among children and adolescents at risk for schizophrenia. The normative process of synaptic pruning that sets in around late childhood and adolescence could interact with the state of reduced tonic glutamatergic neurotransmission, perhaps acting via NMDA receptors, to result in a net excess of synapse elimination in the cortical and subcortical structures. Reduced activity in the corticostriatal glutamatergic neurons would lead to a diminished cortical dopaminergic tone because of a reduced release of mesocortical DA that comes on line during adolescence. Recent data (Scott et al. 2002) suggest that NMDA agonists may shift the balance of dopamine signaling toward the D1 receptor and away from the D2 receptors by recruiting D1 receptors to the plasma membrane; this might account for the therapeutic effects of glutamatergic agonists such as glycine and D-cycloserine in improving negative symptoms and cognitive deficits in schizophrenia. Interpersonal and cognitive deficits could lead to an inability to handle the psychosocial stresses unique to adolescence and early adulthood (Keshavan and Hogarty 1999). Such stresses, in turn, may precipitate an up-regulation of the subcortical DA neurons; the behavioral response to stress-induced phasic glutamate and DA release is therefore likely to be exaggerated, leading to positive psychotic symptoms. If untreated, persistent dopaminergic and consequent phasic glutamatergic excess could cause further excitotoxic brain damage, perhaps by increasing oxidative stress.

Other similar, integrative models view schizophrenia as a lifetime disorder of brain development, plasticity, and aging (Olney and Farber 1995; DeLisi

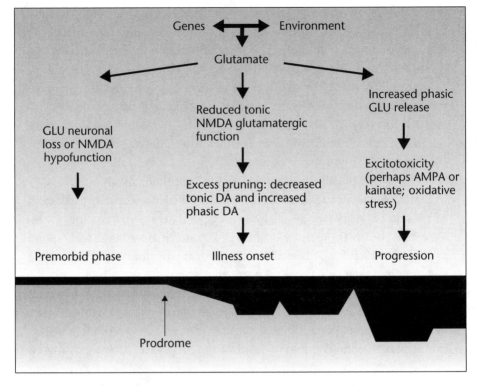

Fig. 2.1. The natural course of schizophrenia and the unitary glutamatergic model.
Note: GLU = glutamatergic; NMDA = *N*-acetyl-D-aspartate; DA = dopaminergic;
AMPA = amino-3-hydroxy-5-methyl-4-isoxazole prolionic acid. *Source:* Adapted from
Keshavan 1999.

1997; Lieberman, Sheitman, and Kinon 1997). I have attempted to extend
these models by proposing that the successive premorbid, morbid, and post-
onset pathology of schizophrenia results from a glutamatergic dysfunction at
critical windows of vulnerability during early and late developmental phases
and during the early course of the illness. In this model, each of the steps of
dysfunction in glutamatergic functioning could increase the risk for the subsequent step, leading to a pathophysiological cascade (see Figure 2.1).

Conclusions and Future Directions

The model of schizophrenia proposed here has considerable heuristic
value. Several specific predictions, outlined below, can be generated from the

model and can be tested using state-of-the-art methods in biological psychiatry.

1. Individuals at risk for schizophrenia (e.g., young relatives of schizophrenic patients) will show evidence of reduced brain glutamatergic function. Noninvasive in vivo neuroimaging techniques such as proton MRS (McClure, Keshavan, and Pettegrew 1998; Stanley, Pettegrew, and Keshavan 2000) may help answer this question. Using high-field magnets (i.e., 3 Tesla or higher), it is possible to delineate the glutamate and glutamine signals reliably with proton MRS.

2. An excessive loss of synapses in glutamatergic neurons may characterize the neuropathology of schizophrenia. Recent, sophisticated neuropathological techniques (Lewis and Akil 1997; Lewis and Lieberman 2000) can help confirm this possibility. An examination of peripheral model systems such as the olfactory neuroepithelium offers a potentially valuable approach to the study of neurodevelopmental processes in schizophrenia.

3. An association may exist between reduced glutamatergic function and evidence for impaired tonic-phasic dopamine regulation in schizophrenia. Neuroimaging techniques such as positron emission tomography (PET) scans may prove useful in addressing this issue (Bressan and Pilowsky 2002).

4. It could be that longitudinal studies of schizophrenia will reveal a progressive pathology in structures containing dopamine and glutamate terminal fields, and such a progression might be associated with increased oxidative stress. Careful longitudinal studies of brain biology in relation to oxidative stress are needed to explore this possibility (Yao, Reddy, and van Kammen 2001).

5. Gene(s) encoding for a glutamate-related receptor or transport protein may be linked to schizophrenia. Recent methodological developments offer new opportunities for the interpretation of findings in molecular genetics and neuropathology. Gene microarray methodologies allow the gene expression of thousands of genes to be examined simultaneously, thereby providing a molecular fingerprint for neuropsychiatric disorders that can be compared to control tissue samples (Mirnics et al. 2000).

6. Treatments that modulate glutamatergic neurotransmission may have

a protective effect on the development and/or progression of schizophrenic illness. Recent studies have suggested the potential benefit of
drugs that reduce glutamate release, such as lamotrigene, and agents
that reduce AMPA receptor activity, such as topiramate, in treating
schizophrenia (Deutsch et al. 2001); such research is worth exploring
further. The beneficial effects of atypical antipsychotic drugs such as
clozapine have also been linked to their ability to modulate glutamatergic neurotransmission (Meltzer 1994; Arnt and Skarsfeldt 1998).
Treatments that seek to enhance glutamatergic neurotransmission,
such as glycine, L-Serine, and D-Cycloserine, likewise seem promising
in the treatment of negative and cognitive symptoms of schizophrenia (Heresco-Levy and Javitt 1998). Another issue yet to be investigated is whether the early introduction of antioxidant treatments can
potentially mitigate the neurotoxic effects of oxidative stress in early
schizophrenia. Carefully designed clinical trials are needed to unravel
these questions further.

ACKNOWLEDGMENTS

This work was supported in part by grants from the National Institute of
Mental Health (MH45156 and MH45203) and by a National Alliance for Research on Schizophrenia and Depression (NARSAD) Investigator Award.

REFERENCES

Akbarian, S., Bunney, W. E., Potkin, S. G., Wigal, S. B., Hagman, J. O., and Sandman, C.
    A. (1993). Altered distribution of nicotamine-adenine dinucleotide phosphate-
    diaphorase cells in frontal lobe of schizophrenics implies disturbances of cortical de-
    velopment. *Archives of General Psychiatry* 50:169–77.
Akbarian, S., Sucher, N., Bradley, D., Tafazzoli, A., Trinh, D., Hetrick, W., et al. (1996). Se-
    lective alterations in gene expression for NMDA receptor subunits in prefrontal cor-
    tex of schizophrenics. *Journal of Neuroscience* 16:19–30.
Anand, A., Charney, D. S., Oren, D. A., Berman, R. M., Hu, X. S., Cappiello, A., et al.
    (2000). Attenuation of the neuropsychiatric effects of ketamine with lamotrigine:
    Support for hyperglutamatergic effects of N-methyl-D-aspartate receptor antagonists.
    Archives of General Psychiatry 57:270–76.
Andreasen, N., Rezai, K., Alliger, R., Swayze, V., 2nd, Flaum, M., Kirchner, P., et al. (1992).
    Hypofrontality in neuroleptic-naive patients with chronic schizophrenia: Assessment

with xenon 133 single-photon emission computed tomography and the Tower of London. *Archives of General Psychiatry* 49:943–58.

Arnt, J., and Skarsfeldt, T. (1998). Do novel antipsychotics have similar pharmacological characteristics? A review of the evidence. *Neuropsychopharmacology* 18:63–101.

Bondy, S., and Lee, D. (1993). Oxidative stress induced by glutamate receptor agonists. *Brain Research* 610:229–33.

Bressan, R. A., and Pilowsky, L. S. (2000). Imaging the glutamatergic system in vivo: Relevance to schizophrenia. *European Journal of Nuclear Medicine* 27(11):1723–31.

Cannon, T. D. (1997). On the nature and mechanisms of obstetric influences in schizophrenia: A review and synthesis of epidemiologic studies. *Internal Review of Psychiatry* 9:387–97.

Cannon, T. D., and Marco, E. (1994). Structural brain abnormalities as indicators of vulnerability to schizophrenia. *Schizophrenia Bulletin* 20:89–102.

Cheramy, A., Barbeito, L., Godeheu, G., Desce, J., Pittaluga, A., Galli, T., et al. (1990). Respective contributions of neuronal activity and presynaptic mechanisms in the control of the in vivo release of dopamine. *Journal of Neural Transmission* Suppl. 29:183–93.

Chugani, H. T., Phelps, M. E., and Mazziotta, J. C. (1987). Positron-emission tomography study of human brain functional development. *Annals of Neurology* 22:487–97.

Collins, R. (1986). Selective vulnerability of the brain: New insights from the excitatory synapse. *Metabolic Brain Disease* 1:231–40.

Constantine-Paton, M. (1994). Effects of NMDA receptor antagonists on the developing brain. *Psychopharmacology Bulletin* 30:561–65.

Coyle, J. T. (1996). The glutamatergic dysfunction hypothesis for schizophrenia. *Harvard Review of Psychiatry* 3:241–53.

Cruzio, W. (1991). The neuropsychology of schizophrenia: A perspective from neurobehavioural genetics. *Behavioral Brain Science* 14:23–24.

DeLisi, L. E. (1995). A prospective follow-up study of brain morphology and cognition in first-episode schizophrenic patients: Preliminary findings. *Biological Psychiatry* 38:349–60.

DeLisi, L. E. (1997). Is schizophrenia a lifetime disorder of brain plasticity, growth, and aging? *Schizophrenia Research* 23:119–29.

Deutsch, S. I., Rosse, R. B., Schwartz, B. L., and Mastropaolo, J. (2001). A revised excitotoxic hypothesis of schizophrenia: Therapeutic implications. *Clinical Neuropharmacology* 24(1):43–49.

Done, D. J., Crow, T. J., Johnstone, E. C., and Sacker, A. (1994). Childhood antecedents of schizophrenia and affective illness: Social adjustment at ages 7 and 11. *British Medical Journal* 309(6956):699–703.

Eastwood, S. L., and Harrison, P. J. (1995). Decreased synaptophysin in the medical temporal lobe in schizophrenia demonstrated using immunoautoradiography. *Neuroscience* 69:339–43.

Elvevag, B., and Goldberg, T. E. (2000).Cognitive impairment in schizophrenia is the core of the disorder. *Critical Review of Neurobiology* 14(1):1–21.

Erlenmeyer-Kimling, L., and Cornblatt, B. A. (1992). A summary of attentional findings in the New York High-Risk Project. *Journal of Psychiatric Research* 26:405–26.

Farber, N. B., Kim, S. H., Dikranian, K., Jiang, X. P., and Heinkel, C. (2002). Receptor mechanisms and circuitry underlying NMDA antagonist neurotoxicity. *Molecular Psychiatry* 7(1):32–43

Farber, N. B., Wozniak, D., Price, M., Labruyere, J., Huss, J., St. Peter, H., et al. (1995). Age-specific neurotoxicity in the rat associated with NMDA receptor blockage: Potential relevance to schizophrenia? *Biological Psychiatry* 38:788–96.

Feinberg, I. (1982–83). Schizophrenia: Caused by a fault in programmed synaptic elimination during adolescence? *Journal of Psychiatry Research* 17:319–34.

Feinberg, I. (1990). Cortical pruning and the development of schizophrenia. *Schizophrenia Bulletin* 16:567–70.

Finlay, J., and Zigmond, M. (1997). The effects of stress on central dopaminergic neurons: Possible clinical implications. *Neurochemical Research* 22:1387–94.

Fish, B. (1987). Infant predictors of the longitudinal course of schizophrenic development. *Schizophrenia Bulletin* 13:395–409.

Floresco, S. B., Todd, C. L., and Grace, A. A. (2001). Glutamatergic afferents from the hippocampus to the nucleus accumbens regulate activity of ventral tegmental area dopamine neurons. *Journal of Neuroscience* 21(13):4915–22.

Garey, L. J., Patel, T., and Ong, W. Y. (1994). Loss on dendritic spines from cortical pyramidal cells in schizophrenia. *Schizophrenia Research* 11:137.

Garside, S., Furtado, J. C., and Mazurek, M. F. (1996). Dopamine-glutamate interactions in the striatum: Behaviourally relevant modification of excitotoxicity by dopamine receptor-mediated mechanisms. *Neuroscience* 75(4):1065–74.

Glantz, L. A., and Lewis, D. A. (1997). Reduction of synaptophysin immunoreactivity in the prefrontal cortex of subjects with schizophrenia: Regional and diagnostic specificity. *Archives of General Psychiatry* 54:943–52.

Goff, D. C., and Coyle, J. T. (2001). The emerging role of glutamate in the pathophysiology and treatment of schizophrenia. *American Journal of Psychiatry* 158:1367–77.

Grace, A. (1993). Cortical regulation of subcortical dopamine systems and its possible relevance to schizophrenia. *Journal of Neural Transmission* 91:111–34.

Haas, G., and Sweeney, J. (1992). Premorbid and onset features of first-episode schizophrenia. *Schizophrenia Bulletin* 18:373–86.

Häfner, H., Maurer, K., Loffler, W., and Riecher-Rossler, A. (1993). The influence of age and sex on the early course of schizophrenia. *British Journal of Psychiatry* 162:80–86.

Heresco-Levy, U., and Javitt, D. (1998). The role of N-methyl-D-aspartate (NMDA) receptor-mediated neurotransmission in the pathophysiology and therapeutics of psychiatric syndromes. *European Neuropsychopharmacology* 8:141–52.

Herkert, M., Rottger, S., and Becker, C. (1998). The NMDA receptor subunit NR2B of neonatal rat brain: Complex formation and enrichment in axonal growth cones. *European Journal of Neuroscience* 10:1553–62.

Hirsch, S., Das, I., Garey, L., and deBelleroche, J. (1997). A pivotal role for glutamate in the pathogenesis of schizophrenia and its cognitive dysfunction. *Pharmacology, Biochemistry, and Behavior* 56:797–802.

Hofer, M., and Constantine-Paton, M. (1994). Regulation of N-methyl-D-aspartate (NMDA) receptor function during the rearrangement of developing neuronal connections. *Progress in Brain Research* 10:227–85.

Hoffman, R., and McGlashan, T. (1997). Synaptic elimination, neurodevelopment, and the mechanism of hallucinated "voices" in schizophrenia. *American Journal of Psychiatry* 154:1683–89.

Ikonomidou, C., Bosch, F., Miksa, M., Bittigau, P., Vockler, J., Dikarnian, K., et al. (1999). Blockade of NMDA receptors and apoptotic neurodegeneration in the developing brain. *Science* 283:70–74.

Itzhak, Y., and Martin, J. L. (2000). Cocaine-induced kindling is associated with elevated NMDA receptor binding in discrete mouse brain regions. *Neuropharmacology* 39:32–39.

Jaskiw, G. E., Juliano, D. M., Goldberg, T. E., Hertzman, M., Urow-Hamell, E., and Weinberger, D. R. (1994). Cerebral ventricular enlargement in schizophreniform disorder does not progress: A seven-year follow-up study. *Schizophrenia Research* 14:23–28.

Javitt, D., Steinschneider, M., Schroeder, C., and Arezzo, J. (1996). Role of cortical N-methyl-D-aspartate receptors in auditory sensory memory and mismatch negativity generation: Implications for schizophrenia. *Proceedings of the National Academy of Sciences, USA* 93:11962–67.

Javitt, D., and Zukin, S. (1991). Recent advances in the phencyclidine model of schizophrenia. *American Journal of Psychiatry* 148:1301–8.

Jernigan, T. L., and Tallal, P. (1990). Late childhood changes in brain morphology observable with MRI. *Developmental Medicine and Child Neurology* 32:379–85.

Johnston, M. (1994). Neuronal death in development, aging, and disease. *Neurobiology of Aging* 15:235–36.

Johnston, M. (1995). Neurotransmitters and vulnerability of the developing brain. *Brain and Development* 17:301–6.

Jones, P., and Cannon, M. (1998). The new epidemiology of schizophrenia. *Child and Adolescent Psychiatric Clinics of North America* 21(1):1–25.

Kalivas, P. (1993). Involvement of N-methyl-D-aspartate receptor stimulation in the ventral tegmental area and amygadala in behavioral sensitization to cocaine. *Journal of Pharmacology and Experimental Therapeutics* 267:486–95.

Karler, R., Calder, L., and Turkanis, S. (1991). DNQX blockade of amphetamine behavioral sensitization. *Brain Research* 552:295–300.

Keshavan, M. S. (1999). Development, disease, and degeneration in schizophrenia: A unitary pathophysiological model. *Journal of Psychiatric Research* 33:513–21.

Keshavan, M. S., Anderson, S., and Pettegrew, J. (1994). Is schizophrenia due to excessive synaptic pruning in the prefrontal cortex? The Feinberg hypothesis revisited. *Journal of Psychiatric Research* 28:239–65.

Keshavan, M. S., Haas, G. L., Kahn, C. E., Aguilar, E., Dick, E. L., Schooler, N. R., (1998). Superior temporal gyrus and the course of early schizophrenia: Progressive, static, or reversible? *Journal of Psychiatric Research* 32:60–65.

Keshavan, M. S., and Hogarty, G. E. (1999). Brain maturational processes and delayed onset in schizophrenia. *Developmental Psychopathology* 11:525–43.

Keshavan, M. S., Montrose, D., Pierri, J., Dick, E., Rosenberg, D., Talagala, L., et al. (1997). Magnetic resonance imaging and spectroscopy in offspring at risk for schizophrenia: Preliminary studies. *Progress in Neuropsychopharmacology and Biological Psychiatry* 21:1285–95.

Keshavan, M. S., Pettegrew, J., Bagwell, W., Haas, G., Sweeney, J., and Schooler, N. (1994). Gray matter volume deficits in first-episode schizophrenia. *Biological Psychiatry* 35:713.

Keshavan, M. S., Reynolds, C. F., Miewald, J. M., Montrose, D. M., Sweeney, J. A., Vasko, R. C., et al. (1998). Delta sleep deficits in schizophrenia: Evidence from automated analyses of sleep data. *Archives of General Psychiatry* 55:443–48.

Kim, J., Kornhuber, H., Schmid-Burgk, W., and Holzmuller, B. (1980). Low cerebrospinal fluid glutamate in schizophrenic patients and a new hypothesis on schizophrenia. *Neuroscience Letters* 20:379–82.

Komuro, H., and Rakic, P. (1993). Modulation of neuronal migration by NMDA receptors. *Science* 260:95–97.

Kotrla, K. J., Sater, A. K., and Weinberger, D. R. (1997). Neuropathology, neurodevelopment, and schizophrenia. In M. S. Keshavan and R. M. Murray (Eds.), *Neurodevelopment and Adult Psychopathology* (pp. 187–98). New York: Cambridge University Press.

Kovelman, J., and Scheibel, A. (1984). A neurohistological correlate of schizophrenia. *Biological Psychiatry* 19:1601–21.

Kraepelin, E. (1919). *Dementia Praecox and Paraphrenia*. Edinburgh: E. and S. Livingstone.

Lawrie, S. M., Whalley, H., Kestelman, J. N., Abukmeil, S. S., Byrne, M., Hodges, A., et al. (1999). Magnetic resonance imaging of brain in people at high risk of developing schizophrenia. *Lancet* 353:30–33.

Lewis, D., and Akil, M. (1997). Cortical dopamine in schizophrenia: Strategies for postmortex studies. *Journal of Psychiatric Research* 31:175–95.

Lewis, D. A., and Lieberman, J. A. (2000). Catching up on schizophrenia: Natural history and neurobiology. *Neuron* 28(2):325–34.

Lieberman, J. (1993). Prediction of outcome in first-episode schizophrenia. *Journal of Clinical Psychiatry* 54(Suppl):13–17.

Lieberman, J., Chakos, M., Wu, H., Alvir, J., Hoffman, E., Robinson, D., et al. (2001). Longitudinal study of brain morphology in first episode schizophrenia. *Biological Psychiatry* 49:487–99.

Lieberman, J., Koreen, A., Chakos, M., Sheitman, B., Woerner, M., Alvir, J., et al. (1996). Factors influencing treatment response and outcome of first-episode schizophrenia: Implications for understanding the pathophysiology of schizophrenia. *Journal of Clinical Psychiatry* 9:5–9.

Lieberman, J., Sheitman, B., and Kinon, B. (1997). Neurochemical sensitization in the pathophysiology of schizophrenia: Deficits and dysfunction in neuronal regulation and plasticity. *Neuropsychopharmacology* 17:205–29.

Loebel, A. D., Liberman, J. A., and Alvir, J. M. (1992). Duration of psychosis and outcome in first-episode schizophrenia. *American Journal of Psychiatry* 149:1183–88.

Mathalon, D. H., Ford, J. M., Rosenbloom, M., and Pfefferbaum, A. (2000). P300 reduction and prolongation with illness duration in schizophrenia. *Biological Psychiatry* 47:413–27.

McClure, R., Keshavan, M., and Pettegrew, J. (1998). Chemical and physiologic brain imaging in schizophrenia. *Psychiatric Clinics of North America* 21:93–122.

McDonald, J., and Johnstone, M. (1990). Physiological and pathophysiological roles of excitatory amino acids during central nervous system development. *Brain Research Review* 15:41–70.

McDonald, J., Silverstein, S., and Johnston, M. (1988). Neurotoxicity of N-methyl-D-aspartate is markedly enhanced in the developing rat central nervous system. *Brain Research* 349:200–203.

McGlashan, T. H., and Fenton, W. (1993). Subtype progression and pathophysiologic deterioration in early schizophrenia. *Schizophrenia Bulletin* 19:71–84.

McGlashan, T. H., and Hoffman, R. E. (2000). Schizophrenia as a disorder of developmentally reduced synaptic connectivity. *Archives of General Psychiatry* 57:637–48.

Mednick, S. A., Machon, R. A., and Huttunen, M. O. (1988). Adult schizophrenia following prenatal exposure to an influenza epidemic. *Archives of General Psychiatry* 45:171–76.

Meltzer, H. (1994). An overview of the mechanism of action of clozapine. *Journal of Clinical Psychiatry* 55:47–52.

Michaelis, E. (1998). Molecular biology of glutamate receptors in the central nervous system and their role in excitotoxicity, oxidative stress, and aging. *Progress in Neurobiology* 54:369–415.

Mirnics, K., Middleton, F. A., Marquez, A., Lewis, D. A., and Levitt, P. (2000). Molecular characterization of schizophrenia viewed by microarray analysis of gene expression in prefrontal cortex. *Neuron* 28(1):53–67.

Moghaddam, B. (2002). Stress activation of glutamate neurotransmission in the prefrontal cortex: implications for dopamine-associated psychiatric disorders. *Biological Psychiatry* 51:775–87.

Mohn, A. R., Gainetdinov, R. R., Caron, M. G., and Koller, B. H. (1999). Mice with reduced NMDA receptor expression display behaviors related to schizophrenia. *Cell* 98(4):427–36.

Murray, R., and Lewis, S. (1987). Is schizophrenia a neurodevelopmental disorder? *British Medical Journal* 295(6600):681–82.

Norman, M. (1996). Malformations of the brain. *Journal of Neuropathology and Experimental Neurology* 55(2):133–43.

Ohno, M., and Watanabe, S. (1995). Persistent increase in dopamine release following activation of metabotropic glutamate receptors in the rat nucleus accumbens. *Neuroscience Letters* 200:113–16.

Olney, J. W., and Farber, N. (1995). Glutamate receptor dysfunction and schizophrenia. *Archives of General Psychiatry* 52:998–1007.

Olney, J. W., Newcomer, J. W., and Farber, N. B. (2002). Is NMDA receptor hypofunction in schizophrenia associated with a primary hyperglutamatergic state? *Archives of General Psychiatry* 59:466–68.

Pettegrew, J. W., and Keshavan, M. S. (1991). Alterations in brain high-energy phosphate and membrane phospholipid metabolism in first-episode, drug-naive schizophrenics. *Archives of General Psychiatry* 48:563–68.

Pettegrew, J. W., McClure, R., Keshavan, M., Minshew, N., Panchalingam, K., and Klunk, W. (1997). 31P magnetic resonance spectroscopy studies of developing brain. In M. Keshavan and R. Murray (Eds.), *Neurodevelopment and Adult Psychopathology* (pp. 71–92). New York: Cambridge University Press.

Rabacchi, S., Bailly, Y., Delhaye-Bouchaud, N., and Mariani, J. (1992). Involvement of the N-methyl-D-aspartate (NMDA) receptor in synapse elimination during cerebellar development. *Science* 256:1823–25.

Reid, M., Hsu, K., and Berger, S. (1997). Cocaine and amphetamine preferentially stimulate glutamate release in the limbic system: Studies on the involvement of dopamine. *Synapse* 27:5–105.

Rice, S. R., Niu, N., Berman, D. B., Heston, L. L., and Sobell, J. L. (2001). Identification of single nucleotide polymorphisms (SNPs) and other sequence changes and estimation of nucleotide diversity in coding and flanking regions of the NMDAR1 receptor gene in schizophrenic patients. *Molecular Psychiatry* 6(3):274–84.

Riley, B., Tahir, E., Rajagopalan, S., Mogudi-Carter, M., Faure, S., Weissenbach, J., et al. (1997). A linkage study of the N-methyl-D-aspartate receptor subunit gene loci and schizophrenia in southern African Bantu-speaking families. *Psychiatric Genetics* 7:57–74.

Scott, L., Kruse, M. S., Forssberg, H., Brismar, H., Greengard, P., and Aperia, A. (2002). Selective up-regulation of dopamine D1 receptors in dendritic spines by NMDA receptor activation. *Proceedings of the National Academy of Sciences, USA* 99:1661–64.

Seidman, L. J., Faraone, S. V., Goldstein, J. M., Goodman, J. M., Kremen, W. S., Matsuda, G., et al. (1997). Reduced subcortical brain volumes in nonpsychotic siblings of schizophrenic patients: A pilot magnetic resonance imaging study. *American Journal of Medical Genetics* 74:507–14.

Selemon, J., Rajkowska, G., and Goldman-Rakic, P. (1995). Abnormally high neuronal density in the schizophrenic cortex. *Archives of General Psychiatry* 52:805–18.

Stanley, J. A., Pettegrew, J. W., and Keshavan, M. S. (2000). Magnetic resonance spectroscopy in schizophrenia: Methodological issues and findings—Part II. *Biological Psychiatry* 48:357–68.

Susser, E. S., and Lin, S. P. (1992). Schizophrenia after prenatal exposure to the Dutch Hunger Winter of 1944–1945. *Archives of General Psychiatry* 49:983–88.

Takahata, R., and Moghaddam, B. (1998). Glutamatergic regulation of basal and stimulus-activated dopamine release in the prefrontal cortex. *Journal of Neurochemistry* 71:1443–49.

Tamminga, C. A. (1998). Schizophrenia and glutamatergic transmission. *Critical Review of Neurobiology* 12:21–36.

Thompson, P. M., Vidal, C., Giedd, J. N., Gochman, P., Blumenthal, J., Nicolson, R., et al. (2001). Mapping adolescent brain change reveals dynamic wave of accelerated gray matter loss in very early-onset schizophrenia. *Proceedings of the National Academy of Sciences, USA.* 98:11650–55.

Tsai, G., Passani, L., Slusher, B., Carter, R., Baer, L., Kleinman, J., et al. (1995). Abnormal excitatory neurotransmitter metabolism in schizophrenia brains. *Archives of General Psychiatry* 52:829–36.

Watt, N. (1978). Patterns of childhood social development in adult schizophrenics. *Archives of General Psychiatry* 35:1052–56.

Weinberger, D. R. (1987). Implications of normal brain development for the pathogenesis of schizophrenia. *Archives of General Psychiatry* 44:660–69.

Weinberger, D. R. (1995). From neuropathology to neurodevelopment. *Lancet* 346(8974): 552–57.

Weinberger, D. R., and McClure, R. K. (2002). Neurotoxicity, neuroplasticity, and magnetic resonance imaging morphometry: What is happening in the schizophrenic brain? *Archives of General Psychiatry* 59:553–58.

Whitton, P. (1997). Glutamatergic control over brain dopamine release in vivo and in vitro. *Neuroscience and Biobehavioral Reviews* 21:481–88.

Wyatt, R. (1991). Neuroleptics and the natural course of schizophrenia. *Schizophrenia Bulletin* 17:325–51.

Wyatt, R., Alexander, R., Egan, M., and Kirch, D. (1988). Schizophrenia, just the facts: What do we know, how well do we know it? *Schizophrenia Research* 1:3–18.

Yao, J. K., Reddy, R. D., and van Kammen, D. P. (2001). Oxidative damage and schizophrenia: An overview of the evidence and its therapeutic implications. *CNS Drugs* 15(4):287–310.

Zecevic, N., Bourgeois, J., and Rakic, P. (1989). Changes in synaptic density in motor cortex of rhesus monkey during fetal and postnatal life. *Developmental Brain Research* 50:11–32.

Zipursky, R. O. (1992). Widespread cerebral gray matter volume deficits in schizophrenia. *Archives of General Psychiatry* 49:195–205.

CHAPTER THREE

Neurobiological Development during Childhood and Adolescence

Tonya White, M.D., and Charles A. Nelson, M.D.

The development of the central nervous system (CNS) can be thought of as a process in which initially inefficient mechanisms are used to generate a highly efficient and adaptable system. Early in development, the brain produces an overabundance of neurons, synapses, and dendrites, the majority of which are subsequently pruned. This process results in the potential for brain plasticity and adaptability and enhances the efficiency of sensation and cognition. As an analogy, consider the process of laying down roads and intersections across North America. If this process were modeled after the brain, considerably more roads and intersections would initially be constructed than were actually required. The laying down of these roads across the continent would take place in an orderly manner, although there would be room for stochastic events.

A person would then be assigned to each road and intersection (neuron and synapse) to keep track of the activity along that particular road or intersection. Although certain major roads—the route from New York to San Francisco, say—would be genetically determined, a large number of roads and intersections would be torn up (apoptosis and synaptic pruning) either because they were not used much or because they resulted in traffic congestion. Although it is inefficient to build roads and then tear them up, only the most well-traveled routes will ultimately survive, and thus efficiency is gained with regard to the flow of traffic. Specific toxins, such as lead or alcohol, can influence the specificity of pruning and create inefficient traffic patterns. Consider what would happen if the people monitoring the traffic flow were lazy, often slept on the job, or out-and-out undermined the integrity of the roads. Clearly, this would adversely affect the optimal flow of traffic. Finally, although some of the main thoroughfares would have originally been laid down in gravel, they would later be paved and become freeways and interstate highways (myelination). This would allow a greater conduction velocity of the vehicles traveling along these roads.

This simple analogy to what is in fact an extremely complex process will provide the backdrop for an overview of normal neurodevelopment, which is summarized in Table 3.1. However, we will focus primarily on those normal developmental processes known to be aberrant in schizophrenia. (For recent reviews of pre- and postnatal neurobiological development, see Monk, Webb, and Nelson 2001 and Webb, Monk, and Nelson 2001.)

The Early Development of the Central Nervous System

Formation of the Neural Tube (Neurulation)

A complex orchestration of events is required to generate the vast network of neurons and supporting cells that make up the CNS from a single original cell. During the second week of uterine life, as cells begin to divide, they differentiate so as to form three distinct layers of tissue: the endoderm, the mesoderm, and the ectoderm. As the cells in these layers continue to differentiate, they produce the various organs of the body, each of which has its own developmental timetable. The gastrointestinal system arises from the endoderm, the vascular and skeletal systems from the mesoderm, and the CNS and skin from the ectoderm. Whereas the skin, kidneys, liver, and intestines are functionally similar at birth to those of an adult, the CNS not only develops later, during embryogenesis, but also follows a protracted developmental course that lasts throughout adolescence and into adulthood.

The differentiation of nerve cells within the ectoderm marks the genesis of CNS development. Initially, the neural plate develops as a differentiated unit within the ectoderm (Kandel, Schwartz, and Jessell 2000; Pomeroy and Kim

Table 3.1. *The neurodevelopmental time line from conception through adolescence*

Developmental event	Time line	Overview of developmental events
Neurulation	18 to 24 prenatal days	• Cells differentiate into one of three layers: endoderm, mesoderm, and ectoderm, which then continue differentiating to form the various organs in the body. • The neural tube (from which the CNS is derived) develops from the ectoderm cells; the neural crest (from which the autonomic nervous system is derived) lies between the ectodermal wall and the neural tube.
Neuronal migration	6 to 24 prenatal weeks	• Neurons migrate at the ventricular zone along radial glial cells to the cerebral cortex. • The neurons migrate in an inside-out manner, with later generations of cells migrating through previously developed cells. • The cortex develops into six layers.
Synaptogenesis	Third trimester to adolescence	• Neurons migrate into the cortical plate and extend apical and basilar dendrites. • Chemical signals guide the developing dendrites toward their final location, where synapses are formed with projections from subcortical structures. • These connections are strengthened through neuronal activity, and connections with very little activity are pruned.

(*continued*)

Table 3.1. (Continued)

Developmental event	Time line	Overview of developmental events
Postnatal neurogenesis	Birth to adulthood	• The development of new cells in several brain regions, including the dentate gyrus of the hippocampus; the olfactory bulb; and possibly the cingulate gyrus; and regions of parietal cortex.
Myelination	Third trimester to middle age	• Neurons are enclosed in a myelin sheath, resulting in an increased speed of action potentials.
Gyrification	Third trimester to adulthood	• The smooth tissue of the brain folds to form gyri and sulci.
Structural development of the prefrontal cortex	Birth to late adulthood	• The prefrontal cortex is the last structure to undergo gyrification during uterine life. • The synaptic density reaches its peak at 12 months; however, myelination of this structure continues into adulthood.
Neurochemical development of the prefrontal cortex	Uterine life to adolescence	• All major neurotransmitter systems undergo initial development during uterine life and are present at birth. • Although neurotransmitter systems have not been well studied in humans, it is thought that most of these systems are not fully developed until adulthood.

Source: Thompson and Nelson 2001, Fig. 1. Reprinted with permission.

2000). This plate undergoes an invagination, forming first a neural groove and then, with the closure of the folds, a neural tube. The cells within the ectoderm that do not help to form the neural tube instead differentiate to produce the epidermal layer of skin. The spinal column develops from the caudal region of the neural tube, and the cortical and subcortical structures from the ventral region. Finally, cells trapped outside the tube, between the tube and the ectodermal wall, give rise to the autonomic nervous system.

The cerebral vesicles become apparent during the fifth week of fetal life. Over the next several weeks the walls surrounding the vesicles thicken, forming the lamina terminalis (Destrieux, Velut, and Kakou 1998). The dorsal region of the lamina terminalis—the lamina reunions—subsequently folds to become the commissural plate (Rakic and Yakovlev 1968). Meanwhile, the ventral region of the neural tube undergoes exuberant growth resulting in an overabundance of neural and glial cells. Clusters of neurons along the midline of the ventral region of the neural tube differentiate further into the thalamus, the basal ganglia, the hypothalamus, and the brain stem (Pomeroy and Kim 2000).

Neuronal Migration

According to the radial unit hypothesis of cortical development, neurons formed via mitosis at the ventricular zone subsequently migrate along radial glial guide cells to the cerebral cortex (Rakic 1988). During the first six weeks of gestation, the proliferative units divide symmetrically along the ventricular zone, with each progenitor cell producing two new progenitor cells in each mitotic cycle (Rakic 1988). Approximately six weeks into gestation, the progenitor cells gradually initiate asymmetric division, with one daughter cell continuing to divide while the other matures into a neuron that migrates to the cortical plate. These neurons migrate in an inside-out pattern in which later generations travel through previously developed cells before reaching their ultimate position in the gray matter (GM) of the cortex (Sidman and Rakic 1973). The GM of the cortex consists of six layers of cells that have migrated in this inside-out fashion.

The thickness of the cortex depends on the number of neurons produced in each unit plate. The surface area of the brain, however, is determined by the number of contributing radial units along the ventricular zone (Rakic 1988, 1995). These radial units, formed by symmetric division during the first six weeks of uterine life, are aligned vertically in the ventricular zone (Sidman and

Rakic 1973; Rakic 1974). A larger number of radial units results in with greater lined projections to the cortical plate and thus a greater surface area of the brain. Irradiation of monkey embryos during the symmetric phase of progenitor cell division results in a decrease in total surface area, whereas irradiation subsequent to this phase leads to a deletion of cortical cell layers and thus a decrement in cortical thickness (Rakic 1995). Since each round of mitosis causes an exponential increase in the number of progenitor cells, it has been postulated that small changes affecting the duration of symmetric growth are responsible for the robust ontogenetic growth of surface area (Rakic 1995).

From an evolutionary perspective, the increase in the total surface area of the human brain has far exceeded the growth in cortical thickness (Welker 1990). For example, the cortical surface area in humans is 1,700 times greater than that in shrews, yet the cortical thickness is only six times greater (Hofman 1989). Similarly, in a comparison of humans to macaque monkeys, the surface area of the human brain was found to be roughly ten times greater but the cortical plate only twice as thick (Rakic 1995). Studies of monozygotic twins have demonstrated lower correlations between the measures of brain surface morphology (Bartley, Jones, and Weinberg 1997; Lohmann, von Cramon, and Steinmetz 1999; White, Andreasen, and Nopoulos 2002), whereas the thickness of the cortex is highly correlated (White, Andreasen, and Nopoulos 2002).

The maturation of cells within the six cortical layers also evolves in an inside-out pattern and follows a dorsal to ventral course. At 7 months gestational age, the innermost or deepest layers, layers V and VI, show a greater degree of development than do layers II and III in the motor and visual cortex (Marin-Padilla 1970; Zilles et al. 1986). The maturation of the cells also includes the formation of interneurons and dendritic structures within the specific cell layers, a process that results in an expansion of the cell layers and a decrease in the packing density of the layers (Blinkov and Glezer 1968; Benes et al. 1996).

Development of Connectivity Between Cortical and Subcortical Structures

As the radial glial cells migrate toward the cortical plate, they meet with afferent cell projections from the thalamus (Rakic 1988). These projections migrate primarily into layer IV of the cortex (Wise and Jones 1978). The connection of these nerve cells allows for communication between the subcortical and cortical structures. Such a direct relation between cortical GM and the thalamus would presume a volumetric relation between the two structures. Studies of twins have indeed demonstrated high correlations between the thalamus and cortical GM (White, Andreasen, and Nopoulos 2002). This relation between the thalamus and cortical GM meshes well with the present neurodevelopmental and neuroanatomic understanding of thalamic/cortical GM connectivity. The decreases in the volume of both the thalamus and cortical regions (i.e., reductions in the volume of both the prefrontal cortex and medialdorsal nucleus of the thalamus) seen in some studies may reflect aberrant patterns of connectivity between the two regions.

As the neurons migrate into the cortical plate, they extend apical and basilar dendrites (Juraska and Fifkova 1979). The apical dendrites subsequently extend additional branches, in an increasingly complex pattern that continues during postnatal development (Conel 1939). Chemical signals guide these developing dendrites toward their ultimate location, where synapses are formed (Sperry 1963). Connections are strengthened through activity, and those connections that see little traffic are eventually pruned. Thus, a certain level of growth and pruning allows for inherent plasticity during neurodevelopment and explains why children in whom large sections of the brain have been removed may meet with minimal consequences as compared to an adult patient with the same resection.

Postnatal Neurodevelopment

Very rapid changes in neurodevelopment take place during the first decade of life (Yakovlev and Lecours 1967; Huttenlocher and de Courten 1987; Huttenlocher 1990; Reiss et al. 1996). Synaptic density is thought to peak in the striate cortex by approximately 4 months of age (Huttenlocher and de Courten 1987) and by approximately 12 months in the prefrontal cortex (Huttenlocher 1979). Brain weight peaks at roughly 10 years of age, and magnetic resonance imaging (MRI) studies have demonstrated only a minimal increase in gross mass after a child reaches 4 to 5 years of age (Pfefferbaum et al. 1994; Reiss et al. 1996).

Postmortem studies evaluating age-related changes in total cell counts of the cortex have yielded mixed results (for a review, see Peters et al. 1998). Since the original studies carried out by Brody (1955), which indicated that as many as half of the neurons in frontal and temporal regions are lost during development, there have been conflicting reports as to the extent of neuronal loss in the cortex (Shefer 1973; Cragg 1975; Devaney and Johnson 1980; Henderson, Tomlinson, and Gibson 1980; Anderson et al. 1983; Haug et al. 1984). The early studies that reveal significant cell loss did not compensate for methodological techniques that resulted in a greater shrinkage of younger brains, with this age-dependent shrinkage leading to an increased density of neurons (Haug et al. 1984; Haug 1986). Later studies using methodologies that control for shrinkage have not replicated this dramatic reduction in neuronal numbers, although considerable variability in the findings persists (Terry, DeTeresa, and Hansen 1987; Leuba and Kraftsik 1994). The present consensus is that cortical neurons are generally preserved during adolescence and adulthood with at most a 10 percent reduction in neuronal numbers (Peters et al. 1998). Since the loss of neuronal cells mainly takes place in older adults, little loss of cells is expected in the adolescent age range.

Even in the absence of considerable neuronal cell loss, regressive changes in the brain occur throughout adolescence and into adult life. Huttenlocher et al. reported substantial decreases in synaptic density in the middle frontal gyrus during those periods but without significant neuronal loss (Huttenlocher et al. 1982; Huttenlocher 1979). This decrease in synaptic density is associated with decreased plasticity and is likely related to the pruning of connections that have less functional efficiency in the developing neuropil (Easter et al. 1985). Histological studies have also demonstrated an age-related decrease in cortical thickness that is associated with the changes taking place in the neuropil (Jacobs, Driscoll, and Schall 1997). The thinning of the cortical GM during late childhood and adolescence primarily involves modulations within the neuropil, namely, synaptic pruning and dendritic arborization. The age-related findings that have been identified histologically have also been obtained in studies employing MRI techniques.

MRI studies have consistently demonstrated a gradual decline in GM starting in late childhood and progressing into adulthood (Jernigan and Tallal 1990; Jernigan, Archibald, et al. 1991; Jernigan, Trauner, et al. 1991; Pfefferbaum et al. 1994; Caviness et al. 1996; Giedd et al. 1996; Reiss et al. 1996; Sowell, Thompson, et al., Localizing age-related changes 1999; Sowell, Thompson, et al., In vivo evidence 1999; Thompson et al. 2000; De Bellis et al. 2001). The age of peak GM volume varies among studies, ranging from 4 years of age (Pfefferbaum et al. 1994) up to the time of puberty (Giedd et al. 1996). An age-related regional specificity in GM volume decreases has also been reported. Between childhood and adolescence, there appears to be a greater GM loss in the parietal lobes (Sowell, Thompson, et al., Localizing age-related changes, 1999), whereas in adolescence the loss occurs more in the frontal and subcortical regions (Sowell, Thompson, et al., In vivo evidence, 1999). MRI studies have also pointed to reductions in the thickness of the cortex within the frontal, parietal, and temporal lobes, with sparing of the occipital cortex (White et al. in preparation). Ventricular volume either declines or remains relatively constant until early adolescence, when a gradual increase in volume, greater in males than females, takes place (Giedd et al. 1996). The postpubertal increase in ventricular volume correlates temporally with the loss of subcortical GM (Giedd et al. 1996).

Postnatal Neurogenesis

For many years it was assumed that the mammalian nervous system has its full complement of neurons at the time of birth, which is to say that no new neurons are subsequently added (with the exception, perhaps, of the olfactory bulb), even in response to injury. This view of development has recently undergone a dramatic shift made possible, in part, by the use of new staining methods for looking at DNA turnover, such as 5'-Bromo-2-deoxyuridine. Work on several fronts, including studies of both human (e.g., Gage 2000) and nonhuman primates (Gould et al. 1999; Kornack and Rakic 1999) and of rodents (Gould et al. 1999), has increasingly suggested that in certain regions of the brain—the dentate gyrus of the hippocampus, for instance, and possibly the cingulate gyrus of the frontal cortex and regions of the parietal cortex (for a review and discussion, see Gould and Gross 2002)—new cells are in fact added for many years after birth. Furthermore, there is some evidence, particularly in the case of rodents, that the addition of such cells can be influenced by the environment (e.g., Gould et al. 1999). For example, an up-regulation of postnatal neurogenesis in the dentate gyrus occurs when rats are placed in contexts that challenge learning and memory systems and a down-regulation of neurogenesis if the rats are placed in stressful environments. By all accounts, these new cells differentiate and appear to be normal in all respects, although recent evidence suggests that they may have a relatively short half-life (Gould et al. 2001). Furthermore, the function of these cells is not yet clear, although van Praag and colleagues (e.g., van Praag et al. 2002) reported that newly generated cells in the hippocampus of the adult mouse exhibit many similarities to mature dentate granule cells (e.g., in display action potentials). It is also unclear how these new cells work their way into existing synaptic circuits. This revised view of neurogenesis is, moreover, not without its critics (see in particular Rakic 2002a, 2002b). Time will tell whether postnatal neurogenesis in regions outside the olfactory bulb and dentate gyrus is a real phenomenon or a product of a misreading of the new staining methods. An enlightening discussion of this topic can be found in a special issue of the *Journal of Neuroscience* (2002, vol. 22[3]).

Myelination

Myelination involves an onionlike layering of neurons in both the central and peripheral nervous system. This sheathing of the neurons greatly speeds the conduction velocity of the action potentials and thus significantly enhances cortical connectivity. Myelination is initiated during the first trimester of uterine life, and in certain regions of the brain, such as the hippocampus and the association cortices, it continues well into the third and fourth decades of life (Yakovlev and Lecours 1967; Benes 1989; Benes et al. 1994; Kinney et al. 1994). The growth of myelinated nerve fibers is greatest during the first two years of life, however. The myelination that takes place in adolescence and early adulthood has been shown histochemically to involve primarily the association cortices of the brain (Yakovlev and Lecours 1967).

In the majority of cases, myelination within the brain follows a well-defined progression (Yakovlev and Lecours 1967; Kinney et al. 1994). The cortical projection fibers myelinate before the association fibers, as can be inferred in evoked potential studies of visual development in newborn infants. These newborns have an early adult response in the occipital lobe region V1 when presented with complex visual stimuli (e.g., symmetric patterns), yet adult electrophysiological patterns for the same stimuli are not present until after 7 to 9 months of age in the association regions. The proximal regions of the fiber pathways myelinate first and at a more rapid rate than the distal regions. Using the same example of the visual system, myelination will initiate in the retina and progress to the lateral geniculate nucleus. Finally, the central cortical regions, that is, the sensorimotor regions, will myelinate before the occipital, frontal, and temporal poles. Additionally, the occipital poles undergo myelination prior to the frontal and temporal poles. Thus, the regions that are among the last to myelinate include the frontal and temporal poles of the brain.

Few studies have evaluated changes in white matter (WM) with age. Lim et al. (1992) studied eight young adults in comparison to six elderly males and found no difference in total WM between the two groups. However, Bartzokis et al. (2001) were able to demonstrate a parabolic curve of WM volumes in a group of males over time. They detected a gradual increase in WM volume up to approximately 45 years of age, after which a gradual decline took place. Paus et al. (1999) traced the diameter of WM fibers in a longitudinal cohort of healthy adolescents and found a gradual increase during this period of age in the diameter of the corticospinal tract and arcuate fasciculus. Finally, Klingberg et al. (1999) used diffusion tensor imaging to evaluate WM in a small group of children in comparison to a small group of adults. Their finding of greater anisotropy, or WM coherence, in the adult group supports the theory that a continued development of WM organization occurs throughout adolescence.

Gyrification

A primary story in the ontology of gyrification, or the folding of the brain surface, is the dramatic increase in surface area of the brain and subsequent increase in cortical GM. In comparison to other mammals, the increased surface area of the human brain is exponentially greater than the increase in the cortical thickness and is in fact one of the defining features of a human being. During the third trimester of fetal life, the brain develops from a smooth, lissencephalic structure into one that more closely resembles the folding patterns of the adult brain (Retzius 1891; Welker 1990; Naidich et al. 1994; Armstrong et al. 1995). Zilles and colleagues (1988) worked out a "gyrification index," which was applied to measure the developmental trajectory of gyrification in humans. They found that the gyrification index—defined as the ratio between a coronal outline of the brain that includes the sulcal outlines and one that excludes them—increases dramatically during the third trimester and then remains relatively constant throughout development (Dareste 1862; Armstrong et al. 1995). Since the brain nearly triples its volume from the time of birth through to adulthood, the process of gyrification continues to develop, maintaining this constant ratio.

The mechanisms behind brain gyrification are as yet unknown, although a number of theories have been advanced that describe the developmental processes underlying the gyrification of the cerebral cortex. Van Essen (1997) proposed that neuronal connectivity during early neurodevelopment is involved in producing tension that draws specific regions closer together, warping the brain. As a result, the transit time of the action potentials is decreased, thus enhancing the overall efficiency of brain function. If the tension produced by the neuronal connections indeed has a role in the mechanisms of gyrification, then changes in the patterns of the gyri and sulci are an expected outcome of pruning. Such a theory could link brain surface morphology with regional neuronal connectivity within a developmental framework.

Meshing the age-related differences in the morphology of the cerebral cortex with changes in neural connectivity is intriguing. Age-related synaptic and dendritic arborization may serve to decrease the tensile forces that are involved in the morphogenesis of the cerebral cortex. Histological studies of the neuronal pathways have shown that neural fibers tend to course horizontally to the surface in the sulci, whereas fiber pathways traverse more tangentially in the gyri (Welker 1990). A release of tension would occur along the line horizontal to the predominance of pruned connections, which would theoretically produce a widening of the sulci and a greater curvature of the gyri. These changes have in fact been observed in a group of healthy adolescents (White et al. in preparation) and adults (Magnotta et al. 1999) through the use of techniques that measure the curvature of the gyri and sulci within the cortex.

The tertiary sulci, which develop mainly after birth, appear to be more prone to the influence of nongenetic factors (Lohmann, von Cramon, and Steinmetz 1999). Measures of gyral and sulcal curvature are significantly less correlated than measures of volumes and midline structures (White, Andreasen, and Nopoulos 2002). It can plausibly be argued that the greater number of nonshared environmental influences that are present for postnatal twins, coupled with the pronounced cortical plasticity of early development, effect changes in the patterns of cortical surface morphology. Bartley et al. demonstrated, however, that the development of cortical patterns is determined primarily by random environmental factors (Bartley, Jones, and Weinberger 1997).

The Development of the Prefrontal Cortex

The prefrontal cortex (PFC) and, more specifically, the dorsolateral prefrontal cortex (DLPFC) not only undergoes a prolonged developmental course in relation to other regions of the brain (Fuster 1997) but also has been implicated in the pathogenesis of schizophrenia (Weinberger and Berman 1988;

Goldman-Rakic and Selemon 1997; Lewis 1997; Goldman-Rakic 1999; Selemon and Goldman-Rakic 1999). Development of the PFC, which continues well into adolescence, overlaps with the typical age of onset of schizophrenia. The longer developmental window equates with greater vulnerability during development as well as with the potential for a greater involvement of epigenetic influences.

From the migration of neurons to the laying down of myelinated fibers, the PFC is one of the final structures to mature (Fuster 1997). Whereas the synaptic density in the striate cortex attains its peak at about 4 months of age, the peak density of the PFC is not reached until approximately 12 months (Huttenlocher and Dabholkar 1997). The PFC, especially its orbitofrontal regions, is the last to undergo gyrification during uterine life (Gilles, Shankle, and Dooling 1983). Myelination also continues well into adolescence and adulthood in the PFC (Yakovlev and Lecours 1967). The comparatively longer period of maturation in the structure of the PFC is reflected in its functional development as well.

Any discussion of the functional development of the PFC must take into account the vast array of neural networks linking the PFC with other regions of the brain. By definition, the PFC involves areas that have direct connectivity with the medialdorsal nucleus of the thalamus. Additionally, neural networks connect the basal ganglia, the limbic system, and other cortical regions to the PFC. Comparative neuroanatomy shows that the PFC is the brain region most closely associated with being human.

The primary functions attributed to the PFC involve the temporal organization and sequencing of goal-directed behavior (Fuster 1997). Subsumed under this process are components of the cognitive domains of attention, working memory, inhibition, and planning. Working memory is defined as the ability to keep either a verbal or visual cue on line, or in short-term memory. A functional approximation of working memory first emerges sometime between 6 and 12 months of life (e.g., Diamond 1985; for a review, see Diamond 2001); however, both the amount of information and the duration of the period that the information can remain on line improve steadily throughout childhood and adolescence (Luciana and Nelson 1998). Functional MRI studies of working memory in children have shown that children demonstrate the same patterns of changes in blood flow (activations) as those seen in adults (Casey, Giedd, and Thomas 2000; Nelson et al. 2000). Assessments of the extent of activation in children have yielded mixed results, indicating both an increase of blood flow in children compared to adults (Thomas et al. 1999) and an increase in blood flow that is positively correlated with increasing age and working memory load (Klingberg, Forssberg, and Westerberg 2002).

Neurochemical Development of the Prefrontal Cortex

Very little is known about human neurodevelopmental trajectories for specific neurotransmitters, and much of the current knowledge has been extrapolated from animal studies (for a review, see Benes 2001). These trajectories are complicated by the inside-out migration of neurons to the various layers of the cortex, as described above, as well as regional differences in neurotransmitter levels, synaptic pruning, changes in neuropil, and variations between and interactions among specific neurotransmitter systems (glutamine, serotonin, GABA, dopamine). The hypothesis that brain regions that are connected will show a similar neurochemical development ("regions that fire together, wire together") may be truer for some areas (cortical-cortical connections) than for others (cortical-subcortical connections) (Johnston 1988).

All of the major neurotransmitter systems initially develop during uterine life and are thus present at birth. Neurotransmitter systems are dynamic and continue to mature throughout childhood and adolescence (Benes 2001). In studies of rats, both the excitatory neurotransmitter glutamate and the inhibitory neurotransmitter GABA show higher rates of receptor binding during the "childhood" phase of neurodevelopment than at adulthood (Candy and Martin 1979; Schliebs, Kullman, and Bigl 1986). The decline in receptor-binding levels throughout adolescence and into adulthood may reflect synaptic pruning and the expansion of neuropil (Vincent, Pabreza, and Benes 1995). Dopamine, serotonin, norepinephrine, and acetylcholine also demonstrate changes in their receptor binding, breakdown, and interactions during development.

Dopaminergic and cholinergic neurons develop in the lower layers (V and VI) of the cortex before they develop in the upper layers (I and II) (Kalsbeek et al. 1988; Voorn et al. 1988). The density of dopaminergic fibers in the PFC gradually increases during childhood and adolescence, with a concomitant rise in dopamine concentration (Johnston 1988; Benes et al. 1996). There is a competitive relation between the dopamine and serotonin fibers such that when the serotonin fiber systems are blocked, a dramatic growth occurs in the number of dopamine fibers (Benes, Taylor, and Cunningham 2000). The dynamic tension between these neurotransmitter systems may explain the efficacy of the newer antipsychotic medications that act on more than just the dopamine (D2) neurotransmitter system. Additionally, the fact that neurotransmitter systems continue to mature during adolescence may explain why the efficacy rates of these drugs differ in childhood- and adolescent-onset schizophrenia versus adult.

Heritability in Cortical Development

Nature has a way of providing unique experimental conditions under which one can explore various aspects of neurodevelopment. Monozygotic twins, for example, are nature's form of cloning. Because this natural phenomenon results in two individuals with an identical genetic complement, it provides an opportunity to study the role of genetic and environmental influences in neurodevelopment. Despite the identical genetic complement of such twins, parents and close friends are generally able to tell one twin from the other, which means that they are not completely identical (Machin 1996). Owing to the complexity of neurodevelopment and the fact that some processes—pruning, for example—are influenced by environmental factors (via mechanisms such as immediate early genes), coupled with the potential for stochastic processes, certain aspects of brain development differ between identical twins.

Initial investigations into brain development in twins evaluated the midline structures, namely, the corpus callosum and the distance between the anterior and posterior commissure. Those MRI studies show that the midline structures of the brain are highly correlated in monozygotic twins (Oppenheim et al. 1989; Tramo et al. 1995; Biondi et al. 1998). This correlation is seen in both the length and the area of the corpus callosum, ranging from 0.73 to 0.90 and 0.90 to 0.99, respectively (Oppenheim et al. 1989; Biondi et al. 1998). Likewise, the correlation for the distance of the line connecting the anterior and posterior commissure is 0.70 (Biondi et al. 1998). Not all midline structures demonstrate such high correlations, however. For example, the length of the perimeter of the corpus callosum, which is considered more a measurement of surface than of volume or area, has an intraclass correlation coefficient of 0.62.

Measures of cerebral and regional volumes also display a high degree of correlation in monozygotic twins—greater than 0.95 for the volumes of the cerebral hemispheres (Bartley, Jones, and Weinberger 1997; White, Andreasen, and Nopoulos 2002; Tramo et al. 1995; Carmelli et al. 1998; Pennington et al.

2000). Unfortunately, not all studies have included both monozygotic and dizygotic twins, a comparison of which is necessary to tease apart the influence of shared environmental factors. The three studies that did include dizygotic twins reported heritability scores of over 90 percent for total brain volume (Bartley, Jones, and Weinberger 1997; Carmelli et al. 1998; Pennington et al. 2000). Dividing the cortex into GM, WM, and cerebrospinal fluid, all demonstrate high correlations between monozygotic twins (White, Andreasen, and Nopoulos 2002). Yet not all the cerebral structures show a high rate of similarity in their volume measurement. For example, Steinmetz et al. (1995) demonstrated that monozygotic twins discordant for handedness exhibited differing degrees of asymmetry of the planum temporale. Epigenetic factors are a probable explanation, not only for asymmetries of the planum temporale but also for other surface measurements of the brain, which show significantly lower correlations than do the volumetric data.

Whereas high correlations exist for brain volumes and midline structures, a greater degree of variability between twins has been reported in the patterns of gyral and sulcal development (Bartley, Jones, and Weinberger 1997; Biondi et al. 1998; Lohmann, von Cramon, and Steinmetz 1999; White, Andreasen, and Nopoulos 2002). Previous MRI studies of the surface of the cerebral cortex have, however, relied on relatively incomplete and/or rudimentary measures. Evaluating sulcal depth, Lohmann et al. found that the deeper primary sulci— those formed earlier in development—displayed more similarities than the shallower tertiary sulci (Lohmann, von Cramon, and Steinmetz 1999). The strongest evidence for surface-pattern dissimilarities between monozygotic twins has been provided by a study by Bartley et al. (Bartley, Jones, and Weinberger 1997) that included both monozygotic and dizygotic twins. This study, which used a cross-correlation algorithm to compare structural brain images, demonstrated that, although influenced by genes, the majority of the morphological variance between monozygotic twins was the result of random environmental effects. In contrast, when Tramo et al. (1995) measured the surface area in ten pairs of monozygotic twins, they found that both hemispheres, especially the left, were highly influenced by genetic factors.

Sexual Dimorphism in Brain Development

Multiple imaging studies have identified sexually dimorphic regions within the brain (Andreasen et al. 1993; Filipek et al. 1994; Schultz et al. 1994; Schlaepfer et al. 1995; Zaidel, Aboitiz, and Clarke 1995; Caviness et al. 1996;

Giedd et al. 1997, 1999; Lange et al. 1997; Passe et al. 1997; Gur et al. 1999; Oka et al. 1999; Nopoulos et al. 2000; Sullivan et al. 2001). Even when one controls for stature, males prove to have greater overall brain size (Andreasen et al. 1993; Filipek et al. 1994; Pfefferbaum et al. 1994; Schultz et al. 1994; Giedd et al. 1996; Nopoulos et al. 2000). In addition, a number of studies have demonstrated greater WM volume in males compared to females (Filipek et al. 1994; Passe et al. 1997; Gur et al. 1999), although this finding has not been consistently reported (cf. Schlaepfer et al. 1995; and Nopoulos et al. 2000). Sex differences in the size and shape of the corpus callosum have also been frequently described (Zaidel, Aboitiz, and Clarke 1995; Bishop and Wahlsten 1997; Lange et al. 1997; Giedd et al. 1999; Oka et al. 1999; Bermudez and Zatorre 2001; Sullivan et al. 2001).

The literature describing sex differences in total and regional GM is mixed. Studies variously report the total percentage of GM as increased in young males (Reiss et al. 1996), increased in females (Gur et al. 1999), or the same in males and females (Schlaepfer et al. 1995; Nopoulos et al. 2000). Gender-specific regional differences have been found for the parietal lobe (Frederikse et al. 1999; Nopoulos et al. 2000), the parietal/occipital region (Coffey et al. 1998), the dorsolateral prefrontal cortex (Schlaepfer et al. 1995), and the superior temporal gyrus (Schlaepfer et al. 1995). Studies of cortical thickness demonstrate a higher rate of thinning in aging males as compared to females (Magnotta et al. 1999). The fact that age-related differences between males and females have also been reported for various structures in the brain (Gunning-Dixon et al. 1998; Magnotta et al. 1999; De Bellis et al. 2001) suggests that studies that control for age or focus on a specific age group might help to account for some of the paradoxical findings in the literature.

In a cross-sectional study of adolescents, De Bellis et al. (2001) compared WM development in male and female adolescents and found that males had a steeper age-related increase in WM than did females. However, when one controlled for total brain volume, no significant difference in the total WM volume of males and females appeared. Evaluating a group of healthy adolescents and adults, we replicated this sexual dimorphism in WM development and extended the findings into early adulthood (White et al. in preparation). Females appeared to experience an increase in WM development earlier on, but with a subsequent plateau. Although males initially had a smaller percentage of WM relative to the total brain volume that percentage continued to increase into early adulthood.

Conclusions

The development of the CNS involves complex and dynamic processes that start in utero and continue throughout life. The genesis of the CNS is marked by a differentiation of cells within the ectoderm into cell lines that are destined to become the cells of the CNS. These cells undergo rapid proliferation, forming first the neural plate and then in the neural tube. Following the formation of the neural tube, a cascade of neurodevelopmental processes continually unfolds during specific windows of time, some of which overlap (see Table 3.1). These processes include cell differentiation, neuronal migration, synaptogenesis, the development of neuropil, apoptosis, synaptic and dendritic pruning, the formation of synaptic junctions, and neurochemical development. Birth is merely one point on a continuum of neurodevelopment.

Although the brain undergoes its most rapid development prenatally and in the early years following birth, changes in brain structure and function persist throughout childhood and adolescence. Structural brain changes, including a decrease in GM, the spreading of cells within the neuropil, and an increase in WM, have been recorded in both postmortem and neuroimaging studies. The development of the PFC is protracted, with a continuation of myelination and cortical restructuring into adolescence and the early years of adulthood. Functions that tap into measures of the PFC (such as working memory) have also been shown to follow a protracted course of development parallel with the structural developmental trajectory for the PFC. With the recent introduction of a number of electrophysiological and neuroimaging tools that are able to delve into the underlying processes of neurodevelopment, it is likely that the upcoming years will be fruitful to our understanding of brain development during childhood and adolescence.

ACKNOWLEDGMENTS

The writing of this chapter was made possible by grants from the National Institute of Health (NS34458 and NS329976). Dr. Nelson wishes also to thank the John D. and Catherine T. MacArthur Foundation for their support of a research network on early experience and brain development.

REFERENCES

Anderson, J. M., Hubbard, B. M., Coghill, G. R., and Slidders, W. (1983). The effect of advanced old age on the neurone content of the cerebral cortex: Observations with an automatic image analyser point counting method. *Journal of the Neurological Sciences* 58:235–46.

Andreasen, N. C., Flaum, M., Swayze, V., 2nd, et al. (1993). Intelligence and brain structure in normal individuals. *American Journal of Psychiatry* 150:130–34.

Armstrong, E., Schleicher, A., Omran, H., Curtis, M., and Zilles, K. (1995). The ontogeny of human gyrification. *Cerebral Cortex* 5:56–63.

Bartley, A. J., Jones, D. W., and Weinberger, D. R. (1997). Genetic variability of human brain size and cortical gyral patterns. *Brain* 120:257–69.

Bartzokis, G., Beckson, M., Lu, P. H., Nuechterlein, K. H., Edwards, N., and Mintz, J. (2001). Age-related changes in frontal and temporal lobe volumes in men: A magnetic resonance imaging study. *Archives of General Psychiatry* 58:461–65.

Benes, F. M. (1989). Myelination of cortical-hippocampal relays during late adolescence. *Schizophrenia Bulletin* 15:585–93.

Benes, F. M. (2001). The development of prefrontal cortex: The maturation of neurotransmitter systems and their interactions. In C. A. Nelson and M. Luciana (Eds.), *Handbook of developmental cognitive neuroscience* (pp. 79–92). Cambridge, MA: MIT Press.

Benes, F. M., Taylor, J. B., and Cunningham, M. C. (2000). Convergence and plasticity of monoaminergic systems in the medial prefrontal cortex during the postnatal period: implications for the development of psychopathology. *Cerebral Cortex* 10:1014–27.

Benes, F. M., Turtle, M., Khan, Y., and Farol, P. (1994). Myelination of a key relay zone in the hippocampal formation occurs in the human brain during childhood, adolescence, and adulthood. *Archives of General Psychiatry* 51:477–84.

Benes, F. M., Vincent, S. L., Molloy, R., and Khan, Y. (1996). Increased interaction of dopamine-immunoreactive varicosities with GABA neurons of rat medial prefrontal cortex occurs during the postweanling period. *Synapse* 23:237–45.

Bermudez, P., and Zatorre, R. J. (2001). Sexual dimorphism in the corpus callosum: Methodological considerations in MRI morphometry. *Neuroimage* 13:1121–30.

Biondi, A., Nogueira, H., Dormont, D., et al. (1998). Are the brains of monozygotic twins similar? A three-dimensional MR study. *American Journal of Neuroradiology* 19:1361–67.

Bishop, K. M., and Wahlsten, D. (1997). Sex differences in the human corpus callosum: Myth or reality? *Neuroscience and Biobehavioral Reviews* 21:581–601.

Blinkov, S. M., and Glezer, I. I. (1968). *The human brain in figures and tables: A quantitative handbook*. New York: Basic Books.

Brody, H. D. (1955). Organization of the cerebral cortex. *Journal of Comparative Neurology* 1023:511–56.

Candy, J. M., and Martin, I. L. (1979). The postnatal development of the benzodiazepine receptor in the cerebral cortex and cerebellum of the rat. *Journal of Neurochemistry* 32:655–58.

Carmelli, D., DeCarli, C., Swan, G. E., et al. (1998). Evidence for genetic variance in white matter hyperintensity volume in normal elderly male twins. *Stroke* 29:1177–81.

Casey, B. J., Giedd, J. N., and Thomas, K. M. (2000). Structural and functional brain development and its relation to cognitive development. *Biological Psychology* 54:241–57.

Caviness, V. S., Jr., Kennedy, D. N., Richelme, C., Rademacher, J., and Filipek, P. A. (1996). The human brain age 7–11 years: A volumetric analysis based on magnetic resonance images. *Cerebral Cortex* 6:726–36.

Coffey, C. E., Lucke, J. F., Saxton, J. A., et al. (1998). Sex differences in brain aging: A quantitative magnetic resonance imaging study. *Archives of Neurology* 55:169–79.

Conel, J. L. (1939). *The postnatal development of the human cerebral cortex.* Cambridge, MA: Harvard University Press.

Cragg, B. G. (1975). The density of synapses and neurons in normal, mentally defective ageing human brains. *Brain* 98:81–90.

Dareste, M. C. (1862). Sur les rapports de la mase encéphalique avec le développement de l'intelligence. *Bulletin of Social Anthropology Paris* 3:26–54.

De Bellis, M. D., Keshavan, M. S., Beers, S. R., et al. (2001). Sex differences in brain maturation during childhood and adolescence. *Cerebral Cortex* 11:552–57.

Destrieux, C., Velut, S., and Kakou, M. (1998). Development of the corpus callosum. *Neurochirurgie* 44:11–16.

Devaney, K. O., and Johnson, H. A. (1980). Neuron loss in the aging visual cortex of man. *Journal of Gerontology* 35:836–41.

Diamond, A. (1985). Development of the ability to use recall to guide action, as indicated by infants' performance on AB. *Child Development* 56:868–83.

Diamond, A. (2001). A model system for studying the role of dopamine in the prefrontal cortex during early development in humans: Early and continuously treated phenylketonuria. In C. A. Nelson and M. Luciana (Eds.), *Handbook of developmental cognitive neuroscience* (pp. 433–72). Cambridge, MA: MIT Press.

Easter, S. S., Purves, D., Rakic, P., and Spitzer, N. C. (1985). The changing view of neural specificity. *Science* 230:507–11.

Filipek, P. A., Richelme, C., Kennedy, D. N., and Caviness, V. S., Jr. (1994). The young adult human brain: An MRI-based morphometric analysis. *Cerebral Cortex* 4:344–60.

Frederikse, M. E., Lu, A., Aylward, E., Barta, P., and Pearlson, G. (1999). Sex differences in the inferior parietal lobule. *Cerebral Cortex* 9:896–901.

Fuster, J. M. (1997). *The prefrontal cortex: Anatomy, physiology, and neuropsychology of the frontal lobe,* 3rd ed. Philadelphia: Lippincott-Raven.

Gage, F. H. (2000). Mammalian neural stem cells. *Science* 287:1433–38.

Giedd, J. N., Blumenthal, J., Jeffries, N. O., et al. (1999). Development of the human corpus callosum during childhood and adolescence: A longitudinal MRI study. *Progress in Neuropsychopharmacology and Biological Psychiatry* 23:571–88.

Giedd, J. N., Castellanos, F. X., Rajapakse, J. C., Vaituzis, A. C., and Rapoport, J. L. (1997). Sexual dimorphism of the developing human brain. *Progress in Neuropsychopharmacology and Biological Psychiatry* 21:1185–201.

Giedd, J. N., Snell, J. W., Lange, N., et al. (1996). Quantitative magnetic resonance imaging of human brain development: Ages 4–18. *Cerebral Cortex* 6:551–60.

Gilles, F. H., Shankle, W., and Dooling, E. C. (1983). Myelinated tracts: Growth patterns. In F. H. Gilles, A. Leviton, and E. C. Dooling (Eds.), *The developing human brain: Growth and epidemiologic neuropathology* (pp. 117–83). Boston: John Wright.

Goldman-Rakic, P. S. (1999). The physiological approach: Functional architecture of working memory and disordered cognition in schizophrenia. *Biological Psychiatry* 46:650–61.

Goldman-Rakic, P. S., and Selemon, L. D. (1997). Functional and anatomical aspects of prefrontal pathology in schizophrenia. *Schizophrenia Bulletin* 23:437–58.

Gould, E., Beylin, A., Tanapat, P., Reeves, A., and Shors, T. J. (1999). Learning enhances adult neurogenesis in the hippocampal formation. *Nature Neuroscience* 2:260–65.

Gould, E., and Gross, C. G. (2002). Neurogenesis in adult mammals: Some progress and problems. *Journal of Neuroscience* 22:619–23.

Gould, E., Vail, N., Wagers, M., and Gross, C. G. (2001). Adult-generated hippocampal and neocortical neurons in macaques have a transient existence. *Proceedings of the National Academy of Science, USA* 98:10910–17.

Gunning-Dixon, F. M., Head, D., McQuain, J., Acker, J. D., and Raz, N. (1998). Differential aging of the human striatum: A prospective MR imaging study. *American Journal of Neuroradiology* 19:1501–7.

Gur, R. C., Turetsky, B. I., Matsui, M., et al. (1999). Sex differences in brain gray and white matter in healthy young adults: Correlations with cognitive performance. *Journal of Neuroscience* 19:4065–72.

Haug, H. (1986). History of neuromorphometry. *Journal of Neuroscience Methods* 18:1–17.

Haug, H., Kuhl, S., Mecke, E., Sass, N. L., and Wasner, K. (1984). The significance of morphometric procedures in the investigation of age changes in cytoarchitectonic structures of human brain. *Journal für Hirnforsch* 25:353–74.

Henderson, G., Tomlinson, B. E., and Gibson, P. H. (1980). Cell counts in human cerebral cortex in normal adults throughout life using an image analysing computer. *Journal of the Neurological Sciences* 46:113–36.

Hofman, M. A. (1989). On the evolution and geometry of the brain in mammals. *Progress in Neurobiology* 32:137–58.

Huttenlocher, P. R. (1979). Synaptic density in human frontal cortex-developmental changes and effects of aging. *Brain Research* 163:195–205.

Huttenlocher, P. R. (1990). Morphometric study of human cerebral cortex development. *Neuropsychologia* 28:517–27.

Huttenlocher, P. R., and Dabholkar, A. S. (1997). Regional differences in synaptogenesis in human cerebral cortex. *Journal of Comparative Neurology* 387:167–78.

Huttenlocher, P. R., and de Courten, C. (1987). The development of synapses in striate cortex of man. *Human Neurobiology* 6:1–9.

Huttenlocher, P. R., de Courten, C., Garey, L. J., and van der Loos, H. (1982). Synaptic development in human cerebral cortex. *International Journal of Neurology* 17:144–54.

Jacobs, B., Driscoll, L., and Schall, M. (1997). Life-span dendritic and spine changes in areas 10 and 18 of human cortex: A quantitative Golgi study. *Journal of Comparative Neurology* 386:661–80.

Jernigan, T. L., Archibald, S. L., Berhow, M. T., Sowell, E. R., Foster, D. S., and Hesselink, J. R. (1991). Cerebral structure on MRI, Pt. 1: Localization of age-related changes. *Biological Psychiatry* 29:55–67.

Jernigan, T. L., and Tallal, P. (1990). Late childhood changes in brain morphology observable with MRI. *Developmental Medicine and Child Neurology* 32:379–85.

Jernigan, T. L., Trauner, D. A., Hesselink, J. R., and Tallal, P. A. (1991). Maturation of human cerebrum observed in vivo during adolescence. *Brain* 114:2037–49.

Johnston, M. V. (1988). Biochemistry of neurotransmitters in cortical development. In

A. Peter and E. G. Jones (Eds.), *Cerebral cortex*, Vol. 7. (pp. 211–36). New York: Plenum Press.

Juraska, J. M., and Fifkova, E. (1979). A Golgi study of the early postnatal development of the visual cortex of the hooded rat. *Journal of Comparative Neurology* 183:247–56.

Kalsbeek, A., Voorn, P., Buijs, R. M., Pool, C. W., and Uylings, H. B. (1988). Development of the dopaminergic innervation in the prefrontal cortex of the rat. *Journal of Comparative Neurology* 269:58–72.

Kandel, E. R., Schwartz, J. H., and Jessell, T. M. (2000). *Principles of neural science*, 4th ed. New York: McGraw-Hill.

Kinney, H. C., Karthigasan, J., Borenshteyn, N. I., Flax, J. D., and Kirschner, D. A. (1994). Myelination in the developing human brain: Biochemical correlates. *Neurochemical Research* 19:983–96.

Klingberg, T., Forssberg, H., and Westerberg, H. (2002). Increased brain activity in frontal and parietal cortex underlies the development of visuospatial working memory capacity during childhood. *Journal of Cognitive Neuroscience* 14:1–10.

Klingberg, T., Vaidya, C. J., Gabrieli, J. D., Moseley, M. E., and Hedehus, M. (1999). Myelination and organization of the frontal white matter in children: A diffusion tensor MRI study. *Neuroreport* 10:2817–21.

Kornack, D. R., and Rakic, P. (1999). Continuation of neurogenesis in the hippocampus of the adult macaque monkey. *Proceedings of the National Academy of Sciences, USA* 96:5768–73.

Lange, N., Giedd, J. N., Castellanos, F. X., Vaituzis, A. C., and Rapoport, J. L. (1997). Variability of human brain structure size: Ages 4–20 years. *Psychiatry Research* 74:1–12.

Leuba, G., and Kraftsik, R. (1994). Changes in volume, surface estimate, three-dimensional shape and total number of neurons of the human primary visual cortex from midgestation until old age. *Anatomy and Embryology* 190:351–66.

Lewis, D. A. (1997). Development of the prefrontal cortex during adolescence: Insights into vulnerable neural circuits in schizophrenia. *Neuropsychopharmacology* 16:385–98.

Lim, K. O., Zipursky, R. B., Watts, M. C., and Pfefferbaum, A. (1992). Decreased gray matter in normal aging: An in vivo magnetic resonance study. *Journal of Gerontology* 47:B26–30.

Lohmann, G., von Cramon, D. Y., and Steinmetz, H. (1999). Sulcal variability of twins. *Cerebral Cortex* 9:754–63.

Luciana, M., and Nelson, C. A. (1998). The functional emergence of prefrontally-guided working memory systems in four- to eight-year-old children. *Neuropsychologia* 36:273–93.

Machin, G. A. (1996). Some causes of genotypic and phenotypic discordance in monozygotic twin pairs. *American Journal of Medical Genetics* 61:216–28.

Magnotta, V. A., Andreasen, N. C., Schultz, S. K., et al. (1999). Quantitative in vivo measurement of gyrification in the human brain: Changes associated with aging. *Cerebral Cortex* 9:151–60.

Marin-Padilla, M. (1970). Prenatal and early postnatal ontogenesis of the human motor cortex: A golgi study, Pt. 1: The sequential development of the cortical layers. *Brain Research* 23:167–83.

Monk, C. S., Webb, S. J., and Nelson, C. A. (2001). Prenatal neurobiological development: Molecular mechanisms and anatomical change. *Developmental Neuropsychology* 19:211–36.

Naidich, T. P., Grant, J. L., Altman, N., et al. (1994). The developing cerebral surface: Preliminary report on the patterns of sulcal and gyral maturation—anatomy, ultrasound, and magnetic resonance imaging. *Neuroimaging Clinics of North America* 4:201–40.

Nelson, C. A., Monk, C. S., Lin, J., Carver, L. J., Thomas, K. M., and Truwit, C. L. (2000). Functional neuroanatomy of spatial working memory in children. *Developmental Psychology* 36:109–16.

Nopoulos, P., Flaum, M., O'Leary, D., and Andreasen, N. C. (2000). Sexual dimorphism in the human brain: Evaluation of tissue volume, tissue composition and surface anatomy using magnetic resonance imaging. *Psychiatry Research* 98:1–13.

Oka, S., Miyamoto, O., Janjua, N. A., et al. (1999). Re-evaluation of sexual dimorphism in human corpus callosum. *Neuroreport* 10:937–40.

Oppenheim, J. S., Skerry, J. E., Tramo, M. J., and Gazzaniga, M. S. (1989). Magnetic resonance imaging morphology of the corpus callosum in monozygotic twins. *Annals of Neurology* 26:100–104.

Passe, T. J., Rajagopalan, P., Tupler, L. A., Byrum, C. E., MacFall, J. R., and Krishnan, K. R. (1997). Age and sex effects on brain morphology. *Progress in Neuropsychopharmacology and Biological Psychiatry* 21:1231–37.

Paus, T., Zijdenbos, A., Worsley, K., et al. (1999). Structural maturation of neural pathways in children and adolescents: In vivo study. *Science* 283:1908–11.

Pennington, B. F., Filipek, P. A., Lefly, D., et al. (2000). A twin MRI study of size variations in human brain. *Journal of Cognitive Neuroscience* 12:223–32.

Peters, A., Morrison, J. H., Rosene, D. L., and Hyman, B. T. (1998). Feature article: Are neurons lost from the primate cerebral cortex during normal aging? *Cerebral Cortex* 8:295–300.

Pfefferbaum, A., Mathalon, D. H., Sullivan, E. V., Rawles, J. M., Zipursky, R. B., and Lim, K. O. (1994). A quantitative magnetic resonance imaging study of changes in brain morphology from infancy to late adulthood. *Archives of Neurology* 51:874–87.

Pomeroy, S. L., and Kim, J. Y. (2000). Biology and pathobiology of neuronal development. *Mental Retardation and Developmental Disabilities Research Reviews* 6:41–46.

Rakic, P. (1974). Neurons in rhesus monkey visual cortex: Systematic relation between time of origin and eventual disposition. *Science* 183:425–27.

Rakic, P. (1988). Specification of cerebral cortical areas. *Science* 241:170–76.

Rakic, P. (1995). A small step for the cell, a giant leap for mankind: A hypothesis of neocortical expansion during evolution. *Trends in Neuroscience* 18:383–88.

Rakic, P. (2002a). Adult neurogenesis in mammals: An identity crisis. *Journal of Neuroscience* 22:614–18.

Rakic, P. (2002b). Neurogenesis in adult primate neocortex: An evaluation of the evidence. *Nature Reviews: Neuroscience* 3:65–71.

Rakic, P., and Yakovlev, P. I. (1968). Development of the corpus callosum and cavum septi in man. *Journal of Comparative Neurology* 132:45–72.

Reiss, A. L., Abrams, M. T., Singer, H. S., Ross, J. L., and Denckla, M. B. (1996). Brain development, gender and IQ in children: A volumetric imaging study. *Brain* 119:1763–74.

Retzius, A. (1891). Über den Bau der Oberflachenschicht der Grosshirnrunde beim Menschen und bei den Saugetieren. *Verhandlungen Biologishe Vereinigung* 3:90–103.

Schlaepfer, T. E., Harris, G. J., Tien, A. Y., Peng, L., Lee, S., and Pearlson, G. D. (1995).

Structural differences in the cerebral cortex of healthy female and male subjects: A magnetic resonance imaging study. *Psychiatry Research* 61:129–35.

Schliebs, R. E., Kullman, E., and Bigl, V. (1986). Development of glutamate binding sites in the visual structures of the rat brain. *Biochimica and Biophysica Acta* 45:4495–506.

Schultz, R. T., Cho, N. K., Staib, L. H., et al. (1994). Brain morphology in normal and dyslexic children: The influence of sex and age. *Annals of Neurology* 35:732–42.

Selemon, L. D., and Goldman-Rakic, P. S. (1999). The reduced neuropil hypothesis: A circuit-based model of schizophrenia. *Biological Psychiatry* 45:17–25.

Shefer, V. F. (1973). Absolute number of neurons and thickness of the cerebral cortex during aging, senile and vascular dementia, and Pick's and Alzheimer's diseases. *Neuroscience and Behavioral Physiology* 6:319–24.

Sidman, R. L., and Rakic, P. (1973). Neuronal migration, with special reference to developing human brain: A review. *Brain Research* 62:1–35.

Sowell, E. R., Thompson, P. M., Holmes, C. J., Batth, R., Jernigan, T. L., and Toga, A. W. (1999). Localizing age-related changes in brain structure between childhood and adolescence using statistical parametric mapping. *Neuroimage* 9:587–97.

Sowell, E. R., Thompson, P. M., Holmes, C. J., Jernigan, T. L., and Toga, A. W. (1999). In vivo evidence for post-adolescent brain maturation in frontal and striatal regions. *Nature Neuroscience* 2:859–61.

Sperry, R. W. (1963). Chemoaffinity in the orderly growth of nerve fiber patterns and connections. *Proceedings of the National Academy of Sciences, USA* 50:703–10.

Steinmetz, H., Herzog, A., Schlaug, G., Huang, Y., and Jancke, L. (1995). Brain (A) symmetry in monozygotic twins. *Cerebral Cortex* 5:296–300.

Sullivan, E. V., Rosenbloom, M. J., Desmond, J. E., and Pfefferbaum, A. (2001). Sex differences in corpus callosum size: Relationship to age and intracranial size. *Neurobiology and Aging* 22:603–11.

Terry, R. D., DeTeresa, R., and Hansen, L. A. (1987). Neocortical cell counts in normal human adult aging. *Annals of Neurology* 21:530–39.

Thomas, K. M., King, S. W., Franzen, P. L., et al. (1999). A developmental functional MRI study of spatial working memory. *Neuroimage* 10:327–38.

Thompson, P. M., Giedd, J. N., Woods, R. P., MacDonald, D., Evans, A. C., and Toga, A. W. (2000). Growth patterns in the developing brain detected by using continuum mechanical tensor maps. *Nature* 404:190–93.

Thompson, R. A., and Nelson, C. A. (2001). Developmental science and the media: Early brain development. *American Psychologist* 56:5–15.

Tramo, M. J., Loftus, W. C., Thomas, C. E., Green, R. L., Mott, L. A., and Gazzaniga, M. S. (1995). Surface area of human cerebral cortex and its gross morphological subdivisions: In vivo measurements in monozygotic twins suggest differential hemisphere effects of genetic factors. *Journal of Cognitive Neuroscience* 7:292–301.

Van Essen, D. C. (1997). A tension-based theory of morphogenesis and compact wiring in the central nervous system. *Nature* 385:313–18.

van Praag, H., Schinder, A. F., Christie, B. R., Toni, N., Palmer, T. D., and Gage, F. H. (2002). Functional neurogenesis in the adult hippocampus. *Nature* 415:1030–34.

Vincent, S. L., Pabreza, L., and Benes, F. M. (1995). Postnatal maturation of GABA-immunoreactive neurons of rat medial prefrontal cortex. *Journal of Comparative Neurology* 355:81–92.

Voorn, P., Kalsbeek, A., Jorritsma-Byham, B., and Groenewegen, H. J. (1988). The pre-

and postnatal development of the dopaminergic cell groups in the ventral mesencephalon and the dopaminergic innervation of the striatum of the rat. *Neuroscience* 25:857–87.

Webb, S. J., Monk, C. S., and Nelson, C. A. (2001). Mechanisms of postnatal neurobiological development: Implications for human development. *Developmental Neuropsychology* 19:147–71.

Weinberger, D. R., and Berman, K. F. (1988). Speculation on the meaning of cerebral metabolic hypofrontality in schizophrenia. *Schizophrenia Bulletin* 14:157–68.

Welker, W. (1990). Why does cerebral cortex fissure and fold? In E. G. Jones and A. Peters (Eds.), *Cerebral cortex,* Vol. 8B (pp. 3–136). New York: Plenum Press.

White, T., Andreasen, N. C., and Nopoulos, P. (2002). Brain volumes and surface morphology in monozygotic twins. *Cerebral Cortex* 12:486–93.

Wise, S. P., and Jones, E. G. (1978). Developmental studies of thalamocortical and commissural connections in the rat somatic sensory cortex. *Journal of Comparative Neurology* 178:187–208.

Yakovlev, P. I., and Lecours, A. R. (1967). The myelogenetic cycles of regional maturation of the brain. In A. Minkowski (Ed.), *Regional development of the brain in early life* (pp. 3–70). Oxford: Blackwell.

Zaidel, E., Aboitiz, F., and Clarke, J. (1995). Sexual dimorphism in interhemispheric relations: Anatomical-behavioral convergence. *Biological Research* 28:27–43.

Zilles, K., Armstrong, E., Schleicher, A., and Kretschmann, H. J. (1988). The human pattern of gyrification in the cerebral cortex. *Anatomy and Embryology* 179:173–79.

Zilles, K., Werners, R., Busching, U., and Schleicher, A. (1986). Ontogenesis of the laminar structure in areas 17 and 18 of the human visual cortex: A quantitative study. *Anatomy and Embryology* 174:339–53.

CHAPTER FOUR

Genetic and Other Risk Factors

Sophia Frangou, M.D., Michael Hadjulis, M.D., and Robin M. Murray, M.D.

Schizophrenia, in line with most common human diseases, represents the cul-mination of lifelong interactions between an individual's genome and envi-ronment. The genetic model that is most compatible with the clinical evidence regarding schizophrenia is the polygenic/multifactorial threshold model, which was first applied to human disorders by Gottesman and Shields (1967) more than three decades ago. The key concept in this model is liability, a term that refers to the relative probability of developing a given disorder: the higher the liability, the greater the chances of developing the disorder. Genes con-tribute to genetic liability, while environmental factors contribute to environ-mental liability; the combined, additive action of genes and environmental factors defines the total liability to the disorder. Total liability is normally dis-tributed, and once it reaches a certain point or threshold, the clinical pheno-type of the disorder is expressed (Murray and McGuffin 1993). In this context, the search for the causes of schizophrenia focuses on the identification of fac-tors, biological or psychosocial, that increase liability. Such conditions are called "risk factors."

Broadly speaking, there are two approaches to determining risk factors. One is to monitor a group of healthy people over a long period of time and compare those who develop a disease to those that do not; the other is to compare a group of people who already have the disease to otherwise similar but healthy individuals. Risk factors consist of specific personal traits as well as particular environmental conditions that appear significantly more frequently in those who develop a disease than in those who do not. It is often difficult to distinguish between true risk factors—those that lie on the causal pathway—and risk indicators, that is, factors that merely signal the presence of a higher degree of liability. In the case of lung cancer, smoking is a causal risk factor, whereas nicotine-stained fingers are a risk indicator. In the absence of a clear-cut pathophysiological model for schizophrenia, distinguishing between the two is not always possible. We will therefore use the term *risk factor* to signify both.

In what follows, we will review the most recent literature concerning the biological, cognitive, developmental, and psychosocial risk factors for schizophrenia, placing particular emphasis on those that are deemed more relevant to the early-onset form of the disorder. The overt clinical syndrome of schizophrenia typically begins in early adulthood (Häfner et al. 1993). However, about 4 percent of cases experience an unusually early onset of the disorder, namely, before 18 years of age (Cannon et al. 1999). Some of the studies reviewed below concentrated specifically on patients who developed the illness before the age of 12 (childhood-onset schizophrenia), while others focused on cases of adolescent-onset schizophrenia, and yet others included both children and adolescents. Because the boundary between childhood- and adolescent-onset schizophrenia reflects traditional divisions in service organization rather than differences in presumed etiology or pathophysiology, unless otherwise specified we will use the term *early-onset schizophrenia* (EOS) to describe both childhood- and adolescent-onset cases.

Genetic Factors

Family and Twin Studies

Schizophrenia aggregates within families, with the risk for the disorder in relatives of schizophrenic patients increasing as genetic proximity to the affected member increases. In first-degree relatives of schizophrenic patients, the lifetime risk of schizophrenia is over ten times that in normal controls (Kendler et al. 1994; Sham et al. 1994). Twin studies have estimated the heritability of schizophrenia to be between 0.60 and 0.80 (Kendler 1983; Onstad et al. 1991; Cannon et al. 1998; Cardno et al. 1999). Two classic studies, conducted by Kallmann and Roth in 1956 and by Kolvin et al. in 1971, indicated an increased familial aggregation for EOS. Additionally, Kallmann and Roth found the disparity in concordance between monozygotic and dizygotic twins to be higher in those who developed schizophrenia at a younger age, thus suggesting that genetic factors may contribute to an earlier onset of the disorder. Similar findings have been reported from other high-risk samples. Cardno et al. (1998) found a significant within-pair association for age of illness onset ($p < .02$) in a sample of sibling pairs, both of whom had been diagnosed with schizophrenia. In a large sample from the family study conducted at University of California, Los Angeles (UCLA), Asarnow et al. (2001) found an increased lifetime morbidity risk for schizophrenia and schizotypal personality disorder in the parents of childhood-onset schizophrenia probands as compared to parents of children with attention deficit hyperactivity disorder (ADHD) and healthy community probands. The authors also compared the risk for schizophrenia identified in their study with historical rates from family studies of adult-onset schizophrenia. The likelihood that parents of childhood-onset probands would themselves have schizophrenia was estimated to be three to six times higher than that reported in studies of adult-onset schizophrenia. Similarly, the relative risk for schizotypal and paranoid personality disorder was higher for the parents of childhood-onset schizophrenia probands than for the parents of the adult-onset patients. Although direct comparisons to historical data are fraught with methodological problems, these findings do suggest that familial, presumed genetic, factors may play a more salient role in EOS. In the ongoing National Institute of Mental Health (NIMH) study of childhood-onset schizophrenia, the rates of schizophrenia and schizoaffective disorder in relatives of childhood-onset patients were similar to those estimated for the relatives of patients with adult-onset schizophrenia (Gordon et al. 1994; Jacobsen and Rapoport 1998). However, an excess of paranoid and schizotypal personality disorders was also found (Nicolson and Rapoport 1999).

Molecular Genetic Studies

The most important finding of molecular genetic studies so far has been that no single gene of large effect determines the genetic predisposition to schizophrenia. Although this is a negative conclusion, it is valuable in setting schizophrenia firmly among those chronic conditions, such as diabetes or hypertension, that arise as a consequence of the combined effects of a number of genes of small effect and environmental factors. Earlier investigations did not find associations for apolipoprotein E alleles (Fernandez et al. 1999) and human leucocyte antigens in childhood-onset schizophrenia (Jacobsen et al. 1998). More recently, however, there have been a number of encouraging reports on possible genetic "hot spots" from linkage studies performed in large multiply-affected pedigrees or samples of nuclear families. Areas implicated include 1q, 4q, 5p, 5q, 6p, 6q, 8p, 9q, 10p, 13q, 15q, 22q, and Xp11 (Baron 2001). Allelic association studies have yielded positive findings for the Ser9Gly polymorphism in exon 1 of the D3 receptor gene (Crocq et al. 1992; Williams et al. 1998), as well as for the T102C polymorphism of the 5-HT2A receptor gene (Inayama et al. 1996; Williams et al. 1996; Williams et al. 1997). The relevance of these candidate regions to EOS is not yet clear, but in view of the increased familial loading for EOS, such studies would seem particularly promising.

Chromosomal Abnormalities

Various chromosomal aberrations have been reported in people with schizophrenia, including translocations such as t(2;18)(p11.2;p11.2) and t(1;7)(p22; q22); inversions such as 9p11-9q13 and 4p15.2-q21.3; trisomies of 5p14.1 and 8 as well as the partial trisomy of 5q11-13; fragile sites at 8q24 and 10q24; deletions at 22q11 and 5q21-23.1; and sex aneuplodies (reviewed in Baron 2001). Of the above, particularly interesting is the 22q11 deletion, which overlaps the region implicated in velocardiofacial syndrome (VCFS), a genetic condition that is associated with schizophrenia-like psychosis (Murphy and Owen 2001).

An increased rate of cytogenetic abnormalities was found in the NIMH childhood-onset schizophrenia cohort as compared to the general population. Specifically, 5 out of the 47 patients exhibited chromosomal abnormalities: a girl with Turner syndrome, a boy with a t(1;7) reciprocal translocation, and two girls and a boy with VCFS. This rate appears to be higher than that in adult-onset schizophrenia and is thus suggestive of a link between chromosomal changes and an earlier age of onset (Usiskin et al. 1999). The association of schizophrenia with VCFS is of particular relevance as it has been estimated that 25 to 30 percent of children with VCFS will eventually develop psychosis (Murphy, Jones, and Owen 1999). Eliez et al. (2001) found that children and adolescents with VCFS show a reduction in gray- and white-matter tissue volumes and attributed a significant gray-matter reduction to a 22q11.2 microdeletion on the maternal chromosome.

Trinucleotide Repeats

In the mid-1990s there was considerable speculation about the role of trinucleotide repeats, a dynamic mutational mechanism, in the pathogenesis of schizophrenia. A typical clinical manifestation of such unstable trinucleotide repeats is the phenomenon of anticipation, whereby the severity of an illness increases and the age of onset decreases through successive generations within multiply-affected families. A number of studies have indeed reported anticipation in families with a history of schizophrenia (Asherson et al. 1994; Bassett and Honer 1994; Yaw et al. 1996), and reports of an association between CAG/CTG trinucleotide repeats and schizophrenia (Burgess et al. 1998) appeared to provide the underlying mechanism. However, the studies reporting anticipation may have been confounded by sampling or cohort bias (Asherson et al. 1994; Yaw et al. 1996), and recent studies of CAG/CTG repeats have largely been negative (Li et al. 1998; Vincent et al. 1998; Hawi et al. 1999; Bowen et al. 2000; Oharal et al. 2000). It is now thought that a major role for unstable trinucleotides in psychosis is unlikely, although involvement at a more modest level may be present in a minority of cases (Vincent et al. 2000).

Prenatal and Perinatal Factors

Obstetric complications are defined as deviations from normal fetal development and the ordinary course of events during pregnancy, labor, delivery, and early neonatal period. According to estimates based on meta-analyses of relevant studies, obstetric complications are associated with a twofold increase in the likelihood of developing schizophrenia (Geddes and Lawrie 1995; Geddes et al. 1999). Further studies, based on large epidemiologically based samples, have confirmed that people who later develop schizophrenia are more likely to have been exposed to obstetric complications, although the magnitude of this effect was more modest (Dalman et al. 1999; Kendell et al. 2000). It is, however, probable that obstetric complications play a more significant role in EOS than in the adult-onset form of the illness (Verdoux et al. 1997). Several studies appear to support this view.

Cannon et al. (2000) identified a linear increase in the odds of developing schizophrenia that correlated with an increasing number of hypoxia-related obstetric complications; this effect was associated with an early age at onset.

Similarly, Rosso et al. (2000) found that hypoxia-associated obstetric complications in a Finnish birth cohort significantly increased the odds of early- (22 years for females and 19 for males) but not of later-onset schizophrenia. Hultman et al. (1999) reported some degree of gender specificity, with multiparity, bleeding during pregnancy, and small size for gestational age being associated with an increased risk for schizophrenia of early onset (15 to 21 years) in males only; O'Callaghan et al. (1992) also found young male patients with schizophrenia to be more likely to show this association.

Given that the effect size of obstetric complications is very modest, it is perhaps not surprising that results from studies based on smaller samples that concentrate solely on EOS are more ambiguous. The NIMH study found no difference in the rate of obstetric complications between subjects with EOS and matched controls. Similarly, our own study, the Maudsley Early Onset Schizophrenia Study failed to detect an increase in the overall rate of complications, although schizophrenic patients did show higher frequencies of fetal distress and forceps delivery (Matsumoto, Simmons, et al., Structural magnetic imaging, 2001). In contrast, findings from Japan have suggested that the rate of obstetric complications in EOS is higher than that in psychiatric controls, and it was estimated that exposure to obstetric complications led to a three-and-a-half-fold increase in risk of schizophrenia (Matsumoto, Takei, et al. 2001).

Brain Structural Abnormalities

Much research has been carried out on brain structural abnormalities in schizophrenia that largely employ magnetic resonance imaging (MRI) techniques. The most consistent findings reported are ventriculomegaly; decreases in the cortical, temporal lobe, and hippocampal volumes; and abnormal hemispheric asymmetry (Wright et al. 2000). The prevailing view is that most of these abnormalities precede the onset of schizophrenia and may be neurodevelopmental in origin, although the possibility of some progression in the abnormalities has recently been reinvestigated (Lieberman 1999; Allin and Murray 2001). Given that aberrant neurodevelopment may be more relevant to EOS, neuroimaging studies of this age group may prove particularly informative about the interaction between brain development and schizophrenia. A number of studies on brain structural abnormalities in EOS are discussed in detail in chapter 10 of this volume. Here we will briefly discuss some of the key findings that differentiate EOS from adult-onset schizophrenia.

Changes in temporal lobe structures do not appear to be a characteristic feature of EOS. As part of the Maudsley Early Onset Schizophrenia Study, brain MRI data were obtained from 40 children and adolescents with schizophrenia of recent onset (illness duration was less than 2 years) and from 40 healthy subjects closely matched on age, gender, ethnicity, and parental socioeconomic status. A comparison of the two groups did not reveal any volume reduction in temporal lobe structures such as the hippocampus (Matsumoto, Simmons, et al., Structural magnetic imaging, 2001), a finding that has been independently confirmed by three other studies: by the NIMH group (Jacobsen et al. 1996), by Findling et al. (1996) at the Case Western Reserve University School of Medicine, and by Levitt et al. (2001) from the UCLA group. Neither the Maudsley Early Onset Schizophrenia Study nor the NIMH group was able to detect volume decrements in the amygdala (Jacobsen et al. 1998), although Yeo et al. (1997) reported smaller amygdala in children with schizophrenia spectrum disorders. In the Maudsley Early Onset Schizophrenia Study the patients with EOS showed a reduction in both the total and the gray-matter volume of the right but not the left superior temporal gyrus (Matsumoto, Simmons, et al., Superior temporal gyrus, 2001). Although in the NIMH study this finding was absent at baseline, a considerable right-sided volume loss was detected in the superior temporal gyrus at a two-year follow-up of a subgroup of these patients (Jacobsen at al 1998). The thalamus appears to be reduced in volume or area in EOS (Frazier et al. 1996; Dasari et al. 1999), and in the Maudsley Early Onset Schizophrenia Study voxel-based analysis of the brain MRI data revealed that this reduction may be primarily localized in the dorsomedial nucleus.

Age at the time of scanning appears to play a significant role in the pattern of changes in brain morphology seen in EOS. Following initial reports of accelerated gray-matter loss occurring during adolescence in frontal, parietal, and temporal regions of schizophrenic adolescents (Rapoport et al. 1999), Thompson et al. (2001) reexamined data from the NIMH cohort using brain-mapping algorithms. This revealed a specific temporal pattern of gray-matter loss over a 5-year period. The earliest deficits were present in parietal brain regions but then progressed anteriorly into the temporal lobes, the sensorimotor and dorsolateral prefrontal cortices, and the frontal eye fields. Evidently, then, patients with EOS studied at different points along this developmental trajectory may display differences in the pattern and degree of their structural brain abnormalities. Moreover, the period of adolescence may be especially critical to the development of the brain pathology in schizophrenia.

Life Events

The interest in the role of life events in schizophrenia is based on the assumption that such events, whether pleasant or unpleasant, are stressful and that patients with schizophrenia are unusually vulnerable to stress. An increased number of life events—particularly clustered in the period from 3 weeks to 3 months prior to the onset of illness—has been observed in patients with schizophrenia in comparison to normal controls but not to groups with other psychiatric disorders (Norman and Malla 1993). This association between life events and the onset of illness is not specific to schizophrenia, however. In fact, the effect sizes appear to be greater for affective disorders (Brown, Harris, and Peto 1973; Paykel 1978; Bebbington et al. 1993). In the Edinburgh High-Risk Study, Miller et al. (2001) demonstrated a correlation between relatively upsetting life events and the appearance of psychotic symptoms in both the control and the high-risk groups. Although the impact of life events specifically in EOS has not yet been investigated, the Maudsley Early Onset Schizophrenia Study noted an excess of first-generation immigrants among EOS patients as compared to controls. Although this finding suggests that immigration may be a trigger for EOS, other interpretations are possible, such as biases in the recruitment of the control sample and the possibility of selective migration on the part of high-risk families (Sharpley et al. 2001), the role of potential environmental triggers in an unusually early onset of schizophrenia is worth exploring further.

Family Interactions

Not surprisingly, the quality of the relationship between patients with schizophrenia and their relatives or caregivers has a significant impact on both the onset and the overall course of the illness. Family members who are highly critical or hostile or who tend to be overinvolved are said to manifest a high level of expressed emotion (Vaughn and Leff 1976). Increased levels of expressed emotion have proven to be a robust predictor of relapse in schizophrenia (Bebbington and Kuipers 1994), although its impact is not specific to schizophrenia and may in fact be greater in mood and eating disorders (Butzlaff and Hooley 1998). Most young people with EOS live with their families and so may be more vulnerable than adult patients to disturbed family relationships. However, Asarnow et al. (1994) did not discover any significant differences in the rates of expressed emotion among parents of children with schizophrenia spectrum disorders and parents of normal controls. In support of their findings the authors pointed out that there are usually high levels of expressed emotion when family members view symptoms as being under the patient's control (Hooley 1987), an assumption that is less likely to be made in the case of children who are ill.

Drug Abuse

It is well established that substance abuse can precipitate the emergence of psychotic symptoms (Connell 1985; Horowitz 1969). Cannabis is of particular interest because of its increasing social acceptability and widespread use. Andreasson et al. found that Swedish conscripts who frequently used cannabis were more likely than their peers to be admitted to hospital with psychosis (Andreasson et al. 1987; Andreasson, Allebeck, and Rydberg 1989). The increased risk conferred by substance abuse may also be associated with an earlier onset of the disorder. Hambrecht and Häfner (2000) found that in a large representative sample of patients with first-episode schizophrenia, 13 percent had a history of cannabis abuse, with males and those who began to abuse drugs at a relatively early age being those most at risk. Indeed, substance abuse in children and adolescents is becoming a major public health issue. Data drawn from a stratified sample of 9,742 children and adolescents in England revealed a rise in illicit drug use from 1.0 percent at age 11 to 14.5 percent at age 16, with illicit drug use most prevalent among 15-year-old boys (Sutherland and Shepherd 2000). Substance abuse may therefore soon become one of the most significant precipitants of psychosis among children and adolescents. At the same time, because it is one of the few modifiable risk factors for psychosis, the importance of interventions to prevent or limit substance abuse among young people cannot be overstated.

Psychomotor Development

Studies of adult-onset schizophrenia have found evidence of developmental delay, primarily in speech and language (Ambelas 1992; Jones et al. 1994) and in motor control (Walker and Lewine 1990; Walker et al. 1993; Cannon et al. 1999; Boks et al. 2000). Delayed speech and language development and/or linguistic impairment has been consistently observed in 43 to 55 percent of patients with childhood-onset schizophrenia (Kolvin et al. 1971; Watkins, Asarnow, and Tanguay 1988; Nicolson et al. 2000). In the Maudsley Early Onset Schizophrenia Study, we found that language impairment was present in 19.4 percent of the cases, a figure lower than that reported in studies of childhood-onset schizophrenia. This discrepancy may, however, be explained by the predominance of adolescents in our sample. Hollis (1995) studied a group of 61 children and adolescents with schizophrenia, with a mean age of onset of 14.3 years, from the Maudsley Children's Department and found that 23 percent of them had speech and/or language impairment. Such impairment was more prevalent in patients who developed schizophrenia before the age of 13 than in those with an adolescent onset.

The earliest study of motor development, by Kolvin et al. (1971), noted that only 3 percent of developmental delays were attributable to delayed motor milestones. However, Hollis (1995) reported motor disturbance in 31 percent of his subjects. His definition of motor impairment included restlessness, stereotyped movements, poor coordination, and delayed milestones. Nicolson et al. (2000) found motor impairment in 57.1 percent of the NIMH sample of patients with childhood-onset schizophrenia, including not only delayed motor milestones but also poor coordination and abnormal repetitive movements. In an earlier analysis of a subgroup of this sample, Alaghband-Rad et al. (1995) reported that the rate of motor impairment when restricted to delayed walking was 17 percent and that developmental motor delays were more common in those schizophrenic children who met at least one or all the criteria for infantile autism (36% and 13%, respectively). In the Maudsley Early Onset Schizophrenia Study the incidence of delayed motor milestones proved to be insignificant. However, about 3 percent of the sample had been unable to walk unsupported by the age of 2 and thus showed gross motor deficits.

Studies of samples at high risk for schizophrenia because of genetic proximity to an affected family member also support the idea that early developmental deviance is a significant risk indicator in schizophrenia. Erlenmeyer-Kimling et al. (2000) assessed neuromotor performance during childhood and adolescence in the offspring of schizophrenic subjects and healthy controls. They demonstrated that impairment in gross motor skills showed a reasonably high specificity and sensitivity. Probands with abnormalities in gross motor skills had a 33 percent probability of developing schizophrenia.

Increased rates of such abnormalities were reported even in the earliest studies of pediatric patients with schizophrenia (Kennard 1960; Gittelman and Birch 1967). Karp et al. (2001) evaluated neurological functioning in a cohort of adolescents with early-onset schizophrenia. The schizophrenic group exhibited a high frequency of neurological abnormalities (mean of 6, SD = 2, range = 2) when compared to normal controls (mean of 4, SD = 2, range = 0–8). Additionally, the number of such abnormalities decreased with age in the healthy controls but not in the subjects with adolescent schizophrenia, which suggested that these patients experienced a delay in or a lack of normal neurological maturation during adolescence.

Premorbid Functioning

Poor premorbid social functioning is one of the most frequently replicated findings in schizophrenia. It has been reported in retrospective studies (Watt 1972; Watt and Lubensky 1976; Lewine et al. 1980; Baum and Walker 1995; Cannon et al. 1997; Malmberg et al. 1998), in prospective birth cohort studies (Done et al. 1994; Jones et al. 1994; Mirsky et al. 1995; Olin, John, and Mednick 1995; Poulton et al. 2000), and in high-risk studies (Amminger et al. 1999; Hans et al. 2000). The most common features of premorbid functioning are poor peer relationships, social withdrawal, suspiciousness, and anxiety (Mirsky et al. 1995; Olin and Mednick 1996).

In their study of EOS cases, Kolvin et al. (1971) found that 87 percent of their subjects were premorbidly odd; 58 percent of them displayed schizoid traits such as an unusually high degree of shyness, withdrawal, timidity, and sensitivity. Hollis (1995) found that a premorbid history of social withdrawal was markedly more common in cases of EOS than in nonpsychotic patients. Two studies on treatment-resistant EOS cases (Alaghband-Rad et al. 1995; Nicolson and Rapoport 1999) found that parents and teachers had voiced concern about the social development and academic performance of more than half of their subjects. The Maudsley Early Onset Schizophrenia Study confirmed the presence of a number of schizophrenia spectrum traits during the premorbid phase of EOS: 70.5 percent of our subjects exhibited at least one such trait, most commonly social isolation (54%), followed by the presence of odd ideas or perceptions (41%). We were also able to identify a significant interaction between a history of developmental deviance and the presence of social isolation and abnormal thoughts and beliefs in those subjects who later developed schizophrenia. Premorbid function further deteriorated as patients progressed into adolescence, with the most striking changes seen in social isolation and poor scholastic performance. In addition, boys were more affected, in terms of peer relationships and social isolation.

Existing evidence suggests that poor academic performance and social isolation may show some degree of specificity to schizophrenia. Asarnow and Ben-Meir (1988) compared children with schizophrenia, schizophrenia spectrum disorder, depression, and dysthymic disorders and found that the first two groups were significantly more impaired. Cannon et al. (2001) reported that social withdrawal and disturbed relationships with peers or adults other than family members were more common in those children who developed schizophrenia as opposed to affective disorders later in life. There may also be a quantitative difference in the occurrence of these premorbid abnormalities in subjects with early- versus adult-onset schizophrenia. Despite the methodological difficulties in comparing ratings from different studies, Cannon-Spoor, Potkin, and Wyatt (1982) and Alaghband-Rad et al. (1995) reported poorer scores on the Premorbid Adjustment Scale for EOS cases than for subjects with adult-onset schizophrenia.

Cognitive Factors

Cognitive deficits are a consistent feature of schizophrenia, having been noted even in the earliest descriptions of the disorder (Bleuler 1950). Abnormalities have been reported in all aspects of cognition, with the largest effect size seen in general intellectual ability, verbal memory, and executive function (Heinrichs and Zakzanis 1998). In a study of 18-year-old male Swedish Army conscripts, David et al. (1997) found that intellectual functioning was a powerful predictor of future schizophrenia, a finding that was replicated in an Israeli cohort of 16- and 17-year-old males tested for eligibility for military service (Davidson et al. 1999). Paradoxically, a study by Isohanni et al. (1999) demonstrated that the distance in either direction from the cognitive norm increases the odds for the disorder, and the proportion of cases falling within the highest IQ category in the study by Davidson et al. was six times higher than that of the comparison subjects.

High-risk studies have provided additional evidence concerning cognitive risk factors for schizophrenia. Erlenmeyer-Kimling et al. (2000) presented findings from the New York High-Risk Project. In a sample of offspring of parents with schizophrenia, childhood abnormalities in verbal memory and in attention span characterized 83 percent and 58 percent, respectively, of those who developed schizophrenia-related psychoses. In the Jerusalem Infant Development Study, Hans et al. (1999) showed that 42 percent of the offspring of schizophrenic parents overall, and 73 percent of the male children, showed poor neurobehavioral functioning, as compared to 22 percent of the offspring of normal controls. These signs were stable over time in a subgroup of these offspring whose cognitive functioning was particularly poor but not among other young people, and were associated with psychopathology, especially schizophrenia spectrum disorders with an onset in adolescence.

Several studies have examined the cognitive profile of EOS cases. Kenny et al. (1997) found that in comparison to normal subjects, adolescents with schizophrenia demonstrated generalized cognitive impairment in measures of attention, memory, and executive functions, with moderate to very large effect sizes, the largest of which were seen in measures of focused and divided attention and working memory. In contrast, Oie and Rund (1999) did not detect attentional deficits in adolescents with schizophrenia but instead noted impairments in abstraction-flexibility and visuospatial abilities. When compared with ADHD subjects, the schizophrenic group appeared to have a selective impairment in visual memory. Kumra et al. (2000) examined cognitive function in EOS patients and in those with psychotic disorder not otherwise specified and discovered that both groups shared a pattern of generalized cognitive deficits including impairment in attention, learning, and abstraction. In the Maudsley Early Onset Schizophrenia Study, comprehensive cognitive assessment was available in 20 of the 40 EOS subjects and in an equal number of closely matched controls. In terms of general intellectual ability, the average impairment of these patients with reference to the normative data ranged between 0.2 and 0.7 standard deviation, with full-scale and performance IQ being significantly lower than in controls. As in the study by Oie and Rund (1999), patients showed no attentional dysfunction but were impaired in all measures of memory, particularly verbal memory, followed by smaller impairments in visual and spatial abilities.

Conclusions

Schizophrenia is now clearly established as a multifactorial disease. Much progress has been made in recent years in identifying risk factors and indicators, but we are still unable to identify the precise contribution of each factor to disease liability, nor do we fully understand their interaction with one another. Each of these risk factors appears to exercise a small to moderate effect, some increasing vulnerability to schizophrenia, others reflecting early manifestations of the illness. Predicting the contribution of various risk factors to complex disorders such as schizophrenia remains a challenge, and determining the interactions between genes and the environment during any disease process is a daunting task. EOS appears to share most if not all of the risk factors that have already been identified in the adult-onset form of the disorder. In particular, abnormalities in psychomotor development and premorbid functioning appear to be either more prevalent or more severe in EOS. There is also evidence for dynamic brain morphological changes taking place in EOS subjects during adolescence. Together these findings suggest that EOS offers an especially useful opportunity to observe the interaction between developmental and disease processes. At the same time, advances in human genome mapping have led to the identification of large numbers of genetic markers that allow systematic searches for multiple disease-susceptibility genes that underlie complex traits. The development of DNA microarrays for genotyping and gene expression promise to make hundreds, if not hundreds of thousands, of genetic measurements feasible in family and general population studies. Studies that carefully report and register risk factors in populations genetically enriched for schizophrenia, including EOS, will be of immense value when combined with genetic risk profiling.

REFERENCES

Alaghband-Rad, J., McKenna, K., Gordon, C. T., Albus, K. E., Hamburger, S. D., Rumsey, J. M., et al. (1995). Childhood-onset schizophrenia: The severity of premorbid course. *Journal of the American Academy of Child and Adolescent Psychiatry* 34:1273–83.
Allin, M., and Murray, R. M. (2001). Schizophrenia: A neurodevelopmental or neurodegenerative disorder? *Current Opinion in Psychiatry* 15:9–15.
Ambelas, A. (1992). Preschizophrenics: Adding to the evidence, sharpening the focus. *British Journal of Psychiatry* 160:401–4.
Amminger, G. P., Pape, S., Rock, D., Roberts, S. A., Ott, S. L., Squires-Wheeler, E., et al. (1999). Relationship between childhood behavioral disturbance and later schizophrenia in the New York High-Risk Project. *American Journal of Psychiatry* 156:525–30.
Andreasson, S., Allebeck, P., Engstrom, A., and Rydberg, U. (1987). Cannabis and schizophrenia: A longitudinal study of Swedish conscripts. *Lancet* 2(8574):1483–86.

Andreasson, S., Allebeck, P., and Rydberg, U. (1989). Schizophrenia in users and nonusers of cannabis: A longitudinal study in Stockholm County. *Acta Psychiatrica Scandinavica* 79:505–10.

Asarnow, J. R., and Ben-Meir, S. (1988). Children with schizophrenia spectrum and depressive disorders: A comparative study of premorbid adjustment, onset pattern and severity of impairment. *Journal of Child Psychology and Psychiatry* 29:477–88.

Asarnow, J. R., Tompson, M., Hamilton, E. B., Goldstein, M. J., and Guthrie, D. (1994). Family-expressed emotion, childhood-onset depression, and childhood-onset schizophrenia spectrum disorders: Is expressed emotion a nonspecific correlate of child psychopathology or a specific risk factor for depression? *Journal of Abnormal Child Psychology* 22:129–46.

Asarnow, R. F., Nuechterlein, K. H., Fogelson, D., Subotnik, K. L., Payne, D. A., Russell, A. T., et al. (2001). Schizophrenia and schizophrenia-spectrum personality disorders in the first-degree relatives of children with schizophrenia: The UCLA family study. *Archives of General Psychiatry* 58:581–88.

Asherson, P., Walsh, C., Williams, J., Sargeant, M., Taylor, C., Clements, A., et al. (1994). Imprinting and anticipation: Are they relevant to genetic studies of schizophrenia? *British Journal of Psychiatry* 164:619–24.

Baron, M. (2001). Genetics of schizophrenia and the new millennium: Progress and pitfalls. *American Journal of Human Genetics* 68:299–312.

Bassett, A. S., and Honer, W. G. (1994). Evidence for anticipation in schizophrenia. *American Journal of Human Genetics* 54:864–70.

Baum, K. M., and Walker, E. F. (1995). Childhood behavioral precursors of adult symptom dimensions in schizophrenia. *Schizophrenia Research* 1:111–20.

Bebbington, P., and Kuipers, E. (1994). The predictive utility of expressed emotion in schizophrenia: An aggregate analysis. *Psychological Medicine* 24:707–18.

Bebbington, P., Wilkins, S., Jones, P., Foerster, A., Murray, R., Toone, B., et al. (1993). Life events and psychosis: Initial results from the Camberwell Collaborative Psychosis Study. *British Journal of Psychiatry* 162:72–79.

Bleuer, E. (1950). *Dementia praecox or the group of schizophrenias*. New York: International Universities Press.

Boks, M. P., Russo, S., Knegtering, R., and van den Bosch, R. J. (2000). The specificity of neurological signs in schizophrenia: A review. *Schizophrenia Research* 43:109–16.

Bowen, T., Guy, C. A., Cardno, A. G., Vincent, J. B., Kennedy, J. L., Jones, L. A., et al. (2000). Repeat sizes at CAG/CTG loci CTG18.1, ERDA1 and TGC13-7a in schizophrenia. *Psychiatric Genetics* 10:33–37.

Boydell, J., van Os, J., McKenzie, K., Allardyce, J., Goel, R., McCreadie, R. G., et al. (2001). Incidence of schizophrenia in ethnic minorities in London: Ecological study into interactions with environment. *British Medical Journal* 323(7325):1336.

Brown, G. W., Harris, T. O., and Peto, J. (1973). Life events and psychiatric disorders, Pt. 2: Nature of causal link. *Psychological Medicine* 3:59–76.

Burgess, C. E., Lindblad, K., Sidransky, E., Yuan, Q. P., Long, R. T., Breschel, T., et al. (1998). Large CAG/CTG repeats are associated with childhood-onset schizophrenia. *Molecular Psychiatry* 3:321–27.

Butzlaff, R. L., and Hooley, J. M. (1998). Expressed emotion and psychiatric relapse: A meta-analysis. *Archives of General Psychiatry* 55:547–52.

Cannon, M., Jones, P., Gilvarry, C., Rifkin, L., McKenzie, K., Foerster, A., et al. (1997).

Premorbid social functioning in schizophrenia and bipolar disorder: Similarities and differences. *American Journal of Psychiatry* 154:1544–50.

Cannon, M., Jones, P., Huttunen, M. O., Tanskanen, A., Huttunen, T., Rabe-Hesketh, S., et al. (1999). School performance in Finnish children and later development of schizophrenia: A population-based longitudinal study. *Archives of General Psychiatry* 56:457–63.

Cannon, M., Walsh, E., Hollis, C., Kargin, M., Taylor, E., Murray, R. M., et al. (2001). Predictors of later schizophrenia and affective psychosis among attendees at a child psychiatry department. *British Journal of Psychiatry* 178:420–26.

Cannon, T. D., Kaprio, J., Lonnqvist, J., Huttunen, M., and Koskenvuo, M. (1998). The genetic epidemiology of schizophrenia in a Finnish twin cohort: A population-based modeling study. *Archives of General Psychiatry* 55:67–74.

Cannon, T. D., Rosso, I. M., Hollister, J. M., Bearden, C. E., Sanchez, L. E., and Hadley, T. (2000). A prospective cohort study of genetic and perinatal influences in the etiology of schizophrenia. *Schizophrenia Bulletin* 26:351–66.

Cannon-Spoor, H. E., Potkin, S. G., and Wyatt, R. J. (1982). Measurement of premorbid adjustment in chronic schizophrenia. *Schizophrenia Bulletin* 8:470–84.

Cardno, A. G., Jones, L. A., Murphy, K. C., Sanders, R. D., Asherson, P., Owen, M. J., et al. (1998). Sibling pairs with schizophrenia or schizoaffective disorder: Associations of subtypes, symptoms and demographic variables. *Psychological Medicine* 28:815–23.

Cardno, A. G., Marshall, E. J., Coid, B., Macdonald, A. M., Ribchester, T. R., Davies, N. J., et al. (1999). Heritability estimates for psychotic disorders: The Maudsley twin psychosis series. *Archives of General Psychiatry* 56:162–68.

Connell, P. H. (1985). *Amphetamine psychosis.* Maudsley Monograph No. 5. London: Chapman & Hall.

Crocq, M. A., Mant, R., Asherson, P., Williams, J., Hode, Y., Mayerova, A., et al. (1992). Association between schizophrenia and homozygosity at the dopamine D3 receptor gene. *American Journal of Medical Genetics* 29:858–60.

Dalman, C., Allebeck, P., Cullberg, J., Grunewald, C., and Koster, M. (1999). Obstetric complications and the risk of schizophrenia: A longitudinal study of a national birth cohort. *Archives of General Psychiatry* 56:234–40.

Dasari, M., Friedman, L., Jesberger, J., Stuve, T. A., Findling, R. L., Swales, T. P., et al. (1999). A magnetic resonance imaging study of thalamic area in adolescent patients with either schizophrenia or bipolar disorder as compared to healthy controls. *Psychiatry Research* 91:155–62.

David, A. S., Malmberg, A., Brandt, L., Allebeck, P., and Lewis, G. (1997). IQ and risk for schizophrenia: A population-based cohort study. *Psychological Medicine* 27:1311–23.

Davidson, M., Reichenberg, A., Rabinowitz, J., Weiser, M., Kaplan, Z., and Mark, M. (1999). Behavioral and intellectual markers for schizophrenia in apparently healthy male adolescents. *American Journal of Psychiatry* 156:1328–35.

Done, D. J., Crow, T. J., Johnstone, E. C., and Sacker, A. (1994). Childhood antecedents of schizophrenia and affective illness: Social adjustment at ages 7 and 11. *British Medical Journal* 309(6956):699–703.

Eliez, S., Antonarakis, S. E., Morris, M. A., Dahoun, S. P., and Reiss, A. L. (2001). Parental origin of the deletion 22q11.2 and brain development in velocardiofacial syndrome: A preliminary study. *Archives of General Psychiatry* 58:64–68.

Erlenmeyer-Kimling, L., Rock, D., Roberts, S. A., Janal, M., Kestenbaum, C., Cornblatt,

B., et al. (2000). Attention, memory, and motor skills as childhood predictors of schizophrenia-related psychoses: The New York High-Risk Project. *American Journal of Psychiatry* 157:1416–22.

Fernandez, T., Yan, W. L., Hamburger, S., Rapoport, J. L., Saunders, A. M., Schapiro, M., et al. (1999). Apolipoprotein E alleles in childhood-onset schizophrenia. *American Journal of Medical Genetics* 88:211–13.

Findling, R. L., Friedman, L., Henny, J. T., Swales, T. P., Cola, D. M., and Schulz, S. C. (1996). Hippocampal volume in adolescent schizophrenia. *Schizophrenia Research* 18:185.

Frangou, S. (1999). The Maudsley Early Onset Schizophrenia Study: Abnormal genes, abnormal brains, abnormal families. *Biological Psychiatry* 45(Suppl.):12.

Frazier, J. A., Giedd, J. N., Hamburger, S. D., Albus, K. E., Kaysen, D., Vaituzis, A. C., et al. (1996). Brain anatomic magnetic resonance imaging in childhood-onset schizophrenia. *Archives of General Psychiatry* 53:617–24.

Geddes, J. R., and Lawrie, S. M. (1995). Obstetric complications and schizophrenia: A meta-analysis. *British Journal of Psychiatry* 167:786–93.

Geddes, J. R., Verdoux, H., Takei, N., Lawrie, S. M., Bovet, P., Eagles, J. M., et al. (1999). Schizophrenia and complications of pregnancy and labor: An individual patient data meta-analysis. *Schizophrenia Bulletin* 25:413–23.

Gittelman, M., and Birch, H. G. (1967). Childhood schizophrenia: Intellect, neurologic status, perinatal risk, prognosis, and family pathology. *Archives of General Psychiatry* 17:16–25.

Gordon, C. T., Frazier, J. A., McKenna, K., Giedd, J., Zametkin, A., Zahn, T., et al. (1994). Childhood-onset schizophrenia: An NIMH study in progress. *Schizophrenia Bulletin* 20:697–712.

Gottesman, I. I., and Shields, J. (1967). A polygenic theory of schizophrenia. *Proceedings of the National Academy of Sciences USA* 58:199–205.

Häfner, H., Maurer, K., Loffler, W., and Riecher-Rossler, A. (1993). The influence of age and sex on the onset and early course of schizophrenia. *British Journal of Psychiatry* 162:80–86.

Hambrecht, M., and Häfner, H. (2000). Cannabis, vulnerability, and the onset of schizophrenia: An epidemiological perspective. *Australian and New Zealand Journal of Psychiatry* 34:468–75.

Hans, S. L., Auerbach, J. G., Asarnow, J. R., Styr, B., and Marcus, J. (2000). Social adjustment of adolescents at risk for schizophrenia: The Jerusalem Infant Development Study. *Journal of the American Academy of Child and Adolescent Psychiatry* 39:1406–14.

Hans, S. L., Marcus, J., Nuechterlein, K. H., Asarnow, R. F., Styr, B., and Auerbach, J. G. (1999). Neurobehavioral deficits at adolescence in children at risk for schizophrenia: The Jerusalem Infant Development Study. *Archives of General Psychiatry* 56:741–48.

Hawi, Z., Mynett-Johnson, L., Murphy, V., Straub, R. E., Kendler, K. S., Walsh, D., et al. (1999). No evidence to support the association of the potassium channel gene hSKCa3 CAG repeat with schizophrenia or bipolar disorder in the Irish population. *Molecular Psychiatry* 4:488–91.

Heinrichs, R. W., and Zakzanis, K. K. (1998). Neurocognitive deficit in schizophrenia: A quantitative review of the evidence. *Neuropsychology* 12:426–45.

Hollis, C. (1995). Child and adolescent (juvenile onset) schizophrenia: A case control study of premorbid developmental impairments. *British Journal of Psychiatry* 166:489–95.

Hooley, J. M. (1987). The nature and origins of expressed emotion. In K. Hahlweg and M. J. Goldstein (Eds.), *Understanding major mental disorder: The contribution of family interaction research.* (pp. 176–94). New York: Family Process Press.

Horowitz, M. J. (1969). Flashbacks: Recurrent intrusive images after the use of LSD. *American Journal of Psychiatry* 126:565–69.

Hultman, C. M., Sparen, P., Takei, N., Murray, R. M., and Cnattingius, S. (1999). Prenatal and perinatal risk factors for schizophrenia, affective psychosis, and reactive psychosis of early onset: Case-control study. *British Medical Journal* 318(7181):421–26.

Inayama, Y., Yoneda, H., Sakai, T., Ishida, T., Nonomura, Y., Kono, Y., et al. (1996). Positive association between a DNA sequence variant in the serotonin 2A receptor gene and schizophrenia. *American Journal of Medical Genetics* 67:103–5.

Isohanni, I., Jarvelin, M. R., Jones, P., Jokelainen, J., and Isohanni, M. (1999). Can excellent school performance be a precursor of schizophrenia? A 28-year follow-up in the Northern Finland 1966 birth cohort. *Acta Psychiatrica Scandinavica* 100:17–26.

Jacobsen, L. K., Giedd, J. N., Castellanos, F. X., Vaituzis, A. C., Hamburger, S. D., Kumra, S., et al. (1998). Progressive reduction of temporal lobe structures in childhood-onset schizophrenia. *American Journal of Psychiatry* 155:678–85.

Jacobsen, L. K., Giedd, J. N., Vaituzis, A. C., Hamburger, S. D., Rajapakse, J. C., Frazier, J. A., et al. (1996). Temporal lobe morphology in childhood-onset schizophrenia. *American Journal of Psychiatry* 153:355–61.

Jacobsen, L. K., Mittleman, B. B., Kumra, S., Lenane, M. C., Barracchini, K. C., Adams, S., et al. (1998). HLA antigens in childhood-onset schizophrenia. *Psychiatry Research* 78:123–32.

Jacobsen, L. K., and Rapoport, J. L. (1998). Research update: Childhood-onset schizophrenia—implications of clinical and neurobiological research. *Journal of Child Psychology and Psychiatry* 39:101–13.

Jones, P., Rodgers, B., Murray, R., and Marmot, M. (1994). Child development risk factors for adult schizophrenia in the British 1946 birth cohort. *Lancet* 344(8934):1398–402.

Kallmann, F. J., and Roth, M. (1956). Genetic aspects of preadolescent schizophrenia. *American Journal of Psychiatry* 112:599–606.

Karp, B. I., Garvey, M., Jacobsen, L. K., Frazier, J. A., Hamburger, S. D., Bedwell, J. S., et al. (2001). Abnormal neurologic maturation in adolescents with early-onset schizophrenia. *American Journal of Psychiatry* 158:118–22.

Kendell, R. E., McInneny, K., Juszczak, E., and Bain, M. (2000). Obstetric complications and schizophrenia: Two case-control studies based on structured obstetric records. *British Journal of Psychiatry* 176:516–22.

Kendler, K. S. (1983). Overview: A current perspective on twin studies of schizophrenia. *American Journal of Psychiatry* 140:1413–25.

Kendler, K. S., McGuire, M., Gruenberg, A. M., and Walsh, D. (1994). Clinical heterogeneity in schizophrenia and the pattern of psychopathology in relatives: Results from an epidemiologically based family study. *Acta Psychiatrica Scandinavica* 89:294–300.

Kennard, M. A. (1960). Value of equivocal signs in neurologic diagnosis. *Neurology* 10:753–64.

Kenny, J. T., Friedman, L., Findling, R. L., Swales, T. P., Strauss, M. E., Jesberger, J. A., et al. (1997). Cognitive impairment in adolescents with schizophrenia. *American Journal of Psychiatry* 154:1613–15.

Kolvin, I., Ounsted, C., Humphrey, M., and McNay, A. (1971). Studies in the childhood psychoses, Pt. 2: The phenomenology of childhood psychoses. *British Journal of Psychiatry* 118:385–95.

Kumra, S., Wiggs, E., Bedwell, J., Smith, A. K., Arling, E., Albus, K., et al. (2000). Neuropsychological deficits in pediatric patients with childhood-onset schizophrenia and psychotic disorder not otherwise specified. *Schizophrenia Research* 42:135–44.

Levitt, J. G., Blanton, R. E., Caplan, R., Asarnow, R., Guthrie, D., Toga, A. W., et al. (2001). Medial temporal lobe in childhood-onset schizophrenia. *Psychiatry Research* 108:17–27.

Lewine, R. R., Watt, N. F., Prentky, R. A., and Fryer, J. H. (1980). Childhood social competence in functionally disordered psychiatric patients and in normals. *Journal of Abnormal Psychology* 89:132–38.

Li, T., Vallada, H. P., Liu, X., Xie, T., Tang, X., Zhao, J., et al. (1998). Analysis of CAG/CTG repeat size in Chinese subjects with schizophrenia and bipolar affective disorder using the repeat expansion detection method. *Biological Psychiatry* 44:1160–65.

Lieberman, J. A. (1999). Is schizophrenia a neurodegenerative disorder? A clinical and neurobiological perspective. *Biological Psychiatry* 46:729–39.

Malmberg, A., Lewis, G., David, A., and Allebeck, P. (1998). Premorbid adjustment and personality in people with schizophrenia. *British Journal of Psychiatry* 172:308–13.

Matsumoto, H., Simmons, A., Williams, S., Hadjulis, M., Pipe, R., Murray, R., et al. (2001). Superior temporal gyrus abnormalities in early-onset schizophrenia: Similarities and differences with adult-onset schizophrenia. *American Journal of Psychiatry* 158:1299–304.

Matsumoto, H., Simmons, A., Williams, S., Pipe, R., Murray, R., and Frangou, S. (2001). Structural magnetic imaging of the hippocampus in early-onset schizophrenia. *Biological Psychiatry* 49:824–31.

Matsumoto, H., Takei, N., Saito, F., Kachi, K., and Mori, N. (2001). The association between obstetric complications and childhood-onset schizophrenia: A replication study. *Psychological Medicine* 31:907–14.

Miller, P., Lawrie, S. M., Hodges, A., Clafferty, R., Cosway, R., and Johnstone, E. C. (2001). Genetic liability, illicit drug use, life stress and psychotic symptoms: Preliminary findings from the Edinburgh study of people at high risk for schizophrenia. *Social Psychiatry and Psychiatric Epidemiology* 36:338–42.

Mirsky, A. F., Kugelmass, S., Ingraham, L. J., Frenkel, E., and Nathan, M. (1995). Overview and summary: Twenty-five-year follow-up of high-risk children. *Schizophrenia Bulletin* 21:227–39.

Murphy, K. C., Jones, L. A., and Owen, M. J. (1999). High rates of schizophrenia in adults with velo-cardio-facial syndrome. *Archives of General Psychiatry* 56:940–45.

Murphy, K. C., and Owen, M. J. (2001). Velo-cardio-facial syndrome: A model for understanding the genetics and pathogenesis of schizophrenia. *British Journal of Psychiatry* 79:397–402.

Murray, R. M., and McGuffin, P. (1993). Genetic aspects of psychiatric disorders. In R. E. Kendell and A. K. Zeally (Eds.), *Companion to psychiatric studies*, 5th ed. (pp. 227–61). Edinburgh: Churchill-Livingstone.

Nicolson, R., and Rapoport, J. L. (1999).Childhood-onset schizophrenia: Rare but worth studying. *Biological Psychiatry* 46:1418–28.

Nicolson, R., Lenane, M., Singaracharlu, S., Malaspina, D., Giedd, J. N., Hamburger, S. D., et al. (2000). Premorbid speech and language impairments in childhood-onset schizophrenia: Association with risk factors. *American Journal of Psychiatry* 157:794–800.

Norman, R. M., and Malla, A. K. (1993). Stressful life events and schizophrenia, Pt. 1: A review of the research. *British Journal of Psychiatry* 162:161–66.

O'Callaghan, E., Gibson, T., Colohan, H. A., Buckley, P., Walshe, D. G., Larkin, C., et al. (1992). Risk of schizophrenia in adults born after obstetric complications and their association with early onset of illness: A controlled study. *British Medical Journal* 305(6864):1256–59.

Oharal, K., Ikeuchi, T., Suzuki, Y., Ohtani, M., Ohara, K., and Tsuji, S. (2000). A CAG tri-nucleotide repeat expansion and familial schizophrenia. *Psychiatry Research* 94:257–62.

Oie, M., and Rund, B. R. (1999). Neuropsychological deficits in adolescent-onset schizophrenia compared with attention deficit hyperactivity disorder. *American Journal of Psychiatry* 156:1216–22.

Olin, S. S., John, R. S., and Mednick, S. A. (1995). Assessing the predictive value of teacher reports in a high risk sample for schizophrenia: A ROC analysis. *Schizophrenia Research* 16:53–66.

Olin, S. C., and Mednick, S. A. (1996). Risk factors of psychosis: Identifying vulnerable populations premorbidly. *Schizophrenia Bulletin* 22:223–40.

Onstad, S., Skre, I., Torgersen, S., and Kringlen, E. (1991). Twin concordance for *DSM-III-R* schizophrenia. *Acta Psychiatrica Scandinavica* 83:395–401.

Paykel, E. S. (1978). Contribution of life events to causation of psychiatric illness. *Psychological Medicine* 8:245–53.

Poulton, R., Caspi, A., Moffitt, T. E., Cannon, M., Murray, R., and Harrington, H. (2000). Children's self-reported psychotic symptoms and adult schizophreniform disorder: A 15-year longitudinal study. *Archives of General Psychiatry* 57:1053–58.

Rapoport, J. L., Giedd, J. N., Blumenthal, J., Hamburger, S., Jeffries, N., Fernandez, T., et al. (1999). Progressive cortical change during adolescence in childhood-onset schizophrenia: A longitudinal magnetic resonance imaging study. *Archives of General Psychiatry* 56:649–54.

Rosso, I. M., Cannon, T. D., Huttunen, T., Huttunen, M. O., Lonnqvist, J., and Gasperoni, T. L. (2000). Obstetric risk factors for early-onset schizophrenia in a Finnish birth cohort. *American Journal of Psychiatry* 157:801–7.

Sham, P. C., Jones, P., Russell, A., Gilvarry, K., Bebbington, P., Lewis, S., et al. (1994). Age at onset, sex, and familial psychiatric morbidity in schizophrenia: Camberwell Collaborative Psychosis Study. *British Journal of Psychiatry* 165:466–73.

Sharpley, M., Hutchinson, G., McKenzie, K., and Murray, R. M. (2001). Understanding the excess of psychosis among the African-Caribbean population in England: Review of current hypotheses. *British Journal of Psychiatry Supplement* 40:s60–s68.

Sutherland, I., and Shepherd, J. (2000). Substance use seems to be increasing among 11-year-olds. *British Medical Journal* 321(7269):1161.

Thompson, P. M., Vidal, C., Giedd, J. N., Gochman, P., Blumenthal, J., Nicolson, R., et al. (2001). Mapping adolescent brain change reveals dynamic wave of accelerated gray matter loss in very early-onset schizophrenia. *Proceedings of the National Academy of Sciences, USA* 98:11650–55.

Usiskin, S. I., Nicolson, R., Krasnewich, D. M., Yan, W., Lenane, M., Wudarsky, M., et al. (1999). Velocardiofacial syndrome in childhood-onset schizophrenia. *Journal of the American Academy of Child and Adolescent Psychiatry* 38:1536–43.

Vaughn, C., and Leff, J. (1976). The measurement of expressed emotion in the families of psychiatric patients. *British Journal of Social and Clinical Psychology* 15:157–65.

Verdoux, H., Geddes, J. R., Takei, N., Lawrie, S. M., Bovet, P., Eagles, J. M., et al. (1997). Obstetric complications and age at onset in schizophrenia: An international collaborative meta-analysis of individual patient data. *American Journal of Psychiatry* 154: 1220–27.

Vincent, J. B., Kalsi, G., Klempan, T., Tatuch, Y., Sherrington, R. P., Breschel, T., et al. (1998). No evidence of expansion of CAG or GAA repeats in schizophrenia families and monozygotic twins. *Human Genetics* 103:41–47.

Vincent, J. B., Paterson, A. D., Strong, E., Petronis, A., and Kennedy, J. L. (2000). The unstable trinucleotide repeat story of major psychosis. *American Journal of Medical Genetics* 97:77–97.

Walker, E. F., Grimes, K. E., Davis, D. M., and Smith, A. J. (1993). Childhood precursors of schizophrenia: Facial expressions of emotion. *American Journal of Psychiatry* 150: 1654–60.

Walker, E. F., and Lewine, R. J. (1990). Prediction of adult-onset schizophrenia from childhood home movies of the patients. *American Journal of Psychiatry* 147:1052–56.

Watkins, J. M., Asarnow, R. F., and Tanguay, P. E. (1988). Symptom development in childhood-onset schizophrenia. *Journal of Child Psychology and Psychiatry* 29:865–78.

Watt, N. F. (1972). Longitudinal changes in the social behavior of children hospitalized for schizophrenia as adults. *Journal of Nervous and Mental Diseases* 155:42–54.

Watt, N. F., and Lubensky, A. W. (1976). Childhood roots of schizophrenia. *Journal of Consulting and Clinical Psychology* 44:363–75.

Williams, J., McGuffin, P., Nothen, M., and Owen, M. J. (1997). Meta-analysis of association between the 5-HT2a receptor T102C polymorphism and schizophrenia. European Multicentre Association Study of Schizophrenia (EMASS) Collaborative Group. *Lancet* 349(9060):1221.

Williams, J., Spurlock, G., Holmans, P., Mant, R., Murphy, K., Jones, L., et al. (1998). A meta-analysis and transmission disequilibrium study of association between the dopamine D3 receptor gene and schizophrenia. *Molecular Psychiatry* 3:141–49.

Williams, J., Spurlock, G., McGuffin, P., Mallet, J., Nothen, M. M., Gill, M., et al. (1996). Association between schizophrenia and T102C polymorphism of the 5-hydroxytryptamine type 2a-receptor gene. European Multicentre Association Study of Schizophrenia (EMASS) Group. *Lancet* 347(9011):1294–96.

Wright, I. C., Rabe-Hesketh, S., Woodruff, P. W., David, A. S., Murray, R. M., and Bullmore, E. T. (2000). Meta-analysis of regional brain volumes in schizophrenia. *American Journal of Psychiatry* 157:16–25.

Yaw, J., Myles-Worsley, M., Hoff, M., Holik, J., Freedman, R., Byerley, W., et al. (1996). Anticipation in multiplex schizophrenia pedigrees. *Psychiatric Genetics* 6:7–11.

Yeo, R. A., Hodde-Vargas, J., Hendren, R. L., Vargas, L. A., Brooks, W. M., Ford, C. C., et al. (1997). Brain abnormalities in schizophrenia-spectrum children: Implications for a neurodevelopmental perspective. *Psychiatry Research* 76:1–13.

CHAPTER FIVE

Neuroimaging in Adolescent Schizophrenia

S. Charles Schulz, M.D., Elizabeth DeOreo, and Johanna Lamm, Psy.D.

Because schizophrenia is most often regarded as an adult disorder or, more rarely, a disorder of childhood, the adolescent population suffering from schizophrenia has frequently been overlooked. Loranger (1984) examined patients with first-episode schizophrenia and noted that 39 percent of men and 23 percent of women had experienced their initial episode of the illness by the time they had reached 19 years of age. Although hardly trivial alone, when coupled with the numerous studies showing that adolescent-onset schizophrenia seems to be more severe than other forms of the illness, these numbers emphasize the need for additional research specifically within this population. Furthermore, because it is now generally accepted that adolescent-onset schizophrenia lies on a continuum with the adult form of the disorder and that the duration of time between diagnosis and treatment can have a substantial impact on outcome, a more thorough understanding of the disease process in this age group is bound to have important implications.

Newer thinking regarding the age of onset of schizophrenia necessitates that etiological theories concerning the disorder be rethought. The neurodevelopmental hypothesis postulates that "abnormalities" in the brain are present from conception onward but are not fully appreciated until the normal stages of neural development are (or should be) completed in adolescence (Weinberger 1987). Evidence supporting the neurodevelopmental hypothesis is drawn in part from neuroimaging studies that have demonstrated abnormalities in brain structure in patients with schizophrenia. Further evidence includes the higher incidence of a history of obstetric complications at birth among those with childhood-onset schizophrenia (COS), which is often associated with abnormal fetal development (Matsumoto, Takei, et al. 2001; Lewis, Owen, and Murray 1989). When taken in association with later neurodevelopmental hypotheses, such as the theory of synaptic pruning and the myelination model of schizophrenia, these findings underscore the need to study teenagers firsthand.

The advent of noninvasive brain imaging has allowed for in vivo studies of young people. Initial studies of teenagers used structural scans, such as computerized tomography (CT) scans, but now, newer techniques of neuroimaging enable us to watch the brain develop and to make volumetric, functional, and metabolic measurements. Neuroimaging thus allows investigators and clinicians to view specific abnormalities in discrete areas and to contrast their development over time. We can, for example, look at images of the brain of an adolescent experiencing a first episode of schizophrenia and compare them with those of an adult who has been ill for many years. Contrasting these populations also offers researchers a superb opportunity to distinguish the abnormalities and other changes that are actually part of the disease process from those caused by a prolonged course of medication. Furthermore, sophisticated image-analysis programs that include color coding related to significant differences between groups and over time may provide us with entirely new ways to view the brain (Thompson et al. 2001).

As theories of etiology evolve, becoming more complex, it is timely to review and analyze the role of neuroimaging during the critical neurodevelopmental stage of adolescence. In what follows, we will aim to extend recent work in this area (Findling et al. 1995; Peterson 1995; Sowell et al. 2000). We will survey specific techniques of neuroimaging—computerized tomography (CT) (previously known as computerized axial tomography, or CAT), positron emission tomography (PET), single photon emission computerized tomography (SPECT), magnetic resonance imaging (MRI), and magnetic resonance spectroscopy (MRS)—and present the research and subsequent findings relevant to each method. In addition, we will consider diagnostic specificity, comparisons between adults and adolescents, and new directions for neuroimaging.

A Brief Summary of Scan Techniques

CT, also known as a CAT scan, is a relatively brief and painless procedure. The scan is conducted by placing the patient in a tube that may or may not (depending on the machine) rotate around the area of the body under scrutiny while emitting a calibrated dose of X rays. The risk to the patient is minimal, consisting merely of the dose of radiation. Some subjects, however, find the X-ray tube very confining and thus experience a certain psychological discomfort. Early research into schizophrenia using neuroimaging was carried out with CT and focused on ventricular and sulcal size—mostly because these were areas that could be measured or rated fairly readily.

MRI is a magnetic imaging technique and, like CT, is safe and painless. Again the patient is placed in a long tube, but in MRI the patient is exposed to a magnetic pulse rather than to X rays. The magnetic force causes the atoms in the body containing hydrogen to align. The nuclei return to their original position and emit their own radio waves, which are converted into a picture image. The advantages to MRI are that images can be obtained in any plane and that they enhance the contrast between normal and abnormal tissue. MRI techniques are divided into subgroups: structural, functional, metabolic, and microstructural. Structural MRI, which makes possible the volumetric, physical, and static imaging of specific structures within the body, allows researchers to see the brain more clearly and to quantify brain structures such as the thalamus and hippocampus. Functional MRI also provides a view of the brain while additionally incorporating information about the blood flow through brain tissue when certain mental tasks are performed. This has allowed for the noninvasive examination of how the brain is working.

MRS works in the same manner as MRI. Instead of being translated into pictures, however, the signals convey information about the concentrations of chemicals and the metabolic state of the structure being studied. Phosphorus MRS measures the amount of phosphorus in a given part of the brain, thereby allowing conclusions to be drawn about the energy status (phosphocreatine, inorganic phosphate, and adenosine triphosphate), membrane integrity (phosphomonoesters), and breakdown by-products (phosphodiesters). Proton MRS measures the amount of N-acetylaspartate (NAA), a neuronal marker in tissues. Choline measurements are also valuable and are suggestive in particular of membrane injury (Brooks et al. 1998). Through MRS, investigators are now able to examine the brain chemistry of living patients. In addition, a recent extension of MRI technology, diffusion tensor imaging (DTI), allows for the visualization and quantification of white-matter tracks in the brain.

PET scans enable researchers to make inferences about the metabolic activity of the brain by monitoring the concentration of an intravenously or arterially injected radioactive chemical. Some ligands allow investigators to assess regional metabolic characteristics of brain, while others target neuroreceptors. When positrons, or particles with a positive charge, from the injected tracer collide with electrons in the body, gamma rays are produced. These gamma rays are detected by a ring surrounding the patient and then translated by computers into images. While the information gained from PET scans is extremely valuable, the procedure is invasive and can be anywhere from uncomfortable to painful. Little research has been done on adolescents using PET scanning owing to the issues of consent that surround subjecting minors to lengthy, possibly painful, and somewhat risky procedures.

SPECT (single photon emission tomography) is similar to PET but uses one photon rather than the two higher-energy photons used in PET. As a result, the images produced have less resolution. However, the availability of new radiopharmaceuticals that can enhance image quality, in combination with economic and practical concerns, make SPECT a legitimate alternative in some instances.

Table 5.1 compares the characteristics of the various scan techniques.

Brain Imaging Studies in Adolescents with Schizophrenia

CT Imaging

CT was the first noninvasive brain imaging technique to be applied to patients with schizophrenia. Two early studies (Johnstone et al. 1976; Weinberger et al. 1979) used a method of quantification of the lateral ventricles by area; Weinberger and colleagues specifically used the ratio of ventricle area to brain (VBR). Both studies demonstrated that schizophrenic patients have statistically larger ventricle size than do controls. These findings naturally raised

Table 5.1. Summary of imaging techniques

	Invasive	Radiation exposure	Nuclear magnetic resonance	Associated risk	Structural	Functional	Metabolic
PET	X	X		Some		X	
SPECT	X	X		Some		X	
CT		X		Minimal	X		
MRI			X	Minimal	X	X (fMRI)	
MRS			X	Minimal			X

the question when the enlargement occurred, leading investigators to design studies to evaluate CT scans taken of adolescents with psychiatric disorders.

Taking advantage of an adolescent inpatient service at the Medical College of Virginia, Schulz and colleagues (1982) initially reported on a group of adolescents with schizophrenia and then extended their work to include a patient control group with borderline personality disorder (Schulz, Koller, et al. 1983). The schizophrenia spectrum patients had larger VBRs than the film-library adolescent controls, while the VBRs of the borderline patients were similar to those of the controls. Furthermore, no correlation was found between the length of illness and VBR, thereby lending support to a developmental concept.

Reiss and colleagues (1983) subsequently carried out a CT study of a group of children and adolescents with psychiatric illness and compared the resulting measurements to those from a neurological control group. In the group studied ($N = 20$) were 11 children or adolescents with a severe and persistent illness, including schizotypal disorder or schizophrenia. As a group, the psychiatric patients proved to have significantly larger VBRs than did the controls. No relationship appeared to exist, however, between such enlargement and specific diagnoses, although the two largest VBRs were those of patients in the schizophrenia spectrum. Like the work of Schulz and colleagues, this study points to the emergence of ventricular enlargement at an early age in psychiatric illness, and, as the authors note, their data supports the idea that severe illness results from early developmental issues. In a later study that bridged CT and MRI, Woody et al. (1987) examined a 10-year-old patient diagnosed with schizophrenia. Both types of scanning detected an enlargement of the lateral and third ventricles as well as cerebellar abnormalities.

Thus, the first forays into noninvasive imaging in subjects with schizophrenia under the age of 18 revealed that the lateral ventricles—the most frequently assessed parameter in CT studies—were typically enlarged. These early studies also began to investigate the timing of the development of ventricular enlargement and the continuity between adolescent and adult forms of the illness.

PET Imaging

Positron emission tomography (PET) was first applied to patients with schizophrenia in the early 1980s, using radioactive labeled glucose. These early studies noted a relative hypofrontality in schizophrenic patients as compared to controls (Buchsbaum et al. 1982). More recent studies have produced similar results, although not invariably. Newer technology allows for the assessment of patients as they are performing specific cognitive tasks.

Jacobsen, Hamburger, et al. (1997) used 18F fluoroxyglucose PET to study 16 adolescents during the administration of a continuous performance test. These patients first experienced symptoms of schizophrenia before their teen years, but the PET scans were performed during their adolescence. To our knowledge, this is the only PET-scan study of adolescent schizophrenics, although some patients under the age of 18 may have been included in first-episode studies. In the present case, the scans showed that adolescent schizophrenic patients had a lower glucose metabolism in the middle frontal gyrus and superior frontal gyrus than did controls and, interestingly, an increased metabolism in the inferior frontal gyrus and supra marginal gyrus. When tested as teenagers, patients with COS thus showed a hypofrontality similar to that seen in adult patients. Granted, these researchers worked with a small sample and were quick to point out that their findings of hypofrontality were "less than robust." Nonetheless, their results do support the hypofrontality hypothesis, which posits that, in comparison to normal subjects, patients with schizophrenia have less metabolic activity in their frontal lobes as compared to their posterior lobes.

SPECT Imaging

Single photon emission computerized tomography (SPECT) has advantages for the study of psychiatric patients in that it is less invasive than PET and that ligands for study use can be more easily obtained. SPECT studies in adults with schizophrenia have allowed researchers to examine brain activity while these patients are actually performing cognitive tasks, another advantage of SPECT over 18F-2-deoxyglucose PET.

Despite these advantages, we could find only one study designed specifically to assess teenagers with schizophrenia. Batista et al. (1995) examined a group of neuroleptic-naïve adolescents with a recent diagnosis of schizophrenia, looking for possible abnormalities in regional cerebral blood flow. SPECT scans did indeed reveal such abnormalities in 12 of the 15 patients. More specifically, there was a decreased uptake of 99mTc-HMPAO in the frontal lobes, primarily in the left hemisphere. Abnormal blood flow, particularly in the anterior superior temporal gyrus, may be associated with auditory hallucinations. This single SPECT study thus supports earlier PET findings of decreased glucose metabolism in the frontal lobes.

MRI Imaging

Besides producing more detailed images, MRI allows for multiple-plane sectioning of the brain, whereby views of specific tissues and structures can be obtained from all desired angles. Multiple-plane sectioning allows for volumetric measures, which are more sensitive than measures of area. Since the introduction of MRI as a method for examining brain structure, the technique has been expanded to allow for functional MRI measurements, in vivo chemical measures by MRS, and microstructure assessment of white matter through DTI. Because of the high resolution MRI provides and because it does not require an intravenous injection, it has been used more frequently than other techniques for studying young people.

Using structural imaging of the brain, Frazier et al. (1996) found that a group of adolescents with COS showed a smaller total cerebral volume, a smaller thalamic area, and increases in the basal ganglia size in comparison to controls. Ventricular size was larger as well, although it did not reach statistical significance ($p = .06$). The authors of the study also noted that the globus pallidus enlargement could be secondary to previous neuroleptic exposure.

Friedman and colleagues (1999) addressed the question of whether certain of the features pinpointed by imaging that seem characteristic of adolescents can be linked to specific psychiatric diagnoses by conducting MRI scans of adolescent schizophrenic patients ($n = 20$), community controls ($n = 16$), and adolescents with bipolar illness ($n = 15$). No differences were found between the two patient groups on the measures assessed, which included an intracranial index, ventricular volumes, regional cortical measures, and external skull measures. The most notable differences between patients and controls were in the frontal cortical area and superior temporal area, where the patients had a significantly greater percentage of cortical fluid than the controls ($p = .007$). Interestingly, there was no difference in ventricular volume between patients and controls ($p = .077$) unless a control outlier was excluded, at which point a difference did appear ($p = .008$). Especially when taken along with Frazier et al. (1996), this study suggests that ventricular volume may not be as enlarged in teenagers as in adult patients. In a further advance in analysis technology, Sowell et al. (2000) assessed COS patients ($n = 9$) and controls ($n = 10$) with MRI, using a voxel-by-voxel volumetric analysis. They noted statistically significant differences between patients and controls in the ventricles, most of which could be accounted for by posterior portion. Differences were also noted in other specific brain regions, such as the thalamus.

For the groups involved in MRI imaging of young people, the general measures described above provided a starting point, but increasingly sophisticated technology has since permitted researchers to examine more specific structures and areas of the brain. Given that the more refined studies have typically been undertaken by the groups who did the original, more general measures, we will discuss them by research group.

The investigators at the Child Psychiatry Branch of the NIMH followed their initial study of childhood-onset schizophrenic patients (Frazier et al. 1996) with a series of specific measures. Jacobsen et al. (1996) examined temporal lobes and related structures but reported no difference between patients and controls for temporal lobe morphology when absolute values were analyzed. Interestingly, when cerebral volumes were included in the analysis, the temporal lobe proved to be larger in patients than in controls. The group then moved on to examine the corpus collosum—the white-matter structure connecting the cerebral hemispheres—and reported that the absolute area of the corpus collosum was similar in COS patients and in controls. Much as in the findings concerning the temporal lobes, moreover, the corpus collosum was shown to be larger in the patients when measurements were adjusted to the smaller cerebral volume (Jacobsen, Hamburger, et al. 1997), which the research team thought might indicate that white matter is spared in the development of the illness. The planum temporale was also assessed, on the theory that its area or asymmetry may be abnormal in the COS patient group, but no differences between the patients and the controls emerged (Jacobsen, Giedd, et al., Quantitative magnetic resonance imaging, 1997). The cerebellum has been studied in relationship to schizophrenia for more than two decades, ever since Weinberger and colleagues noted cerebellar pathology in a CT study (Weinberger, Torrey, and Wyatt 1979). The NIMH group also assessed scans of the cerebellum and fourth ventricle in their patient group and found that, after adjustments for cerebral volume were made, the cerebellar volume and areas of the cerebellum were reduced in the subjects with schizophrenia as compared to controls (Jacobsen, Giedd, et al., Quantitative morphology, 1997).

Our own research group, at Case Western Reserve University, likewise moved on to study specific brain structures after taking the general measures described above. Dasari and colleagues (1999) pursued the size of the thalamus in follow-up study of the findings of reduced size reported by Andreasen

(1994). The thalamic area was similar in the two patient groups, schizophrenic and bipolar, but was significantly smaller in the patient groups than in the control group—even after an adjustment for total brain volume. This study was followed by an analysis of white-matter hyperintensities as a preliminary step to assessing white matter and to investigating whether adolescent patients showed findings similar to those of schizophrenic adults. Pillai et al. (2002) noted a statistically significant increase in the presence of white-matter hyperintensities in the bipolar, but not schizophrenic, adolescents as compared to the controls.

Other research groups working with young patients have focused on specific brain areas and have reported greater frequency and severity of enlarged cavum septi pellucidi in the COS sample at the NIMH (Nopoulos et al. 1998), smaller right superior temporal lobe gyrus in an adolescent sample (Matsumoto, Simmons, et al., Superior temporal gyrus, 2001), equivalent hippocampal volume when adjusted for brain volume (Matsumoto, Simmons, et al., Structural magnetic imaging, 2001), enlargement of the fornix (Davies et al. 2001), and larger volume of amygdala when controlled for brain volume (Levitt et al. 2001).

As we have mentioned, imaging research during the early stages of schizophrenia was undertaken partly in an effort to determine when differences from normal controls first appear. The discovery of enlarged ventricles in the early stages of schizophrenia (Degreef et al. 1992) bolstered the emerging neurodevelopmental argument, which was further supported by follow-up CT studies (Nasrallah et al. 1986; Illowsky et al. 1988; Vita et al. 1988) that showed no significant changes in adult patients. The advent of more sophisticated instruments such as MRI and the availability of cohorts of young patients led the Child Psychiatry Branch group at the NIMH to reexplore the issue of brain structural parameters over time. Rapoport and colleagues (1997) supplemented their original MRI research (Frazier et al. 1996) by a two-year follow-up study of teenagers with COS that revealed a statistically significant increase in the patients' ventricular size, as well as in the area of the thalamus, in comparison to controls ($p = .001$). They noted clinical correlates to these changes, thus extending the implications of progressive ventricular enlargement. A subsequent assessment of temporal lobe structures found progressive changes in the temporal lobes of 10 adolescent schizophrenic patients compared to controls over a two-year period (Jacobsen et al. 1998). Decreases in the volume of the temporal gyral structures as well as in the left hippocampal volume were noted, the authors concluded that the findings suggest that these changes in the temporal lobes take place in "a nonstatic, continuous process" (p. 683).

Further research into the issue of changes in the brain was carried out by Rapoport et al. (1999), in a study that led to an interesting extension of the findings reviewed above. The group focused on the development of the brain cortex over time by comparing adolescent patients with COS to controls and found not only statistically significant differences in decreases in gray-matter volumes between the two groups but also diagnostic regional specificity. Briefly stated, the adolescent patients showed decreases in gray matter in the frontal, prefrontal, and temporal areas. No changes in white matter were seen. The research team concluded that while these findings do not contradict neurodevelopmental hypotheses, they do point to the importance of later neurodevelopmental events.

To address the question why increasing ventricular enlargement is not frequently seen in adults—even in first-episode studies—the group analyzed a larger number of subjects, who were assessed as many as three times, versus controls (Giedd et al. 1999). Sophisticated statistical analysis revealed a nonlinear increase in ventricular volume in the COS patients and decreases in the cerebrum and hippocampus. These changes began to form an asymptotic curve as subjects reached young adulthood, thus suggesting why such changes are so rarely observed in adulthood. Thompson et al. (2001) further analyzed the adolescent COS patients from the NIMH sample using brain-mapping algorithms. Using scans collected over five years, they compared 12 patients with 12 controls and discovered a spreading of cortical deficits beginning in the parietal area and concluding in the prefrontal areas. These changes correlated with psychotic symptoms: the greater the loss of cortical volume, the higher the psychoses ratings.

A different view was recently presented by James and colleagues at Oxford. In their initial study, they noted brain growth, not reduction, in adolescent schizophrenic patients assessed across a span of 13 to 20 years (James et al. 1999). In a control group brain size reached an asymptote at the age of 13, whereas in patients it continued to change, which led the research group to question the possibility of delayed development. A follow-up study of a subset of the adolescent patients and controls undertaken 2.7 years later failed to find a significant difference in measurements over time between the two groups, from which it was concluded that parameters seen in patients at baseline are nonprogressive (James et al. 2002). This study illustrates the need for further research to clarify the varied clinical courses and pathological processes that have already been observed.

MRS Imaging

Proton MRS allows researchers to examine in vivo measurements of aspects of brain biochemistry by detecting signals from compounds located within neurons. These compounds include *N*-acetyl–containing moieties (mainly NAA), choline-containing compounds, and creatine plus phosphocreatine.

Using proton MRS, Bertolino et al. (1998) looked at the frontal cortex of young adolescents with COS and reported that these subjects had diminished NAA measures in their hippocampal areas and in the dorsolateral prefrontal cortex. The availability of MRI images as a supplement further made it possible to determine that these reduced NAA amounts were not the product of reduced volumes in these areas. These results are consistent with the findings of Jacobsen, Giedd, et al. (Three-dimensional, 1997), who demonstrated hypofrontality through the use of PET scans, and are similar to the results seen in adult patients with schizophrenia.

MRS studies have also been employed to examine children who are considered to be at risk for schizophrenia. Brooks et al. (1998) scanned 16 preadolescents who did *not* carry the diagnosis of schizophrenia but rather exhibited some symptoms and/or had family members with schizophrenia spectrum disorders. All 16 were found to have lower NAA/creatine ratios than the children in the control sample. Similarly, Hendren et al. (1995) found that a group of children with schizophrenia spectrum disorders had lower NAA/creatine and choline/creatine ratios as compared to a control group.

Differentiating Among Disorders

Neuroimaging studies may be helpful to investigators seeking to differentiate among disorders and learn about the similarities and differences that exist among specific psychiatric and medical conditions. Brain structure anomalies and disturbances in cognitive functioning in those with schizophrenia have been well documented, and similar patterns of dysfunction and impairment have been observed in other disorders.

Schulz, Sinicrope, et al. (1983) used CAT scans to compare VBRs of adolescent patients suffering from schizophrenia or from borderline personality disorder to those of a control group and found that the schizophrenic patients had significantly enlarged ventricles as compared to the controls and to those with borderline illness. The purpose of the comparison was to determine whether patients without psychotic illness (those with borderline personality disorder) might develop enlarged ventricles secondary to the stress of an inpatient hospitalization. Friedman et al. (1999) subsequently used MRI scans again to compare three groups: adolescents with schizophrenia or with bipolar disorder and normal controls. Both patient groups differed from the control group in the following measures: reduced intracranial volume, increased ventricular volume, and increased percentage of frontal and temporal fluid. No significant differences appeared between the two patient groups in terms of brain structure. Dasari et al. (1999) examined the same adolescents, using MRI scans to compare thalamic size among the three groups. While both patient groups showed a significant reduction in thalamic area as compared to the controls, the adolescents with schizophrenia did not differ from those with bipolar disorder, which raises interesting questions about how to differentiate between bipolar disorder and schizophrenia.

In another study (Kumra et al. 2000), adolescents with a psychotic disorder not otherwise specified were compared to adolescents with COS and normal controls. MRI scans revealed that both patient groups had significantly larger ventricles and smaller total cerebral volume as compared to controls. This study also detected a difference between the patient groups, namely, that the schizophrenia patients had a smaller midsagittal thalamic area as compared to the patients with an undiagnosed psychotic disorder and the control sample. As expected, the research team asserted that the brain morphology of the patients with an unspecified psychotic disorder resembled that of patients with schizophrenia more closely than it resembled that of patients with other neuropsychiatric disorders who had previously been scanned.

Children with attention deficit hyperactivity disorder (ADHD) have been studied using neuroimaging techniques and cognitive testing and have also been compared to adolescents with schizophrenia. It is logical to speculate that those with schizophrenia would exhibit more brain structure abnormalities and more severe and global cognitive deficits, consistent with the relative severity of the two diagnoses. Jacobsen et al. (1996) found that a group of adolescents with schizophrenia had a significantly lower IQ than both a normal control group and a group with ADHD. And while the schizophrenic patients performed more poorly overall on eye-tracking tests, no significant correlation was seen between these results and VBRs taken from MRI data.

Imaging techniques have also proved useful in the study of obsessive-compulsive disorder (OCD). Some clinicians have theorized that early symptoms of OCD could indicate the possible development of schizophrenia later on, and many children and adolescents with schizophrenia also display obsessive-compulsive symptoms. A study by Iida et al. (1995) compared 39 schizophrenic patients under the age of 15 who were divided into two groups: those with obsessive-compulsive symptoms during the prodromal stage ($n = 16$) and those without such symptoms ($n = 23$). CT scans showed that brain abnormalities were more common in the schizophrenic patients with OCD symptoms. Also characteristic of this subgroup were a more insidious onset of the disease, a greater frequency of negative symptoms, and a lesser number of hereditary factors at play. Kurokawa et al. (2000) compared a group of young males with schizophrenia spectrum disorders who had prodromal symptoms of OCD to a group of patients with nonpsychotic OCD. MRI scans revealed that the former group had significantly larger VBRs than both the latter group and a group of normal controls. More recently, Aoyama et al. (2000) used MRI scans to study a group of patients with early-onset schizophrenia, some of whom also showed obsessive-compulsive symptoms and some of whom did not. Scans indicated that the group with obsessive-compulsive symptoms had a significantly smaller left hippocampus in comparison to both the group without OCD symptoms and a control sample.

A study by Lys et al. (1999) compared autistic children with adolescents with schizophrenia—research that is particularly valuable in view of the known biological factors in the development of autism. MRS examinations demonstrated reduced NAA in both patient groups as compared to controls; however, no difference could be seen between the two patient groups themselves. Given that autism has been established as a neurodevelopmental disorder, the finding that adolescents with schizophrenia show similar NAA cortical detriments is especially relevant to current theories about the pathogenesis of schizophrenia.

Further imaging research comparing adolescents with schizophrenia to those with other psychiatric disorders will doubtless prove beneficial to our understanding of the role of neurodevelopment in specific disorders. Furthermore, as additional studies that compare different diagnostic groups are carried out, we may be able to identify characteristics specific to each illness that will help us to distinguish among disorders with greater clarity and thereby refine our diagnostic criteria.

Adolescent Versus Adult Schizophrenia

Neuroimaging techniques offer us an invaluable opportunity to study the differences and similarities between adolescents and adults with schizophrenia. Such studies have important implications for our understanding of both the etiology and the progression of the disease, as well as for our endeavors to develop appropriate treatment interventions and determine prognosis. In addition, comparative analyses of this sort may provide new insights into the pathophysiology of schizophrenia.

As the studies described in this chapter well illustrate, many similarities between adolescent and adult schizophrenic patients have been identified across imaging modalities. Not only structural scans (CT and MRI) but also metabolic imaging (PET and MRS) have demonstrated that adolescents with schizophrenia differ from controls in much the same way as their adult counterparts. These differences may then be subtle, as suggested by Giedd et al. (1999), who noted that adolescence may be a period of differential brain development during which early vulnerabilities or abnormalities progress (which would explain why the first symptoms are likely to appear at adolescence). Evidence for this theory includes a longitudinal study undertaken by the NIMH group in which MRI scans of adolescents with COS revealed a progression of brain abnormalities during adolescence—specifically a decrease in the volume of the cerebrum and hippocampus and an increase in the lateral ventricles—that reached a plateau by early adulthood (Giedd et al. 1999).

New Directions

Clearly, neuroimaging in adolescents has provided key insights into the intricacies of the schizophrenic process. With the advent of more detailed and probing technology, the brains of this pivotal age group have yielded a tremendous amount of information, even though relatively few patients have been studied. Moreover, this information offers support for the neurodevelopmental theory and its role in schizophrenia as well as for the continuity of the disorder between adolescence and adulthood. The longitudinal study carried out at the NIMH has now pointed to a possible progression of the disease during adolescence—an issue that requires further attention (Weinberger and McClure 2002). Indeed, longitudinal studies are another exciting possibility offered by the newer imaging techniques. Because it appears that the brain of an adolescent with schizophrenia is much like that of an adult with schizophrenia, the progression of the disease may largely take place during the adolescent years. Scanning young children at risk for schizophrenia could enhance our understanding of the precise brain structures involved in the disease and the abnormalities to which each is vulnerable.

One hindrance to research has been the stigma attached to "experimenting" on children by having them participate in clinical studies, together with the desire to avoid labeling them as schizophrenic or psychotic at such a young age. Of great importance, then, is the need to educate patients and the public alike about the benefits of participation in clinical research. Whereas it was once considered risky to participate in clinical studies, our advancing knowledge and the use of newer imagining techniques have minimized the risk associated with such research. Once researchers can compile larger group samples and data pools, subsequent studies will be able draw more powerful conclusions.

In the future, scanning may permit researchers to measure better the effectiveness of both current and newly developing approaches to intervention. It may also allow us to make more concise differential diagnoses in children, which will in turn increase the likelihood of patients receiving the most efficacious treatment at the earliest possible juncture. If nothing else, however, clinicians are sure to gain a more thorough understanding of the neurocognitive processes at work over a broad spectrum of neuropsychiatric disorders.

ACKNOWLEDGMENT

The authors wish to thank Gregg Helmberger for his excellent assistance with the manuscript.

REFERENCES

Andreasen, N. C. (1994). Thalamic abnormalities in schizophrenia visualized through magnetic resonance image averaging. *Science* 266:294–98.
Aoyama, J., Iida, J., Inoue, M., Iwasaka, H., Sakiyama, S., Hata, K., et al. (2000). Brain

imaging in childhood- and adolescent-onset schizophrenia associated with obsessive-compulsive symptoms. *Acta Psychiatrica Scandinavica* 102:32–37.

Batista, J. F., Galiano, M. C., Torres, L. A., Hernandez, M. C., Sosa, F., Perera, A., et al. (1995). Brain single-photon emission tomography with technetium-99m hexamethylpropylene amine oxime in adolescents with initial-stage schizophrenia. *European Journal of Nuclear Medicine* 22:1274–77.

Bertolino, A., Kumra, S., Calicott, J. H., Mattay, V. S., Lestz, R. M., Jacobsen, L., et al. (1998). Common pattern of cortical pathology in childhood-onset and adult-onset schizophrenia as identified by proton magnetic resonance spectroscopic imaging. *American Journal of Psychiatry* 155:1376–83.

Brooks, W. M., Hodde-Vargas, J. H., Vargas, L. A., Yeo, R. A., Ford, C. C., Hendren, et al. (1998). Frontal lobe of children with schizophrenia spectrum disorders: A proton magnetic resonance spectroscopy study. *Biological Psychiatry* 43:263–69.

Buchsbaum, M. A., Ingvar, D. H., Kessler, R., Waters, R. N., Cappelletti, J., van Kammen, D. P., et al. (1982). Cerebral glucography with positron tomography: Use in normal subjects and in patients with schizophrenia. *Archives of General Psychiatry* 39:251–59.

Dasari, M., Friedman, L., Jesberger, J., Stuve, T. A., Findling, R. L., Swales, T. P., et al. (1999). A magnetic resonance imaging study of thalamic area in adolescent patients with either schizophrenia or bipolar disorders as compared to healthy controls. *Psychiatry Research: Neuroimaging* 91:155–62.

Davies, D. C., Wardell, A. M., Woolsey, R., and James, A. C. (2001). Enlargement of the fornix in early-onset schizophrenia: A quantitative MRI study. *Neuroscience Letters* 301:163–66.

Degreef, G., Ashtari, M., Bogerts, B., Bilder, R. M., Jody, D. N., Alvir, J. M., et al. (1992). Volumes of ventricular system subdivisions measured from magnetic resonance images in first-episode schizophrenic patients. *Archives of General Psychiatry* 49:531–37.

Findling, R. L., Friedman, L., Kenny, J. T., Swales, T. P., Cola, D. M., and Schulz, S. C. (1995). Adolescent schizophrenia: A methodologic review of the current neuroimaging and neuropsychologic literature. *Journal of Autism and Developmental Disorders* 25:627–93.

Frazier, J. A., Giedd, J. N., Hamburger, S. D., Albus, K. E., Kaysen, D., Vaituzis, A. C., et al. (1996). Brain anatomic magnetic resonance imaging in childhood-onset schizophrenia. *Archives of General Psychiatry* 53:617–24.

Friedman, L., Findling, R. L., Kenny, J. T., Swales, T. P., Stuve, T. A., Jesberger, J. A., et al. (1999). An MRI study of adolescent patients with either schizophrenia or bipolar disorder as compared to healthy control subjects. *Biological Psychiatry* 46:78–88.

Giedd, J. N., Jeffries, N. O., Blumenthal, J., Castellanos, F. X., Vaituzis, A. C., Fernandez, T., et al. (1999). Childhood-onset schizophrenia: Progressive changes during adolescence. *Biological Psychiatry* 46:892–98.

Hendren, R. L., Hodde-Vargas, J., Yeo, R. A., Vargas, L. A., Brooks, W. M., Ford, C., et al. (1995). Neuropsychophysiological study of children at risk for schizophrenia: A preliminary report. *Journal of the American Academy of Child and Adolescent Psychiatry* 34:1284–91.

Iida, J., Iwasaka, H., Hirao, F., Hashino, K., Matsumura, K., Tahara, K., et al. (1995). Clinical features of childhood-onset schizophrenia with obsessive-compulsive symptoms during the prodromal phase. *Psychiatry and Clinical Neurosciences* 49:201–7.

Illowsky, B. P., Juliano, D. M., Bigelow, L. B., and Weinberger, D. R. (1998). Stability of

CT scan findings in schizophrenia: Results of an 8-year follow-up study. *Journal of Neurology and Neurosurgical Psychiatry* 51:209–13.

Jacobsen, L. K., Giedd, J. N., Berquin, P. C., Krain, A. L., Hamburger, S. D., Kumra, S., et al. (1997). Quantitative morphology of the cerebellum and fourth ventricle in childhood-onset schizophrenia. *American Journal of Psychiatry* 154:1663–69.

Jacobsen, L. K., Giedd, J. N., Castellanos, F. X., Vaituzis, A. C., Hamburger, S. D., Kumra, S., et al. (1998). Progressive reduction of temporal lobe structures in childhood-onset schizophrenia. *American Journal of Psychiatry* 155:678–85.

Jacobsen, L. K., Giedd, J. N., Rajapakse, J. C., Hamburger, S. D., Vaituzis, A. C., Frazier, J. A., et al. (1997). Quantitative magnetic resonance imaging of the corpus callosum in childhood-onset schizophrenia. *Psychiatry Research: Neuroimaging* 68:77–86.

Jacobsen, L. K., Giedd, J. N., Tanrikut, C., Brady, D. R., Donohue, B. C., Hamburger, S. D., et al. (1997). Three-dimensional cortical morphometry of the planum temporale in childhood-onset schizophrenia. *American Journal of Psychiatry* 154:685–87.

Jacobsen, L. K., Giedd, J. N., Vaituzis, C. A., Hamburger, S. D., Rajapaske, J. C., Frazier, J. A., et al. (1996). Temporal lobe morphology in childhood-onset schizophrenia. *American Journal of Psychiatry* 153:355–267.

Jacobsen, L. K., Hamburger, S. D., Van Horn, J. D., Vaituzis, A. C., McKenna, K., Frazier, J. A., et al. (1997). Cerebral glucose metabolism in childhood-onset schizophrenia. *Psychiatry Research* 75:131–44.

James, A. C., Crow, T. J., Renowden, S., Wardell, A. M., Smith, D. M., Anslow, P., et al. (1999). Is the course of brain development in schizophrenia delayed? *Schizophrenia Research* 40:1–10.

James, A. C., Javaloyes, A., James, S., and Smith, D. M. (2002). Evidence for non-progressive changes in adolescent-onset schizophrenia: Follow-up magnetic resonance imaging study. *British Journal of Psychiatry* 180:339–44.

Johnstone, E. C., Crow, T. J., Frith, C. D., Husband, J., and Kreel, L. (1976). Cerebral ventricular size and cognitive impairment in chronic schizophrenia. *Lancet* 2(7992):924–26.

Kumra, S., Giedd, J. N., Vaituzis, A. C., Jacobsen, L. K., McKenna, K., Bedwell, J., et al. (2000). Childhood-onset psychotic disorders: Magnetic resonance imaging in volumetric differences in brain structure. *American Journal of Psychiatry* 157:1467–74.

Kurokawa, K., Nakamura, K., Sumiyoshi, T., Hagino, H., Yotsutsuji, T., Yamashita, I., et al. (2000). Ventricular enlargement in schizophrenia spectrum patients' prodromal symptoms of obsessive-compulsive disorder. *Psychiatry Research: Neuroimaging* 99:83–91.

Levitt, J. G., Blanton, R. E., Caplan, R., Asarnow, R., Guthrie, D., Toga, A. W., et al. (2001). Medial temporal lobe in childhood-onset schizophrenia. *Psychiatry Research: Neuroimaging* 108:17–27.

Lewis, S. W., Owen, M. J., and Murray, R. M. (1989). Obstetric complications and schizophrenia: Methodology and mechanisms. In S. C. Schulz and C. A. Tamminga (Eds.), *Schizophrenia: Scientific progress* (pp. 56–68). New York: Oxford University Press.

Loranger, A. W. (1984). Sex differences in age at onset of schizophrenia. *Archives of General Psychiatry* 41:157–61.

Lys, C., Findling, L., Friedman, S., Schulz, S. C., Xue, M., Ng, T., et al. (1999). Frontal lobe metabolism and aberrant neurodevelopment: A comparative MRS study among adolescents with autism, schizophrenia, and healthy subjects. *Schizophrenia Research* 36:226.

Matsumoto, H., Simmons, A., Williams, S., Hadjulis, M., Pipe, R., Murray, R., et al. (2001). Superior temporal gyrus abnormalities in early-onset schizophrenia: Similarities and differences with adult-onset schizophrenia. *American Journal of Psychiatry* 158:1299– 1304.

Matsumoto, H., Simmons, A., Williams, S., Pipe, R., Murray, R., and Frangou, S. (2001). Structural magnetic imaging of the hippocampus in early-onset schizophrenia. *Biological Psychiatry* 49:824–31.

Matsumoto, H., Takei, N., Saito, F., Kachi, K., and Mori, N. (2001). The association between obstetric complications and childhood-onset schizophrenia: A replication study. *Psychological Medicine* 31:901–14.

Nasrallah, H. A., Olson, S. C., McCalley-Whitters, M., Chapman, S., and Jacoby, C. (1986). Cerebral ventricular enlargements in schizophrenia. A preliminary follow-up study. *Archives of General Psychiatry* 43:157–59.

Nopoulos, P. C., Giedd, J. N., Andreasen, N. C., and Rapoport, J. L. (1998). Frequency and severity of enlarged cavum septi pellucidi in childhood-onset schizophrenia. *American Journal of Psychiatry* 155:1074–79.

Peterson, B. S. (1995). Neuroimaging in child and adolescent neuropsychiatric disorders. *Journal of the American Academy of Child and Adolescent Psychiatry* 34:1570–76.

Pillai, J. J., Freidman, L., Stuve, T. A., Trinidad, S., Jesberger, J. A., Lewin, J. S., et al. (2002). Increased presence of white matter hyperintensities in adolescent patients with bipolar disorder. *Psychiatry Research* 225:51–56.

Rapoport, J. L., Giedd, J. N., Blumenthal, J., Hamburger, S., Jeffries, N., Fernandez, T., et al. (1999). Progressive cortical change during adolescence in childhood-onset schizophrenia. *Archives of General Psychiatry* 56:649–54.

Rapoport, J. L., Giedd, J. N., Kumra, S., Jacobsen, L., Smith, A., Lee, P., et al. (1997). Childhood-onset schizophrenia: Progressive ventricular change during adolescence. *Archives of General Psychiatry* 54:887–903.

Reiss, D., Feinstein, C., Weinberger, D. R., King, R., Wyatt, R. J., and Brallier, D. (1983). Ventricular enlargement in child psychiatric patients: A controlled study with planimetric measurements. *American Journal of Psychiatry* 140:453–56.

Schulz, S. C., Koller, M. M., Kishore, P. R., Hamer, R. M., and Friedel, R. O. (1982). Abnormal scans in young schizophrenia. *Psychopharmacology Bulletin* 18:163–64.

Schulz, S. C., Koller, M. M., Kishore, P. R., Hamer, R. M., Gehl, J. J., and Friedel, R. O. (1983). Ventricular enlargement in teenage patients with schizophrenia spectrum disorder. *American Journal of Psychiatry* 140:1592–95.

Schulz, S. C., Sinicrope, P., Kishore, P. R., and Friedel, R. O. (1983). Treatment response and ventricular brain enlargement in young schizophrenic patients. *Psychopharmacology Bulletin* 19:510–12.

Sowell, E. R., Levitt, J., Thompson, P. M., Holmes, C. J., Blanton, R. E., Kornsand, D. S., et al. (2000). Brain abnormalities in early-onset schizophrenia spectrum disorder observed with statistical parametric mapping of structural magnetic resonance images. *American Journal of Psychiatry* 157:1475–84.

Thompson, P. M., Vidal, C., Giedd, J. N., Gochman, P., Blumenthal, J., Nicolson, R., et al. (2001). Mapping adolescent brain change reveals dynamic wave of accelerated gray matter loss in very early-onset schizophrenia. *Proceedings of the National Academy of Sciences, USA* 98:11650–55.

Vita, A., Sacchetti, E., Valvassori, G., and Cazzullo, C. L. (1988). Brain morphology in schizophrenia: A 2- to 5-year CT scan follow-up study. *Acta Psychiatrica Scandinavica* 78:618–21.

Weinberger, D. R. (1987). Implications of normal brain development for the pathogenesis of schizophrenia. *Archives of General Psychiatry* 44:660–69.

Weinberger, D. R., and McClure, R. K. (2002). Neurotoxicity, neuroplasticity, and magnetic resonance imaging morphometry: What is happening to the schizophrenic brain? *Archives of General Psychiatry* 59:553–58.

Weinberger, D. R., Torrey, E. F., Neophytides, A. N., and Wyatt, R. J. (1979). Structural abnormalities in the cerebral cortex of chronic schizophrenic patients. *Archives of General Psychiatry* 36:935–39.

Weinberger, D. R., Torrey, E. F., and Wyatt, R. T. (1979). Cerebellar atrophy in chronic schizophrenia. *Lancet* 1:718–19.

Woody, R. C., Bolyard, K., Eisenhauer, G., and Altschuler, L. (1987). CT scan and MRI findings in a child with schizophrenia. *Journal of Child Neurology* 2:105–10.

CHAPTER SIX

Neuropsychological Factors in Early-Onset Schizophrenia

Jeffrey R. Wozniak, Ph.D., Tonya White, M.D., and S. Charles Schulz, M.D.

One of the hallmarks of schizophrenia, cognitive dysfunction, was initially believed by Kraepelin and other early writers to be a component of the later stages of the disease. Subsequent studies of first-episode patients, however, made it apparent that cognitive deficits are present at the time of, or even before, the onset of symptoms, that is, during the prodromal phase of schizophrenia (Saykin et al. 1994; Hoff et al. 1999). Thus, while cognitive dysfunction was once thought to represent a "consequence" of the disease, it is now recognized as a potential precursor or sign of vulnerability to the illness. Interest in examining childhood- and adolescent-onset forms of schizophrenia has recently grown, in proportion to our new understanding of the importance of early cognitive deficits in the disease.

A number of compelling reasons have led researchers to focus on the neurocognitive aspects of schizophrenia specifically in young people. First, many questions remain about whether the disease is primarily neurodevelopmental, neurodegenerative, or both (Marenco and Weinberger 2000), and the exploration of neurocognitive deficit patterns in young people with schizophrenia can inform our understanding of the developmental aspects of the disease. Second, because the transition between preschizophrenia, prodrome, and schizophrenia occurs within a compressed time frame in the early-onset form, the adolescent population provides an especially valuable opportunity to examine the relationship between cognition and disease stage. Third, brain structure and function continue to develop significantly during adolescence (Huttenlocher 1984; see also chapter 1). Characterizing the cognitive correlates of the disease in this population and the relationship between cognition and neurodevelopment will assist us in determining the underpinnings of schizophrenia. Fourth, it is not yet completely clear whether the early-onset form of schizophrenia is an independent entity or simply a more severe variant of the adult-onset form (Nicolson and Rapoport 1999). Retrospective studies of adult patients with adult-onset versus adolescent-onset schizophrenia have demonstrated that the former is associated with more severe language impairment (Johnstone et al. 1989) and greater deficits in intelligence, memory, attention, and fine motor dexterity (Basso et al. 1997). However, other studies have failed to find an association between age of onset and cognitive outcome (Yang et al. 1995). Exploring the similarities and differences in cognitive deficit patterns in adult-onset and early-onset schizophrenia may offer an effective complementary method of addressing this issue. Finally, it is critical for clinicians working with young psychotic patients to understand the patterns of cognitive deficit specific to this group and to understand the functional implications of these deficits. Thus far, the literature on adult-onset schizophrenia has clearly established a relationship between cognitive dysfunction and clinical outcome (Green 1996), but this relationship has not been well documented and is not yet well understood in patients with the early-onset form of disease.

In what follows, we will review the relatively small but steadily growing literature on cognitive functioning in children and adolescents with schizophrenia spectrum disorders. We will also provide a brief overview of the studies pertaining to cognitive deficits in preschizophrenic and prodromal states. Our discussion will conclude with some remarks on the clinical neuropsychological examination of patients with early-onset schizophrenia.

Developmental Neuropsychological Considerations

Critical to understanding the neuropsychological factors at work in early-onset psychiatric conditions, including psychosis, is the fact that the developing brain is not a static entity. Because the object of study is a moving target, the neuropsychological assessment of young patients differs significantly from the assessment of adults. Perhaps most importantly, a clinical evaluation of children and adolescents requires multiple data points, especially when an emerging condition such as schizophrenia is under study. The developmental process complicates the clinical assessment of young people and also introduces a very significant interaction factor to any scientific study of early-onset schizophrenia.

In addition, it is important to consider the differences between the traditional adult neuropsychological model and the developmental neuropsychological model that applies to children and adolescents. The adult model is based on the assumption that development unfolds normally until a disease or injury occurs, and thus neuropsychological assessment is often viewed as a measure of the gap between the premorbid or preinjury state and the current state. Accordingly, adult instruments have thus traditionally been designed to detect damage or deficit as well as to localize the deficit. In contrast, the developmental model as applied to children and adolescents focuses on the differences in cognitive development revealed by a comparison to healthy same-age peers. The emphasis in the assessment of young patients is usually on measuring their progress or lack of progress through normal neurodevelopmental stages, and instruments are therefore designed to measure developmental status and possible delays in development rather than damage per se. For these reasons, the study of a disorder such as schizophrenia that may involve both delayed development in certain cognitive domains and loss of function in others is particularly complex in young people, whose brains are still undergoing dramatic neurodevelopmental change.

Neuropsychological Domains

Neuropsychologists typically divide cognitive functioning into subdomains based on cognitive neuropsychological theory as well as on evidence for functional modularity in the brain (Lezak 1995). The same domains apply to both young patients and adults. *Intelligence* is a broad construct that most neuropsychologists consider a valuable starting point in the assessment of cognition. The IQ measure lends itself well to analyses of overall cognitive status in relation to development, disease course, and treatment. Numerous studies of schizophrenia have thus examined the impact of the disease on intelligence. *Academic functioning* is a cognitive domain unique to the study of children, adolescents, and young adults. Patients with schizophrenia often undergo a decline in academic function that precedes or accompanies the onset of psychosis. Tracking the onset and course of academic decline can assist us in determining the future course of the illness. Given that for children and adolescents school is the primary arena of performance, school performance—academic, behavioral, and social—is a very useful functional measure of outcome for young patients with mental illness.

Language functioning encompasses not only basic expressive and receptive vocabulary, grammar, and syntax but also the more subtle, pragmatic elements of communication. Understanding developmental abnormalities in social communication is particularly crucial to the study of early-onset schizophrenia. *Attentional functioning* has long been of interest to researchers and clinicians working with psychotic disorders owing to the profound disruptions in concentration that accompany these conditions. The study of attentional and higher-level *executive functioning* has generated a great deal of interest in research into schizophrenia because of the relationship to frontal lobe integrity. Frontal lobe abnormalities are now believed to play a key role in the pathophysiology of the disease. Attention and executive functioning are particularly worth studying in younger patients in view of the profound change that occurs in the frontal cortex during normal adolescent development (Huttenlocher 1984; Luciana and Nelson 1998; Giedd et al. 1999; Sowell et al. 1999).

The study of *memory* processes can potentially to help us appreciate the role of cortical and subcortical systems in schizophrenia. Along with executive functioning deficits, moreover, memory impairment is one of the most debilitating aspects of the cognitive dysfunction in schizophrenia. Finally, *visual-perceptual* and *motor functions* have long been known to be aberrant in schizophrenia. Motor abnormalities are an early, albeit nonspecific, symptom often present in the preschizophrenic state. In short, nearly the entire spectrum of potential cognitive dysfunction is relevant to the study of young patients with schizophrenia.

A Review of the Literature by Cognitive Domain

A relatively small number of studies have examined neurocognitive deficits in young patients with schizophrenia spectrum disorders. Table 6.1 lists, in chronological order, the studies that have specifically measured cognitive functioning in adolescent patients with psychotic disorders. Whereas early studies

Table 6.1. Studies examining neurocognition in early-onset schizophrenia spectrum disorders

Study	Patient group	Comparison group	Domains examined
Erickson et al. 1984	($n = 11$) Schizophrenia and schizophreniform Mean age = 14.2	ADD ($n = 11$) Conduct disorder ($n = 21$) Anxiety disorder ($n = 26$)	Sustained attention
Asarnow et al.·1987	($n = 24$) Schizophrenia Mean age = 10.1	Autism ($n = 23$)	Intelligence
Schneider and Asarnow 1987	($n = 11$) Schizophrenia Mean age = 11.0	Autism ($n =15$) Healthy controls ($n = 28$)	Intelligence, vocabulary, and executive function
Goldberg et al. 1988	($n = 39$) Schizophrenia, schizophreniform, and atypical psychosis Mean age = 14.8	Adjustment disorder ($n = 20$) Conduct disorder ($n = 13$) Dysthymia ($n = 7$) Personality disorder ($n = 1$)	Intelligence, reading, math, visual-motor, and fine motor
Asarnow et al. 1994– (reviews a series of studies in their lab)	($n = 47$) Schizophrenia Mean age = 10.5	Healthy controls ($n =$ unreported)	Language, visual-perception, fine motor, executive function, and visual memory

(continued)

Table 6.1. (Continued)

Study	Patient group	Comparison group	Domains examined
Kenny et al. 1997	(n = 17) Schizophrenia, schizophreniform, and schizoaffective Mean age = 15.7	(n = 17) Healthy controls	Attention, working memory, verbal learning, executive function
	(n = 20) Schizophrenia and schizotypal personality disorder Mean age = 11.0	Healthy controls (n = 20)	IQ, verbal and nonverbal memory, visual-perception, executive function, working memory
Karatekin and Asarnow 1998	(n = 13) Schizophrenia Mean age = 14.5	ADHD (n = 31) Healthy controls (n = 27)	Working memory
Oie and Rund 1999; Oie, Rund, and Sundet 1998; Oie, Sundet, and Rund 1999	(n = 19) Schizophrenia, schizophreniform, schizoaffective disorder, and delusional disorder Mean age = 16.2	ADHD (n = 20) Healthy controls (n = 30)	Covert visual attention, visual and verbal memory, executive function, fine motor

Study	Schizophrenia group	Comparison group	Domains assessed
Zahn et al. 1998	(n = 23) Schizophrenia Mean age = 14.3	Healthy controls (n = 52)	Attention and reaction time
Kumra et al. 2000	(n = 27) Schizophrenia Mean age = 14.4	Normative data and psychosis NOS (n = 24)	Intelligence, attention, vocabulary, visual-perception, visual and verbal memory, academic achievement
Caplan et al. 2001	(n = 88) Schizophrenia Mean age = 12.0	Healthy controls (n = 190) ADHD (n = 115)	Intelligence, attention, memory
Karp et al. 2001	(n = 21) Schizophrenia Mean age = 14.0	Healthy controls (n = 27)	Estimated IQ
McCarthy et al. 2002	(n = 23) Schizophrenia, schizoaffective, and psychosis NOS Mean age = 9.9	ADHD (n = 33) Mood disorder (n = 15) Combined ADHD and mood disorder (n = 11)	Intelligence, visual-motor skill, processing speed, working memory
White et al. 2002	(n = 62) Schizophrenia Mean age = 16.5	Adults with schizophrenia (n = 169)	Attention, language, memory, executive function, fine motor
Kravariti et al. 2003	(n = 40) Schizophrenia Mean age = 16.5	Healthy controls (n = 21)	Intelligence, memory, executive function

Note: ADD = attention deficit disorder; ADHD = attention deficit hyperactivity disorder; NOS = not otherwise specified

incorporated only limited cognitive measures such as IQ tests, subsequent research has included more comprehensive neuropsychological batteries covering multiple domains and has thus yielded much useful data about numerous
facets of cognition.

Intelligence

A great deal of work has explored IQ deficits in adolescents with psychotic
disorders relative to normative expectations and also in comparison to clinical control groups. One early study (Goldberg et al. 1988) examined a group
of adolescent inpatients with schizophrenia spectrum diagnoses using a standardized IQ measure. The patient group's performance was compared to that
of a clinical control group consisting of inpatients with nonpsychotic, mixed
disorders. Patients with schizophrenia scored more than one standard deviation below the clinical control group and about two standard deviations below normative range on performance IQ (PIQ). Comparing psychotic patients
with autistic patients, Schneider and Asarnow (1987) found no significant differences in full-scale IQ (FSIQ). However, the schizophrenic group scored below the autistic group on PIQ in this study and also had below-average FSIQs
(nearly one standard deviation below normal). Using composite measures derived primarily from the subtests of the Wechsler Intelligence Scale for Children—Third Edition, Yeo et al. (1997) discovered impairment on both verbal
and nonverbal composite measures in young patients relative to controls. Caplan et al. (2001) found that FSIQ was about one standard deviation below normal in youth with schizophrenia and was inversely correlated with the degree
of formal thought disorder in their patients. Mild IQ deficits in adolescents
with schizophrenia relative to controls were also apparent in a study by Kravariti et al. (2003), with the most pronounced deficits noted in the performance
domain.

Several other studies have detected even more dramatic impairments in IQ.
One study found a 1.5 standard deviation difference on an estimated IQ measure between a sample of adolescents with schizophrenia and a group of
healthy volunteers (Karp et al. 2001). The authors also reported a significant
relationship between IQ deficit and neurological signs, including primitive re-
flexes and impaired coordination. Similarly, patients with childhood-onset
psychoses—that is, patients younger than 12 years of age—were shown to
have deficits on the order of 1.5 standard deviations from the mean in verbal
IQ (VIQ), PIQ, and FSIQ (McCarthy et al. 2002).

In contrast to these consistent findings of below-average IQ in young patients with schizophrenia, Kenny et al. (1997) found no difference between schizophrenia spectrum patients and a control group. It is likely, however, that the abbreviated IQ measure used in this study, which did not tap processing speed or working memory, reflected generally intact, crystallized functioning in the patients but did not reflect the specific processing deficits that could have resulted in lower scores on a full IQ measure. In fact, the authors did pinpoint numerous other deficits—in working memory and in processing speed, for example—in their patient group on other measures. Moreover, the subjects in this study consisted of outpatients who were stabilized on medication and in treatment and so were presumably less acutely ill than the patients in the other studies. In addition, the control subjects in the study by Kenny et al. were matched to patients in terms of socioeconomic status, which likely contributed to the smaller differences in IQ between groups.

Overall, studies of intelligence reveal that young patients with schizophrenia have unusually low IQ scores that may in fact be evident before the onset of symptoms. Certain aspects of intelligence, especially those related to rapid problem solving and concentration, are more apt to be affected than others. Intellectual deficits in this range are serious enough to have an appreciable impact on the young patient's functioning in school as well as on everyday judgment and decision making.

Academic Functioning

Very few studies have examined academic functioning in adolescents with psychosis. In one early study (Goldberg et al. 1988), adolescent patients performed distinctly below average in comparison to normative data on measures of reading and math, although their performance did not differ significantly from clinical controls. The study further demonstrated that mental illness, broadly defined, was often associated with poor academic achievement. It is worth noting that the patients with psychosis did show a higher-than-expected incidence of learning disabilities, defined by a significant discrepancy between their IQ and academic scores. Another study examined retrospective measures of academic achievement. Although the authors did not specifically study adolescent patients but instead used a retrospective design applied to adult patients, they found that, as children, patients with schizophrenia had lower than average scores on the Iowa Test of Basic Skills (reading, math, and language) for their age (Fuller et al. 2002).

Language

As is well recognized, young patients with psychotic disorders suffer from communication abnormalities similar to those of adults with schizophrenia. These include poverty of speech content, illogical speech, and the use of neologisms (Cantor et al. 1982; Caplan 1994). Typically, such deficits are measured as components of formal thought disorder by administering rating scales. Some studies have employed formal psychometric instruments to measure expressive and receptive language skills in young patients with schizophrenia. Using a broad measure of single-word receptive vocabulary skill, Schneider and Asarnow (1987) could see no differences between youth with schizophrenia and controls. However, the same research group later found evidence for impaired auditory processing (sequencing) and receptive language (direction following) in these patients (Asarnow et al. 1994). In contrast to Schneider and Asarnow (1987), a study by Kumra et al. (2000) did detect vocabulary deficits on the same measure of receptive vocabulary in adolescents with schizophrenia. It is worth noting, however, that the patients in this study were treatment-refractory patients all of whom had developed schizophrenia during childhood and thus may have represented a more severely ill group than that studied by Schneider and Asarnow. A subsequent study (White et al. 2002) that used measures of higher-order language to compare adolescent and adult patients with schizophrenia found language impairments in both groups but more severe impairment in the adolescent group.

Thus, although some communication deficits are evident in young patients with schizophrenia, these patients do not typically display serious problems with core language skills such as syntax, repetition, naming, or word finding. Rather, they struggle with tasks requiring concentration and organized output (e.g., the ability to follow directions). In addition, patients with childhood-onset schizophrenia may experience more widespread difficulties with language than those whose illness had an adolescent onset.

Attention

Attention/concentration variables in young patients with schizophrenia have been another focus of research. On a continuous performance test (CPT) that measured sustained attention, adolescents with schizophrenia spectrum disorders had higher levels of omission errors (a measure of attentional lapses) than patients with conduct disorder and anxiety disorders (Erickson et al. 1984). A later study of attention and reaction time in patients with early-onset schizophrenia showed significant deficits in both domains (Zahn et al. 1998), while White et al. (2002) reported significant attention deficits for adolescent patients on a CPT administered as part of a comprehensive battery.

In contrast, using a measure of covert visual attention, Oie and colleagues did not find deficits in a group of early-onset patients with schizophrenia (Oie, Rund, and Sundet 1998). They also failed to find deficits on a degraded stimulus continuous performance task or a sustained attention test (Oie and Rund 1999). Interestingly, though, a comparison group of adolescents with attention deficit hyperactivity disorder (ADHD) did show impairments on the sustained attention test.

Asarnow et al. (1994) examined different components of attention in a sample of young patients and found evidence for increased distractibility on the "freedom from distractibility" index on an IQ measure. Similarly, a study that employed a comprehensive neurocognitive battery to assess adolescents with schizophrenia demonstrated attention deficits relative to controls on a variety of concentration tasks: serial addition, sustained attention, and inhibitory control (Kenny et al. 1997). Results from pure vigilance measures have been mixed, perhaps because of the variety of CPT measures employed across studies. Higher-level attentional processes are, however, consistently impaired in early-onset schizophrenia.

Executive Functioning

Because executive dysfunction is such a common trait of adults with schizophrenia, numerous studies have sought to explore this domain in adolescent patients. Schneider and Asarnow (1987) demonstrated executive impairment in early-onset patients relative to controls using the Wisconsin Card Sorting Test (WCST). The same research group later reported that patients are impaired in their ability to learn this task even when provided with explicit instructions (Asarnow et al. 1994). Kenny et al. (1997) found that adolescents with schizophrenia spectrum disorders made more perseverative errors on the WCST and had more trouble than control subjects on mazes, a task that requires significant planning skill. Yeo et al. (1997) discovered generalized impairment in patients relative to controls on "frontal ability" measures, such as the WCST and a measure of spontaneous verbal production. Oie et al. (1999) also observed poor WCST performance in adolescents with schizophrenia spectrum disorders and poor performance on a measure of divided attention and sequencing (Oie, Sundet, and Rund 1999).

In a study of patients with early-onset schizophrenia and psychosis not otherwise specified (NOS), both groups scored below average on traditional executive measures including the WCST (Kumra et al. 2000). There were no between-group differences, however. Caplan et al. (2001) found that adolescents with schizophrenia had a lower performance on working memory tasks than patients with ADHD, but no relationship appeared to exist between working memory and formal thought disorder in patients with schizophrenia. White et al. (2002) observed significant executive deficits in adolescent patients relative to controls on a number of measures, including the WCST and several working memory tasks. The authors also noted that their adolescent control group performed below the level of the adult control group, which highlights the fact that many executive skills are still developing during adolescence. Kravariti et al. (2003) subsequently demonstrated significant executive deficits in adolescents with schizophrenia relative to controls using a variety of measures, including a pure planning task, a spatial working memory task, and a measure of divided attention. No studies have been published, however, that report normal executive functioning in young patients with psychotic illness. Thus, deficits in executive functioning appear to be a highly consistent feature of early-onset schizophrenia spectrum disorders.

Learning and Memory

The full range of memory skills has been examined in young patients with schizophrenia spectrum conditions. Asarnow et al. (1994) reported deficits in the visual span of apprehension in a group of young patients with schizophrenia. The span-of-apprehension task measures the patient's capacity for visual memory. Patients with schizophrenia used the same processes of encoding the visual information yet were unable to carry out the task as efficiently as the control subjects, whose IQs nonetheless matched those of the patients. Therefore, the observed visual-memory deficit was not simply a function of general intellectual impairment but represented a deficit specific to the patients. Kenny et al. (1997) administered a battery of verbal-memory measures to adolescent patients and found that they performed more poorly than controls on a number of the tasks, especially those that involved a distraction or a delay. At the same time, no significant deficits in immediate verbal recall emerged.

In the study by Yeo and colleagues (1997), adolescents with schizophrenia spectrum disorders showed significant impairments in both verbal and non-verbal memory on a variety of standardized instruments. Another study revealed that the verbal deficits and the impairment in delayed visual memory exhibited by young patients with schizophrenia were similar in severity to those found in patients with ADHD (Karatekin and Asarnow 1998). However, the former showed greater impairment in immediate verbal memory than the latter. Oie and colleagues also compared adolescents with schizophrenia to patients with ADHD and found that both groups scored below controls on a measure of verbal learning (Oie, Sundet, and Rund 1999). However, only the patients with schizophrenia had deficits in visual memory, specifically figure memory and spatial memory. Kumra et al. (2000) discovered that patients with schizophrenia and with psychosis NOS were both impaired on measures of verbal learning, but the impairment was substantially greater in the patients with schizophrenia. In fact, out of a multiple-domain battery, the relative degree of impairment in verbal learning was the only measure that differentiated the groups. Both groups also scored below average on measures of visual memory. In their study of adolescents with schizophrenia, White et al. (2002) reported deficits in both verbal and nonverbal memory that proved comparable in severity to those seen in adults with schizophrenia. Kravariti et al. (2003) examined memory function in older adolescents with schizophrenia and likewise found impairments, especially within the verbal domain.

In sum, adolescents and children with schizophrenia spectrum conditions often display memory deficits in both the verbal and nonverbal domains, but specific types of visual memory deficits may serve to distinguish patients with schizophrenia from those with other conditions such as ADHD. As a number of studies have also demonstrated, young patients with schizophrenia show inefficiencies in their manner of learning and encoding information. Somewhat inconsistent findings have been reported in the literature concerning immediate verbal memory, but these discrepancies may be related to the severity of the illness.

Visual-Perceptual Skills

In a study by Schneider and Asarnow (1987), adolescents with schizophrenia fared reasonably well on a visual-spatial judgment task requiring them to discriminate among spatial orientations, but they did show impairment on a visual search task. As the authors note, the difference may have been due to the increased attentional load in the case of the visual search task. Asarnow et al. (1994) found no impairment in the performance of adolescent patients on a basic visual discrimination test. However, they did detect significant impairment when a memory component was added. Kumra et al. (2000) noted impairments on measures of spatial organization, including a figure-drawing task, in a sample of young patients with schizophrenia, while White et al. (2002) used a variety of tests to measure visual-perceptual skills in adolescents with schizophrenia and also reported significant deficits. Overall, then, basic visual-perceptual processes such as visual discrimination do not seem especially impaired in cases of early-onset schizophrenia, but higher-level processes that require visual organization or visual search do seem to be impaired.

Fine Motor Skills

Asarnow et al. (1994) administered a measure of fine motor speed and dexterity to young patients with schizophrenia, along with a group of control subjects, and found that the patients performed more poorly whether they were using their dominant hand or their nondominant hand, as well as when both hands were measured simultaneously. Oie and colleagues found similar deficits in a group of adolescents who were assessed on a more complex measure of fine motor dexterity (Oie, Sundet, and Rund 1999). In contrast, Kavariti et al. (2003) did not detect any evidence of impaired fine motor skills in adolescents with schizophrenia, leading the authors to speculate that the deficits seen in other studies may have been related to neuroleptic exposure or to a longer duration of illness. White et al. (2002) reported that adolescent patients with schizophrenia demonstrated greater impairment on fine motor tasks in comparison to both an adolescent control group and adult patients. Approximately one-third of their adolescent patients were neuroleptic-naïve or nearly naïve at the time the neuropsychological testing was carried out, and both the neuroleptic-naïve and neuroleptic-exposed groups exhibited notable deficits in motor skills. The discovery of greater impairment in adolescents than in adults but of no relationship to neuroleptic status suggests that neuroleptic exposure may not explain the motor skill impairment seen in early-onset schizophrenia.

Summary

The existing literature clearly demonstrates that child- and adolescent-onset schizophrenia is associated with many of the same cognitive deficits that accompany the adult-onset form of the disease. In comparison to their healthy peers, young patients with schizophrenia spectrum conditions certainly do show numerous cognitive deficits, including intellectual impairments of about 1.0 to 1.5 standard deviations below the mean for their age. They struggle with academic achievement, various language abilities, sustained attention, avoidance of distractibility, planning and flexibility, verbal and visual memory, visual spatial and visual-organizational processing, and fine motor performance. Although a number of these deficits are not specific to the disorder, two points are worth noting in connection with the level of debilitation often seen in youth with schizophrenia. First, the breadth of the deficits experienced by an adolescent with schizophrenia is typically substantially wider than that seen in other child and adolescent psychiatric conditions such as major depressive disorder, ADHD, and anxiety disorders. Second, there is some evidence that the level of impairment within specific domains, such as intelligence, executive functioning, and memory, may be greater in schizophrenia than in the other conditions. If, however, we wish to understand the full impact of these cognitive deficits on young people with schizophrenia spectrum disorders, we will need to examine patterns of deficit presentation over the course of development and across stages of the disease itself.

The Course of Cognitive Deficits in Early-Onset Schizophrenia

Patients with early-onset schizophrenia display a number of notable premorbid cognitive differences that bear on our understanding the disease. Using a follow-back design with a sample of young patients with schizophrenia, Asarnow (1999) discovered that greater than 70 percent of these patients had histories of early developmental delays, including deficits in language and motor skills. The author reported that many of these language deficits had become less apparent by the time the diagnosis of schizophrenia was made. Preschizophrenic children demonstrated delays in language skill acquisition (such as being unable to speak single words even at two and half years of age), but they did not show permanent language deficits when vocabulary and other verbal skills were measured between the ages of 9 and 11. In general, these findings are consistent with prospective studies of adult-onset schizophrenia. There is also evidence for very early developmental markers of schizophrenia in prepsychotic children, including delayed motor milestones, poor speech development, and below average educational scores (Jones et al. 1994).

A study by Lin et al. (2000), which examined the relationship between WCST performance and schizotypy in a sample of healthy adolescents at moderate risk for schizophrenia, provides insight into the developmental course of executive functioning deficits. These findings are especially valuable because the evaluation of executive functioning before the onset of illness is not typically available in retrospective study designs. The authors could not establish a link between executive functioning as measured by WCST performance and schizotypy, although, as they noted, earlier studies had shown WCST deficits in early-onset schizophrenia to be associated with onset of the disease itself. In contrast, a similar study (Diforio, Walker, and Kestler 2000) did find evidence for executive functioning impairment in adolescents with schizotypal personality disorder; however, these deficits appeared on only one measure, the WCST. Thus, while executive dysfunction is clearly present in early-onset schizophrenia, it is less clear that these deficits are present prior to symptom onset. In this respect, executive dysfunction may be distinct from language impairment and motor dysfunction, both of which are clearly present long before symptom onset. Future longitudinal studies of high-risk populations may help to clarify the developmental course of executive dysfunction in schizophrenia.

Recently, prospective studies of high-risk subjects have begun to shed more light on the course of various cognitive deficits during the preschizophrenic, prodromal, and transitional phases of schizophrenia. These studies have demonstrated that patients who develop schizophrenia as adults have usually exhibited impairment in various cognitive functions as children, well before the onset of psychotic symptoms (Jones et al. 1994; Cornblatt et al. 1999; Cannon et al. 2000; Erlenmeyer-Kimling et al. 2000). Deficits in attention, motor skill, verbal memory, and IQ have also been observed. In addition, research by Cosway et al. (2000) suggests that the onset of psychosis may be preceded by a loss of cognitive function as indicated by a drop in IQ scores. In contrast, a slightly earlier study (Russell et al. 1997) found no evidence of significant cognitive decline from the prepsychotic childhood period to the psychotic state in adulthood.

As of now, there is still a dearth of prospective data specifically describing the trajectory of cognitive function in patients who develop schizophrenia during adolescence. Presumably, these patients will turn out to show some of the same predictive cognitive impairments before the onset of psychotic symptoms as do adults. Until the necessary data are collected, however, we will be unable to evaluate whether, and to what degree, the pattern among adolescents differs from that of patients who develop schizophrenia later in adult-hood.

Unfortunately, very little longitudinal data is available to describe the course of cognitive functioning after the appearance of clinical symptoms in early-onset schizophrenia. Our own ongoing study (Wozniak et al. 2003) of adolescents diagnosed with schizophrenia spectrum disorders indicates a relative stability in cognitive functioning across the first year of illness. We have found stability coefficients in the range of 0.6 to 0.9 for specific cognitive variables: attention, executive functioning, processing speed, and memory. These correlations are noteworthy when compared to lower and nonsignificant stability coefficients for clinical symptom ratings on the Positive and Negative Syndrome Scale, which were in the range of 0.1 to 0.6 over the same time period. This finding of stable neurocognitive impairment in a group of adolescents with psychotic disorders is consistent with a recent longitudinal study using MRI that detected stable, nonprogressive brain abnormalities—in particular, ventricular enlargement—among patients with adolescent-onset schizophrenia (James et al. 2002). Stable cognitive impairments have also been observed in studies of first-episode, adult-onset schizophrenia (Hoff et al. 1999). A definite need remains, however, for additional longitudinal studies of both the cognitive and the neurological changes that accompany the emergence of psychotic symptoms in adolescent patients. The interaction of these variables with the effects of pharmacological methods of treatment, such as the use of the newer, atypical antipsychotic medications, make this type of research particularly challenging.

Neuropsychological Assessment of Patients with Early-Onset Psychotic Disorders

Regardless of the precise approach adopted, the neuropsychological assessment of patients with early-onset schizophrenia can serve a number of important goals in patient care. In addition to providing a baseline against which to measure either cognitive decline or improvement and yielding data about the cognitive effects of treatment, it can aid clinicians in working through the process of differential diagnosis, adjusting academic programming within the school setting, and providing information to families and professionals about the underlying reasons for the functional impairment observed in the patient's daily behavior.

In our outpatient clinic for young people with psychotic disorders, we employ a core neuropsychological battery with optional components as part of a comprehensive team evaluation. Results of the neuropsychological evaluation are incorporated in the team's decisions about diagnosis, suggested academic accommodations, and treatment. We also attempt to collect all available academic records and the results of previous psychological testing. Incorporating these findings into the neuropsychological evaluation allows the team to construct a history of the individual's cognitive development. We also comb this data for evidence of cognitive decline. Patients diagnosed with psychotic disorders are then followed and reevaluated at 6 and 12 months as part of a research protocol. Our team has experimented with various methods of incorporating this neurocognitive data into the feedback given to parents, other professionals, and schools, an approach that has been extremely well received. Parents find explanations of executive functioning deficits and memory problems to be particularly valuable in helping them to understand their affected child. With parental permission, the team neuropsychologist often consults with special education professionals in the school to assist with the development of appropriate individual education programs (IEP) for the student. Given the changing nature of the clinical and cognitive symptoms in early-onset schizophrenia, long-term follow-up is critical to this type of consultation.

Conclusions and Future Directions

The expanding literature concerning young patients with psychotic disorders is consistent with the neurodevelopmental hypothesis of schizophrenia. Cognitive delays, which presumably reflect certain aspects of neuronal maturation and integrity, indicate that early brain development in children who go on to develop schizophrenia is abnormal. Some of the first neurodevelopmental markers may be delays in the normal acquisition of language and motor skills during the infant and toddler years. Attentional deficits, although nonspecific to schizophrenia, are also a common manifestation of the underlying brain abnormalities present in preschizophrenic youth. While these are present early on, they may only be detected when the child enters school. Intellectual and academic functioning may also undergo a decline—usually gradual, although at times rapid—that precedes the onset of clinical symptoms. The trajectory of executive functioning is unknown. There is little available evidence that executive deficits are associated with the preschizophrenic state but considerable evidence that these deficits accompany the onset of clinical symptoms. Because higher-order cognitive functions, such as executive functioning, are not fully developed until later adolescence or early adulthood, it is possible that alterations in the development of these skills are simply more difficult to measure in young people. Although relatively little is known about the course of verbal learning deficits in early-onset schizophrenia, such deficits are clearly implicated in the disorder as well. On the whole, however, despite the discovery of multiple deficits across a number of neuropsychological domains, a specific neuropsychological profile for schizophrenia has yet to be identified, and the considerable heterogeneity of schizophrenia may in fact preclude this. Nevertheless, the use of increasingly sophisticated, developmentally appropriate instruments may uncover patterns that are presently invisible to us.

Further research efforts in this area should be guided by the present gaps in the literature. One such gap currently exists in our understanding of the normal and abnormal development of neuropsychological processes, most notably executive functions. Relatively few studies have investigated the development of planning, organizing, self-monitoring, and other higher-order skills in young people. Studies that demonstrate a clear developmental trajectory for executive functions in young people (Luciana and Nelson 1998) and those that suggest the possible insensitivity of common instruments like the WCST in this age range (Chelune and Baer 1986) highlight the need for new measures of these functions that target development in particular.

Future research on early-onset schizophrenia will likely incorporate design elements that maximize the potential for understanding multiple components of the disease. Longitudinal studies of patients assigned to high-risk categories (on the basis of genetics or early markers such as neurodevelopmental delays) will allow for the detailed study of transitions through the stages of schizophrenia. The selection of appropriate control groups—well matched for key characteristics including age, socioeconomic status, IQ, and perhaps other neurocognitive variables—should eventually boost the specificity of our deficit measures and of our markers for the disease. Serial brain imaging studies during the high-risk stage and the prodrome phase and at the onset of illness will help answer basic questions about the natural course of the disease and the underlying neurodevelopmental, and possibly degenerative, processes at work. Neuropsychological studies employing comprehensive batteries, as opposed to focused tasks, will aid in this process. Also of critical importance will be the continued development of neuropsychological instruments based on the developmental model rather than on the injury or deficit model, along with those with the psychometric characteristics that allow for multiple administrations over time. Together, these new tools will allow researchers simultaneously to examine numerous brain systems and functional aspects of brain integrity across the early course of the disease and thus gain a more comprehensive understanding of the disease process.

REFERENCES

Asarnow, R. F. (1999). Neurocognitive impairments in schizophrenia: A piece of the epigenetic puzzle. *European Child and Adolescent Psychiatry* 8(Suppl. 1):5–8.

Asarnow, R. F., Asamen, J., Granholm, E., Sherman, T., Watkins, J. M., and Williams, J. E. (1994). Cognitive/neuropsychological studies of children with a schizophrenic disorder. *Schizophrenia Bulletin* 29(4):647–69.

Asarnow, R. F., Tanguay, P. E., Bott, L., and Freeman, B. J. (1987). Patterns of intellectual function in non-retarded autistic and schizophrenic children. *Journal of Child Psychology and Psychiatry* 28(2):273–80.

Basso, M. R., Nasrallah, H. A., Olson, S. C., and Bornstein, R. A. (1997). Cognitive deficits distinguish patients with adolescent- and adult-onset schizophrenia. *Neuropsychiatry, Neuropsychology, and Behavioral Neurology* 10(2):107–12.

Cannon, T. D., Bearden, C. E., Hollister, J. M., Rosso, I. M., Sanchez, L. E., and Hadley, T. (2000). Childhood cognitive functioning in schizophrenia patients and their unaffected siblings: A prospective cohort study. *Schizophrenia Bulletin* 26(2):379–93.

Cantor, S., Evans, J. D., Pearce, J., and Pezzot-Pearce, T. (1982). Childhood schizophrenia: Present but not accounted for. *Journal of the American Academy of Child and Adolescent Psychiatry* 26:601–4.

Caplan, R. (1994). Communication deficits in childhood schizophrenia spectrum disorders. *Schizophrenia Bulletin* 20(4):671–83.

Caplan, R., Guthrie, D., Tang, B., Nuechterlein, K. H., and Asarnow, R. E. (2001). Thought disorder in attention-deficit hyperactivity disorder. *Journal of the American Academy of Child and Adolescent Psychiatry* 40(8):965–72.

Chelune, G. J., and Baer, R. A. (1986). Developmental norms for the Wisconsin Card Sorting Test. *Journal of Clinical and Experimental Neuropsychology* 8:219–28.

Cornblatt, B., Obuchowski, M., Roberts, S., Pollack, S., and Erlenmeyer-Kimling, L. (1999). Cognitive and behavioral precursors of schizophrenia. *Development and Psychopathology* 11(3):487–508.

Cosway, R., Byrne, M., Clafferty, R., Hodges, A., Grant, E., Abukmeil, S. S., et al. (2000). Neuropsychological change in young people at high risk for schizophrenia: Results from the first two neuropsychological assessments of the Edinburgh High Risk Study. *Psychological Medicine* 30(5):1111–21.

Diforio, D., Walker, E. F., and Kestler, L. P. (2000). Executive functions in adolescents with schizotypal personality disorder. *Schizophrenia Research* 42(2):125–34.

Erickson, W. D., Yellin, A. M., Hopwood, J. H., Realmuto, G. M., and Greenberg, L. M. (1984). The effects of neuroleptics on attention in adolescent schizophrenics. *Biological Psychiatry* 19(5):745–53.

Erlenmeyer-Kimling, L., Rock, D., Roberts, S. A., Janal, M., Kestenbaum, C., Cornblatt, B., et al. (2000). Attention, memory, and motor skills as childhood predictors of schizophrenia-related psychoses: The New York High-Risk Project. *American Journal of Psychiatry* 157(9):1416–22.

Fuller, R., Nopoulos, P., Arndt, S., O'Leary, D., Ho, B. C., and Andreasen, N. C. (2002). Longitudinal assessment of premorbid cognitive functioning in patients with schizophrenia through examination of standardized scholastic test performance. *American Journal of Psychiatry* 159(7):1183–89.

Giedd, J. N., Jeffries, N. O., Blumenthal, J., Castellanos, F. X., Vaituzis, A. C., Fernandez, T., et al. (1999). Childhood-onset schizophrenia: Progressive brain changes during adolescence. *Biological Psychiatry* 46(7):892–98.

Goldberg, T. E., Karson, C. N., Leleszi, J. P., and Weinberger, D. R. (1988). Intellectual impairment in adolescent psychosis: A controlled psychometric study. *Schizophrenia Research* 1(4):261–66.

Green, M. F. (1996). What are the functional consequences of neurocognitive deficits in schizophrenia? *American Journal of Psychiatry* 153(3):321–30.

Hoff, A. L., Sakuma, M., Wieneke, M., Horon, R., Kushner, M., and DeLisi, L. E. (1999). Longitudinal neuropsychological follow-up study of patients with first-episode schizophrenia. *American Journal of Psychiatry* 156(9):1336–41.

Huttenlocher, P. R. (1984). Synapse elimination and plasticity in developing human cerebral cortex. *American Journal of Mental Deficiency* 88:488–96.

James, A. C., Javaloyes, A., James, S., and Smith, D. M. (2002). Evidence for non-progressive changes in adolescent-onset schizophrenia: Follow-up magnetic resonance imaging study. *British Journal of Psychiatry* 180:339–44.

Johnstone, E. C., Owens, D. G., Bydder, G. M., Colter, N., Crow, T. J., and Frith, C. D. (1989). The spectrum of structural brain changes in schizophrenia: Age of onset as a predictor of cognitive and clinical impairments and their cerebral correlates. *Psychological Medicine* 19(1):91–103.

Jones, P., Rodgers, B., Murray, R., and Marmot, M. (1994). Child development risk factors for adult schizophrenia in the British 1946 birth cohort. *Lancet* 344(8934):1398–1402.

Karatekin, C., and Asarnow, R. F. (1998). Working memory in childhood-onset schizophrenia and attention-deficit hyperactivity disorder. *Psychiatry Research* 80:165–76.

Karp, B. I., Garvey, M., Jacobsen, L. K., Frazier, J. A., Hamburger, S. D., Bedwell, J. S., et al. (2001). Abnormal neurologic maturation in adolescents with early-onset schizophrenia. *American Journal of Psychiatry* 158(1):118–22.

Kenny, J. T., Friedman, L., Findling, R. L., Swales, T. P., Strauss, M. E., Jesberger, J. A., et al. (1997). Cognitive impairment in adolescents with schizophrenia. *American Journal of Psychiatry* 154(11):1613–15.

Kravariti, E., Morris, R. G., Rabe-Hesketh, S., Murray, R. M., and Frangou, S. (2003). The Maudsley Early Onset Schizophrenia Study: Cognitive function in adolescents with recent onset schizophrenia. *Schizophrenia Research* 61(2–3):137–48.

Kumra, S., Wiggs, E., Bedwell, J., Smith, A. K., Arling, E., Albus, K., et al. (2000). Neuropsychological deficits in pediatric patients with childhood-onset schizophrenia and psychotic disorder not otherwise specified. *Schizophrenia Research* 42(2):135–44.

Lezak, M. D. (1995). *Neuropsychological Assessment,* 3rd ed. New York: Oxford University Press.

Lin, C. C., Chen, W. J., Yang, H. J., Hsiao, C. K., and Tien, A. Y. (2000). Performance on the Wisconsin Card Sorting Test among adolescents in Taiwan: Norms, factorial structure, and relation to schizotypy. *Journal of Clinical and Experimental Neuropsychology* 22(1):69–79.

Luciana, M., and Nelson, C. A. (1998). The functional emergence of prefrontally guided working memory systems in four- to eight-year-old children. *Neuropsychologia* 36:273–93.

Marenco, S., and Weinberger, D. R. (2000). The neurodevelopmental hypothesis of schizophrenia: Following a trail of evidence from cradle to grave. *Development and Psychopathology* 12(3):501–7.

McCarthy, J., Rabinowitz, D., Habib, M., Goldman, H., Miley, D., Stefanyshyn, H. Y., et al. (2002). Bender Gestalt Recall as a measure of short-term visual memory in children and adolescents with psychotic and other severe disorders. *Perceptual and Motor Skills* 95(3, Pt. 2):1233–38.

Nicolson, R., and Rapoport, J. L. (1999). Childhood-onset schizophrenia: Rare but worth studying. *Biological Psychiatry* 46(10):1418–28.

Oie, M., and Rund, B. R. (1999). Neuropsychological deficits in adolescent-onset schizophrenia compared with attention deficit hyperactivity disorder. *American Journal of Psychiatry* 156(8):1216–22.

Oie, M., Rund, B. R., and Sundet, K. (1998). Covert visual attention in patients with early-onset schizophrenia. *Schizophrenia Research* 34:195–205.

Oie, M., Sundet, K., and Rund, B. R. (1999). Contrasts in memory functions between adolescents with schizophrenia or ADHD. *Neuropsychologia* 37:1351–58.

Russell, A. J., Munro, J. C., Jones, P. B., Hemsley, D. R., and Murray, R. M. (1997). Schizophrenia and the myth of intellectual decline. *American Journal of Psychiatry* 154(5):635–39.

Saykin, A. J., Shtasel, D. L., Gur, R. E., Kester, D. B., Mozley, L. H., Stafiniak, P., et al. (1994). Neuropsychological deficits in neuroleptic naive patients with first-episode schizophrenia. *Archives of General Psychiatry* 51(2):124–31.

Schneider, S. G., and Asarnow, R. F. (1987). A comparison of cognitive/neuropsychological impairments of nonretarded autistic and schizophrenic children. *Journal of Abnormal Child Psychology* 15(1):29–45.

Sowell, E. R., Thompson, P. M., Homes, C. J., Jernigan, T., and Toga, A. W. (1999). In vivo evidence for post-adolescent brain maturation in frontal and striatal regions. *Nature Neuroscience* 2:859–61.

White, T., Ward, J., Ho, B. C., Arndt, S., O'Leary, D., Alicata, D., et al. (2002). Cognitive function in adolescent-onset schizophrenia: A comparison with adult onset schizophrenia and adolescent controls. *Schizophrenia Research* 53(Suppl. 1):122–23.

Wozniak, J. R., Koehler, D. J., White, T., and Schulz, S. C. (2003). Neurocognitive functioning over the first year of illness in adolescent patients with psychotic disorders. *Schizophrenia Research* 60(Suppl. 1):162.

Yang, P. C., Liu, C. Y., Chiang, S. Q., Chen, J. Y., and Lin, T. S. (1995). Comparison of adult manifestations of schizophrenia with onset before and after 15 years of age. *Acta Psychiatrica Scandinavica* 91(3):209–12.

Yeo, R. A., Hodde-Vargas, J., Hendren, R. L., Vargas, L. A., Brooks, W. M., Ford, C. C., et al. (1997). Brain abnormalities in schizophrenia-spectrum children: Implications for a neurodevelopmental perspective. *Psychiatry Research: Neuroimaging* 67(1):1–13.

Zahn, T., Jacobsen, L. K., Gordon, C. T., McKenna, K., Frazier, J. A., and Rapoport, J. L. (1998). Attention deficits in childhood-onset schizophrenia. *Journal of Abnormal Psychology* 107(1):97–108.

CHAPTER SEVEN

Neurophysiology and the Neurodevelopmental Hypothesis

Endophenotypes, Genetic Risk, and Brain Dysfunction

Randal G. Ross, M.D., Michael A. Kisley, Ph.D., and Jason R. Tregellas, Ph.D.

Schizophrenia is a complicated illness, with a heterogeneous clinical presentation that varies with age and a complex genetic etiology, that involves dysfunction in multiple regions of the brain. Symptoms are primarily internal and are thus difficult to measure quantitatively. Imaging studies can be a challenge to design, as it is often unknown when, for example, a subject is actively hallucinating. Likewise, family genetic studies are often problematic. Although some individuals in a family are clearly ill, others may fall on the borderline in terms of symptoms, making it hard to judge whether they are affected or not. Such problems have led to attempts to identify less complex physiological phenotypes appropriate for genetic, imaging, and developmental studies.

A number of physiological variables have been examined in the context of schizophrenia, including skin conductance (Holzman 1987), prepulse inhibition (Braff, Geyer, and Swerdlow 2001), P300 amplitude (Friedman and Squires-Wheeler 1994), and mismatch negativity (Javitt et al. 1995). This chapter focuses on three phenotypes that best exemplify the potential of physiology. The first, P50 sensory gating, helps to demonstrate how physiological phenotypes can aid us in the search for genes. In addition, saccadic eye movements allow us to explore the role of brain functioning in schizophrenia, and, finally, smooth pursuit eye movements can help us to assess the developmental component of schizophrenia.

P50 Sensory Gating and Genetic Vulnerability

Needless to say, understanding physiological studies of genetic vulnerability requires a grasp of the relevant terminology. Perhaps one of the most confusing concepts in this area is that of an endophenotype. Research on endophenotypes assumes that complex disorders are multigenic and that each disease-associated gene is associated not only with the clinical phenotype itself but also with other phenotypes more closely linked to the gene, which are termed *endophenotypes*. Endophenotypes, such as changes in skin conductance, autonomic responsivity, or eye movement abnormalities, represent phenotypes that derive from the contribution of one, or at most a few, disease-associated genes. Endophenotypes may or may not be directly related to the clinical presentation. However, the identification of genetically simple phenotypes may both facilitate studies that seek to identify candidate genes and improve our knowledge of the pathophysiology of the disorder under consideration.

Figure 7.1 provides a model of the relationship between the clinical phenotype, intermediate phenotypes, and endophenotypes. Intermediate phenotypes can include cognitive changes such as deficits in sensory inhibition or working memory, changes in functional responses in the brain such as might be seen on a functional magnetic resonance image (MRI) or magnetoencephalogram (MEG), or a relevant cellular change such as a reduction in the number of a specific neurotransmitter receptor measured in the hippocampus of postmortem brain. Whereas endophenotypes may or may not be directly associated with the clinical phenotype, intermediate phenotypes do contribute to the symptomatology of a disorder. (The term *extended phenotype* has been understood in multiple ways, from narrow definitions that focus on subclinical symptoms to broad definitions that encompass all phenotypes, including clinical, subclinical, intermediate, and endophenotypes. To avoid the confusion created by these varying definitions, alternatives to the term *extended phenotype* will be used in this chapter.)

As categories, intermediate phenotypes and endophenotypes partially overlap: if an endophenotype contributes to the clinical presentation of the disor-

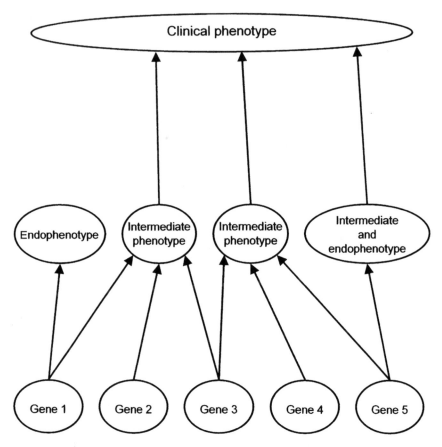

Fig. 7.1. The relationship between the clinical phenotype (such as schizophrenia), intermediate phenotypes, and endophenotypes, and genetic contributions to the disorder.

der, it is also an intermediate phenotype. Conversely, if an intermediate phenotype reflects only a single gene factor, it can also be an endophenotype. Schizophrenia is a complex disorder that develops only as the result of an interaction between multiple genetic and environmental events. In other words, individuals with schizophrenia carry more than one risk-associated allele, and it is the combination of these alleles that may lead to the clinical disorder. Due to genetic segregation, first-degree relatives will share some, but often not all, of the risk-associated alleles. Thus, first-degree relatives carry some of the genetic risk, but not enough to develop the disorder themselves. If an endophenotype is closely linked to a specific risk-associated allele, it will occur in many family members, even though those family members do not carry enough genetic vulnerability to demonstrate clinical symptoms. However, because endophenotypes reflect a smaller number of genetic influences, identifying endophenotypes can enhance the ability of genetic studies, including linkage studies, to identify candidate genes. Given that endophenotypes and intermediate phenotypes are often simple physiological measures, they are also often appropriate targets for imaging studies, which allows them to provide information on fundamental neurophysiological deficits associated with a particular disorder.

An approach based on the identification of a simple phenotype has been successfully used in identifying the genetic basis of hemochromatosis. Serum iron levels proved to be more effective than the clinical phenotype itself at pinpointing genetic contributors to the disorder (Lalouel et al. 1985). Given that elevated serum iron levels are associated with the pathology and clinical course of the disease and also lead to the identification of a specific gene, serum iron levels are both an intermediate phenotype and an endophenotype. Because the etiology of schizophrenia is complex, however, clarifying which physiological measures are endophenotypes, which are intermediate phenotypes, and which are both is an especially delicate task.

P50 Sensory Gating as a Model of a Physiological Endophenotype

The impetus to study sensory gating by means of physiological methods originated with the observation that persons with schizophrenia often complain of an inability to ignore or block out irrelevant sensory stimuli. Perhaps the most detailed account of this phenomenon has been offered by McGhie and Chapman (1961), who interpreted their patients' complaints as stemming from "disturbances in the process of attention" and/or from "perception" (pp. 104, 105). These patients essentially perceived all sounds in the environment, even those in the background, as seminal, and thus their attention was distracted from whatever they were doing. A short time later, Venables (1964) pointed out that these deficits must ultimately be due to some specific neurobiological lesion that could be studied physiologically. Almost twenty years later, his insight was proven correct.

The "paired-click" paradigm, combined with measurements obtained by electroencephalogram, was first used to study the physiological basis of sensory gating (Adler et al. 1982). In this paradigm, a pair of clicks, 0.5 seconds apart, were presented to a subject every 10 seconds. The global brain activity evoked by these stimuli was recorded from an electrode positioned at the vertex and averaged over many stimulus presentations. Sensory gating was assessed by comparing the amplitude of brain potential evoked by the second, or "test," click of the pair to the amplitude evoked by the first, or "conditioning," click. In this design, the test click provides no new information beyond the first click and is therefore redundant and irrelevant. Ideally, then, the brain will not devote neural resources to processing that second click. This inhibition of neural activity is expressed as a greatly diminished amplitude of evoked potential in response to the test click as compared to the conditioning click, that is, as a low T/C ratio (see Figure 7.2). Indeed, for normal controls, this is precisely what was originally observed. In contrast, patients with schizophrenia exhibited T/C ratios close to 1.0, which indicates that their brain was responding approximately equally to both clicks of the pair. Multiple interclick intervals were tested, and three different auditory-evoked potential components were assessed. The largest effect—the difference in sensory gating between patients and controls—was found at the 0.5 second interclick interval for evoked potential component P50, a positive wave that peaks approximately 50 milliseconds after the stimulus (Adler et al. 1982). The basic finding of impaired sensory gating in schizophrenia, as measured with wave P50, has been both confirmed and extended by several independent research groups (Boutros, Zouridakis, and Overall 1991; Erwin et al. 1991; Jerger, Biggins, and Fein 1992; Judd et al. 1992).

Although sensory gating abnormalities are not strictly specific to schizophrenia, deficits found in other clinical populations predominantly result from nongenetic causes. For example, patients with bipolar disorder also exhibit impaired P50 gating but only during mania (Franks et al. 1983). This state-dependence is believed to result from the increased levels of catecholamines associated with the manic phase (Adler et al. 1990). Although impaired P50 gating has been documented in Parkinson's and Alzheimer's diseases (Teo et al. 1997; Jessen et al. 2001), it remains unclear whether the deficits are indirectly caused by an accompanying neurodegeneration. Among environmental insults, illicit drug use (Boutros et al. 2000; Patrick and Struve 2000), traumatic brain injury (Arciniegas et al. 2000), and psychological trauma (Neylan et al. 1999; Skinner et al. 1999) have all been shown to cause impaired sen-

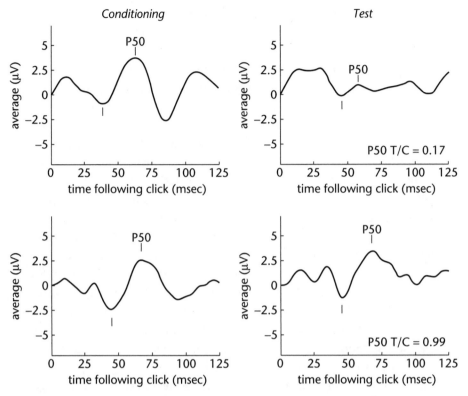

Fig. 7.2. Examples of auditory-evoked potentials, measured by "paired-click" tests, used to assess sensory gating. The graphs at the top show the brain activity of a control individual without a family history of psychosis, while those at the bottom show the activity for a patient with schizophrenia medicated with haloperidol. The graphs on the left trace the average global brain activity evoked by the first, or "conditioning," click of the pair; on the right is the activity evoked by the second, "test," click, which occurs 0.5 seconds (500 ms) later. The amplitude of wave P50 is measured between the positive peak and the preceding negative trough. Note that the control individual exhibits robust suppression of wave P50 in response to the test click. This suppression is expressed numerically as a low "T/C" (test/conditioning) ratio (computed as the amplitude of the test P50 divided by amplitude of the conditioning P50). In contrast, the patient does not suppress wave P50 in response to the test click, yielding a T/C ratio close to 1.0. (Note that positive is shown upward in this figure, which departs from the practice adopted in much of the existing literature on P50 sensory gating.)

sory gating, as measured physiologically. Finally, and somewhat surprisingly given their distractibility, adult ADHD patients generally do *not* exhibit abnormal P50 gating (Olincy et al. 2000).

Because the physiological measure described above was initially developed to facilitate an understanding of genetics, efforts were quickly made to determine whether the sensory gating deficits associated with schizophrenia are heritable. This line of research showed that approximately half the first-degree relatives of a schizophrenic proband will also exhibit the sensory gating impairment (Figure 7.3), regardless of whether they are themselves affected with schizophrenia (Siegel et al. 1984; Waldo et al. 1994; Clementz, Geyer, and Braff 1998). Demonstrating this pattern of autosomal dominant transmission paved the way for genetic linkage studies.

In 1997, Freedman et al. reported a positive linkage of the sensory gating phenotype to chromosome 15q14. The study was conducted with nine families, each having at least two first-degree relatives diagnosed with schizophrenia, and produced a logarithmic odds (LOD) score of 5.3. Although the discovery of a significant linkage to any region of the genome was a boon, researchers were particularly pleased to close in on 15q14, as this region contains the gene for a particular form of brain nicotine receptor—the α7-nicotinic receptor—which had already been determined to be critical for sensory gating in rodents (Luntz-Leybman, Bickford, and Freedman 1992; Stevens et al. 1996). Suggestive evidence that dysfunction in the α7 receptor might be involved in the sensory gating deficits associated with schizophrenia also existed at the time. In particular, it was known that nicotine could restore P50 sensory gating in schizophrenia patients and their first-degree relatives (Adler et al. 1992, 1993) and further that patients with schizophrenia have fewer α7-nicotinic receptors in the hippocampus than do matched controls (Freedman et al. 1995). Although the precise change in the α7 gene that might lead to sensory gating impairment is currently unknown, preliminary mutation screening suggests that single and multiple base-pair changes in the promoter region of the gene could be responsible (Leonard et al. 2001).

Even though a direct causative relationship between changes in a particular candidate gene and the sensory gating phenotype is not yet proven, the original goal of the physiological approach has come to fruition. In particular, by selecting a less complex phenotype than the clinical phenotype of schizophrenia, researchers have created a more tractable genetic problem. And, encouragingly, the same genetic locus identified by physiological studies of sen-

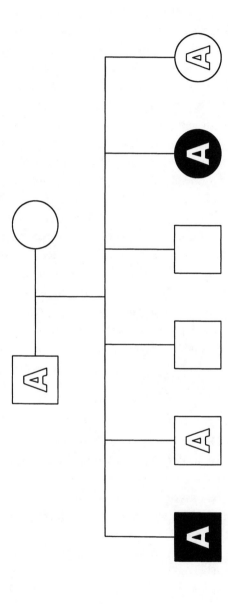

Fig. 7.3. The fictional pedigree of a family containing two siblings affected with schizophrenia (represented by the filled-in symbols). The autosomal dominant trait—in this case a deficit in P50 sensory gating (indicated by A)—appears in the two offspring with schizophrenia but is also expressed in the father and in two of the four other children.

sory gating (15q14) has been linked to the phenotype of schizophrenia itself (reviewed by Freedman and Leonard 2001).

Research on P50 gating in schizophrenia has also suggested a novel treatment strategy. The current hypothesis holds that sensory gating impairments result from underactivation of α7-nicotinic receptors in the central nervous system. Therefore, an increased activation of these receptors should improve a patient's ability to gate out irrelevant stimuli. As we have just seen, nicotine has been shown to be effective in this regard. In fact, it has been suggested that the extremely high smoking rates observed in the schizophrenia population might represent an attempt at self-medication (Leonard et al. 2000). Unfortunately, the reversal of sensory gating deficits by nicotine are temporary, lasting less than twenty minutes (Adler et al. 1993), presumably because the α7-nicotinic receptors desensitize rapidly in the presence of nonspecific ligands such as nicotine or acetylcholine (Griffith et al. 1998). However, compounds that activate α7 receptors but not other types of nicotine receptors (e.g., α4β2) do not appear to produce such rapid desensitization, at least in animal studies (Stevens and Wear 1997). This has led to the hope that such compounds might provide a "cleaner," longer-lasting alleviation of the attention and perception deficits associated with schizophrenia. Thus, study of a physiological phenotype has led to the first notably positive linkage score on chromosome 15, has identified a candidate gene, and has opened a novel target for pharmaceutical development.

Saccades and Brain Imaging

In 1905, Dodge used a cleverly designed machine to record eye movements. He reflected light off the subject's eye onto photographic paper as the photographic paper was being wound from one spool to another. Dodge determined that there were five major classes of eye movements, including slow eye movements designed to maintain the gaze on a moving object, which he termed *smooth pursuit,* and rapid eye movements designed to shift the gaze and foveate a previously peripheral target, which he termed *saccades.* Three years later, Dodge collaborated with Diefendorf on the first study of eye movements in chronically psychotic patients (Diefendorf and Dodge 1908). They reported that, although smooth pursuit tracking was notably impaired in patients with schizophrenia, saccadic eye movements were normal in this group. These original studies focused on the simplest task: rapidly moving the eyes to focus the gaze on a peripheral target. Since 1907, many authors have replicated Diefendorf and Dodge's original report of minimal to no detriments in saccadic task performance (e.g., Fukushima et al. 1990). In contrast to these earlier studies, more recent research, incorporating more complex tasks, has identified schizophrenia-comparison group differences with the largest effect sizes ever reported for a physiological measure in schizophrenia (McDowell et al. 1999). These deficits during saccadic tasks are also more common in relatives of schizophrenic probands (Ross, Harris, et al. 1998; McDowell et al. 1999), including adolescent relatives (Heinlein and Ross 2001). The large schizophrenia-normal effect size and the presence of deficits in family members supports the consideration of a dysfunction during saccadic tasks as an endophenotype, although lack of specificity (Ross, Harris, et al. 2000) may limit the eventual utility of these tasks in genetic studies. Saccadic eye movement tasks may instead play the greatest role in exploring underlying brain pathology.

The two most commonly used tasks are the delayed oculomotor response task (DOR) and the antisaccade task. In the DOR, a subject stares at a central fixation point while a cue flashes in the periphery (see Figure 7.4). The subject is first instructed not to look at the flash (that is, to inhibit response) and then, after a period of time, when cued, to look where the flash used to be. For the antisaccade task, subjects are asked not to look at the flash but instead to look the same distance in the opposite direction (see Figure 7.5). Each of these tasks measures at least two critical cognitive abilities. First, the individual must inhibit responding to task-relevant stimuli. Second, when cued to do so, the individual must look to a known location without a current stimulus—in the case of the DOR to a remembered location and in the case of the antisaccade task to a computed location. Thus inhibitory and spatial working memory measures can be derived from these tasks.

Many of the physiological abnormalities associated with schizophrenia, including impaired P50 sensory gating and deficits in smooth pursuit eye movement, were first applied to schizophrenia on the basis of clinical observation. In other words, clinicians noted a problem, a physiological task was developed to study it, and then questions were raised as to which portions of the brain might be involved in the abnormality. Saccadic tasks were first developed to study nonhuman models of brain functioning and only later applied to schizophrenia research. In particular, the DOR has been extensively used for more than fifteen years to study working memory in primate models. Single-cell recording and lesion studies have suggested that the dorsolateral prefrontal

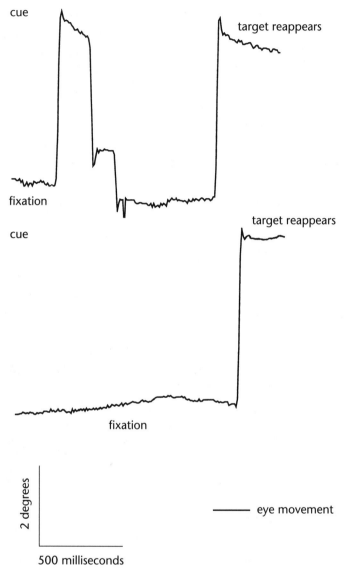

Fig. 7.4. Results of a delayed oculomotor response task (DOR) performed by an 11-year-old male with schizophrenia. In the DOR, the subject stares at a central fixation point while a cue flashes in the periphery. The subject is first instructed not to look at the flash and then, after a period of time, when cued, to look where the flash used to be. Here, the subject initially responds prematurely and looks toward the flash (top graph). The subject then appropriately delays response to the cue until the fixation light goes off (after a 1-second delay), before looking to the remembered location of the cue (bottom graph).

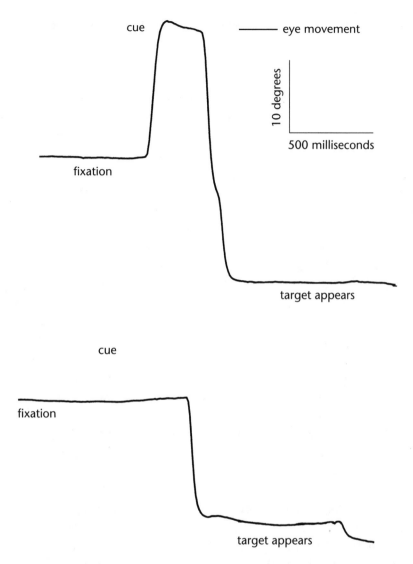

cue

eye movement

10 degrees

500 milliseconds

fixation

target appears

cue

fixation

target appears

Fig. 7.5. The antisaccade task. In this test, the subject is presented with a cue, in the form of a flash, and is instructed *not* to look at the flash when it appears but instead to look immediately the same distance in the opposite direction. As the graph at the top illustrates, the subject at first fails to inhibit response and mistakenly looks toward the cue. The subject then appropriately inhibits response and accurately looks the same distance in the opposite direction. The target light appears after the shift in gaze (the saccade), encouraging a corrective saccade if needed.

cortical neurons maintain information about remembered locations, and it is primarily this work that has confirmed the role of the dorsolateral prefrontal cortex in working memory (see Goldman-Rakic 1987 and Levy and Goldman-Rakic 2000 for reviews). The role of the prefrontal cortex in inhibition and working memory in humans has been established via natural lesion (e.g., cerebral infarct) studies (Guitton, Buchtel, and Douglas 1985). The extensive information already available on brain localization of complex saccadic tasks has made them ideal for the study of working memory deficits in schizophrenia.

Over the last decade, functional neuroimaging has emerged as a valuable tool for studying brain dysfunction in schizophrenia. Positron emission tomography (PET) and functional MRI (fMRI) studies have employed saccadic tasks in an attempt to elucidate the pathology underlying inhibitory failure and working memory dysfunction in the disease. Early studies (e.g., Nakashima et al. 1994) suggested that altered saccadic performance in schizophrenia was associated with reduced activity in frontal brain regions such as the frontal eye fields, which are known to be involved in the generation of saccades (Anderson et al. 1994; O'Driscoll et al. 1995; Sweeney et al. 1996; Law et al. 1997; Petit et al. 1997; Berman et al. 1999), and the dorsolateral prefrontal cortex (DLPFC), a region involved in many higher cognitive processes including working memory. More recent studies, using fMRI, offer even clearer insight into the nature of saccadic dysfunction in schizophrenia. This is largely the result of the greatly improved temporal resolution of fMRI in comparison to PET, which permits a greater sensitivity to brief responses, and the improved experimental design of recent studies, which allows for better parsing out of the different cognitive processes involved in tasks. McDowell and colleagues (2002) reported reduced activation of the DLPFC in subjects with schizophrenia as they performed an antisaccade task. This study used a reflexive, or prosaccade, task (subjects were instructed to move their eyes quickly in response to new stimuli that appeared in the periphery) as a baseline so that the brain activation associated with the motor component of saccade execution could be eliminated. These results suggest that the observed reduction in DLPFC activity is linked to either the inhibitory or the working memory component of saccadic dysfunction in schizophrenia.

Neuroimaging studies of saccadic tasks in schizophrenia have also emphasized the possible role of other brain regions in poor task performance. The cingulate gyrus, insula, and striatum all appear inappropriately active during complex saccadic tasks in patients with schizophrenia (Crawford et al. 1996;

Raemaekers et al. 2002). These results support the suggestion that a cortical-subcortical circuit, which includes the DLFPC, the cingulate gyrus, and the striatum, may be altered in schizophrenic subjects.

Smooth Pursuit Eye Movements and Neurodevelopment

Of all the physiological phenotypes associated with schizophrenia, probably the most extensively studied—with not a single report of a failure to replicate the standard findings—are abnormalities during smooth pursuit eye movement (SPEM) tasks (Levy et al. 1993, 1994). First reported in 1908 (Diefendorf and Dodge 1908), SPEM abnormalities were rediscovered in the 1930s (Couch and Cox 1934) and rediscovered in the 1970s (Holzman, Proctor, and Hughes 1973).

SPEM as an Endophenotype

Holzman and colleagues, working first with monozygotic twins discordant for schizophrenia and later with other nonpsychotic relatives (Holzman et al. 1980, 1988), discovered that abnormalities during SPEM tasks were common not only in individuals with schizophrenia but also in many of their unaffected relatives. This suggested that such abnormalities were related to some of the same genetic risk factors as schizophrenia, although with greater penetrance. It appeared that the same genetic vulnerability could present as abnormal smooth pursuit, as schizophrenia, or as both. However, in the presence of genetic vulnerability, SPEM abnormalities were more likely to be present than the clinical symptoms of schizophrenia, making SPEM dysfunction more suited than the phenotype of the disease itself for identifying genetic vulnerability to schizophrenia. This more frequent or highly penetrant trait was termed a *latent trait* by Holzman and colleagues (1988) and an *endophenotype* by Gottesman and Shields (1967). The increased frequency of SPEM abnormalities in relatives of schizophrenic probands has been replicated in seven large studies (Holzman et al. 1988; Blackwood et al. 1991; Grove et al. 1992; Iacono et al. 1992; Keefe et al. 1997; Lencer et al. 2000; Ross et al. 2002) as well as several smaller ones.

Genetic linkage analyses of SPEM dysfunction have provided suggestive evidence that global measures of SPEM performance are linked to regions on chromosomes 6 and 8, with LOD scores of 2.73 and 1.66 respectively (Arolt et al. 1996, 1999) but these are well below the scores of 5.0 or above generally considered to be strong evidence for linkage. The discrepancy between a highly replicable familial dysfunction and a lack of strongly positive linkage scores may be related to problems in phenotype definition.

While all physiological phenotypes require extensive work to operationalize outcomes, most physiological phenotypes become associated with a single operational outcome. For P50 sensory gating, the most common measure is the testing-to-condition amplitude ratio or, during saccadic tasks, the percentage of trials showing a failure to inhibit task-inappropriate saccades. Conversely, in SPEM research, the optimal dependent measure has been more difficult to identify. While part of this difficulty has been due to nosology issues (different laboratories using the same term to mean different things), much of the difficulty can be attributed to the complex nature of the task.

As we have seen, the ability to maintain the gaze on a moving target while the head is passively restrained has been termed *smooth pursuit eye movement.* However, this is something of a misnomer in that performance on this task actually requires the integration of both saccadic and smooth pursuit eye movements. To differentiate between the smooth pursuit *task* and smooth pursuit *eye movements,* we have adopted the convention of referring to the task by the acronym SPEM while using the spelled-out form, "smooth pursuit," to refer to the eye movements themselves. In other words, smooth pursuit (and saccadic) eye movements are used to complete a SPEM task. Smooth pursuit can be slowed either as a result of impaired smooth pursuit performance or as a compensatory measure for intrusive saccades. In the latter case, a saccade will intrude on an otherwise normal pursuit and move the gaze ahead of the target motion, and then the smooth pursuit system will slow to allow the target to catch up to the direction of gaze. As these saccades appear to represent an anticipation of target motion, they have been termed *anticipatory saccades.* Anticipatory saccades can be further subdivided into large anticipatory saccades (amplitudes greater than 4°) and leading saccades (amplitudes between 1° and 4°). This SPEM nosology is based on empirical data demonstrating that smooth pursuit gain as well as catch-up, leading, and large anticipatory saccades differ in the changes they undergo with normal aging (Ross et al. 1993; Ross, Olincy, et al., Effects of age 1999), in their specificity to schizophrenia (Ross, Olincy, et al. 2000; Olincy et al. 2002), and in their response to pharmacological challenge (Olincy et al. 1998; Olincy and Ross 2003). Figure 7.6 provides examples of SPEM performance. On the basis of family studies, an elevated frequency of leading saccades appears to be the SPEM measure most closely tied to a genetic vulnerability for schizophrenia (Ross, Radant, and Hommer 2002). However, linkage analyses of leading saccades have not yet been attempted, and so the ability of this marker to identify schizophrenia-associated genetic loci remains untested.

Imaging and SPEM

As in the case of saccadic tasks, the locations of the basic brain processes required for accurate visual tracking have been identified; however, the SPEM dysfunction associated with schizophrenia appears to be related to higher cortical function. In the only two studies we are aware of, PET scanning has identified lower frontal eye field activation in schizophrenic subjects during the performance of SPEM tasks (Ross et al. 1995; O'Driscoll et al. 1999).

SPEM and the Neurodevelopmental Hypothesis of Schizophrenia

While SPEM studies show promise in genetic and imaging research, perhaps the most useful contribution of these studies to date is the information they have provided concerning the neurodevelopmental hypothesis of schizophrenia. The hypothesis holds that schizophrenia is the result of alterations in normal brain development. What remains unclear, however, is when during the span of development these alterations occur. Because significant changes in neural organization, including synaptic pruning, take place during adolescence, one possibility is that schizophrenia is produced by alterations in adolescent brain development. Structural imaging studies of adolescents with schizophrenia suggest that they experience a greater loss of gray matter than do nonpsychotic adolescents (Thompson et al. 2001), a finding that supports this theory.

An alternative possibility is that abnormalities in brain development come about much earlier (sometime between conception and early adolescence) and that the adolescent onset of symptoms occurs when normal adolescent changes take place on an abnormal substrate. Children who will later develop schizophrenia present either as asymptomatic or with a nonpsychotic, nonspecific psychopathology (Ross and Compagnon 2001; Schaeffer and Ross 2002) and are thus not easily identified. Consequently, it is difficult to investigate the neurodevelopmental hypothesis beyond a certain point. Physiological alterations, like abnormalities during SPEM, provide a non-symptombased mechanism for studying brain function years before the onset of symptoms.

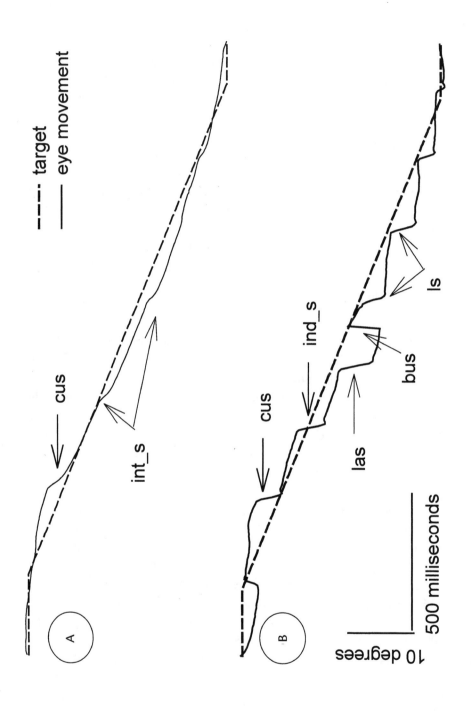

target
eye movement

cus

int_s

A

cus

ind_s

las

bus

ls

B

10 degrees

500 milliseconds

Roughly 82 percent of adults with schizophrenia and 44 percent of their nonpsychotic first-degree adult relatives demonstrate a particular inhibitory deficit during the performance of SPEM tasks, which has been referred to as an increase in leading saccades (Ross et al. 2002). The distribution of these leading saccade scores suggests the influence of a single major gene (Ross, Olincy, et al. 1998; Ross, Olincy, et al., Evidence 1999; Ross et al. 2002). Individuals suffering from bipolar disorder, attention deficit hyperactivity disorder (Ross, Olincy, et al. 2000), and autism do not show this increase in leading saccades, implying that this physiological marker is specific to the genetic vulnerability to schizophrenia. Normally, developing children as young as 6 years of age exhibit leading saccade rates during SPEM tasks at a rate similar to that of young adults. These results suggest that elevated rates of leading saccades reflect a genetically influenced alteration in brain function that appears to be related to a vulnerability to schizophrenia and that the brain functions associated with the ability to inhibit leading saccades are present in school-age children. What is important for the neurodevelopmental hypothesis, however, is whether SPEM abnormalities can be identified during the premorbid period.

The rate of leading saccades during the performance of SPEM tasks has also been assessed in school-age children who have a schizophrenic parent. Because schizophrenia is a multigenetic disorder, it is assumed that the overall risk in these children varies over a continuum: some have inherited many of the genetic risk factors, some a few, and some none at all. However, for a single genetic risk factor, there should be segregation, with some of the children in-

---

Fig. 7.6. opposite The smooth pursuit task (SPEM). Subjects are asked to keep their eyes on a target as it moves back and forth, at 16.7° per second, across a computer screen. This visual tracking movement is called "smooth pursuit." Shown here are tracings from a normally developing 12-year-old male (top graph) and from an 11-year-old with schizophrenia (bottom graph). As can be seen from the graphs, compensatory shifts in gaze, or catch-up saccades (cus), function to correct for impairments in smooth pursuit. In addition, normal subjects will often make small intrusive saccades (int-s), presumably as a refocusing process. Anticipatory saccades, which are subdivided into large anticipatory saccades (las) and small, or leading, saccades (ls), cause the gaze to shift ahead of the target as it moves. The shift in gaze typically produces a slowing of smooth pursuit that allows the moving target to catch up to the position of the gaze. Large anticipatory saccades are often followed by back-up saccades (bus) that return the gaze to the location of the target. Indeterminate saccades (ind-s) cannot be easily classified into one of the subtypes and are discarded from analyses.

heriting the gene and some should not. Research with school-age children (6 to 15 years old) tends to support this hypothesis. In one study, none of the controls but over half (53%) of the children with a schizophrenic parent demonstrated abnormally high rates of leading saccades during SPEM (Ross et al. 1996). Therefore, this genetically influenced physiological marker is already present by school age, years before the risk for psychotic symptomology begins to grow. Similar work with P50 sensory gating likewise reveals physiological abnormalities in school-age children (Myles-Worsley et al. 1996). In sum, these studies suggest that alterations in brain function are present at least by the age of 6. It is currently unknown whether these deficits are present even earlier during brain development, in infancy or even prenatally, but additional work on these younger age groups is in progress.

Adolescent studies aimed at early identification and treatment of schizophrenia, including treatment with antipsychotic medication during the prodromal period, are now underway worldwide. How well we are able to identify premorbid alterations in brain function has considerable implications for treatment in that, to be effective, primary prevention efforts may need to focus on a much earlier period in development, at a time when abnormalities in brain function are first beginning to appear.

Summary: Why Study Physiological Endophenotypes in Adolescents?

In many genetically based disorders, the earlier the age of onset, the greater the genetic loading. Thus, children and adolescents with schizophrenia are likely to have greater genetic loading than individuals in whom the onset of illness is delayed until adulthood. In addition, studying adolescents early on in the disease process can help us to distinguish the effects of the genetic etiology from those that are secondary to the disease (for example, the effects of medication, of institutionalization, or of downward socioeconomic status, etc.). Thus, the inclusion of adolescents can, for a variety of reasons and in a variety of applications, enhance the power of studies of physiological endophenotypes.

To date, much of the focus has been placed on how the inclusion of adolescents can benefit broader studies of physiological measures. However, the fruitful relationship between adolescents and the study of physiological phenotypes is potentially bidirectional in that physiological measures may prove especially helpful in addressing the complex clinical problems often seen in adolescence. The prodromal period in particular is often associated with a functional decline before the onset of readily diagnosable clinical symptoms, making the use of neuroleptic treatment controversial. Physiological measures can signal brain dysfunction that may be the result of etiological processes similar to those of the disease state and thus could potentially act as dependent measures in intervention studies. Unfortunately, the use of such physiological measures has so far been limited to adults with schizophrenia (Adler et al. 1993; Litman et al. 1994; Nagamoto et al. 1996), and hence the potential value of such an approach remains primarily theoretical as far as adolescence is concerned.

Physiological measures are not intended to replace symptoms in the diagnostic formulation. Instead, they are quantifiable reflections of brain function that are useful in identifying genes, isolating problems through the use of functional imaging, and working out the premorbid course of the disorder. Research into these factors should contribute to a more sophisticated understanding of the developmental presentation and progression of schizophrenia, which in turn may help us to devise novel intervention strategies that can be brought into play earlier in the disease process.

REFERENCES

Adler, L. E., Gerhardt, G. A., Franks, R., Baker, N., Nagamoto, H., Drebing, C., et al. (1990). Sensory physiology and catecholamines in schizophrenia and mania. *Psychiatry Research* 31:297–309.

Adler, L. E., Hoffer, L. D., Wiser, A., and Freedman, R. (1993). Normalization of auditory physiology by cigarette smoking in schizophrenic patients. *American Journal of Psychiatry* 150:1856–61.

Adler, L. E., Hoffer, L. J., Griffith, J., Waldo, M. C., and Freedman, R. (1992). Normalization by nicotine of deficient auditory sensory gating in the relatives of schizophrenics. *Biological Psychiatry* 32:607–16.

Adler, L. E., Pachtman, E., Franks, R. D., Pecevich, M., Waldo, M. C., and Freedman, R. (1982). Neurophysiological evidence for a defect in neuronal mechanisms involved in sensory gating in schizophrenia. *Biological Psychiatry* 17:639–54.

Anderson, T. J., Jenkins, I. H., Brooks, D. J., Hawken, M. B., Frackowiak, R. S., and Kennard, C. (1994). Cortical control of saccades and fixation in man: A PET study. *Brain* 117:1073–84.

Arciniegas, D., Olincy, A., Topkoff, J., McRae, K., Cawthra, E., Filley, C. M., et al. (2000). Impaired auditory gating and P50 nonsuppression following traumatic brain injury. *Journal of Neuropsychiatry and Clinical Neurosciences* 12:77–85.

Arolt, V., Lencer, R., Nolte, A., Muller-Myhsok, B., Purmann, S., Schurmann, M., et al. (1996). Eye tracking dysfunction is a putative phenotypic susceptibility marker of schizophrenia and maps to a locus on chromosome 6p in families with multiple occurrences of the disease. *American Journal of Medical Genetics: Neuropsychiatric Genetics* 67:564–79.

Arolt, V., Lencer, R., Purmann, S., Schurmann, M., Muller-Myhsok, B., Krecker, K., et al. (1999). Testing for linkage of eye tracking dysfunction and schizophrenia to markers of chromosomes 6, 8, 9, and 22 in families multiply affected with schizophrenia. *American Journal of Medical Genetics: Neuropsychiatric Genetics* 88:603–6.

Berman, R. A., Colby, C. L., Genovese, C. R., Voyvodic, J. T., Luna, B., Thulborn, K. R., et al. (1999). Cortical networks subserving pursuit and saccadic eye movements in humans: An fMRI study. *Human Brain Mapping* 8:209–25.

Blackwood, D.H.R., St. Clair, D. M., Muir, W. J., and Duffy, J. C. (1991). Auditory P300 and eye tracking dysfunction in schizophrenic pedigrees. *Archives of General Psychiatry* 48:899–909.

Boutros, N. N., Campbell, D., Petrakis, I., Krystal, J., Caporale, M., and Kosten, T. (2000). Cocaine use and the mid-latency auditory evoked responses. *Psychiatry Research* 96:117–26.

Boutros, N. N., Zouridakis, G., and Overall, J. (1991). Replication and extension of P50 findings in schizophrenia. *Clinical Electroencephalography* 22:40–45.

Braff, D. L., Geyer, M. A., and Swerdlow, N. R. (2001). Human studies of prepulse inhibition of startle: Normal subjects, patient groups, and pharmacological studies. *Psychopharmacology* 156:234–58.

Clementz, B. A., Geyer, M. A., and Braff, D. L. (1998). Poor P50 suppression among schizophrenia patients and their first-degree biological relatives. *American Journal of Psychiatry* 155:1691–94.

Couch, R. H., and Cox, J. C. (1934). Photographic study of ocular movements in mental disease. *Archives of Neurology and Psychiatry* 34:556–78.

Crawford, T. J., Puri, B. K., Nijran, K. S., Jones, B., Kennard, C., and Lewis, S. W. (1996). Abnormal saccadic distractibility in patients with schizophrenia: A 99mTc-HMPAO SPET study. *Psychological Medicine* 26:265–77.

Diefendorf, A. R., and Dodge, R. (1908). An experimental study of the ocular reaction on the insane from photographic records. *Brain* 31:451–89.

Dodge, R. (1905). Five types of eye-movement in the horizontal meridian plane of the field of regard. *American Journal of Physiology* 8:307–29.

Erwin, R. J., Mawhinney-Hee, M., Gur, R. C., and Gur, R. E. (1991). Midlatency auditory evoked responses in schizophrenia. *Biological Psychiatry* 30:430–42.

Franks, R. D., Adler, L. E., Waldo, M. C., Alpert, J., and Freedman, R. (1983). Neurophysiological studies of sensory gating in mania: Comparison with schizophrenia. *Biological Psychiatry* 18:989–1005.

Freedman, R., Coon, H., Myles-Worsley, M., Orr-Urtreger, A., Olincy, A., Davis, A., et al. (1997). Linkage of a neurophysiological deficit in schizophrenia to a chromosome 15 locus. *Proceedings of the National Academy of Sciences, USA* 94:587–92.

Freedman, R., Hall, M., Adler, L. E., and Leonard, S. (1995). Evidence in postmortem brain tissue for decreased numbers of hippocampal nicotinic receptors in schizophrenia. *Biological Psychiatry* 38:22–33.

Freedman, R., and Leonard, S. (2001). Genetic linkage to schizophrenia at chromosome 15q14. *American Journal of Medical Genetics: Neuropsychiatric Genetics* 105:655–57.

Freedman, R., Olincy, A., and Leonard, S. (2001). Evidence for multigenic inheritance of schizophrenia. *American Journal of Medical Genetics: Neuropsychiatric Genetics* 105:794–800.

Friedman, D., and Squires-Wheeler, E. (1994). Event-related potentials (ERPs) as indicators of risk for schizophrenia. *Schizophrenia Bulletin* 20:63–74.

Fukushima, J., Morita, N., Fukusima, K., Chiba, T., Tanaka, S., and Yamashita, I. (1990). Voluntary control of saccadic eye movements in patients with schizophrenia and affective disorders. *Journal of Psychiatric Research* 41:9–24.

Goldman-Rakic, P. S. (1987). Circuitry of primate prefrontal cortex and regulation of behavior by representational memory. In F. Plum and V. B. Mountcastle (Eds.), *Handbook of physiology: The nervous system,* Vol. 5 (pp. 373–417). Bethesda, MD: American Physiological Society.

Gottesman, I. I., and Shields, J. (1967). A polygenic theory of schizophrenia. *Proceedings of the National Academy of Sciences, USA* 58:199–205.

Griffith, J. M., O'Neill, J. E., Petty, F., Garver, D., Young, D., and Freedman, R. (1998). Nicotinic receptor desensitization and sensory gating deficits in schizophrenia. *Biological Psychiatry* 44:98–106.

Grove, W. M., Clementz, B. A., Iacono, W. G., and Katsanis, J. (1992). Smooth pursuit ocular motor dysfunction in schizophrenia: Evidence for a major gene. *American Journal of Psychiatry* 149:1362–68.

Guitton, D., Buchtel, H. A., and Douglas, R. M. (1985). Frontal lobe lesions in man cause difficulties in suppressing reflexive glances and in generating goal-directed saccades. *Experimental Brain Research* 58:455–72.

Heinlein, S., and Ross, R. G. (2001). The delayed-oculomotor response task in children at risk for schizophrenia. *Biological Psychiatry* 49:56S.

Holzman, P. S. (1987). Recent studies of psychophysiology in schizophrenia. *Schizophrenia Bulletin* 13:49–75.

Holzman, P. S., Kringlen, E., Levy, D. L., and Haberman, S. J. (1980). Deviant eye tracking in twins discordant for schizophrenia. *Archives of General Psychiatry* 37:627–31.

Holzman, P. S., Kringlen, E., Matthysse, S., Flanagan, S. D., Lipton, R. B., Cramer, G., et al. (1988). A single dominant gene can account for eye tracking dysfunction and schizophrenia in offspring of discordant twins. *Archives of General Psychiatry* 45:641–47.

Holzman, P. S., Proctor, L. R., and Hughes, D. W. (1973). Eye tracking patterns in schizophrenia. *Science* 181:179–81.

Iacono, W. G., Moreau, M., Beiser, M., Fleming, J.A.E., and Lin, T. Y. (1992). Smooth-pursuit eye tracking in first-episode psychotic patients and their relatives. *Journal of Abnormal Psychology* 101:104–16.

Javitt, D. C., Doneshka, P., Grochowski, S., and Ritter, W. (1995). Impaired mismatch negativity generation reflects widespread dysfunction in working memory in schizophrenia. *Archives of General Psychiatry* 52:550–58.

Jerger, K., Biggins, C., and Fein, G. (1992). P50 suppression is not affected by attentional manipulations. *Biological Psychiatry* 31:365–77.

Jessen, F., Kucharski, C., Fries, T., Papassotiropoulos, A., Hoenig, K., Maier, W., et al.

(2001). Sensory gating deficit expressed by a disturbed suppression of the P50 event-related potential in patients with Alzheimer's disease. *American Journal of Psychiatry* 158:1319–21.

Judd, L. L., McAdams, L., Budnick, B., and Braff, D. L. (1992). Sensory gating deficits in schizophrenia: New results. *American Journal of Psychiatry* 149:488–93.

Keefe, R.S.E., Silverman, J. M., Mohs, R. C., Siever, L. J., Harvey, P. D., Friedman, L., et al. (1997). Eye tracking, attention, and schizotypal symptoms in nonpsychotic relatives of patients with schizophrenia. *Archives of General Psychiatry* 54:169–76.

Lalouel, J. M., Le Mignon, L., Simon, M., Fauchet, R., Bourel, M., Rao, D. C., et al. (1985). Genetic analysis of idiopathic hemochromatosis using both qualitative (disease status) and quantitative (serum iron) information. *American Journal of Medical Genetics: Neuropsychiatric Genetics* 37:700–718.

Law, I., Svarer, C., Holm, S., and Paulson, O. B. (1997). The activation pattern in normal humans during suppression, imagination and performance of saccadic eye movements. *Acta Physiologica Scandinavica* 161:419–34.

Lencer, R., Malchow, C. P., Trillenberg-Krecker, K., Schwinger, E., and Arolt, V. (2000). Eye tracking dysfunction (ETD) in families with sporadic and familial schizophrenia. *Biological Psychiatry* 47:391–401.

Leonard, S., Breese, C., Adams, C., Benhammou, K., Gault, J., Stevens, K., et al. (2000). Smoking and schizophrenia: abnormal nicotinic receptor expression. *European Journal of Pharmacology* 393:237–42.

Leonard, S., Gault, J., Hopkins, J., Logel, J., Ross, R., Olincy, A., et al. (2001). Mapping and mutation screening of the α7 nicotinic receptor gene cluster on chromosome 15 that is linked to schizophrenia and bipolar disorder. *Schizophrenia Research* 49:54.

Levy, D. L., Holzman, P. S., Matthysse, S., and Mendell, N. R. (1993). Eye dysfunction and schizophrenia: A critical review. *Schizophrenia Research* 19:461–536.

Levy, D. L., Holzman, P. S., Matthysse, S., and Mendell, N. R. (1994). Eye tracking and schizophrenia: A selective review. *Schizophrenia Bulletin* 20:47–62.

Levy, R., and Goldman-Rakic, P. S. (2000). Segregation of working memory functions within the dorsolateral prefrontal cortex. *Experimental Brain Research* 133:23–32.

Litman, R., Hommer, D. W., Radant, A. D., Clem, T., and Pickar, D. (1994). Quantitative effects of typical and atypical neuroleptics on smooth pursuit eye tracking in schizophrenia. *Schizophrenia Research* 12:107–20.

Luntz-Leybman, V., Bickford, P. C., and Freedman, R. (1992). Cholinergic gating of response to auditory stimuli in rat hippocampus. *Brain Research* 587:130–36.

McDowell, J. E., Brown, G. G., Paulus, M., Martinez, A., Stewart, S. E., Dubowitz, D. J., et al. (2002). Neural correlates of refixation saccades and antisaccades in normal and schizophrenia subjects. *Biological Psychiatry* 51:216–23.

McDowell, J. E., Myles-Worsley, M., Coon, H., Byerly, W., and Clementz, B. A. (1999). Measuring liability for schizophrenia using optimized antisaccade stimulus. *Psychophysiology* 36:138–41.

McGhie, A., and Chapman, J. (1961). Disorders of attention and perception in early schizophrenia. *British Journal of Medical Psychology* 34:103–16.

Myles-Worsley, M., Coon, H., Byerley, W., Waldo, M., Young, D. A, and Freedman, R. (1996). Developmental and genetic influences on the P50 sensory gating phenotype. *Biological Psychiatry* 39:289–95.

Nagamoto, H. T., Adler, L. E., Hea, R. A., Griffith, J. M., McRae, K. A., and Freedman, R.

(1996). Gating of auditory P50 in schizophrenics: Unique effects of clozapine. *Biological Psychiatry* 40:181–88.

Nakashima, Y., Momose, T., Sano, I., Katayama, S., Nakajima, T., Niwa, S., et al. (1994). Cortical control of saccade in normal and schizophrenic subjects: A PET study using a task-evoked rCBF paradigm. *Schizophrenia Research* 12:259–64.

Neylan, T. C., Fletcher, D. J., Lenoci, M., McCallin, K., Weiss, D. S., Schoenfeld, F. B., et al. (1999). Sensory gating in chronic posttraumatic stress disorder: Reduced auditory P50 suppression in combat veterans. *Biological Psychiatry* 46:1656–64.

O'Driscoll, G. A., Alpert, N. M., Matthysse, S. W., Levy, D. L., Rauch, S. L., and Holzman, P. S. (1995). Functional neuroanatomy of antisaccade eye movements investigated with positron emission tomography. *Proceedings of the National Academy of Sciences, USA* 92:925–29.

O'Driscoll, G. A., Benkelfat, C., Florencio, P. S., Wolff, A.V.G., Joober, R., Lal, S., et al. (1999). Neural correlates of eye tracking deficits in first-degree relatives of schizophrenic patients: A positron emission tomography study. *Archives of General Psychiatry* 56:1127–34.

Olincy, A., Giordano, L., Ross, R. G., and Freedman, R. (2002). Diagnostic specificity of a smooth pursuit eye movement task. Paper presented at the annual meeting of the American College of Neuropsychopharmacology, San Diego, December.

Olincy, A., and Ross, R. G. (2003). Differential effects of cigarette smoking on performance of a smooth pursuit and a saccadic eye movement task in schizophrenia. *Psychiatry Research* 117:223–36.

Olincy, A., Ross, R. G., Harris, J. G., Young, D. A., McAndrews, M. A., Cawthra, E., et al. (2000). The P50 auditory event-evoked potential in adult attention-deficit disorder: Comparison with schizophrenia. *Biological Psychiatry* 47:969–77.

Olincy, A., Ross, R. G., Young, D. A., Roath, M., and Freedman, R. (1998). Improvement in smooth pursuit eye movements after cigarette smoking in schizophrenic patients. *Neuropsychopharmacology* 18:175–85.

Patrick, G., and Struve, F. A. (2000). Reduction of auditory P50 gating response in marihuana users: Further supporting data. *Clinical Electroencephalography* 31:88–93.

Petit, L., Clark, V. P., Ingeholm, J., and Haxby, J. V. (1997). Dissociation of saccade-related and pursuit-related activation in human frontal eye fields as revealed by fMRI. *Journal of Neurophysiology* 77:3386–90.

Raemaekers, M., Jansma, J. M., Cahn, W., van der Geest, J. N., van der Linden, J. A., Kahn, R. S., et al. (2002). Neuronal substrate of the saccadic inhibition deficit in schizophrenia investigated with three-dimensional event-related functional magnetic resonance imaging. *Archives of General Psychiatry* 59:313–20.

Ross, D. E., Thaker, G. K., Holcomb, H. H., Cascella, N. G., Medoff, D. R., and Tamminga, C. A. (1995). Abnormal smooth pursuit eye movements in schizophrenic patients are associated with cerebral glucose metabolism in oculomotor regions. *Psychiatry Research* 58:53–67.

Ross, R. G., and Compagnon, N. (2001). Diagnosis and treatment of psychiatric disorders in children with a schizophrenic parent. *Schizophrenia Research* 50:123–31.

Ross, R. G., Harris, J. G., Olincy, A., and Radant, A. (2000). Eye movement task measures inhibition and spatial working memory in adults with schizophrenia, ADHD, and a normal comparison group. *Psychiatry Research* 95:35–42.

Ross, R. G., Harris, J. G., Olincy, A., Radant, A. D., Adler, L. E., and Freedman, R. (1998).

Familial transmission of two independent saccadic abnormalities in schizophrenia. *Schizophrenia Research* 30:59–70.

Ross, R. G., Hommer, D. W., Radant, A. D., Roath, M., and Freedman, R. (1996). Early expression of smooth pursuit eye movement abnormalities in children of schizophrenic parents. *Journal of the American Academy of Child and Adolescent Psychiatry* 35:941–49.

Ross, R. G., Olincy, A., Harris, J. G., Radant, A., Adler, L. E., Compagnon, N., et al. (1999). The effects of age on a smooth pursuit tracking task in adults with schizophrenia and normals. *Biological Psychiatry* 46:383–91.

Ross, R. G., Olincy, A., Harris, J. G., Radant, A. D., Adler, L. E., and Freedman, R. (1998). Anticipatory saccades during smooth pursuit eye movements and familial transmission of schizophrenia. *Biological Psychiatry* 8:690–97.

Ross, R. G., Olincy, A., Harris, J. G., Radant, A. D., Hawkins, M., Adler, L. E., et al. (1999). Evidence for bilineal inheritance of physiological indicators of risk in childhood-onset schizophrenia. *American Journal of Medical Genetics: Neuropsychiatric Genetics* 88:188–99.

Ross, R. G., Olincy, A., Harris, J. G., Sullivan, B., and Radant, A. (2000). Smooth pursuit eye movements in schizophrenia and attentional dysfunction: Adults with schizophrenia, ADHD, and a normal comparison group. *Biological Psychiatry* 48:197–203.

Ross, R. G., Olincy, A., Mikulich, S. K., Radant, A. D., Harris, J. G., Waldo, M., et al. (2002). Admixture analysis of smooth pursuit eye movements in probands with schizophrenia and their relatives suggests gain and leading saccades are potential endophenotypes. *Psychophysiology* 39:809–19.

Ross, R. G., Radant, A. D., and Hommer, D. W. (1993). A developmental study of smooth pursuit eye movements in normal children from 7 to 15 years of age. *Journal of the American Academy of Child and Adolescent Psychiatry* 32:783–91.

Schaeffer, J., and Ross, R. G. (2002). Childhood-onset schizophrenia: Premorbid and prodromal diagnosis and treatment histories. *Journal of the American Academy of Child and Adolescent Psychiatry* 41:538–45.

Siegel, C., Waldo, M., Mizner, G., Adler, L. E., and Freedman, R. (1984). Deficits in sensory gating in schizophrenic patients and their relatives: Evidence obtained with auditory evoked responses. *Archives of General Psychiatry* 41:607–12.

Skinner, R. D., Rasco, L. M., Fitzgerald, J., Karson, C. N., Matthew, M., Williams, D. K., et al. (1999). Reduced sensory gating of the P1 potential in rape victims and combat veterans with posttraumatic stress disorder. *Depression and Anxiety* 9:122–30.

Stevens, K. E., Freedman, R., Collins, A. C., Hall, M., Leonard, S., Marks, M. J., et al. (1996). Genetic correlation of inhibitory gating of hippocampal auditory evoked response and alpha-bungarotoxin-binding nicotinic cholinergic receptors in inbred mouse strains. *Neuropsychopharmacology* 15:152–62.

Stevens, K. E., and Wear, K. D. (1997). Normalizing effects of nicotine and a novel nicotinic agonist on hippocampal auditory gating in two animal models. *Pharmacology, Biochemistry and Behavior* 57:869–74.

Sweeney, J. A., Mintun, M. A., Kwee, S., Wiseman, M. B., Brown, D. L., Rosenberg, D. R., et al. (1996). Positron emission tomography study of voluntary saccadic eye movements and spatial working memory. *Journal of Neurophysiology* 75:454–68.

Teo, C., Rasco, L., al-Mefty, K., Skinner, R. D., Boop, F. A., and Garcia-Rill, E. (1997). Decreased habituation of midlatency auditory evoked responses in Parkinson's disease. *Movement Disorders* 12:655–64.

Thompson, P. M., Vidal, C., Giedd, J. N., Gochman, P., Blumental, J., Nicolson, R., et al. (2001). Mapping adolescent brain change reveals dynamic wave of accelerated gray matter loss in very early-onset schizophrenia. *Proceedings of the National Academy of Sciences, USA* 98:11650–55.

Venables, P. (1964). Input dysfunction in schizophrenia. *Progress in Experimental Personality Research* 1:1–47.

Waldo, M. C., Cawthra, E., Adler, L. E., Dubester, S., Staunton, M., Nagamoto, H., et al. (1994). Auditory sensory gating, hippocampal volume, and catecholamine metabolism in schizophrenics and their siblings. *Schizophrenia Research* 12:93–106.

CHAPTER EIGHT

Development during Childhood and Adolescence

The Manifestations of Impending Schizophrenia

Elaine F. Walker, Ph.D., Lisa P. Kestler, M.A.,
Karen M. Hochman, M.D., and
Annie M. Bollini, M.A.

Although the syndrome labeled schizophrenia is typically an adult-onset disorder, decades of research have demonstrated that nonclinical signs of dysfunction characterize children and adolescents who eventually succumb to the illness. These premorbid manifestations have influenced the way researchers conceptualize the development of schizophrenia, and they also have the potential to inform us about underlying neuropathological processes.

It is clear that the temporal course of schizophrenia, including the premorbid period, is not random (Walker 1994). Examination of the research findings reveals a clear modal pattern. Subtle signs of developmental delay are already present during the early childhood years. Middle childhood is often associated with academic and social difficulties, although these are usually not severe enough to warrant intervention. In adolescence, adjustment problems set in that escalate in number and increase in severity with the passage of time. In late adolescence subclinical perceptual and ideational abnormalities typically appear that signal the impending psychotic symptomatology in early adulthood.

This temporal pattern, in combination with other research findings, suggests that there are at least two critical periods in the development of schizophrenia. One is the fetal period. Evidence has accumulated from diverse sources to suggest that prenatal neurodevelopmental abnormalities confer a susceptibility to schizophrenia that may be subtly apparent at birth (Walker and Diforio 1997). But, unlike many congenital central nervous system vulnerabilities, the vulnerability to schizophrenia is not expressed as a clinical disorder until later in life. Adolescence is the critical period for the emergence of preclinical signs of dysfunction. Thus, it is not until postpubertal development commences that there is a marked exacerbation of behavioral dysfunction, culminating in the onset of illness.

In this chapter, we will review some of the research findings that have helped to elucidate the premorbid and prodromal developmental course. Although we will address early and middle childhood, we will primarily be concerned with the adolescent and young adult periods, the potential etiological significance of which has become increasingly apparent. The past five years have in fact seen a burgeoning of scientific and public interest in adolescent development (McGlashan and Hoffman 2000; Spear 2000; Walker 2002). This fascination stems, in part, from striking new research findings on human brain development. Although scientists have long acknowledged the significant psychological and bodily changes that accompany pubertal maturation, until recently there was little evidence to suggest structural changes in the brain. The application of neuroimaging techniques to research on normal brain development, however, has changed the perspective of both scientists and the general public (Walker 2002). Plasticity appears to be a feature of the brain that, while extending across the life span, seems to be accelerated in young adulthood.

Increasingly, researchers in the field of schizophrenia are speculating on the adolescent neurodevelopmental processes that might be involved in the unfolding of the schizophrenic syndrome. A variety of postpubertal neurodevelopmental events could be implicated in the cognitive aberrations associated with psychosis. Following our review of the premorbid and prodromal aspects of schizophrenia, we will turn to a brief discussion of potential neural mechanisms. The central question to be addressed in this regard is, how might neurodevelopmental processes occurring during this critical period trigger the expression of the diathesis for schizophrenia?

The Development of Children at Genetic Risk for Schizophrenia

Behavioral genetic research has demonstrated that inherited liabilities are involved in at least some cases of schizophrenia. The rate of schizophrenia in individuals who have a first-degree relative affected by the illness is around 10 to 15 percent (Gottesman 1991). Given these findings, investigators have focused on the unaffected biological relatives of patients in order to identify indicators of risk. The prospective genetic high-risk (HR) paradigm was designed to pinpoint the phenotypic indicators that occur more frequently in HR groups and ultimately to provide a better understanding of the origins of the illness. The research design involves prospective longitudinal study, sometimes beginning at birth, of the offspring of schizophrenic patients (OSPs) throughout the age period of maximal risk for the development of schizophrenia. These studies have focused on two comparisons: OSPs versus children of normal parents or those with other psychiatric disorders, and OSPs who develop schizophrenia versus OSPs with nonschizophrenic outcomes. Of course, the latter comparison can be made only when subjects have been followed into the peak risk period for the onset of illness, namely, early adulthood.

At least a dozen prospective HR studies have followed OSPs from infancy, childhood, or adolescence, and five of these studies have followed samples wholly or partially through the period of greatest risk for the onset of schizophrenia (20 to 30 years of age). Virtually all these projects have examined adjustment, social behavior, and cognitive functions during childhood and adolescence, and several have also looked at neuromotor functions. Early HR projects focused on comparisons of OSPs with children whose biological parents did not suffer from mental illness. Reports from these studies provided some leads in the search for risk markers. However, because most OSPs—at least 80 percent—will not ultimately fall ill with schizophrenia, it cannot be inferred that the factors differentiating them from the children of healthy parents are indicators of risk for schizophrenia. Thus researchers have awaited the opportunity to conduct comparisons of those who eventually develop schizophrenia and those who do not.

Neurobehavioral Signs

Diathesis-stress models of schizophrenia assume that vulnerability is congenital, and some researchers have proposed that the earliest signs of the illness are subtle neuromotor abnormalities and sensorimotor dysfunction. In a seminal article, Fish (1977) described a syndrome she observed in OSPs called "pandysmaturation," which involved deficits and delays in motor development and sensorimotor integration and which she proposed was a manifestation of the "inherited neurointegrative defect in schizophrenia" (p. 1297). Subsequent research findings have provided general support for this theory. A recent review article by Erlenmeyer-Kimling (2000) noted that neurological and neuromotor deficits appear fairly consistently in OSPs. Neurobehavioral deficits have also been found to be stable from infancy to childhood (Marcus et al. 1993) and from childhood through adolescence (Dworkin et al. 1993).

Additional studies have also shown that neurobehavioral abnormalities can be indicative of later psychopathology. Fish (1987) found that pandysmaturation in infancy predicted the severity of psychopathology at 10 years of age and schizophrenia spectrum disorders at 22 years. Similarly, in the Israeli High-Risk Study, neurobehavioral signs, such as hyperkinesis, motor dyscoordination, and perceptual signs, assessed in late childhood (mean age 11.4 years) were associated with subsequent schizophrenia spectrum disorders (Marcus et al. 1987). Of course, the presence of neuromotor deficits in only a subgroup of individuals who later develop schizophrenia could yield a significant group difference. In a recent study, investigators from the New York High-Risk Project sought to determine the prevalence of neuromotor signs in preschizophrenic children (Erlenmeyer-Kimling et al. 2000). They discovered that neuromotor signs are observable in a high proportion of preschizophrenic OSPs: 75 percent of those who developed schizophrenia-like psychoses as adults were identified by childhood neuromotor dysfunction.

For some preschizophrenic children neuromotor dysfunction extends into adolescence. In the Israeli High-Risk Study, a comparison of adolescent OSPs without psychiatric disorders to those with spectrum disorders revealed that neuromotor performance was more impaired in the spectrum group (Hans et al. 1999). Similarly, among OSPs in the Danish High-Risk Project, those who developed adult-onset schizophrenia showed greater deficits in motor coordination during early adolescence than those who developed affective disorders or who had normal outcomes (Olin and Mednick 1996). Because of the lack of standardized procedures for assessing motor and sensorimotor functions across age levels, however, we do not know whether the nature of these impairments changes as HR children develop.

Cognitive Deficits

In addition to neurobehavioral indices, several prospective studies of OSPs have identified specific cognitive measures, such as attention, memory, and general IQ, as liability indicators. A comprehensive review of the findings on attention, memory, and other cognitive functions in OSPs was recently published by Erlenmeyer-Kimling (2000). She concluded that, according to most HR studies, cognitive deficits not only differentiate OSPs from comparison subjects but can also predict spectrum disorders or schizophrenia-related psychoses in adolescence and adulthood. For example, in the New York High-Risk Project, a summary measure of several attention tasks administered in mid-childhood predicted 58 percent of the OSPs who developed adult-onset schizophrenia, and verbal memory scores predicted 83 percent (Erlenmeyer-Kimling et al. 2000). Other investigators have also found that HR children who do poorly on attention tests are more likely to develop schizophrenia in early adulthood (Mirsky, Ingraham, and Kugelmass 1995).

Given the findings on attentional functions, it is not surprising that measures of general intelligence are also linked to an increased risk for a later onset of schizophrenia in OSPs. For example, the Israeli High-Risk Study showed that OSPs who later succumbed to schizophrenia had lower childhood IQ scores than those who developed affective disorders or else remained healthy (Mirsky et al. 1995). Findings from the New York High-Risk Project also suggest that low IQ may be especially characteristic of the risk for schizophrenia, given that those who developed major affective disorder in adulthood did not show IQ deficits in childhood (Ott et al. 1998).

Adjustment Problems and Social Behavior

Poor social adjustment is, of course, a salient feature of schizophrenia and is associated with poor clinical outcome in patients (Bailer, Braeuer, and Rey 1996). Several studies have shown that OSPs tend to experience relatively more serious social adjustment problems in childhood and adolescence. But the differences between OSPs and control children are less pronounced during early childhood. Indeed, some of the HR studies of the social behavior of OSPs in early childhood were unable to find evidence of abnormalities. For example, an HR study undertaken in Sweden did not uncover significant impairments in personal-social competence among 6-year-old children with a psychotic parent (McNeil et al. 1993).

In contrast, among older children, particularly adolescents, researchers have found significant differences between OSPs and comparison groups. For example, the Edinburgh High-Risk Project showed that OSPs manifested a greater tendency toward social isolation that could be detected in childhood and was exacerbated in adolescence (Hodges et al. 1999). In addition, this study pointed to a heightened sensitivity to interpersonal stimuli in the adolescent OSPs. In the St. Louis High-Risk Project, OSPs and control groups did not differ in their behavior during elementary school or their social competence during high school, but OSPs demonstrated a lesser degree of emotional stability and scholastic motivation in later childhood and adolescence (Worland et al. 1984).

When OSPs are compared to groups of children whose parents suffer from nonschizophrenic mental disorders, the OSPs typically appear to be characterized by greater social deficits. The New York High-Risk Project revealed that social dysfunction was more pronounced in OSPs than in the offspring of parents with other mental disorders (Watt, Grubb, and Erlenmeyer-Kimling 1982; Ott et al. 1998). Adolescent OSPs also exhibited higher levels of aggression and lower levels of social comprehension when compared to the offspring of parents who either had affective disorders or had no psychiatric illness at all. Similarly, in the Israeli High-Risk Study, a higher degree of social withdrawal (poor peer engagement) and more pervasive social problems (immaturity and unpopularity with peers) were observed among adolescent OSPs in comparison to the offspring of parents with either nonschizophrenic mental disorders or no psychiatric disorder (Hans et al. 1992, 2000). In contrast, findings from the Stony Brook High-Risk Project did not reveal a difference between OSPs and a comparison group of children whose parents suffered from nonschizophrenic disorders. Teachers rated both groups of at-risk children as more aggressive and/or disruptive and less socially competent than the children of healthy parents (Weintraub and Neale 1984).

In sum, several studies have found evidence of social maladjustment and behavioral problems in OSPs as compared to the offspring both of normal parents and of parents with other psychiatric illnesses. Nonetheless, as Weintraub and Neale (1984) pointed out, OSPs are *not* grossly deviant in middle childhood, and the behavioral differences between them and comparison children are usually subtle. Deficits in social adjustment typically become more pronounced with age and are most apparent during adolescence. Of course, as noted above, the majority of the offspring of parents with schizophrenia will not develop the disorder. Thus, the social adjustment problems observed in OSPs are not necessarily precursors of illness but may instead be a consequence of exposure to a parent with mental illness. For efforts to identify markers of vulnerability, the optimal comparison is that between those OSPs who ultimately develop schizophrenia and those who do not. The results of these comparisons clearly indicate that signs of vulnerability to the illness are at least subtly visible in early childhood but become more openly evident with increased age.

In her study of HR infants, Fish (1987) found that OSPs who later developed schizophrenia spectrum disorders exhibited greater social-affective impairment between 3 and 6 years of age. Similarly, OSPs in the Israeli High-Risk Study who later manifested schizophrenia spectrum disorders could be identified on the basis of problematic social behavior or personality traits in early and middle childhood (Mirsky et al. 1995). The Israeli study also showed that, compared with those who later developed affective disorders or who never became ill, OSPs destined for schizophrenia spectrum disorders tended to be antisocial, withdrawn, suspicious, and unpopular with peers and suffered from low self-esteem and poor communication skills.

There is reason to believe that multivariate indices of adolescent behavior may prove useful in identifying individuals at risk. The Danish High-Risk Project revealed that a multivariate index based on problems of social adjustment in adolescence (mean age 15 years) as rated by teachers was highly predictive of the ultimate diagnostic outcome in OSPs (Olin, John, and Mednick 1995; Tyrka et al. 1995; Olin and Mednick 1996). This index was able to differentiate those who eventually succumbed to schizophrenia from those who did not with a high level of sensitivity and specificity.

Conclusion

The main objective of prospective HR studies has been to identify factors that distinguish OSPs who develop schizophrenia or other psychiatric illnesses from those who remain unaffected. Taken together, the results of these investigations have provided us with valuable insights into the behavioral precursors of schizophrenia. Deviations in neuromotor functioning, cognition, and socioemotional behavior have all been shown to distinguish those who go on to develop a schizophrenia spectrum disorder from those with healthy outcomes.

However, as mentioned above, the vast majority of those diagnosed with schizophrenia do not have a first-degree relative with the illness. The subjects of high-risk research thus constitute a select and nonrepresentative sample of patients with schizophrenia. OSPs may represent a category of patients with a more virulent genetic diathesis. Further, OSPs have, as a group, been brought up in an environment that is at best nonoptimal and in many cases highly stressful. The potential relevance of family environment is highlighted by findings that the risk for psychopathology in the biological offspring of schizophrenic parents who have been adopted into other families is significantly increased when they are reared in stressful family environments (Tienari et al. 1985; Wahlberg et al. 1997). High-risk studies may therefore be best able to document the most extreme premorbid developmental course associated with schizophrenia, one in which both the genetic liability and the level of environmental stress are high.

This raises the question of whether other research methods might reveal a similar developmental course. Rather than following OSPs prospectively, a number of studies have begun with the identification of adult schizophrenia patients and then traced their developmental trajectories back in time. Such studies have the advantage that their samples are more representative of the general population of schizophrenia patients.

Follow-Back Studies of Preschizophrenic Children

The findings from follow-back studies exhibit striking parallels with those from HR research. First, like HR studies, research on non-HR samples of patients with schizophrenia has disclosed premorbid impairment in multiple domains of functioning—motor, cognitive, and socioemotional. Second, follow-back studies have also revealed an age-related increase in functional deficits that is characterized by a marked rise in early adolescence.

Neuromotor Functions

Researchers in Finland followed up a 1996 birth cohort of more than 120,000 individuals who had undergone repeated psychiatric assessments in childhood (Isohanni et al. 2000). Of these, 100 were diagnosed with schizophrenia by the age of 31. Those who developed schizophrenia as young adults were more likely to have manifested delays in the acquisition of motor skills during infancy. Along these same lines, our studies of home movies made when adult-onset schizophrenia patients were children have revealed significant delays and abnormalities in motor functions during the first two years of life (Walker, Savoie, and Davis 1994). Compared to their healthy siblings, the preschizophrenic children manifested a greater degree of postural and movement abnormalities, as well as asymmetries in motor development. Thus, signs of neuromotor impairment are not unique to HR subjects who later become ill but rather are apparent in the general population of patients with schizophrenia.

Adjustment and Socioemotional Functions

A systematic examination of teachers' comments in the elementary and high school records of adult-onset schizophrenia patients was undertaken by Watt and colleagues in the 1970s (Watt and Saiz 1991). When compared to classroom and sibling controls, the preschizophrenic children showed greater deficits in social behavior and were temperamentally more difficult. Again, this divergence from controls became more pronounced in the postpubescent period.

In a novel study using data from the Israeli draft board, Davidson and colleagues (1999) also found that adolescent characteristics were highly predictive of subsequent onset of schizophrenia. Healthy adolescent recruits who were later hospitalized for schizophrenia had poorer social functioning and organizational ability than those whose names were not listed in the psychiatric registry. By considering these premorbid adolescent traits in tandem with scores from cognitive tests, the research team was able to achieve a high level of statistical power for predicting psychiatric outcomes. There is also evidence that more dramatic premorbid declines during adolescence are linked to a greater incidence of negative symptomatology in adult patients. Using retrospective reports from informants, Kelley and colleagues (1992) found that patients with negative symptoms had shown significantly lower levels of premorbid functioning, both social and intellectual, during late adolescence and significantly greater deterioration between childhood and early adolescence. The authors viewed the premorbid deterioration as an "early" prodrome of the disorder.

In previous research on the precursors of schizophrenia, we asked parents of adult-onset patients to provide retrospective reports on the behavior of all their offspring (Neumann et al. 1995). We used a standardized scale, the Achenbach Child Behavior Checklist (CBCL), that contains over a hundred questions concerning a child's behavior and skills. Ratings were obtained for four age periods, extending from infancy to adolescence. Differences among diagnostic groups were observed with regard to most of the factors covered by the scale, including social problems, depression, attentional problems, and thought problems. The group that later developed schizophrenia showed more behavioral problems; the problems increased with age and were most dramatic after 12 years of age. For this same sample of patients with adult-onset schizophrenia, we also used home movies as a source of data on premorbid functioning (Walker et al. 1993). When compared to their healthy siblings depicted in the same films, the preschizophrenic children typically exhibited more frequent negative emotion and a lower rate of positive facial emotion, a diagnostic difference that was apparent in infancy and extended throughout adolescence. The roots of the social-behavior deficits observed in the premorbid course may thus originate in emotional abnormalities that are present at birth.

In subsequent investigations, we have sought to determine whether youth with an Axis II spectrum disorder—namely, schizotypal personality disorder—revealed a developmental trajectory of adjustment problems that resembled that of schizophrenia patients (Walker, Baum, and Diforio 1998). Using the same version of the CBCL we had employed in studies of adult-onset schizophrenia patients, we compared the schizotypal subjects to groups of adolescents with other personality disorders (OPDs) or normal control (NC). In comparison to the other groups, the adolescents with schizotypal personality disorder showed elevated scores on most of the behavioral problem scales. Further, as with the preschizophrenic subjects, these behavior problems became more pronounced with age and, in particular, underwent a dramatic rise in adolescence.

How parents rated their children on the items from the social problems scale of the CBCL for each of four age periods are illustrated in Figure 8.1. As can be seen from the figure, according to parent ratings, the social problems exhibited by children with schizotypal personality disorders (SPD) gradually rose during childhood and then sharply increased after the child entered the adolescent period (12 to 16 years of age). In contrast, the OPD and NC groups appear to experience fewer social problems than the SPD group throughout childhood, and no significant change takes place with their entry into adolescence.

As Figure 8.2 shows, attention problems follow a similar pattern. These findings are consistent with reports of attention deficits from both the HR and follow-back studies of schizophrenia.

Figure 8.3 contains the scores for the thought problems scale of the CBCL. Here we see a somewhat different pattern, with a greater resemblance among the three groups during childhood followed by a steep rise for the SPD group

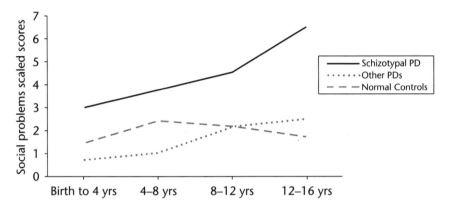

Fig. 8.1. Scores on the social problem scale of the Achenbach Child Behavior Checklist by age and diagnostic group (SPD = schizotypal personality disorder, OPD = other personality disorder, NC = normal control)

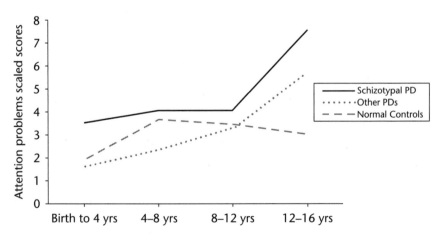

Fig. 8.2. Scores on the attention problem scale of the Achenbach Child Behavior Checklist by age and diagnostic group (SPD = schizotypal personality disorder, OPD = other personality disorder, NC = normal control)

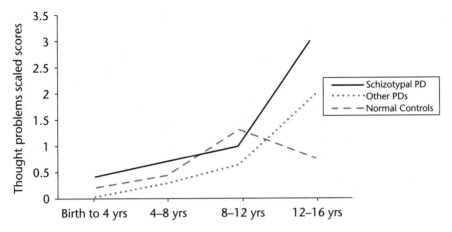

Fig. 8.3. Scores on the thought problem scale of the Achenbach Child Behavior Checklist by age and diagnostic group (SPD = schizotypal personality disorder, OPD = other personality disorder, NC = normal control)

in adolescence. This is, in fact, precisely the pattern we observed when the parents of patients diagnosed with schizophrenia completed the CBCL. Thus, in accordance with both clinical assumptions and empirical findings, abnormalities of thought are usually not detected until adolescence.

Cognitive Functions

In 1984, on the basis of a comprehensive review and meta-analysis of the research to date, Aylward and colleagues drew two general conclusions regarding IQ in preschizophrenic children (Aylward, Walker, and Bettes 1984). First, preschizophrenic children perform more poorly on standardized intelligence tests in comparison to their siblings and to control children drawn from the same classroom. Second, siblings of preschizophrenic children showed lower IQ scores when compared to school controls, which suggests that moderate intellectual deficits may be present in family members of schizophrenic individuals. Indeed, studies published since this review confirm that intellectual deficits are a precursor of schizophrenia. For example, using a birth cohort data set, T. Cannon and colleagues (2000) compared the IQ scores of preschizophrenic children to those of their unaffected siblings and normal controls, first at the age of 4 and again at age 7, and found that the preschizophrenic children had lower IQ scores than their siblings and the controls. The authors also reported that the odds of a schizophrenia diagnosis in adulthood increased by

1.5 for each unit decrease in IQ score. It is noteworthy that preschizophrenic children were significantly overrepresented in the lowest quartile of IQ scores, where the chances of an adult diagnosis were 5.3 times greater.

Similarly, research using a British birth cohort revealed that at the ages of 8, 11, and 15, preschizophrenic children, including those with preschizoaffective disorders, had lower mean scores on a variety of educational tests—verbal, nonverbal, and arithmetic—in comparison to those who remained healthy (Jones et al. 1994). Paralleling the findings of T. Cannon et al. (2000), preschizophrenic children were overrepresented in the lowest IQ tertile and were progressively underrepresented in higher IQ groups. Further, the relation between low IQ and a later onset of schizophrenia became more striking still as the child grew older.

David and colleagues (1997) conducted a study of 18-year-old military inductees and, like other researchers, found that the odds of eventually developing schizophrenia were higher for individuals in the lower IQ range. The authors reported that while general intellectual deficits may predict a subsequent diagnosis of schizophrenia, deficits in particular areas, such as verbal and mechanical knowledge, may confer an additional risk for the illness.

In contrast to these reports, a study based on a Finnish birth cohort by M. Cannon and colleagues (1999) did not yield evidence of deficits in school grades, obtained at ages 7 and 11, among preschizophrenic children. However, the preschizophrenic group, which included children with schizoaffective and schizophreniform disorders, was only half as likely as controls to attend school after the fourth grade. This suggests that measurable academic performance deficits did not develop in the preschizophrenic children until after they reached the age of 11.

Summary: Childhood and Adolescent Precursors of Schizophrenia

There is now ample evidence that significant differences exist between preschizophrenic children and those who remain healthy. The deficits manifested by preschizophrenic children extend across functional domains. In the area of social adjustment, these deficits increase sharply during adolescence. In addition, some findings indicate that the strength of the relation between premorbid intellectual functioning and the risk for schizophrenia increases with age, which argues that the test scores of older children are more reliable predictors of psychiatric outcome.

Because the onset of schizophrenia before late adolescence is uncommon, there have been very few studies of premorbid development in patients with childhood-onset schizophrenia. The limited data available indicate that a childhood onset of the illness is more closely associated with impaired premorbid functioning than is adult-onset schizophrenia. Although, as in adult-onset cases, interpersonal deficits tend to predominate during the premorbid period (Eggers, Bunk, and Krause 2000), some of the premorbid deficits in childhood-onset schizophrenia may be qualitatively different from those observed in adult-onset patients. Eggers et al. found that the majority of those who developed schizophrenia during childhood manifested premorbid developmental abnormalities in cognition and language that standard approaches to the measurement of premorbid functioning were not designed to assess.

The Psychotic Prodrome in Adolescence and Early Adulthood

Over the past decade, interest in the prodromal period has burgeoned. The psychotic prodrome is defined as the phase immediately preceding the onset of illness, during which the first nonspecific indicators of the active psychosis become evident. The standard criteria for defining the prodrome, which are listed in Table 8.1, include both positive and negative signs, although research findings indicate that the negative signs usually precede the positive (Edwards et al. 1999).

The duration and course of prodromal signs varies among patients. For most, the prodrome continues until the psychotic syndrome erupts (Häfner and Heiden 1997), but in some cases the first prodromal phase gradually decreases in intensity and is not the prelude to an onset of schizophrenia. In these cases, the prodromal syndrome is described as an "outpost" syndrome. It occurs in about half of schizophrenia patients, on an average of ten years before the first episode of the illness (Parnas 1999). Of course, the psychotic prodrome is a retrospective concept. That is, one can say with certainty that an individual's nonspecific neurotic and attenuated psychotic symptoms are the prodrome to a psychotic illness only after the definitive characteristics of the disorder are present. As a result, the main investigative approaches have taken the form of retrospective studies of subjects who have already developed schizophrenia or prospective studies of individuals who are exhibiting purported prodromal signs. Further, although most empirical studies of the prodrome include some subjects who developed schizophrenia in their late teens, most

Table 8.1. DSM-III-R *criteria for the prodromal phase of schizophrenia*

A clear deterioration in functioning before the active phase of the disturbance that is not due to a disturbance in mood or to a psychoactive substance use disorder and that involves at least two of the following symptoms:
1. Marked social isolation or withdrawal
2. Marked impairment in role functioning as wage earner, student, or homemaker
3. Markedly peculiar behavior (e.g., collecting garbage, talking to self in public, hoarding food)
4. Marked impairment in personal hygiene and grooming
5. Blunted or inappropriate affect
6. Digressive, vague, overly elaborate, or circumstantial speech, or poverty of speech, or poverty of content of speech
7. Odd beliefs or magical thinking influencing behavior and inconsistent with cultural norms (e.g., superstitiousness, belief in clairvoyance, telepathy, "sixth sense," belief that "others can feel my feelings," overvalued ideas, ideas of reference)
8. Unusual perceptual experiences (e.g., recurrent illusions, sensing the presence of a force or person not actually present)
9. Marked lack of initiative, interests, or energy

Source: American Psychiatric Association 1987

focus on adult-onset schizophrenia, and investigators have not usually distinguished the early-onset patients from the more typical, adult-onset cases in their samples. Nonetheless, as is consistent with the evidence of deficits in multiple domains during the premorbid period, the findings to date indicate that a variety of signs and symptoms mark the impending psychosis. In other words, like the premorbid period, the prodrome is multifaceted.

In 1996, Yung and McGorry reported on prodromal phenomena and sequence patterns in first-episode patients, drawing attention to the diverse signs and symptoms that characterize the prodromal stage. These included a mixture of neurotic and mood symptoms, attenuated psychotic symptoms, cognitive deficits, physical symptoms, and changes in speech, motivation, energy, and behavior. Some of the symptoms experienced were disabling, and some were of potential danger to the subject or others, such as suicidal thoughts and overly aggressive behavior.

A more recent study of the prodrome in first-episode patients showed that distinct qualitative changes in inner experience were reported long before overt behavioral signs created serious family concern (Moller and Husby 2000). In this sample, all of the subjects had experienced a prodromal phase of illness, ranging from one week to more than eleven years in duration. Prodromal phenomena were explored in depth, using both patients and family members as informants. Most patients reported serious difficulty in interpreting and communicating the early changes they experienced in their inner state. Among the prodromal experiences they recalled were disturbances in the perception of self, extreme preoccupation with overvalued ideas, neurotic symptoms, disruptions in formal thought, attenuated delusional ideas or perceptions, difficulties with mental or emotional control, and disturbances in simple perception. Of these, disturbances in perception of self and extreme preoccupation with overvalued ideas were reported almost ubiquitously. In addition to these interior symptoms, both the patients and their families reported a number of observable behaviors, including quitting a job or school or major problems with truancy, changes in physical appearance or behavior, shifts in interests, and social passivity, withdrawal, or isolation.

Along much these same lines, researchers in Germany have examined self-perceived prodromal experiences using the Bonn Scale for the Assessment of Basic Symptoms (BSABS). Basic symptoms are defined as troublesome disturbances experienced within the self, and thus typically not yet observable in outward expression and behavior, that occur during the prodromal period before it evolves into psychosis (Huber and Gross 1998). These symptoms are referred to as "basic" symptoms because they are presumed to be the starting point in the development of the positive first-rank phenomena of schizophrenia (Gross 1997).

Based on a follow-up study of patients who had been administered the BSABS eight years earlier, Klosterkötter et al. (1997) reported that basic symptoms had been detected in the majority of subjects (78 out of 96) during the index examination. Of these patients, 66 percent had developed psychosis by the time of the follow-up, in contrast to the patients who did not give evidence of basic symptoms at the initial examination, none of whom had subsequently become ill. Similar findings were reported in a later study by this group (Klösterkotter et al. 2001). This investigation also identified a cluster of symptoms that seemed most likely to be predictive of the future development of a schizophrenic disorder, namely, disturbances in thought, language, perception, and motor functions.

Finally, it is worth noting that gender differences may exist in the duration of the psychotic prodrome, although research findings are inconsistent on this issue. Häfner and colleagues (1993) reported a longer prodromal period in women than in men, results that were recently replicated in a study by Cohen and colleagues (Cohen, Gotowiec, and Seeman 2000). The latter study demonstrated that even though the first signs of behavioral disturbance were likely to occur at approximately the same age in women and men (18.5 to 19.8 years), the psychotic prodrome lasted almost twice as long for women as for men (7.1 versus 3.9 years). In contrast to these findings, however, Klosterkötter et al. (2001) reported the psychotic prodrome to be of shorter duration in women than in men, with a mean of 4.3 years for women as opposed to 6.7 years for men. Although the reason for these discrepancies is not readily apparent, it is plausible that measures of prodromal signs could vary in their sensitivity to sex differences owing to the qualitative element in prodromal indicators.

In sum, although prodromal symptoms are not uniform across individuals, certain signs are reported with regularity. These include nonspecific psychiatric symptoms, as well as changes in behavior, the perception of self, appearance, and role functioning, and the presence of attenuated psychotic symptoms. Given the progress that has been made in characterizing the prodromal stage, future research should be directed at identifying biological indicators of risk that might be combined with these subjective experiences and behavioral indicators to yield greater predictive accuracy.

In interpreting the results of investigations into the prodrome, several caveats must be kept in mind. First, as mentioned, most studies of the prodrome, regardless of the specific study design, focus on the adolescent and young adult period. This is due, in part, to the natural history and course of schizophrenia. Consequently, much of what has been studied relates to the prodrome in adult-onset schizophrenia, which is to say that we know relatively little about the prodrome in childhood-onset schizophrenia. Further, few studies have differentiated between adolescence and young adulthood in the presentation of the prodrome.

It is possible that differences exist between the prodrome of adult-onset schizophrenia and that of early-onset schizophrenia (EOS) and very early-onset schizophrenia (VEOS). EOS and VEOS are defined as schizophrenia with an onset before the age of 18 years and before the age of 13 years, respectively (American Academy of Child and Adolescent Psychiatry 2001). It has been shown that the onset of the disorder tends to be more insidious in EOS and VEOS (Iida et al. 1995; Eggers, Bunk, and Krause 2000) than in adult-onset schizophrenia. Moreover, demographic differences have been identified that appear to be a function of age at onset. For example, in EOS and VEOS, the ratio of men to women is close to 2:1, whereas in adult-onset schizophrenia the ratio is 1:1 (Häfner and Heiden 1997). The disorder also tends to be more severe and treatment refractory, and the premorbid developmental anomalies more pronounced. Given the above, establishing the onset of the prodrome is a particular challenge in EOS and VEOS. It has been estimated that at least 55 percent of childhood-onset cases are preceded by a prodromal phase (Eggers 1978), but data are limited. Clearly, then, much research remains to be done on the characteristics of the psychotic prodrome in EOS and VEOS.

Another vexing problem has been the fact that prodromal symptoms are relatively common in the general population, particularly young people. A community survey of Australian high school students, published by McGorry et al. in 1995, found a high level of endorsement of *DSM-III-R* prodromal features. At the time of the study, nearly half the sample—49.2 percent—had endorsed two or more prodromal features and thus met the criteria for the *DSM-III-R* schizophrenic prodrome (American Psychiatric Association 1987). However, when the authors raised the threshold for diagnosis by including only the more positive of the nine symptoms (such as magical ideation and unusual perceptual experiences) and by adding the specification that symptoms must have been present for more than one week but less than five years, only 10 to 15 percent of the group met the criteria for the schizophrenic prodrome.

Last, it is generally assumed that the premorbid period and the prodrome can be distinguished. However, findings from research on EOS raise questions about this assumption. Some argue that making the distinction may be impossible for EOS and VEOS patients (Kelley et al. 1992; Eggers, Bunk, and Krause 2000). Many cases of EOS and especially of VEOS are characterized by persistent behavioral abnormality that extends from infancy to the point of clinical onset, and it is not clear that a qualitative shift occurs at any point in the developmental course. This pattern stands in contrast to the findings for patients who follow the modal developmental trajectory, with a late-adolescent or early-adult onset of illness. In these individuals—who constitute the overwhelming majority of cases—the beginning of adolescence marks an abrupt escalation in behavioral dysfunction. One of the most challenging tasks facing investigators in the field is to determine why this developmental epoch is linked with a shift toward more pronounced premorbid deficits.

Speculations on Neurodevelopmental Triggers in Adolescence

In the 1980s, a few pioneering investigators, such as Feinberg (1983), put forward hypotheses concerning the neural mechanisms that might precipitate the onset of schizophrenia in early adulthood. Feinberg proposed that a defect in the normative process of synaptic pruning might be responsible for the late-adolescent or early-adult onset of schizophrenia. Even though Feinberg did not have the benefit of the information subsequently generated by the neuro-imaging revolution, his theory has proved compatible with more recent findings. Furthermore, it is now possible to formulate a more detailed picture of how normal neurodevelopmental processes might go awry, beginning at the molecular level.

We recently offered an updated model of adolescent neurodevelopment in schizophrenia (Walker and Bollini 2002). The model draws on the following lines of evidence from neuroscience: (1) there are receptors for gonadal and adrenal hormones throughout the human brain (Osterlund, Keller, and Hurd 2000; Kawata et al. 2001), (2) neurons contain surface and intranuclear hormone receptors (McEwen 1994), and (3) activation of these receptors can alter the expression of genes that influence neurodevelopmental and neurodegenerative processes (Ojeda and Ma 1999). A schematic of the model is presented in Figure 8.4. The upper tier of the diagram lists the presumed chain of events involved in normal adolescent brain changes, while the lower tier indicates ways that each step in the process might deviate from the norm and thereby lead to the manifestation of schizophrenia.

Of course, to be plausible, the model must be able to incorporate established findings on schizophrenia, including evidence of heritability and manifestations of dysfunction in early childhood. One example of an inherited predisposition for brain disorder that is relatively silent in childhood but then activated by later maturational processes is the ApoE genotype epsilon4, which confers risk for Alzheimer disease. Although clinical dementia is not apparent until later adulthood, negative childhood temperament is linked with the presence of the gene (Keltikangas-Jarvinen, Raikkonen, and Lehtimaki 1993). It is thus reasonable to speculate that schizophrenia involves a genetic liability that results in faulty adolescent neurodevelopment and escalating adjustment problems, culminating in the clinical manifestation of psychosis.

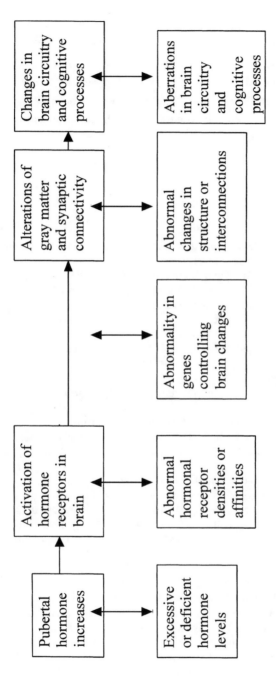

Fig. 8.4. Postulated mechanisms in the hormonally triggered expression of genetic liability for schizophrenia during adolescence

Needless to say, any etiological framework for explaining schizophrenia must be considered tentative at this juncture. Nonetheless, it is clear that our understanding of the developmental course of behavioral dysfunction in schizophrenia can both guide and constrain theorizing. Further, as our knowledge of normal human neurodevelopment expands, we will have a firmer basis from which to generate more precise theories about the neurodevelopmental mechanisms at work in schizophrenia.

REFERENCES

Ambelas, A. (1992). Preschizophrenics: Adding to the evidence, sharpening the focus. *British Journal of Psychiatry* 160:401–4.
American Academy of Child and Adolescent Psychiatry. (2001). Practice parameter for the assessment and treatment of children and adolescents with schizophrenia. *Journal of American Academy of Child and Adolescent Psychiatry* 40(Suppl. 7):4–23.
American Psychiatric Association. (1987). *Diagnostic and statistical manual of mental disorders*, 3rd ed., revised. Washington, D.C.: APA Press.
Aylward, E., Walker, E., and Bettes, B. (1984). Intelligence in schizophrenia: Meta-analysis of the research. *Schizophrenia Bulletin* 10:430–59.
Bailer, J., Braeuer, W., and Rey, E. R. (1996). Premorbid adjustment as predictor of outcome in schizophrenia: Results of a prospective study. *Acta Psychiatrica Scandinavica* 93:368–77.
Cannon, M., Jones, P., Huttunen, M. O., Tanskanen, A., Huttunen, T., Rabe-Hesketh, S., et al. (1999). School performance in Finnish children and later development of schizophrenia: A population-based longitudinal study. *Archives of General Psychiatry* 56:457–63.
Cannon, T. D., Bearden, C. E., Hollister, J. M., Rosso, I. M., Sanchez, L. E., and Hadley, T. (2000). Childhood cognitive functioning in schizophrenia patients and their unaffected siblings: A prospective cohort study. *Schizophrenia Bulletin* 26:379–93.
Castro, J. R., Costoya, J. A., Gallego, R., Prieto, A., Arce, V. M., and Senaris, R. (2000). Expression of growth hormone receptor in the human brain. *Neuroscience Letters* 281:147–50.
Cohen, R. Z., Gotowiec, A., and Seeman, M. V. (2000). Duration of pretreatment phases in schizophrenia: Women and men. *Canadian Journal of Psychiatry* 45:544–47.
David, A. S., Malmberg, A., Brandt, L., Allebeck, P., and Lewis, G. (1997). IQ and risk for schizophrenia: A population-based cohort study. *Psychological Medicine* 27:1311–23.
Davidson, M., Reichenberg, A., Rabinowitz, J., Weiser, M., Kaplan, Z., and Mark, M. (1999). Behavioral and intellectual markers for schizophrenia in apparently healthy male adolescents. *American Journal of Psychiatry* 156:1328–35.
Dworkin, R. H., Cornblatt, B. A., Friedmann, R., Kaplansky, L. M., Lewis, J. A., Rinaldi, A., et al. (1993). Childhood precursors of affective vs. social deficits in adolescents at risk for schizophrenia. *Schizophrenia Bulletin* 19:563–77.

Edwards, J., McGorry, P. D., Waddell, F. M., and Harrigan, S. M. (1999). Enduring negative symptoms in first-episode psychosis: Comparison of six methods using follow-up data. *Schizophrenia Research* 40:147–58.

Eggers, C. (1978). Course and prognosis of childhood schizophrenia. *Journal of Autism and Childhood Schizophrenia* 8:21–36.

Eggers, C., Bunk, D., and Krause, D. (2000). Schizophrenia with onset before the age of eleven: Clinical characteristics of onset and course. *Journal of Autism and Developmental Disorders* 30:29–38.

Erlenmeyer-Kimling, L. (2000). Neurobehavioral deficits in offspring of schizophrenic parents: Liability indicators and predictors of illness. *American Journal of Medical Genetics* 97:65–71.

Erlenmeyer-Kimling, L., Rock, D., Roberts, S. A., Janal, M., Kestenbaum, C., Cornblatt, B., et al. (2000). Attention, memory, and motor skills as childhood predictors of schizophrenia-related psychoses: The New York High-Risk Project. *American Journal of Psychiatry* 157:1416–22.

Feinberg, I. (1983). Schizophrenia: Caused by a fault in programmed synaptic elimination during adolescence? *Journal of Psychiatric Research* 17:319–34.

Fish, B. (1977). Neurobiologic antecedents of schizophrenia in children: Evidence for an inherited, congenital neurointegrative defect. *Archives of General Psychiatry* 34:1297–313.

Fish, B. (1987). Infant predictors of the longitudinal course of schizophrenic development. *Schizophrenia Bulletin* 13:395–409.

Gottesman, I. I. (1991). *Schizophrenia genesis: The origins of madness.* New York: W. H. Freeman.

Gross, G. (1997). The onset of schizophrenia. *Schizophrenia Research* 28:187–98.

Häfner, H., and Heiden, W. (1997). Epidemiology of schizophrenia. *Canadian Journal of Psychiatry/Revue Canadienne de Psychiatrie* 42:139–51.

Häfner, H., Maurer, K., Loffler, W., and Riecher-Rossler, A. (1993). The influence of age and sex on the onset and early course of schizophrenia. *British Journal of Psychiatry* 162:80–86.

Häfner, H., Riecher-Rossler, A., Fatkenheuer, B., Maurer, K., Meissner, S., Loffler, W., et al. (1992). Interview for the retrospective assessment of the onset of schizophrenia. *Schizophrenia Research* 6:209–23.

Hans, S. L., Auerbach, J. G., Asarnow, J. R., Styr, B., and Marcus, J. (2000). Social adjustment of adolescents at risk for schizophrenia: The Jerusalem Infant Development Study. *Journal of the American Academy of Child and Adolescent Psychiatry* 39:1406–14.

Hans, S. L., Marcus, J., Henson, L., Auerbach, J. G., and Mirsky, A. F. (1992). Interpersonal behavior of children at risk for schizophrenia. *Psychiatry* 55:314–35.

Hans, S. L., Marcus, J., Nuechterlein, K. H., Asarnow, R. F., Styr, B., and Auerbach, J. G. (1999). Neurobehavioral deficits at adolescence in children at risk for schizophrenia: The Jerusalem Infant Development Study. *Archives of General Psychiatry* 56:741–48.

Hodges, A., Byrne, M., Grant, E., and Johnstone, E. (1999). People at risk of schizophrenia. *British Journal of Psychiatry* 174:547–53.

Huber, G., and Gross, G. (1998). Basic symptom concept: Historical aspects in view of early detection of schizophrenia. *Neurology, Psychiatry, and Brain Research* 5:183–90.

Iida, J., Iwasaka, H., Hirao, F., Hashino, K., Matsumura K., Tahara, K., et al. (1995). Clinical features of childhood-onset schizophrenia with obsessive-compulsive symptoms during the prodromal phase. *Psychiatry and Clinical Neurosciences* 49:201–7.

Isohanni, M., Jones, P., Kemppainen, L., Croudace, T., Isohanni, I., Veijola, J., et al. (2000). Childhood and adolescent predictors of schizophrenia in the Northern Finland 1966 birth cohort—A descriptive life-span model. *European Archives of Psychiatry and Clinical Neuroscience* 250:311–19.

Jones, P., Rodgers, B., Murray, R., and Marmot, M. (1994). Child development risk factors for adult schizophrenia in the British 1946 birth cohort. *Lancet* 344(7280):1398–1402.

Kawata, M., Matsuda, K., Nishi, M., Ogawa, H., and Ochiai, I. (2001). Intracellular dynamics of steroid hormone receptor. *Neuroscience Research* 40:197–203.

Kelley, M. E., Gilbertson, M., Mouton, A., and van Kammen, D. P. (1992). Deterioration in premorbid functioning in schizophrenia: A developmental model of negative symptoms in drug-free patients. *American Journal of Psychiatry* 149:1543–48.

Keltikangas-Jarvinen, L., Raikkonen K., and Lehtimaki T. (1993). Dependence between apolipoprotein E phenotypes and temperament in children, adolescents, and young adults. *Psychosomatic Medicine* 55:155–63.

Klosterkötter, J., Hellmich, M., Steinmeyer, E., and Schultze-Lutter, F. (2001). Diagnosing schizophrenia in the initial prodromal phase. *Archives of General Psychiatry* 58:158–64.

Klosterkötter, J., Schultze-Lutter, F., Gross, G., Huber, G., and Steinmeyer, E. M. (1997). Early self-experienced neuropsychological deficits and subsequent schizophrenic diseases: An 8-year average follow-up prospective study. *Acta Psychiatrica Scandinavica* 95:396–404.

Marcus, J., Hans, S. L., Auerbach, J. G., and Auerbach, A. G. (1993). Children at risk for schizophrenia: The Jerusalem Infant Development Study, Pt. 2: Neurobehavioral deficits at school age. *Archives of General Psychiatry* 50:797–809.

Marcus, J., Hans, S. L., Nagler, S., Auerbach, J. G., Mirsky, A. F., and Aubrey, A. (1987). Review of the NIMH Israeli Kibbutz-City study and the Jerusalem Infant Development Study. *Schizophrenia Bulletin* 13:425–38.

McEwen, B. S. (1994). Steroid hormone actions on the brain: When is the genome involved? *Hormones and Behavior* 28:396–405.

McGlashan, T. H., and Hoffman, R. E. (2000). Schizophrenia as a disorder of developmentally reduced synaptic connectivity. *Archives of General Psychiatry* 57:637–48.

McGorry, P. D., McFarlane, C., Patton, G. C., Bell, R., Hibbert, M. E., Jackson, H. J., et al. (1995). The prevalence of prodromal features of schizophrenia in adolescence: A preliminary survey. *Acta Psychiatrica Scandinavica* 92:241–49.

McNeil, T. F., Harty, B., Blennow, G., and Cantor-Graae, E. (1993). Neuromotor deviation in offspring of psychotic mothers: A selective developmental deficiency in two groups of children at heightened psychiatric risk? *Journal of Psychiatric Research* 27:39–54.

Meehl, P. E. (1962). Schizotaxia, schizotypy, schizophrenia. *American Psychology* 17:827–38.

Miller, T. J., McGlashan, T. H., Woods, S. W., Stein, K., Driesen, N., Corcoran, C. M., et al. (1999). Symptom assessment in schizophrenic prodromal states. *Psychiatric Quarterly* 70:273–87.

Mirsky, A. F., Ingraham, L. J., and Kugelmass, S. (1995). Neuropsychological assessment of attention and its pathology in the Israeli cohort. *Schizophrenia Bulletin* 21:193–204.

Mirsky, A. F., Kugelmass, S., Ingraham, L. J., Frenkel, E., and Nathan, M. (1995). Overview and summary: Twenty-five-year follow-up of high-risk children. *Schizophrenia Bulletin* 21:227–39.

Moller, P., and Husby, R. (2000). The initial prodrome in schizophrenia: Searching for naturalistic core dimensions of experience and behavior. *Schizophrenia Bulletin* 26: 217–32.

Neumann, C. S., Grimes, K., Walker, E. F., and Baum, K. (1995). Developmental pathways to schizophrenia: Behavioral stereotypes. *Journal of Abnormal Psychology* 104:558–66.

Ojeda, S. R., and Ma, Y. J. (1999). Glial-neuronal interactions in the neuroendocrine control of mammalian puberty: Facilitatory effects of gonadal steroids. *Journal of Neurobiology* 40:528–40.

Olin, S. C., and Mednick, S. A. (1996). Risk factors of psychosis: Identifying vulnerable populations premorbidly. *Schizophrenia Bulletin* 22:223–40.

Olin, S. S., John, R. S., and Mednick, S. A. (1995). Assessing the predictive value of teacher reports in a high-risk sample for schizophrenia: A ROC analysis. *Schizophrenia Research* 16:53–66.

Osterlund, M. K., Keller, E., and Hurd, Y. L. (2000). The human forebrain has discrete estrogen receptor alpha messenger RNA expression: High levels in the amygdaloid complex. *Neuroscience* 95:333–42.

Ott, S. L., Spinelli, S., Rock, D., Roberts, S., Amminger, G. P., and Erlenmeyer-Kimling, L. (1998). The New York High-Risk Project: Social and general intelligence in children at risk for schizophrenia. *Schizophrenia Research* 31:1–11.

Parnas, J. (1999). From predisposition to psychosis: Progression of symptoms in schizophrenia. *Acta Psychiatrica Scandinavica* 99(Suppl. 395):20–29.

Rosenthal, R. (1978). Combining result of independent studies. *Psychological Bulletin* 85:185–93.

Sameroff, A. J., Barocas, R., and Seifer, R. (1984). The early development of children born to mentally ill women. In N. F. Watt, E. J. Anthony, L. C. Wynne, and J. E. Rolf (Eds.), *Children at risk for schizophrenia: A longitudinal perspective* (pp. 482–514). New York: Cambridge University Press.

Spear, L. P. (2000). The adolescent brain and age-related behavioral manifestations. *Neuroscience and Biobehavioral Reviews* 24:417–63

Tienari, P. J., Sori, A., Lahti, I., and Naarala, M. (1985). Interaction of genetic and psychosocial factors in schizophrenia. *Acta Psychiatrica Scandinavica* 71:19–30.

Tyrka, A. R., Cannon, T. D., Haslam, N., Mednick, S. A., Schulsinger, F., Schulsinger, H., et al. (1995). The latent structure of schizotypy, Pt. 1: Premorbid indicators of a taxon of individuals at risk for schizophrenia-spectrum disorders. *Journal of Abnormal Psychology* 104:173–83.

Wahlberg, K.-E., Wynne, L. C., Oja, H., and Keskitalo, P. (1997). Gene-environment interaction invulnerability to schizophrenia: Findings from the Finnish family study of schizophrenia. *American Journal of Psychiatry* 154:355–62.

Walker, E. F. (1994). Developmentally moderated expressions of the neuropathology underlying schizophrenia. *Schizophrenia Bulletin* 20:453–80.

Walker, E. F. (2002). Adolescent neurodevelopment and psychopathology. *Current Directions in Psychological Science* 11:24–28.

Walker, E. F., Baum, K. M., and Diforio, D. (1998). Developmental changes in the behavioral expression of vulnerability for schizophrenia. In M. F. Lenzenweger and R.

H. Dworkin (Eds.), *Origins and development of schizophrenia: Advances in experimental psychopathology* (pp. 469–91). Washington, D.C.: American Psychological Association.

Walker, E. F., and Bollini, A. M. (2002). Pubertal neurodevelopment and the emergence of psychotic symptoms. *Schizophrenia Research* 54:17–23.

Walker, E. F, and Diforio, D. (1997). Schizophrenia: A neural diathesis-stress model. *Psychological Review* 104:1–19.

Walker, E. F., Grimes, K., Davis, D., and Smith, A. (1993). Childhood precursors of schizophrenia: Facial expressions of emotion. *American Journal of Psychiatry* 150:1654–60.

Walker, E. F., Savoie, T., and Davis, D. (1994). Neuromotor precursors of schizophrenia. *Schizophrenia Bulletin* 20:441–51.

Watt, N. F., Grubb, T. W., and Erlenmeyer-Kimling, L. (1982). Social, emotional, and intellectual behavior at school among children at high risk for schizophrenia. *Journal of Consulting and Clinical Psychology* 50:171–81.

Watt, N. F., and Saiz, C. (1991). Longitudinal studies of premorbid development of adult schizophrenics. In E. F. Walker (Ed.), *Schizophrenia: A life-course developmental perspective*. Personality and psychopathology series, Vol. 18 (pp. 157–92). San Diego: Academic Press.

Weinstein, D., Diforio, D., Schiffman, J., Walker, E., and Bonsall, B. (1999). Minor physical anomalies, dermatoglyphic asymmetries, and cortisol levels in adolescents with schizotypal personality disorder. *American Journal of Psychiatry* 156:617–23.

Weintraub, S., and Neale, J. M. (1984). Social behavior of children at risk for schizophrenia. In N. F. Watt et al. (Eds.), *Children at risk for schizophrenia: A longitudinal perspective* (pp. 279–85). New York: Cambridge University Press.

Worland, J., Janes, C. L., Anthony, E. J., McGinnis, M., and Cass, L. (1984). St. Louis Risk Research Project: Comprehensive progress report of experimental studies. In N. F. Watt et al. (Eds.), *Children at risk for schizophrenia: A longitudinal perspective* (pp. 105–47). New York: Cambridge University Press.

Yung, A. R., and McGorry, P. D. (1996). The initial prodrome in psychosis: Descriptive and qualitative aspects. *Australian and New Zealand Journal of Psychiatry* 30:587–99.

Yung, A. R., Phillips, L. J., McGorry, P. D., McFarlane, C. A., Francey, S., Harrigan, S., et al. (1998). Prediction of psychosis. *British Journal of Psychiatry* 172(Suppl. 33):14–20.

CHAPTER NINE

The Prodromal Course

G. Paul Amminger, M.D.,
Steven Leicester, M.Psych., Shona Francey, Ph.D.,
and Patrick D. McGorry, M.D., Ph.D.

Schizophrenia and other psychotic disorders are often preceded by prodromal changes, lasting for periods from several days to several years, that foreshadow the onset of illness. The prodromal phase is potentially important in defining markers of risk for a progression into psychotic illness and investigating novel biological and psychological treatments that might prevent a transition to psychosis (Heinssen et al. 2001). In what follows, we will describe the prodromal phase of schizophrenia and other psychotic disorders, review and compare prodrome rating scales, and explore age-specific characteristics of the prodrome and the transition to psychosis. Empirical data have been drawn from studies conducted in the Personal Assistance and Crisis Evaluation (PACE) Clinic in Melbourne, Australia. PACE is a service for the treatment of and research on adolescents and young adults aged 15 to 29 years who are experiencing perceptual or cognitive changes, unusual thoughts or behavior patterns, or a significant deterioration in role functioning (McGorry et al. 2002).

Characteristics of the Prodrome

Prodrome refers to the early symptoms of an illness that precede the manifestation of the fully developed disorder or to a period of disturbance that represents a deviation from a person's previous experience and behavior (Yung and McGorry 1996a). Prodromal symptoms such as perceptual distortions, short transient hallucinations, or mild paranoia are common in schizophrenia and can be thought of as the earliest form of emergent psychosis. However, these symptoms are far more prevalent in the general population than in clinical cases of psychotic disorders (McGorry et al. 1995; van Os et al. 2001), and not all individuals who experience psychotic symptoms go on to develop a psychotic illness. Accordingly, disturbances in individuals who have not yet experienced a psychotic episode should be viewed as indicators of a risk for psychosis rather than as signs that inevitably signal the start of a progression into a psychotic disorder. The term *at-risk mental state* has been used to describe such symptoms. The concept of an at-risk mental state can be applied prospectively, whereas a prodrome can be defined only retrospectively, once a disorder has been diagnosed (McGorry and Singh 1995).

Most research on the prodrome in psychosis has been conducted in individuals with schizophrenia. Research techniques include retrospective reconstruction of symptoms and events through interviews with patients while they are acutely psychotic or after their symptoms have remitted. Researchers also employ interviews with other informants such as parents, siblings and teachers, and, to much lesser extent, prospective observation of individuals during the development of psychosis.

Clinicians have used retrospective reconstruction to characterize the prodrome of schizophrenia ever since the concept of the illness was first defined by Bleuler (1911/1950) and others. In this tradition, Yung and McGorry (1996b) studied 21 first-episode patients (14 male, 7 female; mean age 23.1 years, standard deviation 4.9 years) who were referred to the Early Psychosis Prevention Intervention Centre in Melbourne, a specialized service for 15- to 29-year-olds with psychosis of recent onset. A prodromal phase was detected in all cases, ranging in duration from 3 days to 6 years. The most frequently reported symptoms were sleep disturbance, anxiety, and irritability, occurring in 100 percent, 86 percent, and 86 percent of individuals, respectively. Other common symptoms were a deterioration in role functioning (76%), depressed mood (76%), social withdrawal (71%), poor concentration (71%), suspiciousness (71%), loss of motivation (68%), perceptual disturbances (62%), motor changes (62%), and weight loss (57%). A sense of confusion, perplexity, and bewilderment was described in 50 percent of individuals as a late phenomenon, occurring just before frank psychosis. Obsessive-compulsive symptoms occurred in 19 percent, while suicidal thoughts and self-harm were reported by 24 percent and 15 percent, respectively. Half the patients identified specific events as "triggers" that precipitated prodromal changes. The broad range of symptoms observed in this sample was consistent with previous descriptions of the schizophrenia prodrome (e.g., Klosterkötter 1988; Ebel et al. 1989). The range also highlights the restrictive nature of the *DSM-III-R* conceptualization of the prodrome, which focused on behavioral features (American Psychiatric Association 1987). The most detailed list of symptoms and signs that have been found to herald psychosis has been provided by Yung and McGorry (1996a, table 2).

Prodrome Criteria and Assessment Scales

Psychosis usually develops gradually, and thus it may be difficult to define the point at which a person can be defined as psychotic. The boundary between "different but not psychotic" ("prepsychotic") and "frankly psychotic" is often blurred (Yung and McGorry 1996a). However, a detailed characterization of typical signs and symptoms is necessary to assist classification and to guide early intervention. Research on the prodrome of schizophrenia has a long tradition in Germany, but most of this research has been retrospective (Huber et al. 1980; Klosterkötter 1988; Häfner et al. 1999). Because patients, their families, and other informants tend to distort retrospective accounts, however, the prospective assessment of a developing psychosis is crucial.

BSABS

The Bonn Scale for the Assessment of Basic Symptoms (BSABS) was the first instrument in which operational definitions of prepsychotic experiences were listed, along with typical statements from patients and examples of questions to be used in assessments during a semistructured interview (Gross et al. 1987). The BSABS measures disturbances of thought, language, perception, bodily perception, stress tolerance, affect, energy, concentration, memory, emotional reactivity, social contacts, and nonverbal expressions.

Klosterkötter and colleagues (2001) prospectively investigated 160 individuals, of whom 110 met the description of the prodromal state according to BSABS criteria. At follow-up after a mean of 9.6 years, 49 percent (79 of 160) had developed *DSM-IV* schizophrenia (American Psychiatric Association 1994). Of those, 98 percent (77 of 79) met BSABS prodromal criteria at the first assessment. Only 2 of the 50 individuals who were not considered prodromal at baseline developed schizophrenia. The absence of prodromal symptoms excluded subsequent schizophrenia with a probability of 96 percent (sensitivity 0.98; false-negative predictions 1.3%), whereas the presence of prodromal symptoms predicted the illness with a probability of 70 percent (specificity 0.59; false-positive predictions 20%). Among the 66 BSABS symptoms, those most predictive of schizophrenia were thought interference, disturbances of receptive language, and visual distortions. The transition to psychosis was observed after a mean of 6.7 years in males and 4.3 years in females following the onset of the prodrome.

CAARMS

On the basis of studies conducted in the PACE Clinic in Melbourne, Yung and colleagues examined prodromal criteria intended to identify individuals at risk of developing psychosis in the near future using the Comprehensive Assessment of At-Risk Mental States (CAARMS; Yung et al. 1998). The CAARMS defines three prodromal subgroups characterized by a recent functional decline plus genetic risk, the recent onset of subthreshold psychotic symptoms, or the onset of brief transient psychotic symptoms (see Table 9.1). Between 30 and 40 percent of individuals who fulfilled the at-risk criteria developed psychosis within 6 to 12 months (Yung et al. 1998; Phillips et al. 2000).

About 31 percent of individuals registered at PACE between 1996 and 1999 met the criteria for more than one prodromal subgroup (McGorry et al. 2002). Diagnoses of the Attenuated Group and the Brief Limited Intermittent Psychosis (BLIP) Group are based on the experience of positive symptoms as rated on a checklist that includes disorders of thought content, perceptual abnormalities, and disorganized speech. Each item is rated by severity, frequency, and duration. Additional ratings record the relation of symptoms to stressful experiences and/or the use of drugs or alcohol. In contrast to the BSABS, the CAARMS assesses the severity, frequency, and duration of the symptoms of prodromal experiences—an important advance from approaches that focused

Table 9.1. Definition of at-risk mental state

State and trait risk factors
1. First-degree relative with any history of psychotic disorder or bipolar disorder or schizotypal personality disorder
2. Reduction on Global Assessment of Functioning scale (American Psychiatric Association 1994) of 30 percent or more points from premorbid level

Attenuated psychotic symptoms
1. At least one of ideas of reference, odd beliefs or magical thinking, perceptual disturbance, digressive speech or thought, odd behavior or appearance
2. Occurrence at least several times per week
3. Change in mental state present for at least one week

Transient psychotic symptoms
At least one of perceptual disturbance or hallucinations, ideas of reference, magical thinking or delusions, digressive speech or formal thought disorder, odd behavior or appearance. Duration of each is less than one week, and symptom resolves spontaneously.

Source: Yung et al. 1998

solely on the quality of the symptoms. The complete CAARMS is more detailed than the PACE intake criteria (see Table 9.1) and rates seven groups of symptoms: positive symptoms, cognitive change, emotional disturbance, negative symptoms, behavioral change, motor/physical change, and general psychopathology. The CAARMS aims not just to determine whether an individual meets the PACE intake criteria of an at-risk mental state but also to either rule out or confirm acute psychosis (see Table 9.1), and to map out a trajectory of psychopathology and functioning over time.

SIPS, SOPS, and COPS

The Structured Interview for Prodromal Symptoms (SIPS, a diagnostic semi-structured interview) and the Scale of Prodromal Symptoms (SOPS, a severity scale) are closely modeled on the CAARMS. McGlashan and colleagues at the Yale University PRIME Research Clinic (Prevention through Risk Identification, Management, and Education) used these instruments to define, diagnose, and measure psychopathological symptoms in individuals who may be in a prepsychotic state (Miller et al., 1999). Prodrome classification using SIPS and SOPS yielded an acceptable interrater reliability (kappa = 0.81) (Miller et al. 2002). Diagnosis is accomplished using the Criteria of Prodromal States (COPS), modeled after the PACE intake criteria. The cutoff point for confirming or ruling out psychosis in the COPS is more conservative than in the CAARMS, allowing fewer subthreshold psychotic experiences. Nevertheless, 7 of the 13 at-risk patients (54%) had made the transition to psychosis within 12 months (Miller et al. 2002).

Defining Prodromal State with the PANSS

A relatively high transition rate of at-risk individuals has been noted by researchers in the United Kingdom. In accordance with the criteria established by the PACE Clinic, a study by Morrison et al. (2002) defined "at risk" by the presence of transient psychotic symptoms, attenuated (subclinical) psychotic symptoms, or family history plus functional decline. The study used the Positive and Negative Syndromes of Schizophrenia Scale (PANSS; Kay, Fiszbein, and Opler 1987) to characterize the duration and severity of subthreshold psychotic symptoms. Transient psychosis was defined by symptoms that scored 4 or more for hallucinations, 4 or more for delusions, and/or 5 or more for conceptual disorganization that lasted less than one week and were resolved without antipsychotic medication. Attenuated psychosis was defined by the presence of symptoms that scored 3 for delusions, 2 to 3 for hallucinations, and 3 to 4 for suspiciousness or for conceptual disorganization. The research group observed the transition to psychosis in 5 of the 23 individuals in the sample (22%) at 6 months.

Predictors for Psychosis in Individuals with Prodromal Symptoms

Specific characteristics of 49 PACE clients were evaluated monthly to assess the predictive validity of clinical risk indicators of schizophrenia (McGorry, Phillips, and Yung 2001). The assessments included a comprehensive rating of psychopathological variables such as the presence of psychotic symptoms, depressive features, manic features, Huber's basic symptoms (Klosterkötter et al. 2001), anxiety symptoms, drug and/or alcohol use, and general functioning. Of 49 subjects, 20 (40.8%) developed a psychotic disorder within 12 months. Highly significant clinical predictors of psychosis at intake were a long duration of prodromal symptoms (greater than 900 days), poor functioning (a GAF [global assessment functioning] score under 51), low-grade psychotic symptoms (a total score on the brief psychiatric rating scale [BPRS] of more than 15 and on the BPRS psychotic subscale of more than 2), depression (a Hamilton Rating Scale for Depression [HRSD] score over 18), disorganization (an attention score greater than 1 on the Scale for the Assessment of Negative Symptoms [SANS]), and cannabis dependence. (On the GAF scale, the BPRS, the HRSD, and the SANS, see, respectively, American Psychiatric Association 1994; Overall and Gorham 1962; Hamilton 1960; and Andreasen 1983.)

A recent analysis that combined some of the predictive clinical variables in the PACE sample yielded a strategy for the prediction of psychosis that demonstrated a high degree of sensitivity (86%), specificity (91%), positive predictive value (80%), and negative predictive value (94%) at a 6-month follow-up (Yung et al. 2003).

Researchers at the PACE Clinic have also investigated neuroimaging, neurocognitive, and neurodevelopmental variables as potential predictors of psychosis. When compared with normal controls, individuals who met the PACE intake criteria exhibited reduced left hippocampal volumes similar to those seen in patients with first-episode psychosis (Velakoulis et al. 1999). However, contrary to our expectations, smaller hippocampal volumes predicted a lower rather than a higher risk of transition to psychosis (Phillips et al. 2003). Neurocognitive functions were impaired in the total sample but did not predict transition, nor did developmental milestones, perinatal complications, or childhood behavioral disturbances.

The incidence of schizophrenia and other psychotic disorders, as well as symptomatic expression in schizophrenia, vary with age and gender. In a study of 391 individuals, aged 14 to 74 years, diagnosed with schizophrenia spectrum disorders, the older subjects exhibited significantly fewer positive and disorganized symptoms (Schultz et al. 1997). Older age was also associated with fewer hallucinations, delusions, bizarre behavior, and inappropriate affect. There was no age effect for formal thought disorder or for negative symptoms. In consistency with these findings, another survey of individuals who had no history of psychiatric disorder reported a negative association between psychotic experiences and age (Verdoux et al. 1998). The authors concluded that normal neuronal developmental processes (e.g., Weinberger 1987) may underlie the influence of age on delusion formation and psychosis.

Prompted by these observations, McGorry et al. (2002) studied the role of age and gender in the transition to psychosis in 92 PACE clients (48 male, 44 female; mean age 20.0 years, SD 3.7 years) who were participating in a randomized controlled intervention study. Cox regression analysis revealed that, after an adjustment for the effects of differing treatments (low-dose neuroleptics, standard treatment, treatment refusal), younger age and female gender proved to be significant predictors of psychosis. Among 14- to 19-year-olds, 19 of the 42 individuals (45%) developed psychosis during a 12-month follow-up, compared to a transition rate of 17 percent in both the 20- to 24-year-old and 25- to 29-year-old groups. These findings emphasize that adolescents, particularly females, with prodromal symptoms have the highest risk of developing a psychosis.

Age-Specific Characteristics of the Prodromal Phase of Schizophrenia

To our knowledge, no one has studied the age-specific characteristics of the prodrome in schizophrenia or in other psychoses. In the sample of 92 individuals in the PACE study described above, no differences were observed in global functioning, quality of life, negative symptoms, positive symptoms, manic symptoms, depressive symptoms, and anxiety among the three age groups (14 to 19 years, 20 to 24 years, and 25 to 29 years). A Structured Clinical Interview for *DSM-IV* (SCID) Axis I section (First et al. 1996) conducted at intake revealed a substantial proportion of comorbid *DSM-IV* disorders alongside the prodromal symptomatology. The proportion of individuals with a *DSM-IV* disorder at baseline were 71 percent, 76 percent, and 83 percent in the three age groups, respectively, which thus did not differ significantly. Affective and anxiety disorders were the most prevalent Axis I disorders (Leicester et al. 2002).

In a study by Francey (2002) a wide-ranging neuropsychological test battery was used to compare three groups of subjects: 71 patients from the PACE Clinic, 32 young people with a first episode of psychosis, and 51 matched normal controls. In general, the PACE group performed at a level somewhere between that of the two comparison groups on almost all the tests administered. However, the PACE group was distinguished by particular impairments that showed up on tests of verbal memory and attentional or executive functioning, although their performance on these tests improved with age. The research team speculated that neuropsychological impairment in the prodromal phase is likely to reflect neurodevelopmental compromise, which may be more severe in those experiencing prodromal symptoms at an earlier age.

Intervention in the Prodromal Phase

Clinical Management

Given the broad variety of nonspecific symptoms that occur in the prodromal phase and their relatively high prevalence in the general population,
an awareness of the risk of false positives is crucial for those designing intervention strategies for individuals considered at immediate risk for psychosis.
Until more knowledge about the nature of the transition to psychosis has
been gathered, preventative interventions will necessarily remain limited.
Despite the current lack of knowledge, however, certain approaches can be
recommended. Early recognition, easy access to care, and close follow-up are
key to intervention in the prodromal phase (Edwards and McGorry 2002).
Young people with prodromal symptoms often seek help, and when they do,
they need to be engaged and offered regular assessment and support and offered as well treatment for syndromes such as depression, anxiety, and substance abuse. Family education and support are often needed in addition. If
young people with prodromal symptoms are not seeking help themselves,
then regular contact with family members can be an appropriate strategy.
Families should be provided with information about the risks for psychosis
and other mental disorders as well as about existing syndromes and problems,
and this information needs to be delivered clearly and carefully and in a flexible format.

Despite psychosocial treatment and the active treatment of syndromes
such as depression and anxiety, the transition rate to psychosis is high
among young people with prodromal symptoms. Until the 1990s it was considered clinically and ethically correct to delay psychosis-specific treatments
until a definite diagnosis of psychosis had been made (McGlashan 2001).
Over the last decade, however, a growing body of evidence has suggested that
early intervention might not just serve as a palliative but might also ameliorate the natural course of psychotic disorders. Support for early intervention has been strengthened by the advent of new atypical neuroleptic agents
that have fewer serious side effects, such as tardive dyskinesia or neuroleptic malignant syndrome, and equal or better efficacy than traditional neuroleptic drugs. However, as part of the routine clinical management, antipsychotic medication should be considered only when suicidal behavior or
hostility is present.

Treatment Studies

On the basis of findings concerning established psychotic disorders, neuroleptics and cognitive behavior therapy have been considered potentially helpful during the prodromal state. Several clinical trials have been launched to investigate how these approaches compare to standard care such as antidepressants, anxiolytics, and mood stabilizers. The first intervention study conducted at the PACE Clinic examined the efficacy of atypical neuroleptics plus cognitive behavior therapy versus standard treatment in 33 individuals. Over the following 12 months, 35.7 percent of those receiving standard care developed psychosis as opposed to only 9.7 percent of those who received atypical neuroleptics plus psychotherapy. Two years after ceasing treatment, only 2 more individuals from the specific treatment group had developed psychosis. The mean dose of risperidone in the PACE intervention study was 1.3 mg (range 0.5 to 2.0 mg), usually administered at night. Treatment was initiated with 0.5 mg daily and increased by 0.5 mg weekly to 2.0 mg per day if the drug was well tolerated. The most common side effects were akathisia, sedation, and weight gain (McGorry et al. 2002).

Novel Approaches

A clinical and ethical controversy exists regarding neuroleptic treatment during the prodromal phase. The main ethical criticism turns on the fact that only about one-third of individuals who exhibit prodromal symptoms go on to develop psychosis. Thus the remaining two-thirds are exposed to potentially harmful medication for no reason. Indeed, the effects of antipsychotics on the developing brain are unknown. Although atypical antipsychotics are associated with fewer extrapyramidal side effects, other side effects, such as weight gain and changes in lipids and glucose metabolism, are not uncommon (Meyer 2002). Novel pharmacological strategies that might be helpful in the phase of emerging psychosis therefore need to be pursued.

Dysfunction of glutamatergic neurotransmission seems important in the pathophysiology of schizophrenia and is thus a promising target for drug development (Goff and Coyle 2001). The N-methyl-D-aspartate (NMDA) subtype of the glutamate receptor may be particularly important, as blockade by substances such as phencyclidine (PCP) or ketamine causes schizophrenialike psychosis in humans and increases dopamine release in the mesolimbic system.

Agents that indirectly enhance NMDA receptor function can diminish negative symptoms and improve cognitive functioning in individuals with schizophrenia (Javitt 1999). It has been suggested that a reduced function of the NMDA receptor might be linked to glutamate-mediated neurotoxicity involving calcium release from nerve cells and a subsequent release of neurotoxic nucleases and proteases. Nitrous oxide and probably hydrogen dioxide are also released, which could lead to an excessive pruning of cells in the central nervous system (CNS) (Farber et al. 2002). Substances that influence the process of neurodegeneration and cell death may be therapeutic or curative in the onset phase of psychosis, even if those substances are not helpful in later stages of the disorder. Lithium and lamotrigine, which have been shown to be neuroprotective in animal models, are also candidates for further investigation in connection with prodromal schizophrenia and other psychoses.

Lipids might play an important role in schizophrenia. By weight, the dry brain of a human being is 50 to 60 percent lipid. A major proportion of these lipids consists of bioactive lipids such as arachidonic acid (AA) and its metabolites, also known as derived essential fatty acids (EFA). In the brain, EFA are mainly bound to glycerophospholipids (GPL). Owing to their unique chemical structure, GPL spontaneously form bilayers and are the basic molecules of all cell membranes. Bioactive lipids are released through direct and indirect enzymatic pathways (e.g., phospholipases) from membrane GPL. AA is one of the main bioactive lipids in the brain released through phospholipase action and is the precursor of eicosanoids such as prostaglandins, thromboxanes, leukotriens, and prostacyclins. Preclinical studies have demonstrated that EFA deficiency and EFA supplementation influenced nearly every receptor system in the CNS. Of particular interest in the context of schizophrenia was the finding that the number of dopamine D_2 receptors in the nucleus accumbens of EFA-deficient rats was increased by 35 percent over the number in rats who were fed a standard diet. Animal studies and preliminary studies in humans have demonstrated an association between bioactive lipid metabolism, behavior, and cognition (Zimmer et al. 2000).

A recent review of fifteen published studies confirmed a depletion of bioactive lipids in cell membranes of patients with schizophrenia (Fenton, Hibbeln, and Knable 2000). The most consistent findings were reductions in AA and its precursors, and these were independent of drug treatment (Yao, van Kammen, and Gurklis 1996). Reductions in AA and its precursors have also been found in postmortem brains of patients with schizophrenia, relative to normal control brains (Yao, Leonard, and Reddy 2000). Three randomized controlled treatment studies conducted over 12 weeks found a 2.0 g per day dose of ethyleicosapentaenoic acid (EPA) significantly more effective than a placebo in reducing psychopathological symptoms in individuals with schizophrenia (Peet et al. 2001; Emsley et al. 2002). The decrease in prodromal symptoms seen in those studies was both clinically relevant and statistically significant. In contrast, Fenton and colleagues (2002) investigated the effect of augmenting neuroleptics with a 3.0 g per day dose of EPA on symptoms and cognition in patients with schizophrenia or schizoaffective disorder and reported no significant improvements. The patients in this study, however, had been ill for two decades and continued to have substantial symptoms despite treatment with newer neuroleptics, including clozapine. The patients in other studies who apparently benefited from EPA were younger and had a shorter duration of illness.

In all EPA treatment studies, no treatment-related side effects or adverse biochemical or hematological effects have been observed. EPA proved safe to administer to schizophrenic patients as an adjunct therapy and did not, by itself, cause side effects other than mild gastrointestinal symptoms, nor did it enhance the side effects of existing drugs. Patients found EPA highly tolerable (Peet et al. 2001). Because EPA combines the acceptance of a natural product that has no significant side effects with a potency potentially similar to that of neuroleptic drugs, EPA seems an ideal candidate for use in intervention studies of the prodromal phase.

Psychotherapeutic Interventions in the Prodromal Phase

Developmental changes during adolescence, including neurobiological and neurocognitive changes, may contribute to an individual's vulnerability to psychosis. Environmental stressors such as relationship problems, difficulties in managing societal commitments, or problems with lifestyle generally appear to increase the vulnerability. Together, these factors are described in the stress-vulnerability model. Integrated psychotherapy developed at the PACE Clinic employs cognitive strategies to strengthen the individual's coping resources. Table 9.2 lists the goals of psychotherapeutic intervention during the prodromal phase.

The following vignettes are typical of adolescents and young adults during the initial assessment, treatment, and follow-up at the PACE Clinic.

Table 9.2. *Goals of psychotherapeutic intervention in the prodromal phase*

- To engage the patient proactively, extending the therapeutic alliance to accomodate the patient's individual needs and possible reluctance to undergo treatment
- To accurately assess and develop an understanding of the reasons for contacting the clinic. A core component of the PACE therapy is the development of an explanatory model for the precipitation and manifestation of presenting symptomatology. This formulation is developed collaboratively between the patient and the therapist and is used as a basis for ongoing planning and review of therapeutic treatment.
- To develop adaptive ways of enhancing coping behaviors and to advocate health awareness
- To recognize and challenge factors that may damage or erode self-esteem
- To assist the patient in understanding and managing subthreshold psychotic symptoms with the aim of preventing or reducing the impact of their development

Sarah, 15 Years Old

Sarah was referred to PACE by her general practitioner and school counselor after she had been experiencing episodes of brief auditory hallucinations, disorientation, and panic for about three months.

Initial Assessment

Sarah reported that changes had started occurring at a school camp three months earlier, when she experienced an episode that began with sensations of anxiety and confusion but escalated to disorientation. Extreme panic ensued, accompanied by auditory hallucinations in which derogatory comments were made about her, thereby exacerbating her panic and confusion. Sarah noticed a number of subsequent changes including periods of anger and agitation lasting up to 30 minutes, as well as disorientation and hallucinatory experiences that occurred two or three times a week, lasting 20 to 30 minutes each time and leaving her tired and confused.

Sarah's parents said they had noticed she had a very variable mood and was increasingly irritable. She had also become isolated from family and friends and had experienced a decline in academic performance. Sarah had previously been an excellent student, however, and was socially outgoing, as well as being an active participant in sports.

At the initial assessment, Sarah offered minimal insight into her experiences and provided very little information about her mood or level of functioning, but she was notably concerned about her mood variation and what she described as "outbursts" at school. Although the hallucinations were disturbing, they had not been a motivating factor in the decision to seek treatment. She was accepted to the clinic on the grounds of attenuated psychotic symptoms.

Family Background

Sarah's father had a history of depression and had been treated with antidepressants, and there was a family history of psychotic disorder as well. Conflict between Sarah and her father had been a significant stressor for the previous 18 months. Sarah's father said her recent difficulties were particularly frustrating and had worsened their already strained relationship.

Progress

Sarah attended weekly psychotherapy sessions at PACE for five months and maintained regular contact with the medical staff. Sessions focused on her relationships with family and friends, with particular attention paid to coping with conflict and adversity. Although she continued to have difficulty providing information about her episodes of panic, she improved considerably in coping with social, family, and personal challenges.

After six months of treatment, the frequency of her episodes had decreased to less than one every two months; the auditory hallucinations had ceased, and her disturbances now consisted mainly of dissociation, panic, and confusion. Her relationship with her father had improved notably, social conflict had diminished, and her school performance was improving. Sessions were reduced to once monthly, and a pattern of steady improvement continued. Her parents stated that her mood at home was noticeably more upbeat and that she was more engaged with the family.

Twelve months after commencing treatment, Sarah had not experienced any paniclike incidents for five months. At the time of her discharge her treating team felt that her risk of developing psychosis was substantially reduced.

John, 19 Years Old

John was referred to the PACE Clinic by a counselor at a community health center who was concerned about his depressive symptoms, social isolation, auditory hallucinations, and overall poor functioning.

Initial Assessment

John had experienced a long-standing major depressive disorder characterized by very low self-esteem, sadness and melancholia, lack of interest in activities, minimal social interaction, and disturbed sleep patterns. He said these symptoms had been present in varying degrees since he was 6 years old.

During the initial consultation John described the origins and persistence of his depression in some detail. He had been a victim of bullying throughout primary school because of his poor posture and awkward gait, which were the result of a spinal condition. He had fallen into a pattern of isolating himself to avoid further harassment, thereby exacerbating his sense of "being different." John continued to be verbally and physically harassed at secondary school, which confirmed to him that he was unable to interact "normally" with others.

Since leaving school two years earlier, John said his self-esteem had steadily decreased and was further worsened yet more by unemployment, social isolation, and a lack of engagement in regular activity. He was rigid in his conviction that he would always be different and did not believe he would ever develop significant relationships with others. He also experienced great discomfort in public because he thought others perceived him as unusual. In addition, he reported that for the past two or three months he had experienced intermittent auditory hallucinations, which occurred when he was particularly distressed and in which he was the subject of derogatory remarks. In the previous few weeks he had also experienced a scratching sensation behind his rib cage as if something was trying to come out from inside him, again during periods of heightened anxiety and distress.

John was accepted to the PACE Clinic as having attenuated psychotic symptoms. He was keen to overcome his depression and concerned that if he was left without support, his functioning would decrease even further. Although his unusual perceptual experiences were of some concern, they were not a strong factor in his agreeing to attend the clinic.

Family Background

John lived with his biological parents and two younger sisters. Both parents had an extended history of depression, treated with medication. John was emotionally distant from his family and believed they had little understanding of his difficulties.

Progress

John was started on an SSRI (selective serotonin reuptake inhibitor) antidepressant because of his acute depressive symptoms. With his consent, the PACE staff contacted his family to offer information about his presenting symptoms and the role of the clinic. Within two weeks John reported a considerable improvement in mood, motivation, and self-esteem, and he was no longer experiencing perceptual abnormalities. He progressively developed considerable insight into the onset and course of his distress and displayed substantial improvement at coping with adversity and reducing his patterns of isolation. After seven months of treatment John's functioning had improved a great deal. He had engaged well with a number of friends from whom he been isolated for two years, returned to studying so that he could complete his final school exams, and fostered interests that had been dormant for several years such as playing the guitar, writing, and reading.

At the time of discharge John's depression was in full remission, and he was no longer taking SSRI medication. Nor had he experienced perceptual abnormalities for almost a year.

Brian, 24 Years Old

Brian was referred for assessment by a family doctor who was concerned about his social isolation and apparent depression, and by a family history of psychosis, specifically in one of his brothers.

Initial Assessment

Brian said that his confidence had been steadily decreasing for the past year, particularly with regard to social interaction. At first this was evident only with people he had just met, but recently he was increasingly anxious around established friends and acquaintances. Brian also described feeling panic in outside environments such as public transport because he thought people were staring at him. He believed this indicated there was something "strange" about him, and his beliefs worsened his social anxiety. Although at the time of assessment Brian was able to question the idea that he was particularly unusual, he was often unable to question these thoughts when he was in public.

Brian was accepted to the clinic because his functioning had deteriorated substantially over the past twelve months and because he had a first-degree relative with a history of psychotic illness. His suspicion and paranoid thinking were considered as possible attenuated psychotic symptoms. Brian was also thought to be developing social phobia and to be at considerable risk of developing a depressive illness.

Family Background

Brian was the youngest of four siblings, and one of his brothers had been diagnosed with a psychotic disorder at a similar age. Brian's father had been living in the family's country of origin for several years and had no intention of returning.

Progress

Brian commenced antipsychotic medication and attended weekly psychotherapy sessions after consenting to participate in a clinical trial. He engaged well and was very compliant with therapy. He felt that his social anxiety had reduced, and he had stayed in contact with a small group of friends with whom he was able to discuss his difficulties and concerns. After six months of treatment he requested that his appointments be reduced to once monthly, with telephone support if needed, because of his marked improvement. His fears about others in public and his paranoid beliefs had greatly diminished, and he was able to recognize that his background levels of anxiety and self-doubt contributed to his paranoia.

After eight months Brian had found a job. He was functioning well, and he showed minimal concerns and a stable mood during clinical sessions. Subsequently, however, he missed several appointments and did not return telephone messages for several weeks. When he was seen again after two months, it was clear his functioning had deteriorated significantly: he was agitated, disheveled, and thought-disordered. He had left his job because he believed other employees were judging him and had remained isolated ever since. He believed his friends were controlling his cognitive processes and so had confronted them, accusing them of conspiring against him. The treating team diagnosed him as having progressed to acute psychosis, and he was immediately transferred to a first-episode psychosis team.

Conclusions

At present there is no general indication for treatments aimed specifically at reducing the risk of a progression to psychosis. Moreover, antipsychotic medications are not usually indicated unless the person meets the criteria for a *DSM-IV* and/or ICD-10 psychotic disorder, although certain exceptions should be considered—when a rapid deterioration is taking place, for example, or when the risk of suicide is very high and the treatment of severe depression has proved ineffective, or when aggression or hostility is increasing and poses a risk to others. If antipsychotics are prescribed, then low doses of atypical medications are preferred and should be regarded as a therapeutic trial for a limited period. If the patient is apparently benefiting after six weeks, the medication may be continued with the patient's consent for a further six months to two years, following an explanation of the risks and benefits. After this period, a gradual withdrawal of the medication should be attempted if the patient agrees and a solid recovery has been made. If the patient has not responded to one atypical antipsychotic, another may be tried if medication is still indicated.

Studies at the PACE clinic have provided encouraging preliminary information on treatments intended to reduce the risk of a transition to psychosis. However, the risk/benefit ratio of specific approaches to intervention has yet to be determined. Further research into the prodromal phase of schizophrenia is therefore needed. Such research promises not only to make a valuable contribution to our understanding of the illness but also to allow us to refine our approaches to treatment.

REFERENCES

American Psychiatric Association. (1987). *Diagnostic and statistical manual of mental disorders,* 3rd ed., revised. Washington, D.C.: APA Press.
American Psychiatric Association. (1994). *Diagnostic and statistical manual of mental disorders,* 4th ed. Washington, D.C.: APA Press.
Andreasen, N. C. (1983). *The Scale for the Assessment of Negative Symptoms (SANS).* Iowa City: University of Iowa.
Andreasen N. C., Flaum, M., and Arndt, S. (1992). The Comprehensive Assessment of Symptoms and History (CASH): An instrument for assessing diagnosis and psychopathology. *Archives of General Psychiatry* 49:615–23.
Bleuler, E. (1950). *Dementia praecox or the group of schizophrenias.* (J. Zinkin, Trans.). New York: International Universities Press. (Original work published 1911.)
Ebel, H., Gross, G., Klosterkötter, J., and Huber, G. (1989). Basic symptoms in schizophrenic and affective psychoses. *Psychopathology* 22:224–32.
Edwards, J., and McGorry, P. D. (2002). *Implementing early intervention in psychosis: A guide to establishing early psychosis services.* London: Dunitz.
Emsley, R., Myburgh, C., Oosthuizen, P., and von Rensburg, S. J. (2002). Randomized, placebo-controlled study of ethyl-eicosapentaenoic acid as supplemental treatment in schizophrenia. *American Journal of Psychiatry* 159:1596–98.
Farber, N. B., Kim, S. H., Dikranian, K., Jiang, X. P., and Heinkel, C. (2002). Receptor mechanisms and circuitry underlying NMDA antagonist neurotoxicity. *Molecular Psychiatry* 7:32–43.
Fenton, W. S., Hibbeln, J., and Knable, M. (2000). Essential fatty acids, lipid membrane abnormalities, and the diagnosis and treatment of schizophrenia. *Biological Psychiatry* 47:8–21.
First, M. B., Spitzer, R. L., Gibbon, M., and Williams, J. B. W. (1996). *Structured clinical in-*

terview for DSM-IV Axis I disorders—patient edition (SCID-I/P, version 2.0). New York: New York State Psychiatric Institute.

Francey, S. M. (2002). Predicting psychosis: A longitudinal investigation of prodromal features and neurocognitive vulnerability indicators in young people at risk of psychosis. Unpublished D.Phil. thesis, University of Melbourne, Melbourne, Australia.

Goff, D. C., and Coyle, J. T. (2001). The emerging role of glutamate in the pathophysiology and treatment of schizophrenia. *American Journal of Psychiatry* 158:1367–77.

Gross, G., Huber, G., Klosterkötter, J., and Linz, M. (1987). *Bonner Skala für die Beurteilung von Basissymptomen.* Berlin: Springer-Verlag.

Hafner, H., Loffler, W., Maurer, K., Hambrecht, M., and der Heiden, W. (1999). Depression, negative symptoms, social stagnation and social decline in the early course of schizophrenia. *Acta Psychiatrica Scandinavica* 100:105–18.

Hamilton, M. (1960). A rating scale for depression. *Journal of Neurology, Neurosurgy, and Psychiatry* 23:56–62.

Heinssen, R. K., Perkins, D. O., Appelbaum, P. S., and Fenton, W. S. (2000). Informed consent in early psychosis research: National Institute of Mental Health workshop, November 15, 2000. *Schizophrenia Bulletin* 27:571–83.

Huber, G., Gross, G., Schuttler, R., and Linz, M. (1980). Longitudinal studies of schizophrenic patients. *Schizophrenia Bulletin* 6:592–605.

Javitt, D. C. (1999). Treatment of negative and cognitive symptoms. *Current Psychiatry Reports* 1:25–30.

Kay, S. R., Fiszbein, A., and Opler, L. A. (1987). The Positive and Negative Syndrome Scale (PANSS) for schizophrenia. *Schizophrenia Bulletin* 13:261–76.

Klosterkötter, J. (1988). Basic symptoms and end phenomena of schizophrenia: An empirical study of psychopathologic transitional signs between deficit and productive symptoms of schizophrenia. *Monographien aus dem Gesamtgebiete der Psychiatrie* 52:1–267.

Klosterkötter, J., Hellmich, M., Steinmeyer, E. M., and Schultze-Lutter, F. (2001). Diagnosing schizophrenia in the initial prodromal phase. *Archives of General Psychiatry* 58:158–64.

Leicester, S., Amminger, G. P., Phillips, L., et al. (2002). *DSM-IV* Axis I disorders in individuals at ultra-high risk for psychosis. *Acta Psychiatrica Scandinavica* 106(Suppl. 413):27.

McGlashan, T. H. (2001). Psychosis treatment prior to psychosis onset: Ethical issues. *Schizophrenia Research* 51:47–54.

McGlashan, T. H., Miller, T. J., and Woods, S. W. (2001). Pre-onset detection and intervention research in schizophrenia psychoses: Current estimates of benefit and risk. *Schizophrenia Bulletin* 27:563–70.

McGorry, P. D., McFarlane, C., Patton, G. C., Bell, R., Hibbert, M. E., Jackson, H. J., et al. (1995). The prevalence of prodromal features of schizophrenia in adolescence: A preliminary survey. *Acta Psychiatrica Scandinavica* 92:241–49.

McGorry, P. D., Phillips, L. J., and Yung, A. R. (2001). Recognition and treatment of the pre-psychotic phase of psychotic disorders: Frontier or fantasy? In T. Miller, S. A. Mednick, T. H. McGlashan, J. Libiger, and J. O. Johannessen (Eds.), *Early intervention in psychiatric disorders* (pp. 101–22). Amsterdam: Kluwer.

McGorry, P. D., and Singh, B., S. (1995). Schizophrenia: Risk and possibility. In B. Raphael and G. D. Burrows (Eds.), *Handbook of studies on preventative psychiatry* (pp. 491–514). Amsterdam: Elsevier.

McGorry, P. D., Yung, A. R., Phillips, L. J., Yuen, H. P., Francey, S., Cosgrave, E. M., et al. (2002). Randomized controlled trial of interventions designed to reduce the risk of progression to first-episode psychosis in a clinical sample with subthreshold symptoms. *Archives of General Psychiatry* 59:921–28.

Meyer, J. M. (2002). A retrospective comparison of weight, lipid, and glucose changes between risperidone- and olanzapine-treated inpatients: Metabolic outcomes after 1 year. *Journal of Clinical Psychiatry* 63:425–33.

Miller, T. J., McGlashan, T. H., Rosen, J. L., Somjee, L., Markovich, P. J., Stein, K., et al. (2002). Prospective diagnosis of the initial prodrome for schizophrenia based on the Structured Interview for Prodromal Syndromes: Preliminary evidence of interrater reliability and predictive validity. *American Journal of Psychiatry* 159:863–65.

Miller, T. J., McGlashan, T. H., Woods, S. W., Stein, K., Driesen, N., Corcoran, C. M., et al. (1999). Symptom assessment in schizophrenic prodromal states. *Psychiatric Quarterly* 70:273–87.

Morrison, A. P., Bentall, R. P., French, P., Walford, L., Kilcommons, A., Knight, A., et al. (2002). Randomised controlled trial of early detection and cognitive therapy for preventing transition to psychosis in high-risk individuals: Study design and interim analysis of transition rate and psychological risk factors. *British Journal of Psychiatry* 43(Suppl.):s78–s84.

Overall, J. E., and Gorham, D. R. (1962). The Brief Psychiatric Rating Scale. *Psychology Report* 10:799–812.

Peet, M., Brind, J., Ramchand, C. N., Shah, S., and Vankar, G. K. (2001). Two double-blind placebo-controlled pilot studies of eicosapentaenoic acid in the treatment of schizophrenia. *Schizophrenia Research* 49:243–51.

Phillips, L. J., Velakoulis, D., Pantelis, C., Wood, S., Yuen, H. P., Yung, A. R., et al. (2002). Non-reduction of hippocampal volumes is associated with higher risk of psychosis. *Schizophrenia Research* 58:145–58.

Phillips, L. J., Yung, A. R., and McGorry, P. D. (2000). Identification of young people at risk of psychosis: Validation of Personal Assessment and Crisis Evaluation Clinic intake criteria. *Australian and New Zealand Journal of Psychiatry* 34 (Suppl.):s164–69.

Schultz, S. K., Miller, D. D., Oliver, S. E., Arndt, S., Flaum, M., and Andreasen, N. C. (1997). The life course of schizophrenia: Age and symptom dimensions. *Schizophrenia Research* 23:15–23.

van Os, J., Hanssen, M., Bijl, R. V., and Vollebergh, W. (2001). Prevalence of psychotic disorder and community level of psychotic symptoms: An urban-rural comparison. *Archives of General Psychiatry* 58:663–68.

Velakoulis, D., Pantelis, C., McGorry, P. D., Dudgeon, P., Brewer, W., Cook, M., et al. (1999). Hippocampal volume in first-episode psychoses and chronic schizophrenia: A high-resolution magnetic resonance imaging study. *Archives of General Psychiatry* 56:133–41.

Verdoux, H., van Os, J., Maurice-Tison, S., Gay, B., Salamon, R., and Bourgeois, M. (1998). Is early adulthood a critical developmental stage for psychosis proneness? A survey of delusional ideation in normal subjects. *Schizophrenia Research* 29:247–54.

Weinberger, D. R. (1987). Implications of normal brain development for the pathogenesis of schizophrenia. *Archives of General Psychiatry* 44:660–69.

Yao, J. K., Leonard, S., and Reddy, R. D. (2000). Membrane phospholipid abnormalities in postmortem brains from schizophrenic patients. *Schizophrenia Research* 42:7–17.

Yao, J. K., van Kammen, D. P., and Gurklis, J. A. (1996). Abnormal incorporation of arachidonic acid into platelets of drug-free patients with schizophrenia. *Psychiatry Research* 60:11–21.

Yung, A. R., and McGorry, P. D. (1996a). The prodromal phase of first-episode psychosis: Past and current conceptualizations. *Schizophrenia Bulletin* 22:353–70.

Yung, A. R., and McGorry, P. D. (1996b). The initial prodrome in psychosis: Descriptive and qualitative aspects. *Australian and New Zealand Journal of Psychiatry* 30:587–99.

Yung, A. R., Phillips, L. J., McGorry, P. D., McFarlane, C. A., Francey, S., Harrigan, S., et al. (1998). Prediction of psychosis: A step towards indicated prevention of schizophrenia. *British Journal of Psychiatry Supplement* 172:14–20.

Yung, A. R., Phillips, L. J., Yuen, H. P., Francey, S. M., McFarlane, C. A., Hallgren, M., et al. (2003). Psychosis prediction: 12-month follow-up of a high-risk ("prodromal") group. *Schizophrenia Research* 60:21–32.

Zimmer, L., Delpal, S., Guilloteau, D., Aioun, J., Durand, G., and Chalon, S. (2000). Chronic n-3 polyunsaturated fatty acid deficiency alters dopamine vesicle density in the rat frontal cortex. *Neuroscience Letters* 284:25–28.

CHAPTER TEN

Other Psychotic Disorders in Childhood and Adolescence

Nitin Gogtay, M.D., and Judith L. Rapoport, M.D.

Transient psychotic phenomena are more common in healthy and mildly disturbed children than is generally recognized (Caplan 1994; Schreier 1999; McGee, Williams, and Poulton 2000). At the same time, serious psychotic disorders of childhood are often misdiagnosed, in part because of their rarity. When such disorders do occur, however, the disruption of cognitive and social development and the burden to the family are usually devastating. Our relatively sparse knowledge of psychotic processes in children, together with diagnostic uncertainty, has hampered research in this area, which has in turn limited our understanding about the prognostic significance of such phenomena in childhood (Nicolson and Rapoport 1999).

Childhood-onset schizophrenia and psychoses that are secondary to mood and affective disorders have been somewhat better studied. In this chapter, we will focus on the clinical phenomenology and neurobiology of childhood-onset psychoses that cannot be classified within any major *DSM* syndrome. In particular, one such group of *patients* displays significant but transient psychotic symptoms and comorbid deficits across multiple domains and has been labeled provisionally as multidimensionally impaired (MDI). Such children are probably more common in clinical practice than those with any other child-hood psychosis. The heterogeneous nature of these cases is becoming increas-ingly apparent with long-term monitoring.

Background and History

For many years the term *psychosis* was used broadly in relation to children, and the varied disorders that could produce psychotic phenomena were not recognized as separate entities. As a result, a spectrum of behavioral disorders and also autism were grouped into the category of childhood schizophrenia (Volkmar 1996). In 1971, landmark studies by Kolvin established the clinical distinction between autism and other psychotic disorders of childhood (Kolvin 1971). Even today, however, high rates of initial misdiagnosis remain owing to symptom overlap, particularly for mood disorders, and the appearance of hal-lucinations and delusions in nonpsychotic pediatric patients (McKenna et al. 1994).

Hallucinatory and delusional phenomena have been described in nonpsy-chotic pediatric populations for many years (Lukianowicz 1969). Healthy preschoolers may manifest "disordered thought," which usually diminishes af-ter age 6 (Caplan 1994). In addition, transient anxiety and stress-related visual hallucinations are occasionally reported in preschool children (Rothstein 1981). The prognosis of these phenomena is benign. School-age children also display hallucinatory phenomena (Schreier 1999; McGee, Williams, and Poul-ton 2000), but psychotic phenomena at this age tend to be more persistent and are often associated with drug toxicity or more serious mental illness (Davison 1983; Abramowicz 1993).

The NIMH Experience

A study of childhood-onset schizophrenia (COS) employing nationwide re-cruitment has been underway at the National Institute of Mental Health (NIMH) since 1990. Inclusion criteria are an onset of psychosis before age 12, a premorbid IQ of 70 or above, and the absence of any major neurological prob-lem. Over the past eleven years, about 1,800 charts have been reviewed, of which 80 percent were rejected from further consideration because the patient failed to meet the criteria for childhood-onset schizophrenia. More than 250 children have been screened in person, of whom about 60 percent were diagnosed with other psychiatric illnesses such as affective disorders, pervasive developmental disorder, and anxiety or behavioral disorders. About 100 children who appeared likely to meet the criteria for COS were admitted to the research unit and underwent an initial observation period followed by a complete medication washout. Once off medication, these children were observed for up to three weeks. At this point, an additional 20 percent turned out not to meet the criteria for childhood-onset schizophrenia, most frequently because an affective disorder had instead been diagnosed (McKenna et al. 1994; Kumra et al. 1999; Nicolson and Rapoport 1999). A recent 4- to 6-year follow-up study of 33 of these cases indicated that the diagnosis of a nonschizophrenic disorder had generally proved stable (Calderoni et al. 2001).

A subgroup of patients referred to the NIMH as cases of childhood-onset schizophrenia showed only transient psychotic symptoms at screening or after medication washout but had impairment secondary to disruptive and aggressive behavior. These cases have been studied in parallel with the COS sample. The subjects in this group reported brief hallucinations and delusions, typically under stress, although there was no evidence of thought disorder. They also exhibited dramatic mood outbursts and heightened levels of aggression. On presentation, these individuals could not be categorized according to existing *DSM* criteria other than those for comorbid attention deficit hyperactivity disorder (ADHD) and/or specific developmental disorders. In view of their impairments in multiple domains these children were provisionally called "multidimensionally impaired" and, together with their families, have been followed longitudinally alongside the patients with childhood-onset schizophrenia (Kumra et al. 1998; Nicolson et al. 2001). The heterogeneous long-term outcome of these patients is only just emerging, as discussed below.

The MDI Group

Over the past fifteen years, a sizeable group of group of children has been identified who have complex developmental disorders, which include affective dysregulation, problems in social interaction, and transient psychotic symptoms. Because their symptoms fail to conform to a specific *DSM* syndrome, these children have posed a diagnostic dilemma (Towbin et al. 1993). Historically, they received multiple *DSM* diagnoses or were described as cases of "childhood schizophrenia" or, in some instances, as examples of a "borderline syndrome of children" (Dahl, Cohen, and Provence 1986; Petti and Vela 1990; Towbin et al. 1993; van der Gaag et al. 1995). Later, a behavioral syndrome was identified that was again characterized by affective dysregulation and impairments in social behavior, but in which more prominent symptoms of autistic spectrum disorders were apparent. This syndrome was labeled "multiplex developmental disorder." However, in comparison to the group described above, these children diagnosed with this disorder showed more pronounced symptoms of pervasive developmental disorder as well as greater evidence of formal thought disorder. Moreover, the onset of their illness occurred before they were 5 (Cohen, Paul, and Volkmar 1986; Towbin et al. 1993; Ad-Dab'bagh and Greenfield 2001).

Clinical Features

Although the MDI group showed similarities with both the COS group and the group diagnosed with multiplex development disorder, the MDI sample proved to have some distinct features (McKenna et al. 1994; Kumra et al. 1998):

1. Brief, transient episodes of psychosis and perceptual disturbance, typically in response to stress
2. Nearly daily periods of emotional lability disproportionate to precipitants
3. Impaired interpersonal skills despite the desire to initiate peer friendships (a distinction from childhood-onset schizophrenia)
4. Cognitive deficits as indicated by multiple deficits in information processing
5. No obvious thought disorder (although clinically this can be difficult to define, especially in presence of a communication disorder)

Differential Diagnosis for the MDI Group

1. Hallucinations are relatively common in affective disorders such as bipolar disorder and major depression, and both the manic and the depressed states are associated with irritability and aggression (Chambers et al. 1982; Varanka et al. 1988). However, the psychotic symptoms and affective dysregulation in these conditions tend to be mood congruent (Garralda 1984b; Ulloa et al. 2000).
2. Organic psychosis and substance abuse disorders (which may show psychosis and irritability) will present with hallucinations (Garralda

1984a; Caplan et al. 1991). In adults, schizophrenia and substance abuse are frequently comorbid.

3. Conduct disorder and various other behavioral disturbances can be accompanied by hallucinations and disruptive overreactive behaviors (Garralda 1984a, 1984b).
4. Pervasive developmental disorders including autism and childhood disintegrative disorder may also show mood lability.

Demographics of the MDI Cohort

To date, the MDI cohort of the NIMH sample consists of 30 children, all with transient psychotic symptoms noted before their thirteenth birthday, who have been given a catch-all diagnosis of psychosis not otherwise specified. The mean age at the time of initial contact was 11.6 ± 2.6 years. The large majority of these patients are male (26, or 86%), a significantly higher proportion than in the COS group ($\chi^2 = 5.92$, df = 1, $p = .01$). Their psychotic symptoms were brief (usually only a few minutes), infrequent (a few times a month), and usually occurred in response to stress, and none showed the disorganized speech or negative symptoms common in children with schizophrenia. While the MDI children had few if any friends, this was due to poor social skills rather than the lack of a desire for friendship. All were characterized by dramatic affective instability and associated aggressive behavior, along with transient hallucinations and no thought disorganization, and thus were initially labeled as MDI patients (Nicolson et al. 2001). On first contact, none met the criteria for mood disorder or post-traumatic stress disorder, but all were diagnosed with comorbid disruptive behavior disorders: ADHD ($n = 20$), oppositional defiant disorder, or ODD ($n = 8$), and conduct disorder ($n = 2$), including two cases given dual diagnoses.

Risk Factors

The probands in the MDI cohort exhibited high rates of premorbid language abnormalities (62%), motor impairments (58%), and deviant social development (58%). In addition, 73 percent had been placed in special education, a proportion comparable to that in the COS group (Nicolson, Lenane, et al. 2001). In addition, preliminary analyses have shown the families of MDI children to be strikingly dysfunctional, as is evident from the high rates of Axis I and/or Axis II diagnoses (85%) in parents of MDI probands (53% were diagnosed with major mood disorder, 23% with substance abuse, and 26% with cluster B personality disorder) in comparison to the parents of patients with COS. These are more often single-parent families (33%), and seven of the fathers have been in jail. Intriguingly, the rate of schizophrenia spectrum disorders in MDI parents (20%) was comparable to that seen in COS parents (24%) but considerably higher than for a community control population (1.5%) (Nicolson et al. 2001).

Neurobiological and Neuropsychological Studies

Neurobiological and neuropsychological studies provide an opportunity to study the pathophysiology of the MDI syndrome. Unique phenotypic features may reflect an underlying genetic risk, thereby providing biological trait markers. Parallel endophenotypic studies of MDI probands and their families may help us to distinguish the genetic or epigenetic phenomena underpinning the psychotic process.

Eye Tracking

Abnormalities in eye tracking (the ability to follow a moving target) are of interest as indirect indicators of frontal lobe function (Levy et al. 1994). Like the COS group, the MDI patients exhibited qualitatively poorer eye tracking (a higher root mean square error and lower gain), although the COS group also showed a greater frequency of catch-up saccades (Jacobsen et al. 1996; Kumra et al. 1998; Kumra et al. 2001; Nicolson et al. 2001). Again like the COS patients, MDI children exhibited significantly greater impairments in eye tracking than did control subjects, which might reflect some common underlying genetic susceptibility in MDI and COS children.

Neuropsychological Functioning

Neurocognitive deficits in the domains of memory, verbal learning, attention, and motor speed tend to remain stable over the years and are considered trait markers of schizophrenia (Nopoulos et al. 1994; Elvevag and Goldberg 2002). Kumra et al. (2000) compared the neuropsychological test performance of 24 MDI children and 27 COS children and found that the former showed deficits in attention, learning, and abstraction, a profile not significantly different from that of the COS group. Even though the study was limited by the lack of IQ-matched controls, as in the case of eye-tracking abnormalities, the nonspecificity of the test profile may reflect a shared susceptibility (Kumra et al. 2000). Preliminary family data for the MDI group indicate that, in contrast to the parents of the COS children, the MDI parents did not differ significantly from community controls on any of the neuropsychological measures (Trails A and B, Wechsler Intelligence Scale for Children, and vocabulary or digit span). This may, however, reflect the relatively small sample size.

Brain Imaging

Anatomic brain MRI scans were obtained from all MDI children and their full siblings at the time of admission, with the scanning repeated at 2-year intervals thereafter. Because most of these children received neuroleptic medications similar to those given the COS group, they also functioned as a medication- and IQ-matched contrast group. Initial brain MRI scans revealed abnormalities for the MDI group not unlike those seen in the COS patients, including reduced total cerebral volume and enlarged lateral ventricles (Kumra et al. 2000). However, longitudinal scans on 20 of the MDI patients revealed a static pattern of gray matter loss and ventricular enlargement not apparent in healthy controls. The lack of progressive deterioration observed in the MDI group differed significantly from the striking back-to-front loss of cortical gray matter seen in schizophrenia (Thompson et al. 2001). These intriguing findings, which in fact pointed to certain small, highly localized loss patterns in MDI cases, are being explored further as subpopulations of the MDI cohort emerge in the course of follow-up outcome studies.

Treatment History

As one would expect from their initial referral as cases of COS, MDI patients had developed psychotic symptoms at an early age (mean $\pm$ SD = 7.5 $\pm$ 2.0)— even earlier than the age at which psychotic symptoms appeared in the COS group (10.3 $\pm$ 1.7) ($p < .0001$). The MDI children had frequently been treated with psychotropic medications (1.9 $\pm$ 2.0 years) (Kumra et al. 1998), and the majority were on a combination of an antipsychotic (45% on an atypical one and 35% on a standard neuroleptic), a mood stabilizer, and/or an anticonvulsant (60%, most often valproic acid or lithium), as well as a stimulant and/or antidepressant. At 4- to 6-year follow-up, 60 percent were being treated with atypical agents, and 10 percent were on a combination of a typical and an atypical agent. The use of anticonvulsants and/or mood stabilizers remained at 60 percent, while 7 patients (15%) were medication free.

Clinical Follow-up

MDI children have had better outcomes than the COS children, particularly with respect to psychotic symptoms, but treatment is still indicated for problems of aggression and behavioral dyscontrol. Of the 29 MDI children who have been followed up over a period of 2 to 8 years, about half (15) are now diagnosed with a mood or psychotic disorder including schizoaffective disorder, depressed type (1), bipolar disorder (12), and major depressive disorder (2). One of the patients diagnosed as depressed had had an episode of mania after initiation of fluoxetine, suggesting a bipolar diathesis (Akiskal et al. 1983). Patients in this group showed significant morbidity even between mood episodes and a poor response to medication, and had also undergone multiple hospitalizations and/or had been placed in a residential treatment facility. Their high level of comorbidity was relatively unchanged, 8 patients continuing to meet criteria for ADHD, 3 for ODD, and 1 for conduct disorder.

For the remaining 16 no evidence of mood or psychotic disorder could be detected at follow-up, although developmental learning problems, elevated levels of aggression, and emotional dyscontrol persisted. Of these 16—who continued to be characterized as MDI patients—5 had remained free of hallucinations and delusions once treatment with antipsychotics was discontinued, suggesting that their psychosis had indeed remitted. The other 8 patients who remained with the diagnosis of psychosis not otherwise specified continued to be treated with antipsychotic medication, primarily to control aggressive and/or impulsive behavior. This treatment may, however, have obscured symptoms of psychosis (Nicolson et al. 2001).

Although none of the MDI children has progressed to schizophrenia, the MDI label to date best predicts affective disorder for continued behavioral dyscontrol. This is likely to change, given that none have yet passed the age of risk for schizophrenia.

Conclusions

Psychotic phenomena such as hallucinations and delusions are relatively common in children and rarely imply a diagnosis of schizophrenia. The NIMH experience with MDI children highlights the importance of a careful diagnostic evaluation. In the case of a diagnosis of schizophrenia, this evaluation should include a period of observation during which the child is off medication. For other school-age children who display even transient psychotic symptoms a long-term follow-up should be undertaken.

It is becoming clear that our MDI designation covers a large heterogeneous group of children at high risk for chronic affective disorders. In contrast, in a 10- to 20-year follow-up study of 19 children deemed to be "borderline" or to have "multiplex" disorders, none met the criteria for affective or psychotic disorder; instead, the majority fit the criteria for a personality disorder (Lofgren et al. 1991). The resemblance of the MDI syndrome to schizophrenia in terms of premorbid development, risk factors, and clinical presentation suggests that the two share certain risk factors, which perhaps reflects an underlying genetic susceptibility common to schizophrenia and affective psychosis (Cannon et al. 1993).

To date, research indicates the family profile of the MDI group differs from that typically seen in cases of childhood-onset schizophrenia. In comparison to their COS counterparts, MDI families have a higher rate of nonspectrum psychiatric diagnoses on Axis I and II, and they tend to do better on neurocognitive testing as well. MDI probands, however, exhibit a neuropsychological profile similar to that of COS probands, and thus their psychosis may share certain endophenotypes with schizophrenia. Schatzberg et al. (2000) showed that patients with psychotic depression and with schizophrenia demonstrate similar impairments in neurocognitive function mediated through frontal cortex and mediotemporal lobes. Thus, the neurocognitive parallels between the MDI and schizophrenia probands might reflect the nonspecificity of these measures. Long-term follow-up of these children as they develop affective and behavioral syndromes may reveal more specific predictors of these illnesses and may ultimately allow long-term risk to be determined on the basis of neuropsychological evaluations.

The high comorbidity of ADHD and the behavioral disturbances in MDI children are reminiscent of the early bipolar syndrome described by Biederman and colleagues (Biederman and Faraone 1995; Wozniak et al. 1995). At their initial evaluation, however, none of the MDI children met the criteria for mania, but a significant number (40%) had developed a bipolar disorder at follow-up. Whether a subgroup of MDI children can in fact be classified as cases of early bipolar disorder will likely become clear through long-term follow-up studies of a larger sample. In addition, although significantly less progressive gray matter loss has already been detected in MDI children, with continued subject accrual we expect to be able to recognize more subtle individual patterns of cortical brain development that can be related to neurocognitive performance and to eventual outcome. Diagnostically specific patterns of selective regional loss will be of great value to our efforts to distinguish MDI from COS patients and to predict long-term outcome. Encouragingly, these studies are currently in progress at the NIMH.

REFERENCES

Abramowicz, M. (1993). Drugs that cause psychiatric symptoms. *Medical Letters in Drugs and Therapeutics* 3565–70.

Ad-Dab'bagh, Y., and Greenfield, B. (2001). Multiple complex developmental disorder: The "multiple and complex" evolution of the "childhood borderline syndrome" construct. *Journal of the American Academy of Child and Adolescent Psychiatry* 40(8):954–64.

Akiskal, H. S., Walker, P., Puzantian, V. R., King, D., Rosenthal, T. L., and Dranon, M. (1983). Bipolar outcome in the course of depressive illness: Phenomenologic, familial, and pharmacologic predictors. *Journal of Affective Disorders* 5(2):115–28.

Biederman, J., and Faraone, S. V. (1995). Childhood mania revisited. *Israeli Journal of Medical Science* 31(11):647–51.

Calderoni, D., Wudarsky, M., Bhangoo, R., Dell, M. L., Nicolson, R., Hamburger, S. D., et al. (2001). Differentiating childhood-onset schizophrenia from psychotic mood disorders. *Journal of the American Academy of Child and Adolescent Psychiatry* 40(10):1190–96.

Cannon, T. D., Mednick, S. A., Parnas, J., Schulsinger, F., Praestholm, J., and Vestergaard, A. (1993). Developmental brain abnormalities in the offspring of schizophrenic mothers, Pt. 1: Contributions of genetic and perinatal factors. *Archives of General Psychiatry* 50(7):551–64.

Caplan, R. (1994). Thought disorder in childhood. *Journal of the American Academy of Child and Adolescent Psychiatry* 33(5):605–15.

Caplan, R., Shields, W. D., Mori, L., and Yudovin, S. (1991). Middle childhood onset of interictal psychosis. *Journal of the American Academy of Child and Adolescent Psychiatry* 30(6):893–96.

Chambers, W. J., Puig-Antich, J., Tabrizi, M. A., and Davies, M. (1982). Psychotic symptoms in prepubertal major depressive disorder. *Archives of General Psychiatry* 30(8): 921–27.

Cohen, D. J., Paul, R., and Volkmar, F. R. (1986). Issues in the classification of pervasive and other developmental disorders: Toward *DSM-IV*. *Journal of the American Academy of Child and Adolescent Psychiatry* 25(2):213–20.

Dahl, E. K., Cohen, D. J., and Provence, S. (1986). Clinical and multivariate approaches to the nosology of pervasive developmental disorders. *Journal of the American Academy of Child and Adolescent Psychiatry* 25(2):170–80.

Davison, K. (1983). Schizophrenia-like psychoses associated with organic cerebral disorders: A review. *Psychiatric Development* 1(1):1–33.

Elvevag, B., and Goldberg, T. E. (2002). Cognitive impairment in schizophrenia is the core of the disorder. *Critical Review of Neurobiology* 14(1):1–21.

Garralda, M. E. (1984a). Hallucinations in children with conduct and emotional disorders, Pt. 1: The clinical phenomena. *Psychological Medicine* 14(3):589–96.

Garralda, M. E. (1984b). Hallucinations in children with conduct and emotional disorders, Pt. 2: The follow-up study. *Psychological Medicine* 14(3):597–604.

Jacobsen, L. K., Hong, W. L., Hommer, D. W., Hamburger, S. D., Castellanos, F. X., Frazier, J. A., et al. (1996). Smooth pursuit eye movements in childhood-onset schizophrenia: Comparison with attention-deficit hyperactivity disorder and normal controls. *Biological Psychiatry* 40(11):1144–54.

Kolvin, I. (1971). Studies in the childhood psychoses, Pt. 1: Diagnostic criteria and classification. *British Journal of Psychiatry* 118(545):381–84.

Kumra, S., Briguglio, C., Lenane, M., Goldhar, L., Bedwell, J., Venuchekov, J., et al. (1999). Including children and adolescents with schizophrenia in medication-free research. *American Journal of Psychiatry* 156(7):1065–68.

Kumra, S., Giedd, J. N., Vaituzis, A. C., Jacobsen, L. K., McKenna, K., Bedwell, J., et al. (2000). Childhood-onset psychotic disorders: Magnetic resonance imaging of volumetric differences in brain structure. *American Journal of Psychiatry* 157(9):1467–74.

Kumra, S., Jacobsen, L. K., Lenane, M., Zahn, T. P., Wiggs, E., Alaghband-Rad, J., et al. (1998). "Multidimensionally impaired disorder": Is it a variant of very early-onset schizophrenia? *Journal of the American Academy of Child and Adolescent Psychiatry* 37(1):91–99.

Kumra, S., Sporn, A., Hommer, D. W., Nicolson, R., Thaker, G., Israel, E., et al. (2001). Smooth pursuit eye-tracking impairment in childhood-onset psychotic disorders. *American Journal of Psychiatry* 158(8):1291–98.

Kumra, S., Wiggs, E., Bedwell, J., Smith, A. K., Arling, E., Albus, K., et al. (2000). Neuropsychological deficits in pediatric patients with childhood-onset schizophrenia and psychotic disorder not otherwise specified. *Schizophrenia Research* 42(2):135–44.

Levy, D. L., Holzman, P. S., Matthysse, S., and Mendell, N. R. (1994). Eye tracking and schizophrenia: A selective review. *Schizophrenia Bulletin* 20(1):47–62.

Lofgren, D. P., Bemporad, J., King, J., Lindem, K., and O'Driscoll, G. (1991). A prospective follow-up study of so-called borderline children. *American Journal of Psychiatry* 148(11):1541–47.

Lukianowicz, N. (1969). Hallucinations in non-psychotic children. *Psychiatric Clinics (Basel)* 2(6):321–37.

McGee, R., Williams, S., and Poulton, R. (2000). Hallucinations in nonpsychotic children. *Journal of the American Academy of Child and Adolescent Psychiatry* 39(1):12–13.

McKenna, K., Gordon, C. T., Lenane, M., Kaysen, D., Fahey, K., and Rapoport, J. L. (1994). Looking for childhood-onset schizophrenia: The first 71 cases screened. *Journal of the American Academy of Child and Adolescent Psychiatry* 33(5):636–44.

Nicolson, R., Lenane, M., Brookner, F., Gochman, P., Kumra, S., Spechler, L., et al. (2001). Children and adolescents with psychotic disorder not otherwise specified: A two- to eight-year follow-up. *Comprehensive Psychiatry* 42(4):319–25.

Nicolson, R., and Rapoport, J. L. (1999). Childhood-onset schizophrenia: Rare but worth studying. *Biological Psychiatry* 46(10):1418–28.

Nopoulos, P., Flashman, L., Flaum, M., Arndt, S., and Andreasen, N. (1994). Stability of cognitive functioning early in the course of schizophrenia. *Schizophrenia Research* 14(1):29–37.

Petti, T. A., and Vela, R. M. (1990). Borderline disorders of childhood: An overview. *Journal of the American Academy of Child and Adolescent Psychiatry* 29(3):327–37.

Rothstein, A. (1981). Hallucinatory phenomena in childhood: A critique of the literature. *Journal of the American Academy of Child and Adolescent Psychiatry* 20(3):623–35.

Schatzberg, A. F., Posener, J. A., DeBattista, C., Kalehzan, B. M., Rothschild, A. J., and Shear, P. K. (2000). Neuropsychological deficits in psychotic versus nonpsychotic major depression and no mental illness. *American Journal of Psychiatry* 157(7):1095–100.

Schreier, H. A. (1999). Hallucinations in nonpsychotic children: more common than we think? *Journal of the American Academy of Child and Adolescent Psychiatry* 38(5):623–25.

Thompson, P. M., Vidal, C., Giedd, J. N., Gochman, P., Blumenthal, J., Nicolson, R., et al. (2001). From the cover: Mapping adolescent brain change reveals dynamic wave of accelerated gray matter loss in very early-onset schizophrenia. *Proceedings of the National Academy of Sciences, USA* 98(20):11650–55.

Towbin, K. E., Dykens, E. M., Pearson, G. S., and Cohen, D. J. (1993). Conceptualizing "borderline syndrome of childhood" and "childhood schizophrenia" as a developmental disorder. *Journal of the American Academy of Child and Adolescent Psychiatry* 32(4):775–82.

Ulloa, R. E., Birmaher, B., Axelson, D., Williamson, D. E., Brent, D. A., Ryan, N. D., et al. (2000). Psychosis in a pediatric mood and anxiety disorders clinic: Phenomenology and correlates. *Journal of the American Academy of Child and Adolescent Psychiatry* 39(3):337–45.

van der Gaag, R. J., Buitelaar, J., Van den Ban, E., Bezemer, M., Njio, L., and Van Engeland, H. (1995). A controlled multivariate chart review of multiple complex developmental disorder. *Journal of the American Academy of Child and Adolescent Psychiatry* 34(8):1096–106.

Varanka, T. M., Weller, R. A., Weller, E. B., and Fristad, M. A. (1988). Lithium treatment of manic episodes with psychotic features in prepubertal children. *American Journal of Psychiatry* 145(12):1557–59.

Volkmar, F. R. (1996). Childhood and adolescent psychosis: A review of the past 10 years. *Journal of the American Academy of Child and Adolescent Psychiatry* 35(7):843–51.

Wozniak, J., Biederman, J., Kiely, K., Ablon, J. S., Faraone, S. V., Mundy, E., et al. (1995). Mania-like symptoms suggestive of childhood-onset bipolar disorder in clinically referred children. *Journal of the American Academy of Child and Adolescent Psychiatry* 34(7):867–76.

CHAPTER ELEVEN

Pharmacological Treatment

Shermeil Dass, M.D., Nora K. McNamara, M.D., and Robert L. Findling, M.D.

In comparison to what is known about the pharmacological treatment of schizophrenia and its related disorders in adults, little is known about this topic in regard to children and adolescents. Whereas scores of clinical trials have been devoted to adults with schizophrenia, only a handful of studies have focused on juveniles with this condition. This paucity of studies poses quite a problem, because what is true about the pharmacotherapy of adults with neuropsychiatric disorders does not necessarily apply to children or teenagers. For example, although historically the tricyclic antidepressants were the gold standard to which other treatments for depression were compared in adults, these agents have consistently been shown to be ineffective as a treatment for depression in both children and teenagers (Findling, Reed, and Blumer 1999; Keller et al. 2001). In addition to differences in effectiveness, tolerability, and safety for adults and young people, an individual's biodisposition may vary considerably across the life cycle (Clein and Riddle 1995). For this reason, weight-based dosing changes may not adequately address how best to treat young patients with such medication.

It is unfortunate that so few data exist about the treatment of juvenile schizophrenia and other psychotic spectrum disorders. Part of the problem is that young people rarely suffer from schizophrenia. Estimates indicate that approximately one in 10,000 children under the age of 12 has the illness (Burd and Kerbeshian 1987). Similarly, retrospective data from studies of adults with schizophrenia indicate that fewer than 5 percent of the patients who develop schizophrenia do so during the first decade of life (Loranger 1984). Adolescent-onset schizophrenia appears to be somewhat more common than the childhood-onset form of the illness. It appears that roughly 30 percent of patients with schizophrenia develop their first positive symptoms before the age of 18 (Häfner et al. 1993; Beratis, Gabriel, and Hoidas 1994). In addition, it may be that adolescents with schizophrenia are a particularly vulnerable population. Findings to date indicate that the clinical course of early-onset schizophrenia is associated with a poorer outcome than is generally seen when the illness develops in adulthood (Gillberg, Hellgren, and Gillberg 1993; Krausz and Müller-Thomsen 1993; Cawthron et al. 1994). Treatments are therefore needed that not only relieve symptoms, but can also allow patients to function better. In what follows, we will review what is currently known about the pharmacotherapy of psychotic illnesses in juveniles. Particular attention will be paid to comparing and contrasting the data available regarding young people as opposed to adults and to providing a clinical perspective on these data.

Typical Antipsychotics (Neuroleptics)

For a long time, the so-called typical antipsychotics, or neuroleptics, were the standard pharmacotherapy for schizophrenia. At present, fourteen such antipsychotics are available for use in the United States as a treatment for adults with psychosis (Findling et al. 1998). These agents have been marketed on the basis of their demonstrated efficacy in patients older than 18 years of age. However, only three prospective studies have specifically considered the use of typical antipsychotics in juveniles with schizophrenia (see Table 11.1).

In the first and largest study to date, 75 adolescents between the ages of 13 and 18 were randomly selected to receive haloperidol (Haldol), loxapine (Loxitane), or a placebo in a double-blind fashion for 4 weeks (Pool et al. 1976)—the placebo-controlled design being one noteworthy feature of this study. Medications were administered twice daily in divided doses, and the amount of medication administered to each subject could be adjusted in accordance

Table 11.1. Selected prospective trials of typical antipsychotics in children and adolescents with schizophrenia

	Study design	Sample size (N)	Age (years)	Medication (no. of subjects dosed)	Mean medication dose (mg/day)	Study length	Rate of EPS (%)
Pool et al. 1976	Double-blind, placebo-controlled, with flexible dosing	75	13 to 18	Loxapine (26) Haloperidol (25) Placebo (24)	Loxapine (87.5) Haloperidol (9.8)	4 weeks	Loxapine (73) Haloperidol (72) Placebo (4)
Realmuto et al. 1984	Randomized, single-blind, flexible dose	21	11 to 18	Thiothixene (13) Thioridazine (8)	Thiothixene (16.2) Thioridazine (17.8)	4–6 weeks	Thiothixene (54) Thioridazine (0)
Spencer and Campbell 1994	Double-blind, placebo-controlled crossover study with flexible dosing	16	5 to 11	Haloperidol (16) Placebo (16)	Haloperidol (1.9)	10 weeks	Not reported

Note: EPS = extrapyramidal symptoms

with the patient's response. The final mean dose of haloperidol prescribed was 9.8 mg per day, while that of loxapine was 87.5 mg per day. The authors reported that both active compounds were superior to the placebo in ameliorating positive symptoms of psychosis. However, as the authors noted, a substantial proportion of the patients did not respond adequately: 15 percent of those treated with loxapine and 30 percent of those treated with haloperidol showed no improvement. Side effects, particularly extrapyramidal side effects (EPS) and sedation, were commonly reported. EPS was seen in 18 out of the 25 patients treated with haloperidol (72%) and in 19 out of the 26 subjects given loxapine (73%), but in only 1 out of the 24 who were administered placebo (4%). Sedation was also a frequent side effect, occurring in 13 out of the 25 subjects treated with haloperidol (52%), 21 out of the 26 given loxapine (81%), and in 6 out of the 24 patients (25%) in the placebo group. The prevalence of these side effects is a major concern because issues surrounding the tolerability of specific medications is likely to adversely affect the long-term adherence to pharmacotherapy on the part of patients suffering from a chronic, potentially debilitating illness.

A second prospective study (Realmuto et al. 1984), which drew on a sample of 21 youths between the ages of 11 and 18, set out to describe and compare the treatment response and the side-effect profiles of thioridazine (Mellaril) with thiothixene (Navane) using a single-blind design. The mean doses were 178 mg per day of thioridazine and 16.2 mg per day of thiothixene. Although both agents seemed to be equally effective in reducing the symptoms of psychosis, a large proportion of these teenagers (43%) were described as only slightly improved or unchanged, or even in worse condition, as a result of their pharmacotherapy. In addition, much as in the case of haloperidol and loxapine, more than half of the patients treated with thiothixene developed EPS, and sedation was again another troublesome side effect, occurring in 75 percent of the patients treated with thioridazine and 50 percent of those treated with thiothixene.

A third study has the distinction of being the only double-blind placebo-controlled trial of neuroleptics ever to focus on children with schizophrenia (Spencer and Campbell 1994). This 10-week study of 16 children between the ages of 5 and 11 compared the efficacy of haloperidol to that of a placebo using a crossover design and flexible dosing. After a 2-week placebo baseline period, patients who continued to show active symptoms of psychosis were randomized to receive an initial four weeks of treatment with either haloperidol or the placebo. After the 4-week trial period, the subjects were treated with the other agent for an additional 4 weeks. Treatment with haloperidol at a mean dose of 1.9 mg per day proved to be associated with greater symptom amelioration than treatment with the placebo.

Despite the different medications under review and the relatively small sample sizes of the study cohorts, the results of these three studies suggest that, even though most patients benefit from treatment, a substantial portion of young patients with schizophrenia exhibit suboptimal symptom amelioration during neuroleptic pharmacotherapy. This conclusion subsequently found support in a retrospective study of adults with schizophrenia, the results of which indicated that an earlier age of onset for schizophrenia is associated with treatment resistance to typical antipsychotic agents (Meltzer et al. 1997).

As these studies also demonstrate, significant side effects, particularly EPS, commonly occur when juveniles are treated with high potency antipsychotics. In fact, results from other studies suggest that young people are at a higher risk than adults for developing EPS during neuroleptic pharmacotherapy (Keepers, Clappison, and Casey 1983; Findling et al. 1998). Not only can EPS be distressing to both patients and their families, but the appearance of such side effects can also lead to stigmatization of the patient by his or her peers. For these reasons, EPS can ultimately have a negative impact on treatment adherence. There is, moreover, evidence to suggest that children may be at a particularly high risk for developing withdrawal dyskinesias (Campbell et al. 1997). In view of these considerations, there was clearly a need for safer, more effective treatments than had historically been available for the juvenile population.

Atypical Antipsychotics

As we have seen, children and adolescents appear to run a higher risk than do adults for developing neurological side effects as a result of treatment with typical antipsychotics, and these side effects, whether acute or long-term, can substantially reduce the likelihood that patients will continue to adhere to treatment. The literature on the use of typical antipsychotics in young people further suggests that a sizeable proportion of these patients do not receive adequate symptomatic relief from these medications. Clinicians have therefore begun to consider using atypical antipsychotics in the treatment of early-onset schizophrenia.

Clozapine

The first atypical antipsychotic released in the United States was clozapine, and both case reports and clinical trials suggest that the drug may be an effective therapy for young patients with treatment-resistant schizophrenia (Siefen and Remschmidt 1986; Birmaher et al. 1992; Boxer and Davidson 1992; Blanz and Schmidt 1993; Mandoki 1993; Jacobsen et al. 1994; Mandoki 1994; Mozes et al. 1994; Remschmidt, Schulz, and Martin 1994; Towbin, Dykens, and Pugliese 1994; Levkovitch et al. 1995; MacEwan and Morton 1996; Usiskin et al. 2000; Reitzle et al. 2001). However, owing to the risk of neutropenia or agranulocytosis associated with the drug, clozapine has been approved only as a therapy for treatment-resistant schizophrenia and, accordingly, has generally been reserved for use only in treatment-refractory cases of child and adolescent schizophrenia. As Table 11.2 illustrates, research on the use of clozapine in young people has not typically taken the form of prospective clinical trials. At present, only three prospective studies of juveniles with schizophrenia have been carried out.

In the first of these studies, 11 patients between the ages and 12 and 17 years with childhood-onset, neuroleptic-resistant schizophrenia were treated in an open fashion for 6 weeks (Frazier et al. 1994). Clozapine was initiated at a dose of either 12.5 or 25 mg per day; the dose was increased every 4 days as clinically indicated, provided the patient was able to tolerate the higher dose. Dosages were adjusted so as to minimize adverse side effects and to optimize symptom reduction. As the authors noted, sedation and tachycardia were the side effects that most often contributed to dose limitations. At a mean clozapine dose of 370.5 mg per day (range = 125 to 825 mg per day), the patients experienced a 58 percent reduction in symptoms from baseline as measured on the Scale for the Assessment of Positive Symptoms (SAPS) (Andreasen 1984) and a 42 percent reduction on the Scale for the Assessment of Negative Symptoms (SANS) (Andreasen 1983). In addition, 9 of the 11 patients (82 %) demonstrated a greater than 30 percent reduction in their scores on the Brief Psychiatric Rating Scale (BPRS) (Overall and Gorham 1962) in comparison to baseline ratings. From baseline through to the end of week 6, there was also a 58 percent reduction in scores on the Clinical Global Impressions (CGI) Scale (National Institute of Mental Health 1985b). The most common side effects of

Table 11.2. Selected reports of clozapine in children and adolescents

	Type of report	Sample size (N)	Age (years)	Diagnosis	Clozapine dosage in mg/day (range/mean)	Length of treatment	Comments
Siefen and Remschmidt 1986	Case series	21	Mean = 18	TR schizophrenia	254–700/352	Not reported	Most patients improved
Birmaher et al. 1992	Case series	3	17 to 18	TR schizophrenia	100–300/233	Up to 1 year	All patients benefited
Boxer and Davidson 1992	Case report	1	17	TR schizophrenia	600	9 months	Patient experienced salutary effects
Blanz and Schmidt 1993	Case series	57	10 to 21	Mostly TR schizophrenia	75–800/285	Mean = 311 days	Most patients were improved; new-onset EEG abnormalities were common (25%)
Mandoki 1993	Case series	2	14 to 16	TR schizophrenia	300–400	12 months	Both patients benefited
Frazier et al. 1994	Open prospective	11	12 to 17	TR schizophrenia	125–825/370.5	6 weeks	Most patients improved
Jacobsen et al. 1994	Case report	1	14	TR schizophrenia	500	Over 14 months	Patient showed a positive response
Mandoki 1994	Case series	6	Not reported	TR psychosis	Mean = 300	Not reported	Effective in reducing psychosis and aggressive behavior
Mozes et al. 1994	Case series	4	10 to 12	TR schizophrenia	150–300/225	23 to 70 weeks	All patients benefited significantly, but 75% showed EEG changes

Study	Design	N	Age	Diagnosis	Dose (mg/day)	Duration	Outcome
Remschmidt, Schulz, and Martin 1994	Chart review	36	Mean = 18	TR schizophrenia	50–800/330	Mean = 154 days	Most patients responded; 6 patients dicontinued due to side effects
Towbin, Dykens, and Pugliese 1994	Case report	1	13	TR schizophrenia	400	15 months	Moderate improvement described
Levkovitch et al. 1995	Case series	2	15 to 16	TR schizophrenia + TD	450–550	"Several months"	Both psychosis and TD were reduced
Kumra et al. 1996	Randomized clinical trial	10	Mean = 14	TR schizophrenia	25–525/176	6 weeks	Clozapine showed superiority to haloperidol but led to seizures and neutropenia
MacEwan and Morton 1996	Case report	1	10	TR schizophrenia + TD	325	16 months	Both psychosis and TD were reduced
Turetz et al. 1997	Open prospective	11	9 to 13	TR schizophrenia	200–300/227.3	16 weeks	Substantial improvements although 82% showed EEG changes
Usiskin et al. 2000	Case report	1	19	TR schizophrenia	300	3 months	Clozapine successfully reintroduced with prophylactic gabapentin in a teen with prior clozapine-induced seizures
Reitzle et al. 2001	Case report	1	12	TR schizophrenia	350	15 weeks	Clozapine-induced agranulocytosis managed with granulocyte colony-stimulating factor

Note: TR = treatment resistant; TD = tardive dyskinesia; EEG = electroencephalogram the medication were sedation, sialorrhea, weight gain, and enuresis. Overall, however, the authors considered clozapine to be "generally well tolerated." As in other, similar studies, the weight gain observed in this adolescent population—15.4 pounds in 6 weeks—was more substantial than that previously observed in adults. Together, these results led the authors to conclude that clozapine seemed like a promising option for severely impaired young patients with schizophrenia who did not respond well to neuroleptics.

In the only double-blind, randomized control trial to focus on the use of clozapine in juvenile psychosis, members of this same research team examined 21 patients with childhood-onset, neuroleptic-resistant schizophrenia in a 6-week prospective study of parallel-arm design. Of the 21 in the group, 10 were treated with clozapine and 11 with haloperidol. The mean age of the patients who received clozapine was 14.4 years, and that of those who received haloperidol was 13.7 years. Patients randomized to receive clozapine could receive up to 525 mg per day, and those receiving haloperidol up to 27 mg per day. Doses of each drug were adjusted in order to maximize clinical benefit while minimizing adverse side effects. For clozapine, the final average dose was 176 mg per day and for haloperidol 16 mg per day. When the patients were assessed using the BPRS (Overall and Gorham 1962), SANS and SAPS (Andreasen 1983, 1984), and the Children's Global Assessment Scale (CGAS) (Shaffer et al. 1983), treatment with clozapine proved to be of greater benefit than treatment with haloperidol. However, the authors also noted that patients treated with clozapine had high rates of potentially serious side effects in addition to the anticipated side effects of weight gain, sedation, and sialorrhea. A reduction in absolute neutrophil count to below 1500 mm^3 was observed in 5 patients, 2 of whom needed to be discontinued from the drug owing to neutropenia. Furthermore, 2 of the patients treated with clozapine experienced seizures, while 3 others required treatment with anticonvulsants because of changes in electroencephalogram (EEG) readings, and 1 other patient experienced sustained tachycardia requiring treatment with a beta-blocker. Clozapine may therefore be a reasonable treatment choice for select patients, but it should be used with caution on account of safety issues (Kumra et al. 1996).

Whereas the work of Frazier et al. (1994) and Kumra et al. (1996) focused on adolescents with childhood-onset schizophrenia, only one prospective trial has targeted neuroleptic-resistant children with schizophrenia. In this study, 11 treatment-refractory children between the ages of 9 to 13 (average age = 11.3 years) were treated prospectively with clozapine over a period of 16 weeks

(Turetz et al. 1997). The medication was initiated at a dose of either 12.5 or 25 mg per day, with 12.5 mg increases able to be made every five days. The average dose at the end of the study was 227 mg per day, at which point the authors found substantial decreases in the patients' scores on the CGI, BPRS, and Positive and Negative Syndrome Scale (PANSS) (Kay, Fiszbein, and Opler 1987). As in previous studies, high rates (90%) of sedation and sialorrhea were observed, while EEG changes occurred in 82 percent of the study cohort. Interestingly, however, no neutropenia or agranulocytosis was observed. The authors concluded that, despite the high rates of side effects, because of the marked amelioration of symptoms it produced clozapine could be a promising treatment for adolescents with schizophrenia.

In short, clozapine is considered a useful medication for adolescent patients who are treatment resistant, but the drug's utility is limited by its profile of side effects. As with adults, sedation and sialorrhea appear to be the most common and most bothersome of these effects. Although the risk of reduced white blood cell counts is a definite concern when young people are treated with clozapine, children and adolescents do not appear to be at any higher risk than adults. As compared to adults, however, younger patients tend to gain more weight. Rather more important, youths treated with clozapine seem to be at particularly high risk for either EEG changes or frank seizures.

Risperidone

Risperidone was the earliest first-line atypical antipsychotic marketed in the United States. Given the shortcomings of the typical antipsychotics and the recommendation that clozapine be used only with treatment-refractory patients, risperidone has become a commonly used agent for addressing a variety of different neuropsychiatric disorders in young people (Findling, McNamara, and Gracious 2000). As is evident from Table 11.3, a number of case series and case reports have appeared that describe the advantages of risperidone in treating juvenile schizophrenia (Cozza and Edison 1994; Mandoki 1995; Quintana and Keshavan 1995; Simeon et al. 1995; Grcevich et al. 1996; Sourander 1997; Kopala and Caudle 1998; Hirose 2000; Kozlova et al. 2001). The sole prospective study of the topic available in English, however, is that by Armenteros et al. (1997). In this study, 10 adolescents with schizophrenia underwent treatment with risperidone for 6 weeks. Patients were initially given 1.0 mg twice daily with increments of 1 mg made every other day to a maximum daily dose of 10 mg. At the end of the study, 6 of the subjects showed a 20 percent re-

Table 11.3. Selected reports of risperidone in children and adolescents

	Type of report	Sample size (N)	Age (years)	Diagnosis	Risperidone dosage in mg/day (range/mean)	Length of treatment	Comments
Cozza and Edison 1994	Case report	2	15	Schizophrenia	2	Not reported	EPS noted at 6 mg/day in both patients
Mandoki 1995	Case series	10	7 to 17	Various	3–8/5.2	6 to 16 weeks	6 of 10 developed EPS
Quintana and Keshavan 1995	Case series	4	12 to 17	Schizophrenia	4–5/4.25	6 months	2 of 4 showed substantial improvements
Simeon et al. 1995	Case series	3	11 to 17	Schizophrenia	2–4/2.8	6 to 12 months	"Marked" benefit in all 3 patients
Grcevich et al. 1996	Chart review	16	9 to 20	Schizophrenia	2–10/5.9	1 to 11 months	15 of 16 responded; 3 had EPS[a]
Armenteros et al. 1997	Open, prospective	10	11 to 18	Schizophrenia	4–10/6.6	6 weeks	Clinical benefit noted
Sourander 1997	Case report	1	8	Schizophrenia	0.5–2	4 months	Good response described
Kopala and Caudle 1998	Case report	1	18	Schizophrenia	4	3.5 years	Rapid response in a catatonic patient
Hirose 2000	Case report	1	15	Simple schizo-phrenia	3	9 months	Salutary effects described
Kozlova et al. 2001	Open, prospective	32	6 to 16	Schizophrenia spectrum	4–8	6 weeks	Significant benefit noted; EPS seen only at higher doses

Note: EPS = extrapyramidal side effects

duction in their total PANSS score. Similarly 6 patients were considered "much" or "very much improved" when assessed on the CGI, and none had worsened. Statistically significant reductions were noted on the BPRS as well. On the whole, the treatment was well tolerated, with sedation and EPS the most commonly reported side effects. Out of the 10 subjects, 8 exhibited mild, transient sedation, 3 developed Parkinsonism, and 2 had acute dystonic reactions. On the strength of these results, the authors considered risperidone promising enough to warrant further study.

The literature to date thus suggests that risperidone may indeed be an effective treatment for young patients with psychosis. When compared to the typical antipsychotics, risperidone seems less likely to cause EPS. It appears that rapid rates of titration and high final doses of the medication increase the risk that EPS will develop. Sedation is another side effect that can limit the tolerability of risperidone early in the course of treatment. However, the most annoying side effect to occur over long-term treatment with risperidone is weight gain.

Olanzapine

The next first-line atypical antipsychotic marketed as a treatment for schizophrenia in the United States was olanzapine (Zyprexa). The first studies on the use of this compound focused on young patients with treatment-resistant schizophrenia (see Table 11.4). In one such study (Mandoki 1997), olanzapine was revealed to be an effective substitute for clozapine in adolescent patients who had previously been stabilized on that medication. In contrast, Kumra et al. (1998) reported that even though treatment with olanzapine was associated with salutary effects in the juvenile population, clozapine did a superior job of alleviating symptoms. These discrepant findings may well reflect the fact that the first study was performed at an academic medical center whereas the latter took place at the National Institute of Mental Health, where a more gravely affected group of young patients was seen.

Several studies, including chart reviews, case series, and open prospective studies, have examined the use of olanzapine in adolescents with psychotic illnesses (Dittman and Junghanß 1999; Maagensen and Aarkrog 1999; Sholevar, Baron, and Hardie 2000; Dittmann et al. 2001; Findling, McNamara, et al. 2001; Haapasalo-Pesu and Saarijärvi 2001). Collectively, these data suggest that olanzapine can effectively reduce symptoms in young people suffering from psychosis. Moreover, EPS do not generally pose serious difficulties. The prob-

Table 11.4. Selected reports of olanzapine in children and adolescents

	Type of report	Sample size (N)	Age (years)	Diagnosis	Olanzapine dosage in mg/day (range/mean)	Length of treatment	Comments
Mandoki 1997	Case series	8	Not reported	Schizophrenia, clozapine responsive	5–20	—	Olanzapine noted to be effective in clozapine-treated patients
Kumra et al. 1998	Open prospective	8	10 to 18	Schizophrenia	12–20/17.5	8 weeks	Olanzapine of some benefit (but less than clozapine) in treatment-resistant childhood-onset schizophrenia
Dittmann and Junghanß 1999	Chart review	24	13 to 19	Schizophrenia, other psychotic disorders	10–30/16.8	28 to 200 days (mean = 77)	75% much or very much improved but significant weight gain noted
Maagensen and Aarkrog 1999	Chart review	7	13 to 17	Schizophrenia, other related illnesses	2.5–17.5/12.5	4.5 to 11 months	Symptom reduction with weight gain noted
Sholevar, Baron, and Hardie 2000	Open prospective	15	6 to 13	Schizophrenia	2.5–5	Mean = 11.3 days	Most benefited from olanzapine; sedation was most common side effect
Dittmann and Junghanß 2001	Open prospective	55	12 to 21	Schizophrenia	5–20/16.5	6 weeks	Effectiveness noted but weight gain common
Findling, McNamara, et al. 2001	Open prospective	14	12 to 17	Schizophrenia, schizoaffective	Mean = 11.9	8 weeks	Effective in symptom reduction; sedation and weight gain were most common side effects
Haapasalo-Pesu and Saarijärvi 2001	Case series	3	14 to 17	Psychosis	10	5 to 16 months	Effective in reducing psychosis but substantial weight gain noted

lem of sedation can place limitations on dosage early in the course of therapy, however, and, as with clozapine and risperidone, weight gain becomes the most troublesome side effect during the later stages of treatment. It should also be noted that pharmacokinetic data are available regarding the use of olanzapine in teenagers (Grothe et al. 2000). These data demonstrate that the pharmacokinetics of olanzapine are similar in adolescents and adults. Unfortunately, no information is presently available regarding the pharmacokinetics of olanzapine in prepubertal children, where the greatest difference from adults would be expected.

Quetiapine

Given that quetiapine (Seroquel) was released in the United States more recently than olanzapine, it is not surprising that fewer data are available for this agent than for olanzapine (see Table 11.5). To the best of our knowledge, no studies are yet available that examine whether quetiapine is a helpful treatment for younger, school-aged children. Rather, initial research on the use of quetiapine focused on its effectiveness in teenagers who had failed to respond to other atypical agents (Szigethy, Brent, and Findling 1998; Healy, Subotsky, and Pipe 1999). Despite the fact that each case report described only one patient, the observation that patients who failed to respond to one first-line atypical antipsychotic might respond to another has important clinical implications. It suggests that the first-line atypical antipsychotics may differ sufficiently from one another, so that that failure to respond to one of them does not imply that treatment with any such agent should not be considered. In contrast, when a patient with a psychotic disorder failed to respond to one neuroleptic agent, the probability that they would respond to treatment with another was low (Kinon et al. 1993).

The first prospective clinical trial to be published that pertained to the use of quetiapine in adolescents was an open-label effectiveness study that included pharmacokinetic sampling (McConville, Arvanitis, et al. 2000). In this study, 10 teenagers with either schizoaffective disorder ($n = 7$) or bipolar disorder ($n = 3$) were treated for 23 days with quetiapine. The medication was initiated at a dose of 50 mg per day and increased over 3 weeks to a total daily dose of 800 mg. The medication was well tolerated: no subjects were dropped from the study owing to side effects, nor did any subjects require treatment for EPS with an anti-Parkinsonian agent. More encouraging still, the patients' symptoms of psychosis receded over the course of the trial. Overall, the phar-

Table 11.5. Selected reports of quetiapine in children and adolescents

	Type of report	Sample size (N)	Age (years)	Diagnosis	Quetiapine dosage in mg/day (range/mean)	Length of treatment	Comments
Szigethy, Brent, and Findling 1998	Case report	1	14	Schizophrenia	200	2 months	Failed prior treatment with risperidone and olanzapine
Healy, Subotsky, and Pipe 1999	Case report	1	15	Psychosis NOS	200	4 months	Failed prior trial with risperidone
McConville, Wong, et al. 2000	Open prospective, with pharmacokinetic sampling	10	12 to 15	7 schizoaffective, 3 bipolar	800	23 days	Safety and effectiveness seen; pharmacokinetics similar to those reported in adult studies
McConville, Arvanitis, et al. 2000	Open label extension	10	12 to 16	7 schizoaffective, 3 bipolar	300–800	Up to 104 weeks	Evidence for continued effectiveness and safety noted
Shaw et al. 2001	Open prospective	15	13 to 17	Mostly schizophrenia	300–800/467	8 weeks	Effective in reducing psychosis

Note: NOS = not otherwise specified

macokinetic profile of quetiapine in adolescents was similar to that in adults. The open-label extension study to this trial further suggested that quetiapine might have good long-term effectiveness in the treatment of teens with psychosis (McConville, Wong, et al. 2000).

A second prospective clinical trial of quetiapine involved the open-label treatment of 15 teenagers, aged 13 to 17, with quetiapine for up to 8 weeks (Shaw et al. 2001). Out of the 15 subjects, 5 had schizophrenia, while 4 had been diagnosed with schizoaffective disorder, 3 with psychosis not otherwise specified, and 3 with an affective disorder. At a mean dose of 467 mg per day, significant reductions in psychotic symptoms were apparent. The medication was well tolerated and not notably associated with EPS, the most common side effects being somnolence and headache. Remarkably, 93 percent of the patients were found to be "much" or "very much" improved in comparison to baseline. Thus, even though the amount of data to date is modest, these early reports indicate that quetiapine may well be a valuable treatment for adolescents with psychosis.

Ziprasidone

At present, ziprasidone (Geodon) is marketed in the United States as a treatment for schizophrenia in adults. Results from controlled clinical trials have led to a recommended dose between 40 and 160 mg per day in that group (Keck et al. 1998; Daniel et al. 1999). Unfortunately, no data exist regarding the safety or effectiveness of ziprasidone in the treatment of schizophrenia in adolescents or children. However, one study has evaluated the use of ziprasidone in pediatric patients with Tourette's syndrome (Sallee et al. 2000). In the study, 16 children were given ziprasidone and 12 received a placebo for up to 8 consecutive weeks. Ziprasidone proved to be an effective treatment for tic disorders such as those seen in Tourette's at an average total daily dose of 28.2 mg. However, the fact that a drug is effective in treating movement disorders does not necessarily imply that it will be effective in psychotic illnesses (or vice versa).

Similarly, just because a compound is apparently safe for use in youngsters with Tourette's syndrome and related conditions does not necessarily mean that the agent is safe to use in children and adolescents with psychosis. Inasmuch as ziprasidone can lead to increases in QTc intervals in adults (see Glassman and Bigger 2001 for a review), safety is a particularly important consideration. Although in the study of youngsters with tic disorders ziprasidone was reported to be safe and was not associated with significant cardiovascular changes, one must bear in mind that the doses of antipsychotics used to treat psychosis are on the whole substantially greater than those used to treat tics. In addition, the sample size of the study by Sallee and colleagues was relatively small. Whether ziprasidone will prove safe and effective as a treatment for young people with psychosis is a topic for future study.

Aripiprazole has recently been marketed in the United States for the treatment of adults with psychotic illnesses, including schizophrenia. Currently, however, nothing is known about the use of this agent in adolescents or children with psychosis.

Practical Management Issues

Diagnostic Accuracy

Making an accurate diagnosis of schizophrenia in a young person is often not an easy task. Numerous psychiatric disorders, general medical conditions, and nonsyndromal circumstances constitute the differential diagnosis of a psychotic disorder (Findling, Schulz, et al. 2001). In fact, many youngsters who present with symptoms of psychosis are not actually suffering from a psychotic illness (McKenna et al. 1994). For this reason, although it might seem obvious, a meticulous diagnostic evaluation is essential before pharmacotherapy is initiated in a youngster suspected of having a psychotic disorder.

Medication Selection

In the case of a patient with schizophrenia, we generally recommend that pharmacotherapy begin with risperidone, olanzapine, or quetiapine, given that data exist to support their safety and effectiveness in young people with psychotic illnesses. If a patient fails to respond to one of these agents, we typically initiate another trial with one of these other two medications.

In our practice, typical antipsychotics are not considered first-line compounds, largely because of the high rates of EPS reported with these compounds and the increased risk of tardive dyskinesia in children. For two reasons, ziprasidone is also not considered a first-line treatment for youngsters with psychotic illnesses. The lack of knowledge about the safety of this compound at higher doses is one, and the other is that effectiveness studies have yet to be completed in this population. In addition, we generally reserve clozapine for the most treatment-resistant of patients. Clozapine is thus prescribed only for young people who have failed a therapeutic trial with three or four other agents, including a typical antispsychotic.

Medication Dosing

When treating a youngster with a psychotic illness, one should remember the adage "start low and go slow." The reason for this is that higher rates of side effects seem to occur at increased rates in young patients when their medication doses are rapidly escalated or when higher absolute doses of drugs are employed. We also recommend titration of only one medication at a time to avoid the risks associated with polypharmacy. The literature to date suggests that adolescents with schizophrenia respond to antipsychotic medications at doses similar to those given adults. For younger children, the optimal dosage seems to be one-half to two-thirds of the adult dose.

Data suggest that obtaining plasma levels of clozapine or olanzapine may be useful in the clinical management of adults (Buur-Rasmussen and Brøsen 1999; Perry et al. 2001). In addition, the evaluation of clozapine levels may be of value in the management of youths with schizophrenia (Piscitelli et al. 1994). In contrast, assessing the plasma levels of other antipsychotics does not appear to facilitate the treatment of young people with psychosis. For this reason, we do not typically monitor drug levels during antipsychotic pharmacotherapy except when concerns exist regarding adherence.

Safety Management

During the acute phase of treatment with atypical antipsychotics, the most common dose-limiting side effect is sedation. As noted above, we generally recommend that dosages begin low and gradual rates of titration be employed. This dosing strategy usually minimizes the risk of sedation. At the same time, some patients with psychosis can be quite agitated. To avoid treatment with unnecessarily high doses of antipsychotics, we tend to favor adjunctive treatment with either benzodiazepines or antihistamines as a method of addressing this concern. Such an approach allows the antipsychotics to be prescribed specifically as a treatment for psychosis rather than as a treatment for acute agitation. When higher potency typical antipsychotics are prescribed, another potential problem during the acute phase of treatment is EPS. In order to minimize the risk of such symptoms, prophylactic treatment with anticholinergic agents such as benztropine or trihexyphenidyl is the approach we most often employ.

Over the long term, with the advent of the atypical antipsychotics perhaps the most pervasive drug-related side effect has become weight gain. We presently lack a definitive means by which weight gain can be treated or prevented. However, we use an "anticipatory guidance" model for patients and parents regarding the increase in appetite that patients treated with antipsychotics almost invariably experience. Healthy food and beverage choices as well as a reasonable regime of physical activity are consistently encouraged from the start of treatment. We also measure height and weight at baseline and then at each subsequent visit.

Another long-term concern for patients treated with antipsychotics is tardive movement disorders. Although it is likely that, in comparison to the neuroleptics, newer agents will reduce the likelihood of these conditions, there is no proof that any antipsychotic is free of the risk of tardive dyskinesia in young people. For this reason, it is recommended that involuntary movements be tracked prior to the start of treatment and then longitudinally. The Abnormal Involuntary Movement Scale (National Institute of Mental Health 1985a) is the instrument most clinicians use. This measure should be completed at baseline, during monthly visits for the first 6 to 12 months of treatment, and at least every three months thereafter. In addition, because young patients appear to be at a greater risk for clozapine-related EEG changes, we generally prefer that a baseline EEG be obtained prior to initiating clozapine treatment. A follow-up EEG is then obtained if either an acute behavioral change or a frank seizure occurs.

As we have seen, only limited data are available concerning the use of ziprasidone in young people. Owing to concerns about this agent's effect on intracardiac electrical conduction, however, it is best to follow the guidelines recommended by the American Heart Association (Gutgesell et al. 1999). These include obtaining a careful medical history from the patient, baseline and sequential monitoring by electrocardiogram, and inquiring about other agents that could lead to drug-drug interactions.

Conclusions

A small but growing body of evidence exists relating to the use of antipsychotic agents in adolescents and children with schizophrenia and its related conditions. However, large-scale, definitive studies regarding the efficacy of such medications are still lacking, on top of which very little is known about the long-term safety of antipsychotics in young people. Whereas the typical antipsychotics differ from one another chiefly in their relative propensity for causing EPS and sedation, it appears that the atypical antipsychotics are truly distinct agents. For this reason, failure to respond to one atypical medication does not imply that a patient will respond poorly to another. Unfortunately, no prospective trials have undertaken "head-to-head" comparisons among the atypical antipsychotic agents in adolescents or children.

For at least two reasons, young patients with psychotic illnesses are an especially vulnerable population. One of these relates to the difficulties associated with their illness; the other is the fact that these patients appear to run a higher risk than adults of responding poorly to pharmacotherapy. Fortunately, much more research is underway than ever before concerning the treatment of young people with schizophrenia. Nonetheless, data remain scarce regarding the pharmacological treatment of these children and adolescents who are so badly in need of help. Only with further research will the gap between the scientific literature and the clinical demands of these patients be bridged.

ACKNOWLEDGMENTS

The authors wish to thank the patients and their families.

REFERENCES

Andreasen, N. C. (1983). *The Scale for the Assessment of Negative Symptoms (SANS)*. Iowa City: University of Iowa.

Andreasen, N. C. (1984). *The Scale for the Assessment of Positive Symptoms (SAPS)*. Iowa City: University of Iowa.

Armenteros, J. L., Whitaker, A. H., Welikson, M., Stedge, D. J., and Gorman, J. (1997). Risperidone in adolescents with schizophrenia. *Journal of the American Academy of Child and Adolescent Psychiatry* 36:694–700.

Beratis, S., Gabriel, J., and Hoidas, S. (1994). Age at onset in subtypes of schizophrenic disorders. *Schizophrenia Bulletin* 20:287–96.

Birmaher, B., Baker, R., Kapur, S., Quintana, H., and Ganguli, R. (1992). Clozapine for the treatment of adolescents with schizophrenia. *Journal of the American Academy of Child and Adolescent Psychiatry* 31:160–64.

Blanz, B., and Schmidt, M. H. (1993). Clozapine for schizophrenia. *Journal of the American Academy of Child and Adolescent Psychiatry* 32:223–24.

Boxer, G. H., and Davidson, J. (1992). More on clozapine. *Journal of the American Academy of Child and Adolescent Psychiatry* 31:993–94.

Burd, L., and Kerbeshian, J. (1987). A North Dakota prevalence study of schizophrenia presenting in childhood. *Journal of the American Academy of Child and Adolescent Psychiatry* 26:347–50.

Buur-Rasmussen, B., and Brøsen, K. (1999). Cytochrome P450 and therapeutic monitoring with respect to clozapine. *European Neuropsychopharmacology* 9:453–59.

Campbell, M., Armenteros, J. L., Malone, R. P., Adams, P. B., Eisenberg, Z. W., and Overall, J. E. (1997). Neuroleptic-related dyskinesias in autistic children: A prospective, longitudinal study. *Journal of the American Academy of Child and Adolescent Psychiatry* 36:835–43.

Cawthron, P., James, A., Dell, J., and Seagroatt, V. (1994). Adolescent onset psychosis: A clinical and outcome study. *Journal of Child Psychology and Psychiatry* 35:1321–32.

Clein, P. D., and Riddle, M. A. (1995). Pharmacokinetics in children and adolescents. *Child and Adolescent Psychiatric Clinics of North America* 4:59–75.

Cozza, S. J., and Edison, D. L. (1994). Risperidone in adolescents. *Journal of the American Academy of Child and Adolescent Psychiatry* 33:1211.

Daniel, D. G., Zimbroff, D. L., Potkin, S. G., Reeves, K. R., Harrigan, E. P., Lakshminarayanan, M., et al. (1999). Ziprasidone 80 mg/day and 160 mg/day in the acute exacerbation of schizophrenia and schizoaffective disorder: A 6-week placebo-controlled trial. *Neuropsychopharmacology* 20:491–505.

Dittmann, R. W., Hagenah, U., Junghans, J., Maestele, A., Mehler, C., Meyer, E., et al. (2001). Olanzapine in a Ph III trial with adolescent schizophrenic patients: First results on drug safety. Poster presentation. In S. Villani (Ed.), *Proceedings of the Forty-eighth Annual Meeting of the American Academy of Child and Adolescent Psychiatry* (p. 155). Honolulu, Hawaii.

Dittman, R. W., and Junghanß, J. (1999). Olanzapine treatment of psychotic adolescents-change of body weight and adverse event profile. *European Neuropsychopharmacology* 9(Suppl. 5): S269–70.

Findling, R. L., McNamara, N. K., Branicky, L. A., and Schulz, S. C. (2001). Olanzapine in adolescent psychosis. *Schizophrenia Research* 49:227.

Findling, R. L., McNamara, N. K., and Gracious, B. L. (2000). Pediatric uses of atypical antipsychotics. *Expert Opinion on Pharmacotherapy* 1:935–45.

Findling, R. L., Reed, M. D., and Blumer, J. L. (1999). Pharmacological treatment of depression in children and adolescents. *Pediatric Drugs* 1:161–82.

Findling, R. L., Schulz, S. C., Kashani, J. H., and Harlan, E., eds. (2001). *Psychotic disorders in children and adolescents.* Thousand Oaks, CA: Sage Publications.

Findling, R. L., Schulz, S. C., Reed, M. D., and Blumer, J. L. (1998). The antipsychotics: A pediatric perspective. *Pediatric Clinics of North America* 45:1205–32.

Frazier, J. A., Gordon, C. T., McKenna, K., Lenane, M. C., Jih, D., and Rapoport, J. L. (1994). An open trial of clozapine in 11 adolescents with childhood-onset schizophrenia. *Journal of the American Academy of Child and Adolescent Psychiatry* 33:658–63.

Gillberg, I. C., Hellgren, L., and Gillberg, C. (1993). Psychotic disorders diagnosed in adolescence: Outcome at age 30 years. *Journal of Child Psychology and Psychiatry* 34:1173–85.

Glassman, A. H., and Bigger, J. T., Jr. (2001). Antipsychotic drugs: Prolonged QTc interval, torsade de pointes, and sudden death. *American Journal of Psychiatry* 158:1774–82.

Grcevich, S. J., Findling, R. L., Rowane, W. A., Friedman, L., and Schulz, S. C. (1996). Risperidone in the treatment of children and adolescents with schizophrenia: A retrospective study. *Journal of Child and Adolescent Psychopharmacology* 6:251–57.

Grothe, D. R., Calis, K. A., Jacobsen, L., Kumra, S., DeVane, C. L., Rapoport, J. L., et al. (2000). Olanzapine pharmacokinetics in pediatric and adolescent inpatients with childhood-onset schizophrenia. *Journal of Clinical Psychopharmacology* 20:220–25.

Gutgesell, H., Atkins, D., Barst, R., Buck, M., Franklin, W., Humes, R., et al. (1999). AHA Scientific Statement: Cardiovascular monitoring of children and adolescents receiving psychotropic drugs. *Journal of the American Academy of Child and Adolescent Psychiatry* 38:1047–50.

Haapasalo-Pesu, K.-M., and Saarijärvi, S. (2001). Olanzapine induces remarkable weight gain in adolescent patients. *European Child and Adolescent Psychiatry* 10:205–8.

Häfner, H., Maurer, K., Löffler, W., and Riecher-Rössler, A. (1993). The influence of age and sex on the onset and early course of schizophrenia. *British Journal of Psychiatry* 162:80–86.

Healy, E., Subotsky, F., and Pipe, R. (1999). Quetiapine in adolescent psychosis. *Journal of the American Academy of Child and Adolescent Psychiatry* 38:1329.

Hirose, S. (2000). Effectiveness of risperidone in simple schizophrenia: A single case report. *Journal of Clinical Psychiatry* 61:300–301.

Jacobsen, L. K., Walker, M. C., Edwards, J. E., and Chappell, P. B. (1994). Clozapine in the treatment of a young adolescent with schizophrenia. *Journal of the American Academy of Child and Adolescent Psychiatry* 33:645–50.

Kay, S. R., Fiszbein, A., and Opler, L. A. (1987). The Positive and Negative Syndrome Scale (PANSS) for schizophrenia. *Schizophrenia Bulletin* 13:261–76.

Keck, P., Jr., Buffenstein, A., Ferguson, J., Feighner, J., Jaffe, W., Harrigan, E. P., et al. (1998). Ziprasidone 40 and 120 mg/day in the acute exacerbation of schizophrenia and schizoaffective disorder: A 4-week placebo-controlled trial. *Psychopharmacology* 140:173–84.

Keepers, G. A., Clappison, V. J., and Casey, D. E. (1983). Initial anticholinergic prophylaxis for neuroleptic-induced extrapyramidal syndromes. *Archives of General Psychiatry* 40:1113–17.

Keller, M. B., Ryan, N. D., Strober, M., Klein, R. G., Kutcher, S. P., Birmaher, B., et al. (2001). Efficacy of paroxetine in the treatment of adolescent major depression: A randomized, controlled trial. *Journal of the American Academy of Child and Adolescent Psychiatry* 40:762–72.

Kinon, B. J., Kane, J. M., Johns, C., Perovich, R., Ismi, M., Koreen, A., et al. (1993). Treatment of neuroleptic-resistant schizophrenic relapse. *Psychopharmacology Bulletin* 29: 309–14.

Kopala, L. C., and Caudle, C. (1998). Acute and longer-term effects of risperidone in a case of first-episode catatonic schizophrenia. *Journal of Psychopharmacology* 12:314–17.

Kozlova, I. A., Burelomova, I. V., Goriunov, A. V., Grebchenko, I. F., and Masikhina, S. N. (2001). An experience of the application of rispolept in childhood schizophrenia. *Zhurnal Nevrologii Psiklhiatrii Im S S Korsakova* 101:35–38.

Krausz, M., and Müller-Thomsen, T. (1993). Schizophrenia with onset in adolescence: An 11-year follow-up. *Schizophrenia Bulletin* 19:831–41.

Kumra, S., Frazier, J. A., Jacobsen, L. K., McKenna, K., Gordon, C. T., Lenane, M. C., et al. (1996). Childhood-onset schizophrenia: A double-blind clozapine-haloperidol comparison. *Archives of General Psychiatry* 53:1090–97.

Kumra, S., Jacobsen, L. K., Lenane, M., Karp, B. I., Frazier, J. A., Smith, A. K., et al. (1998). Childhood-onset schizophrenia: An open-label study of olanzapine in adolescents. *Journal of the American Academy of Child and Adolescent Psychiatry* 37:377–85.

Levkovitch, Y., Kronenberg, J., Kayser, N., Zvyagelski, M., Gaoni, B., and Gadoth, N. (1995). Clozapine for tardive dyskinesia in adolescents. *Brain and Development* 17:213–15.

Loranger, A. W. (1984). Sex difference in age at onset in schizophrenia. *Archives of General Psychiatry* 41:157–61.

Maagensen, M., and Aarkrog, T. (1999). Treatment of adolescent psychoses with olanzapine. A preliminary report. *Nordic Journal of Psychiatry* 53:435–38.

MacEwan, T. H., and Morton, M.J.S. (1996). Use of clozapine in a child with treatment-resistant schizophrenia. *British Journal of Psychiatry* 168:376–78.

Mandoki, M. W. (1993). Clozapine for adolescents with psychosis: Literature review and two case reports. *Journal of Child and Adolescent Psychopharmacology* 3:213–21.

Mandoki, M. W. (1994). Anti-aggressive effects of clozapine in children and adolescents. *Biological Psychiatry* 35:744–45.

Mandoki, M. W. (1995). Risperidone treatment of children and adolescents: Increased risk of extrapyramidal side effects? *Journal of Child and Adolescent Psychopharmacology* 5:49–67.

Mandoki, M. W. (1997). Olanzapine in the treatment of early onset schizophrenia in children and adolescents. *Biological Psychiatry* 41(Suppl.):22S.

McConville, B. J., Arvanitis, L. A., Thyrum, P. T., Yeh, C., Wilkinson, L. A., Chaney, R. O., et al. (2000). Pharmacokinetics, tolerability, and clinical effectiveness of quetiapine fumarate: An open-label trial in adolescents with psychotic disorders. *Journal of Clinical Psychiatry* 61:252–60.

McConville, B. J., Wong, J., Yeh, C., Wilkinson, L., Chaney, R., Foster, K., et al. (2000). Safety, tolerability, and clinical effectiveness of quetiapine in adolescents with selected psychotic disorders: A long-term, open-label study. *Journal of Child and Adolescent Psychopharmacology* 10:254–55.

McKenna, K., Gordon, C. T., Lenane, M., Kaysen, D., Fahey, K., and Rapoport, J. L. (1994). Looking for childhood-onset schizophrenia: The first 71 cases screened. *Journal of the American Academy of Child and Adolescent Psychiatry* 33:636–44.

Meltzer, H. Y., Rabinowitz, J., Lee, M. A., Cola, P. A., Ranjan, R., Findling, R. L., et al. (1997). Age at onset and gender of schizophrenic patients in relation to neuroleptic resistance. *American Journal of Psychiatry* 154:475–82.

Mozes, T., Toren, P., Chernauzan, N., Mester, R., Yoran-Hegesh, R., Blumensohn, R., et al. (1994). Clozapine treatment in very early onset schizophrenia. *Journal of the American Academy of Child and Adolescent Psychiatry* 33:65–70.

National Institute of Mental Health. (1985a). Abnormal Involuntary Movement Scale (AIMS). *Psychopharmacology Bulletin* 21:1077–80.

National Institute of Mental Health. (1985b). Clinical Global Impressions Scale. *Psychopharmacology Bulletin* 21:839–43.

Overall, J. E., and Gorham, D. R. (1962). The Brief Psychiatric Rating Scale. *Psychological Reports* 10:799–812.

Perry, P. J., Lund, B. C., Sanger, T., and Beasley, C. (2001). Olanzapine plasma concentrations and clinical response: Acute phase results of the North American olanzapine trial. *Journal of Clinical Psychopharmacology* 21:14–20.

Piscitelli, S. C., Frazier, J. A., McKenna, K., Albus, K. E., Grothe, D. R., Gordon, C. T., et al. (1994). Plasma clozapine and haloperidol concentrations in adolescents with childhood-onset schizophrenia: Association with response. *Journal of Clinical Psychiatry* 55(9, Suppl. B):94–97.

Pool, D., Bloom, W., Mielke, D. H., Roniger, J. J., Jr., and Gallant, D. M. (1976). A controlled evaluation of loxitane in seventy-five adolescent schizophrenic patients. *Current Therapeutic Research: Clinical and Experimental* 19:99–104.

Quintana, H., and Keshavan, M. (1995). Case study: Risperidone in children and adolescents with schizophrenia. *Journal of the American Academy of Child and Adolescent Psychiatry* 34:1292–96.

Realmuto, G. M., Erickson, W. D., Yellin, A. M., Hopwood, J. H., and Greenberg, L. M. (1984). Clinical comparison of thiothixene and thioridazine in schizophrenic adolescents. *American Journal of Psychiatry* 141:440–42.

Reitzle, K., Warnke, A., Wewetzer, C., and Muller, H. (2001). Agranulozytose bei einem Kind mit Schizophrenie unter Clozapintherapie-klinisches Bild und Therapie: Eine Kasuistik. *Zeitschrift für Kinder- und Jugenpsychiatrie und Psychotherapie* 29:137–43.

Remschmidt, H., Schulz, E., and Martin, P.D.M. (1994). An open trial of clozapine in 36 adolescents with schizophrenia. *Journal of Child and Adolescent Psychopharmacology* 4:31–41.

Sallee, F. R., Kurlan, R., Goetz, C. G., Singer, H., Scahill, L., Law, G., et al. (2000). Ziprasidone treatment of children and adolescents with Tourette's syndrome: A pilot study. *Journal of the American Academy of Child and Adolescent Psychiatry* 39:292–99.

Shaffer, D., Gould, M. S., Brasic, J., Ambrosini, P., Fisher, P., Bird, H., et al. (1983). A Children's Global Assessment Scale (CGAS). *Archives of General Psychiatry* 40:1228–31.

Shaw, J. A., Lewis, J. E., Pascal, S., Sharma, R. K., Rodriquez, R. A., Guillen, R., et al. (2001). A study of quetiapine: Efficacy and tolerability in psychotic adolescents. *Journal of Child and Adolescent Psychopharmacology* 11:415–24.

Sholevar, E. H., Baron, D. A., and Hardie, T. L. (2000). Treatment of childhood-onset schizophrenia with olanzapine. *Journal of Child and Adolescent Psychopharmacology* 10:69–78.

Siefen, G., and Remschmidt, H. (1986). Behandlungsergebnisse mit Clozapine bei schizophrenen Jugendlichen. *Zeitschrift für Kinder- und Jugenpsychiatrie und Psychotherapie* 14:245–57.

Simeon, J. G., Carrey, N. J., Wiggins, D. M., Milin, R. P., and Hosenbocus, S. N. (1995). Risperidone effects in treatment-resistant adolescents: Preliminary case reports. *Journal of Child and Adolescent Psychopharmacology* 5:69–79.

Sourander, A. (1997). Risperidone for treatment of childhood schizophrenia. *American Journal of Psychiatry* 154:1476.

Spencer, E. K., and Campbell, M. (1994). Children with schizophrenia: Diagnosis, phenomenology, and pharmacotherapy. *Schizophrenia Bulletin* 20:713–25.

Szigethy, E., Brent, S., and Findling, R. L. (1998). Quetiapine for refractory schizophrenia. *Journal of the American Academy of Child and Adolescent Psychiatry* 37:1127–28.

Towbin, K. E., Dykens, E. M., and Pugliese, R. G. (1994). Clozapine for early developmental delays with childhood-onset schizophrenia: Protocol and 15-month outcome. *Journal of the American Academy of Child and Adolescent Psychiatry* 33:651–57.

Turetz, M., Mozes, T., Toren, P., Chernauzan, N., Yoran-Hegesh, R., Mester, R., et al. (1997). An open trial of clozapine in neuroleptic-resistant childhood-onset schizophrenia. *British Journal of Psychiatry* 170:507–10.

Usiskin, S. I., Nicolson, R., Lenane, M., and Rapoport, J. L. (2000). Gabapentic prophylaxis of clozapine-induced seizures. *American Journal of Psychiatry* 157:482–83.

CHAPTER TWELVE

Individual Psychotherapy and School Interventions for Psychotic Youth

Linmarie Sikich, M.D.

Children and adolescents suffering from psychotic symptoms experience changes in almost all areas of their lives. For many, their symptoms mark the beginning of a chronic illness that will present lifelong challenges. Treatment provided during the early stages of a psychotic illness can greatly improve its biological course. More important, such treatment will have a profound impact on how patients understand and approach both their illness and its treatment. Ideally, a young person suffering from psychosis will learn to view the disorder as one aspect of life rather than as the defining feature of his or her identity and to regard treatment as a valued tool rather than an onerous demand.

Effective treatment must go beyond the use of medications to alleviate psychotic symptoms to address the emotional, cognitive, and environmental issues facing each child, so as to optimize his or her ability to meet age-appropriate developmental tasks. Doing so requires a complex variety of therapeutic and environmental interventions (American Academy of Child and Adolescent Psychiatry 2001). Psychotherapeutic interventions typically include psycho-education, supportive psychotherapy, cognitive behavioral therapy, coping skills training, and social skills training. The efficacy of these interventions is enhanced by tailoring their content to the patient's life circumstances and to the phase of the illness. Psychotherapy can often be provided in either an individual setting or a group setting, although it is unlikely that most clinicians will see more than one or two children or adolescent patients who are at similar stages in their illness at any given time. Environmental interventions include taking immediate steps to reduce the stress experienced by the child or adolescent; psychoeducation of family members, teachers, and other persons involved in the child's life; and the development of educational, social, and vocational activities at which the child can succeed and thus acquire the skills and confidence necessary to proceed to the next developmental task.

Although these treatment goals are widely embraced, they are often overshadowed by the pressing need to bring dangerous psychotic symptoms under control or overlooked once the initial crises pass. Further, very little information is available that describes specific goals, strategies, and techniques of intervention that can be applied to the juvenile population, nor have there been studies that rigorously evaluate the efficacy of such interventions. Consequently, many well-intentioned clinicians may feel at a loss to know what to do or how to implement the necessary therapies. In the discussion to follow, I will briefly review the three existing studies that focus on psychotherapy in youth with psychotic symptoms and will summarize the literature on individual psychotherapeutic interventions in adults with schizophrenia spectrum illnesses. A model for approaching individual psychotherapy with adolescents suffering from psychotic illnesses will then be presented, along with information on specific techniques that may prove useful during particular phases of the illness. Finally, I will consider potential educational interventions for affected children and adolescents.

Previous Reports of Individual Psychotherapy in Schizophrenia Spectrum Disorders

Adolescent Studies

Only one study, by Jenner and van de Willige (2001), has systematically assessed the utility of individual psychotherapeutic interventions in psychotic youth. The study examined a particular cognitive behavioral method, known as HIT (hallucination-focused integrative treatment), for monitoring and coping with persistent auditory hallucinations (mean duration 3.4 years) in a group of 14 adolescents. Although no details were provided about the frequency or duration of treatment, the authors noted significant symptomatic and functional improvements. Of the 14 patients, 9 were free of hallucinatory voices for at least two months, and 8 showed substantial improvement in their ability to attend and succeed at school or to hold a job.

In addition, there have been two studies specifically related to psychotherapeutic interventions in early-onset schizophrenia. Linszen and colleagues (1998) evaluated two intensive treatment models that used a combination of individual psychotherapy and ongoing pharmacological management with or without adjunct family behavioral intervention, in a sample of 76 young people, most of whom were experiencing their first psychotic break. The rate or relapse over the 15 months of combined psychosocial and mediation treatment was 16 percent and did not differ between the two groups. However, when the psychosocial treatments were discontinued, the relapse rates increased dramatically, to 45 percent in the following 15 months and 70 percent 36 months after discontinuing psychosocial treatments. In the other study, which focused on 12 teenagers with schizophrenia, Rund and colleagues (1994) set up a 2-year program that included problem-solving sessions undertaken jointly by affected teens and their parents, as well as family-therapy sessions for the parents. A group of 12 individuals matched for age, sex, psychosocial functioning, and diagnosis who had been treated in the same hospital during an earlier period (1980–87) were used as a comparison group. Little difference was seen in the overall rates of relapse over the 2 years following the index hospitalization: 7 of the 12 in the experimental group versus 9 in the control group. However, all but one of those in the experimental group who relapsed were rehospitalized only a single time, whereas 8 in the control group who relapsed had multiple or continuous hospitalizations.

Adult Studies

There is a more substantial body of literature describing and examining psychotherapeutic interventions in adults (Penn and Mueser 1996; Mojtabai, Nicholson, and Carpenter 1998; Brenner and Pfammatter 2000; Bustillo et al. 2001). These interventions, which are summarized in Table 12.1, can be roughly divided into psychoeducational approaches (McGorry 1995; Perkins et al. 2000); cognitive behavioral approaches (studies by Tarrier et al. 1993, 1998, 1999, 2000; Kuipers et al. 1997, 1998; Turkington and Kingdon 2000; and Turkington, Kingdon, and Turner 2002; reviewed by Dickerson 2000 and

Table 12.1. Controlled trials of psychotherapy for psychosis

	Intervention	Population	N	Acute outcome	Outcome on follow-up	Effect size
Teen specific						
Jenner and van de Willige 2001	Cognitive therapy focused on AH; no comparison group; duration unknown	Adolescent and young adult (average age = 20 years); approximately 3 have AH	14	9 of 14 free of AH; 8 of 14 showed substantial vocational improvement	No follow-up	Not able to calculate
Linszen et al. 1998	Individual vs. individual and family, for 15 months	Adolescent and young adult (average age = 20 years); more than half in first episode	76	At 15 months, 16% relapsed; decrease in negative symptoms, $p \leq .01$; ND in Tx's	At 36 months, 70% relapsed; ND in Tx's	Not able to calculate
Rund et al. 1994	Parent education plus problem-solving therapy vs. historical control	Adolescent (average age = 16 years)	24	At 24 months, 1 vs. 8 with 2 or more hospitalizations	No follow-up	Not able to calculate
Supportive						
Sjostrom 1985	Dynamic therapy vs. routine care, for 72 to 96 months	Inpatient and outpatient, chronic	24	Not available	Decrease in symptoms and hospitalizations; improved social and vocational functioning	Not able to calculate

Gunderson et al. 1984	Supportive vs. insight-oriented therapy	Outpatient	47	Better vocational functioning after supportive therapy than after insight-oriented	No follow-up	Not able to calculate
Cognitive behavioral						
Turkington et al. 2002	CBT vs. routine care, for 5 months	Stable outpatient; (average age = 40 years)	422	Decrease in symptoms	No follow-up and depression; improved insight	In acute phase, more than 1.0
Drury et al. 1996a, 1996b; Drury, Birchwood, and Cochrane 2000	CBT vs. RT + supportive therapy, for 3 months	Inpatient; 70% within 5 years of first episode	40	Decrease in symptoms; difference in symptoms became apparent at 7 weeks	9 months: 5% of CBT group showed moderate to severe symptoms vs. 56% of control group; at 5 years, minimal change	In acute phase, 1.26 At follow-up, 1.77
Tarrier et al. 1998, 1999, 2000	CT vs. support vs. routine care; for 10 weeks	Stable outpatient	87	For decrease in CT, symptoms and in days hospitalized	At 12 months, decrease in symptoms and in days hospitalized; at 24 months, CT = supportive therapy > routine care	In acute phase, 0.63; At 24-month follow-up, 0.77

(*continued*)

Table 12.1. (Continued)

	Intervention	Population	N	Acute outcome	Outcome on follow-up	Effect size
Sensky et al. 2000	CBT vs. befriending; for 9 months	Stable outpatient (average age = 39 years)	90	Decrease in symptoms; CBT sleep > ($p < .02$ on 1 scale)	At 18 months, increase in small benefits with CBT; some CBT > decrease in benefits with befriending	In acute phase, 0.20 At follow-up, 0.52
Pinto et al. 1999	CBT plus SST vs. supportive therapy	Stable outpatient on clozapine (average age = 35 years)	37	Decrease in symptoms; CBT + SST >, $p < .001$	No follow-up	In acute phase, 0.44
Kuipers et al. 1997, 1998	CT vs. routine care, for 9 months	Stable outpatient	60	Decrease in symptoms; CBT >> $p = .009$	At 18 months, decrease in symptoms; CBT >> $p = .001$; 65% receiving CBT much better vs. 17% receiving routine care	In acute phase, 0.37 At follow-up, 0.64
Hogarty, Greenwald, et al. 1997; Hogarty, Kornblith, et al. 1997	Personal Tx (PT) vs. family vs. supportive therapy, for 36 months	Stable outpatient (average age = 31 years)	151	Not available	At 36 months, relapse delayed with PT vs. family therapy, $p = .02$, and with PT vs. other approaches, $p = .06$	Not able to calculate

Study	Intervention	Population	N	Outcome measure	Results	Effect size
Marder et al. 1996*	SST vs. supportive therapy, for 24 months	Stable outpatient (average age = 38 years)	80	Not available	At 24 months, some improvement in social functioning SS > p = .02; greater improvement if onset before 24 years of age	Not able to calculate
Garety et al. 1994	CT vs. wait list, for 6 months	Stable outpatient	20	Decrease in symptoms	No follow-up	In acute phase, 0.59
Tarrier et al. 1993	CT vs. problem-solving therapy vs. wait list, for 5 weeks	Stable outpatient	27	Decrease in symptoms	At 6 months, decrease in symptoms; CT > PS > wait	At follow-up, 0.67 with CT, 0.48 with problem-solving therapy
Hogarty et al. 1986, 1991	SST vs. family therapy vs. family therapy with SST, for 24 months	Stable outpatient		Decrease in symptoms	At 12 months, no relapse with family therapy plus SST; 50% reduction in relapse with SST or family therapy; at 24 months, fewer relapses with family therapy or family therapy plus SST, but not with SST alone	Not able to calculate
Milton, Patwa, and Häfner 1978	Belief modification vs. confrontation, for 5 sessions	Stable outpatient	16	Decrease in symptoms	No follow-up	In acute phase, 0.78

*Marder and colleagues employed a group therapy intervention

Note: AH = auditory hallucinations; CBT = cognitive behavioral therapy; RT = relaxation training; CT = cognitive therapy; SST = social skills training; PT = placebo treatment; Tx = treatment

Gould et al. 2001); cognitive retraining approaches (Hogarty and Flesher 1999a, 1999b; Rund and Borg 1999; Kurtz et al. 2001); and multimodal therapies (Marder et al. 1996; Hogarty, Greenwald, et al. 1997; Hogarty, Kornblith, et al. 1997). Most of these therapies can be undertaken either in a group or an individual format but in either case must be adapted in ways appropriate to the experiences of the specific participants.

Several conclusions can be drawn from this body of work. First and most important, psychotherapy does seem to be of considerable benefit to individuals with schizophrenia. In their overview of different possible approaches to the treatment of schizophrenia, Mojtabai, Nicholson, and Carpenter (1998) found that the effect size of combined psychosocial and pharmacological treatment compared to no treatment at all was large (0.85), while the effect size of pharmacological treatment alone was only moderate (0.37) and the effect size of psychotherapy alone was smaller still (0.23). These results are summarized in Figure 12.1. Second, it seems to matter less which method of intervention is chosen than that the intervention be sufficiently intense. The effect sizes of different forms of psychotherapy (other than psychodynamic therapy) tend to be quite similar, ranging from 0.41 to 0.56 (Mojtabai, Nicholson, and Carpenter 1998). Gould and colleagues (2001) observed a similar effect size (0.65) for cognitive behavioral therapy. Third, the benefits of these interventions often recede once the treatment is discontinued. Thus, psychosocial therapies

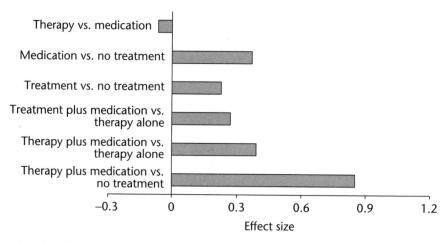

Fig. 12.1. Effect sizes of specific methods of intervention for schizophrenia

should be viewed as an ongoing part of the management of psychotic illnesses rather than as a time limited intervention. Finally, it is essential that the particular psychotherapeutic methods adopted reflect the patient's history and current situation. These therapies will naturally evolve over time as the patient's skill level varies, improving during periods of stability and potentially regressing during relapses. At whatever the stage of treatment, however, both cognitive and psychoeducational approaches should aim to build on the skills the patient has already acquired and become adept at using.

A Potential Approach to Psychotherapy with Children and Adolescents with Psychosis

The Importance of Engagement

The initial step in beginning any treatment is to build a therapeutic alliance. In work with children, that alliance must be established both with the child and with his or her caregivers. Granted, this can be difficult because the two parties may have very different conceptions of what is wrong, and neither of these conceptions may match the clinician's. Often motivational interviewing affords the best place to start. This technique has been summarized by Amador (2002), who refers to it as L-E-A-P (listen, empathize, agree, partner). In conducting a motivational interview, the therapist should try as far as possible to observe the following instructions:

1. *Listen* as closely as possible to the patient and his or her family in an effort to understand their experiences as well as their interpretation of their experiences. Also seek to understand their fears, frustrations, and desires, whether these are related to the illness or to more general matters. In doing this, remember to be very nonjudgmental. Ask, for instance, "How do you *know* that?" rather than "What makes you *think* that?"

2. *Empathize* with the patient and family members. Try to ask yourself how you would respond if the situation the patient is describing were true. If you are unclear how the child is feeling, encourage him or her to say more. Empathizing will also aid your efforts to normalize the child's experience.

3. Identify areas in which you can all *agree* that problems exist. Initially

these areas may center around somatic issues, such as problems with eating or sleeping, or around the distress the individual is experiencing in response to delusions or hallucinations.

4. View yourself as the patient's *partner* in pursuing the goals that you, the patient, and his or her family have jointly identified. Bear in mind that additional treatment goals currently unrecognized by the patient may also exist.

Phases of Treatment

The treatment of schizophrenia proceeds in stages that correspond to stages in the illness (Hogarty, Greenwald, et al. 1997; Hogarty, Kornblith, et al. 1997; Bradshaw 2000; Fenton 2000). These stages are listed in Table 12.2 and may include: a *prodromal period,* in which there is a clear decline in social, academic, and/or vocational functioning but the absence of frank psychosis; *acute periods* of very active, predominantly positive symptoms; *convalescent* or *subacute periods; adaptive plateaus,* also known as moratoriums or "woodshedding" (Strauss et al. 1985), in which the individual is developing new coping skills but has not yet begun to use them systematically; *change points,* with the potential either for significant improvement or for decompensation into an acute period of illness; and finally *stable plateaus.* In all stages of treatment, one must remain aware that many individuals with schizophrenia have a reduced capacity to tolerate intensive therapeutic interventions and adjust the frequency and duration of psychosocial interventions accordingly.

Treatment during the prodromal period is often limited by an uncertainty about whether the symptoms will progress and a concern about stigmatizing or otherwise increasing the anxiety of the affected person. It is often useful to provide psychoeducation based on the vulnerability-stress model of psychosis depicted in Figure 12.2 and to encourage the person to identify specific warning signs that could signal the development of frank psychosis. Many patients will benefit from personalizing and referring back to the vulnerability-stress diagram. A therapist must also be an empathic listener in hopes that the patient will perceive mental health professionals as caring and helpful. Although this approach has not been widely described, it seems likely that cognitive behavioral therapy could help to reduce the discomfort associated with prodromal symptoms and to improve social and relaxation skills. The question of whether treatment with antipsychotics can be beneficial during the prodromal period is currently under investigation.

Table 12.2. Stages of psychotic illnesses and treatment

Stage of illness	Characteristics	Treatment goals	Treatment modalities	Typical duration
Prodromal	Reduced function No clear psychosis	Recognize worsening of symptoms Form alliance Forestall acute symptoms	Supportive therapy Psychoeducation Social skills training Antipsychotics	2 months to 4 years
Acute	Clear positive symptoms May have negative or cognitive symptoms but overshadowed by positive symptoms	Maintain safety Reduce positive symptoms Form alliance	Antipsychotics Supportive therapy Basic psychoeducation Medication management	2 weeks to months
Convalescent	Diminishing positive symptoms Negative and cognitive symptoms may be prominent Often depression presents	Maintain safety Promote adherence to medications Address comorbidities (mood, drug and/or alcohol use) Start to teach coping and cognitive skills	Psychoeducation Medication management Monitoring of symptoms Social skills Relaxation skills Cognitive skills	3 months to 8 months
Adaptive plateau	Outwardly stable but often impaired symptoms prominent Negative symptoms prominent but gain in skills noted	Promote adherence to medications Enhance and build coping and cognitive skills	Social skills Relaxation skills Cognitive skills Monitoring of symptoms Cognitive therapy Role playing Medication management Psychoeducation	3 months to 4 months

(continued)

Table 12.2. (Continued)

Stage of illness	Characteristics	Treatment goals	Treatment modalities	Typical duration
Change points	Period of increased internal or external demands Symptoms or skills may change suddenly leading to higher plateau or relapse to acute phase	Minimize relapse by reducing stress and supporting coping skills Promote adherence to medications Maintain safety	Psychoeducation Supportive therapy Behavioral therapy Environmental changes	Days to weeks
Stable plateau	Symptoms, skills, and level of functioning are relatively stable	Promote adherence to medications Improve ability to cope with residual symptoms Prevent relapse	Cognitive behavioral therapy to deal with persistent symptoms Medication management Supportive therapy	Months to years

During the acute stage of illness, treatment focuses chiefly on reducing symptoms and environmental sources of stress as much as possible. Although antipsychotics and modifications to the patient's environment, such as creating a quiet place to go when upset, or avoiding chaotic situations, such as a busy school cafeteria, are the mainstays of treatment, it is essential that a therapist take time to truly listen to the patient, even one who is suffering from marked thought disorganization. By listening closely, a therapist not only gains valuable diagnostic information but also gradually establishes a relationship with the patient that is likely to be crucial to the patient's attitude toward future treatment. During this stage therapists also need to be sensitive to the emotional trauma that may accompany the psychotic symptoms themselves and, to an even greater extent, other people's reactions to the symptoms. As many as 46 percent of those with recent-onset psychosis experience post-traumatic stress disorder related to involuntary hospitalization, physical restraint, and forced medication (McGorry et al. 1991). Failure to acknowledge and effectively address such trauma both in the acute phase and over the long term may considerably hinder ongoing treatment (Williams-Keeler, Milliken, and Jones 1994). During the acute stage of illness, a manageable amount of psychoeducation can reduce the patient's fears regarding the initial symptoms and provide hope for the future. The therapist should explain to the patient that the unusual perceptions and beliefs that he or she is currently experiencing are commonly the result of a problem with the brain's functioning and are often observed in individuals with psychotic illnesses. The patient also needs to know that medications can gradually reduce the frequency and the intensity of these perceptions and beliefs or make them go away entirely. More extensive psychoeducation should be provided to family members.

Over the next several weeks to months, as the patient enters the convalescent phase, the symptoms will generally become less severe or at least more familiar and therefore less frightening. The reduction in positive symptoms is frequently more dramatic than the reduction in negative symptoms. During this period, the clinician should provide further psychoeducation, again making use of the vulnerability-stress model (see Figure 12.2). As in the prodromal period, the child or adolescent should be given help in identifying personal warning signs that could indicate the reemergence of acute symptoms. He or she should also be encouraged to become aware of particular activities and situations that tend to be personally stressful—for example, crowded, noisy en-

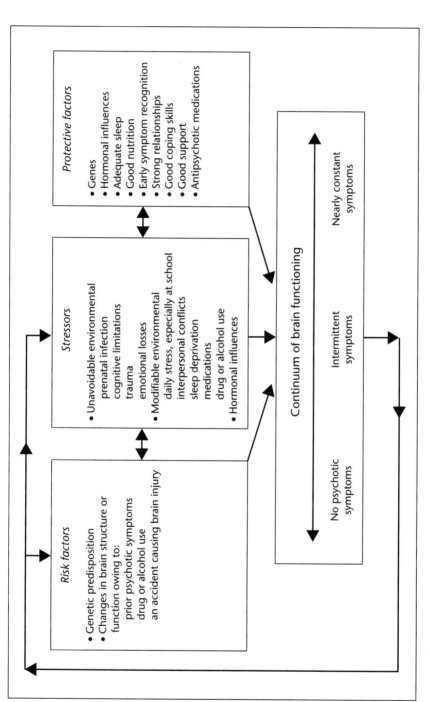

Fig. 12.2. The vulnerability-stress model of psychosis

vironments such as ball games—and, if possible, to avoid them or at least find ways to change them, such as sitting in a relatively quiet seat in the outfield rather than in one of the front rows behind home plate. Concurrent depression, mania, anxiety, or substance abuse act as stressors and should be actively treated. Such treatment can often provide a model for reducing other stresses. The child should be encouraged to communicate fully and work closely with the doctor to maximize benefits from the medication and minimize any associated side effects. The convalescent period is often a fruitful time to begin teaching patients basic skills that will enable them to relax, accurately assess social situations, and monitor symptoms. Ideally, a patient's symptoms and pharmacological treatments will have stabilized at this point, and he or she will have begun to make use of basic coping and social skills as a stepping-stone to the adaptive plateau phase.

The adaptive plateau is a highly productive period for psychotherapeutic interventions partly because, once their symptoms have largely subsided, patients are often particularly receptive to learning and practicing cognitive behavioral strategies that can help them deal with their illness. Patients should build on basic skills by first applying them to fairly concrete situations, then to hypothetical situations, and finally to actual life situations. Once child or adolescent patients have become facile at these techniques, they will usually be poised to make fundamental changes that will allow them to resume age-appropriate developmental tasks.

During change points, the clinician may need to be very active in supporting the patient's developing coping skills and in minimizing situations likely to promote relapse. Such situations may include extreme transitions (e.g., going to camp or college or beginning a job), losses, or factors such as troublesome side effects, drug or alcohol use, or problems with transportation to and from doctors' appointments, all of which can reduce the likelihood that the patient will take medication as prescribed. Both ongoing psychoeducation that emphasizes the patient's ability to reduce or avoid stress and the active management of medication programs are critical.

During the stable plateau, psychotherapeutic interventions primarily center on coping with the distress caused by ongoing symptoms, encouraging a focus on activities related to the person's overarching goals rather than to his or her illness, and instilling hope that the patient can achieve some of these aspirations despite persistent symptoms. That said, considerable work may be needed to foster situations in which the patient can succeed.

Psychoeducation

As we have seen, psychoeducation should be provided to both patients and their families. It begins by identifying the specific experiences that the clinician, patients, and their families perceive as symptoms of psychosis and by reassuring the patients that people with similar illnesses share such experiences. Patients should then be given information about other sorts of psychotic symptoms, including negative and cognitive symptoms, in order to help them understand their illness and make it easier for them to report additional symptoms now and in the future. The typical waxing and waning of psychotic symptoms should be described, possibly with recourse to the vulnerability-stress model depicted in Figure 12.2. In this model, psychotic symptoms result when the combination of a person's vulnerability and his or her level of stress exceeds a certain threshold. If an individual has a low vulnerability to psychotic disorders, a greater intensity or amount of stress is required to elicit psychotic symptoms, whereas if a person is highly vulnerable, relatively mild stresses might do so.

Furthermore, because this balance of stress and vulnerability changes constantly, the presence, intensity, and frequency of psychotic symptoms is also dynamic. Even healthy people with no particular predisposition to psychosis may experience brief visual or auditory illusions owing to exceptionally stressful conditions such as an extreme lack of sleep. Alternatively, a relatively minor source of stress may produce noticeably persistent or intense symptoms in someone who is unusually vulnerable to psychotic illness to begin with. In the context of psychoeducation, the dynamic tension between vulnerability and stress can be used to explain the risk of relapse after recovery from acute symptoms. It is helpful to emphasize that just because one has a chronic vulnerability to psychosis, the psychotic symptoms themselves will not necessarily be chronic. It is also often useful to describe the various disorders that may be associated with psychotic illness and to explain that a significant diagnostic uncertainty can exist when an individual first experiences psychotic symptoms. This diagnostic uncertainty is often greater with children than with adults because a child may find it difficult to describe symptoms or because the symptoms may be less elaborate and less obvious than in adults.

During the second phase of psychoeducation, patients and their families should be educated about their medications and the vital role they have in optimizing their own pharmacologic treatment. In addition to standard information about medications' indications and potential side effects, they should also be told that while antipsychotics act to help the brain function better over the long term, they are often not immediately effective. Rather, it is likely to take weeks to months for the antipsychotic to reduce the patient's symptoms to a significant degree. Over subsequent months to years, symptoms are likely to improve further. The analogy of anticonvulsant treatment for a seizure disorder—in the shorter term the anticonvulsant acts to stop the seizures and in the longer term to prevent further seizures—can often be useful. In addition, both patients and their families should be told that even though the medication may cause side effects, these can generally be controlled by changing the timing and/or the dose of medication, by prescribing adjunct medications, or by switching to a different antipsychotic. Patients and their families should also be strongly encouraged to play an active role in managing the patient's medications by informing their doctor about both the beneficial and adverse effects of the medication they experience. It is often helpful to have a non-physician therapist demonstrate or role-play such conversations.

The third phase of psychoeducation focuses on preventing relapse. In this phase, protective factors such as continuing to take medication, getting adequate rest and nutrition, and pursuing healthy relationships are identified, as are factors that instead increase the risk of psychotic symptoms recurring, such as stopping medication or therapy, drug or alcohol use, or traumatic events (see Figure 12.2). Likewise, it is essential that the patient be aware of factors that will make it more or less likely he or she will continue with treatment (see Figure 12.3).

Ideally, psychoeducation will be pursued throughout the course of a patient's illness, with the sophistication of the material presented varying in accordance with the patient's developmental status and current level of functioning, as well as his or her understanding of the illness and its symptoms and ability to tolerate discussions of the future. Similar education must also be provided to the child's parents, siblings, and teachers so that they can better understand what the child or adolescent suffering from psychosis is experiencing. Such education will also allow family members to aid the patient by continuing to emphasize the vulnerability-stress model of the illness outside of the therapeutic setting.

Cognitive Behavioral Therapies

The literature on adult-onset schizophrenia outlines several different cognitive behavioral therapies, each with a slightly different focus. These include

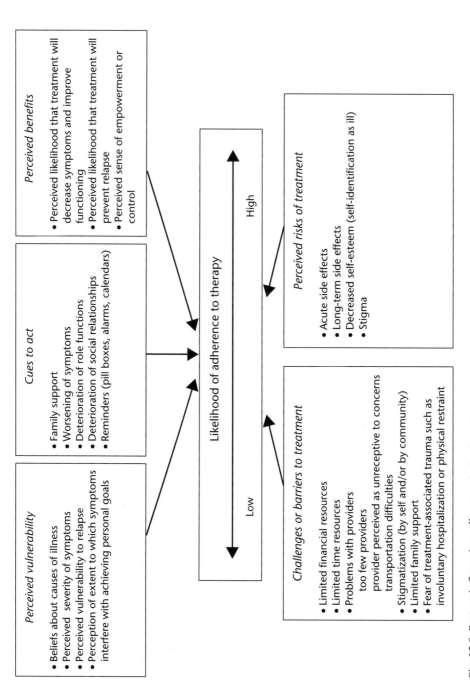

Fig. 12.3. Factors influencing adherence to treatment

the Adherence Coping Education (ACE) therapy developed by Perkins and colleagues (2000), strategies for dealing with persistent positive and negative symptoms, social skills training, and cognitive skills training. Each of these approaches typically begins with the patient's recognizing distressing situations or experiences, followed by the patient's learning specific skills to reduce his or her reaction to the distressing experiences. The patient first practices these skills in a concrete, emotionally neutral situation, then uses the skills with the therapist in hypothetical situations designed to be increasingly relevant to the patient's life, and finally applies the skills in concrete life situations. Skills range from fairly basic measures such as making eye contact or taking deep breaths, to self-talk strategies, to more complex tasks involving problem solving or the questioning of delusions. Although the various cognitive behavioral therapies are often regarded as independent, they can and should be melded so as to address the patient's current needs, as well as his or her long-term goals. Regardless of the specific approach, however, therapy typically progresses from an initial focus on symptom awareness and medication management, to the acquisition of basic skills, and then to social problem solving and methods of coping with ongoing symptoms. Cognitive enhancement strategies (e.g., using mnemonics) are typically introduced in later stages of treatment.

Adapting these strategies in work with children demands that a therapist be alert to the cognitive and language levels at which the children are operating and the developmental tasks they are facing. For instance, children functioning below the level of a typical 11-year-old are likely to require very simple specific instructions and to rely on relatively concrete skills such as self-talk. Self-talk scripts should be kept short and simple. Further, younger children will benefit from ongoing assistance in the use of these techniques from other adults, such as parents and teachers, who are close to them. Adolescents are generally able to use and benefit from the full range of cognitive behavioral techniques, including thought monitoring and alternative explanations and attributions (Dush, Hirt, and Schroeder 1989). In therapy with younger children, greater emphasis is placed on regulating situational influences. As children develop, the focus of therapy shifts from less stressful environments to efforts to increase patients' abilities to respond flexibly to challenging situations. Children and adolescents are usually more responsive to modeling techniques, such as role-playing, reinforcing, and mirroring, than to a trial-and-error approach. Bandura (1977) found that children are especially receptive to videotapes that depict a child of about the same age who is competent but not highly skilled at the approach being taught. After a session of modeling, the therapist should explicitly discuss the component skills and strategies that were used. In the case of younger children, it could also be helpful to provide some general rules for dealing with specific situations.

Adherence Coping Education

The goal of ACE therapy is to reduce the extremely high levels of medication noncompliance observed in individuals recovering from their first episode of schizophrenia (Perkins et al. 2000). Indeed, prior to the introduction of atypical antipsychotics, 75 percent of those hospitalized with a first schizophrenic break stopped taking their medications within one year (Kissling 1992). Similar discontinuation rates have been observed among young adults whose schizophrenic symptoms were treated with atypical agents, despite the fact that these newer drugs produce fewer side effects (Ratakonda et al. 1997). These findings are particularly important because the majority of individuals whose symptoms remit will relapse within two years of stopping their antipsychotics (Gitlin et al. 2001). ACE therapy is based on the health belief model, which posits that patients choose to adhere or not to adhere to recommended treatments based on their beliefs about the seriousness of their illness and the risks associated with it, about the benefits of treatment, and about the costs associated with treatment. This model further emphasizes the sensitivity of these beliefs to a patient's level of education, the severity of his or her symptoms, and the medications at issue. Among the techniques used in ACE therapy are reflective listening, motivational interviewing, inductive questioning, summarizing, reframing, normalizing, and selective validation. Written materials, including symptom rating sheets and videos that help the patient structure their ongoing therapeutic work, are often helpful, as are materials that facilitate adherence to medication, such as calendars, pill boxes, and alarm clocks. A pivotal element in early sessions is the identification of the participant's short- and long-term goals, after which coping strategies and problem-solving skills are taught that will help patients meet the specific goals they have identified. In the treatment of children and adolescents, similar strategies should be utilized to help the patient's parents recognize their own beliefs about their child's illness and treatment and to develop more objective ways to assess the benefits and drawbacks of treatment. This is critical since parents play a key role in ensuring that their children receive the suggested treatments.

Cognitive Behavioral Techniques for Persistent Symptoms

Cognitive behavioral therapy should target symptoms that are selected by the patient on the basis of the distress these symptoms cause or the patient's reactions to the symptoms. Patients often find it easier to address hallucinations first, then delusions, and finally negative symptoms. The therapy begins by normalizing the patient's psychotic experiences by pointing out that many people experience auditory or visual illusions. Then, patients should be assisted in recognizing their hallucinations as different from perceptions of real phenomena. If patients have a hard time identifying perceptions as hallucinations, narrowing the focus to perceptions that elicit particularly strong emotions can be of considerable benefit. The child should be taught to monitor the intensity and characteristics of psychotic phenomena as well as the situations in which they occur. The therapist and the child can then discuss possible ways to determine whether a particular phenomenon was real. For instance, patients could be encouraged to ask themselves whether other people acted as if they had seen or heard the same thing. Once the patient recognizes that the perception was not accurate, he or she can be taught to use scripted self-talk as a means of challenging the perception. Examples of scripts for both normalizing and challenging self-talk are provided in Table 12.3. It is important that patients have alternative explanations available before challenging delusions. Further, if they are to be accepted, these explanations need to be more acceptable and useful to the child than the content of the delusions (Nelson 1997). Particularly in the early stages of treatment, patients often prefer to believe persecutory explanations than to accept the fact that they have a serious, probably chronic, brain illness. The latter explanation becomes less threatening as the patients gradually come to accept that such disorders are not entirely uncommon and develop confidence that the illness can be treated and that they can choose how to respond to the manifestations of the illness.

Also, children can be taught various coping strategies as another way of dealing with the symptoms. Such strategies include relaxation and distraction techniques listed in Table 12.4. Above all, however, the therapist should underscore the fact that having such experiences does not make the child weird or "bad" and that the existence of the symptoms matters less than how he or she reacts to them.

Table 12.3. Examples of positive self-talk

Detective questions to use when feeling scared or angry

Do other people act as if they hear, see, or feel what I am hearing, seeing, or feeling?

Is there any reason this person would try to hurt me?

If this person is really mad at me or trying to hurt me, why would they try to help me in this other way?

Challenging statements

Thinking something is true doesn't always mean it is true.

Just because something seems obvious and true doesn't necessarily mean it is true.

Being certain inside that something is true is not a guarantee that it is true.

Things don't happen just because I imagine them.

Imagining things doesn't make them any more likely to happen.

Normalizing statements

Anyone can have an odd experience if his or her brain is not working well.

People's brains often misinterpret things and give them the wrong information.

People's brains can cause them to have very strange experiences that can be completely wrong or impossible but seem completely real at the time.

I am not weird or peculiar because I hear voices. It is just an extreme of what happens to lots of people.

Believing something to be true that isn't actually true is very common and not weird or peculiar.

We all have some beliefs that do not accurately reflect reality. We are not aware of their inaccuracy when we believe them.

We can imagine things that are impossible in the "real" world.

Everyone's brain produces lots of automatic thoughts, both pleasant and unpleasant, both sensible and silly. No one can control these automatic thoughts.

Self-affirming statements

I am not weird or peculiar or crazy if I hear voices.

Hearing voices, seeing things, or having odd ideas matters only if I act in a dangerous way or if they bother me.

I should not feel guilty or ashamed of what my voices say.

I am a good person even if I have mean or bad automatic thoughts.

I am a good person even if my voices say bad things.

I should not feel guilty or ashamed of my automatic thoughts.

I should not feel guilty or ashamed of the ideas that go through my head or the beliefs that develop from them.

It is OK to realize I was wrong about a particular belief and change it.

Strategies for dealing with negative symptoms are less well developed than those for dealing with positive symptoms. Typically, patients are encouraged to examine past activities that were pleasurable or satisfying, along with the challenges associated with those activities, following which problem-solving

Table 12.4. Strategies for coping with persistent symptoms

Relaxation strategies	Distraction strategies
Take deep breaths	Listen to music
Visualization	Do your favorite hobby
Progressive muscle relaxation	Hum or sing
Rapid cued relaxation	Talk with friends
Self-hypnosis	Watch a movie
Medication	Read
	Watch television
	Exercise
	Take a nap
	Write a letter

strategies can be used to develop a plan for addressing the challenges. Patients can then be asked to monitor the activities that they enjoy or that give them a sense of mastery. A paced activity schedule might subsequently be employed (Sensky et al. 2000). For example, an adolescent patient could be expected to undertake one brief social interaction between appointments and report back on the positive and negative features of the interaction, paying special attention to identifying automatic thoughts that could create difficulties for the patient. The patient can then develop a plan aimed at overcoming some of the negative features during a similar interaction the following week. The frequency and intensity of such interactions can gradually be increased. For instance, the adolescent patient might begin with leaving his or her room to be with other family members for fifteen minutes and go on eventually to participate in a community function such as a school dance.

When cognitive behavioral therapy is employed to address psychotic symptoms, both the patient and the therapist must have realistic goals (Nelson 1997). Improvements are likely to occur slowly and on a small scale, and progress is apt to be erratic. It is helpful to bear in mind that patients are likely to benefit from the therapeutic relationship and from the therapist's conviction that they will ultimately be able to gain some control over the psychotic symptoms and their reaction to them.

Social Skills Training

The value of social skills training in adults with schizophrenia has been given its most rigorous assessment to date by Marder and colleagues (1996).

Interestingly, they found that individuals whose psychotic symptoms set in before the age of 24 were much more responsive to social skills training than those whose symptoms began after that age (p = .0007). This suggests that social skills training may be especially helpful in treating younger patients who suffer from psychotic disorders. Social skills training has also been evaluated extensively in children with nonpsychotic behavioral problems (Beelman, Pfingset, and Lösel 1994). For the most part, the benefits of social skills training programs appear to generalize to her settings if both behavioral and cognitive strategies are employed as part of the program.

In social skills training, the therapist typically begins by discussing the way specific behavioral characteristics such as eye contact, facial expression, posture, tone of speech, and speech volume influence how we respond to social situations. The youths are encouraged to examine how they feel when confronted with one or another of these modes of expression and at the same time to become more aware of how they behave. The therapist can also choose a specific social behavior and then have the patients practice prosocial forms of that behavior. In addition, the child can be taught how to use basic relaxation techniques such as imagery, rapid cued relaxation, progressive muscle relaxation, meditation, and self-hypnosis as a way of fostering successful social interactions. Providing the child with an audiotape that gives step-by-step instructions for use in specific social situations can be a helpful approach as well, especially at the outset of the training.

As patients master these fundamental skills, the therapist shifts the focus to increasing the accuracy of the patients' social perceptions, often by asking what they think other people feel when they act in specified ways. The next step is to begin to apply these various skills to complex social situations. Initially, these social situations are hypothetical, centering at first on relatively simple matters such as how to join a conversation, how to request help, or how to deal with teasing. The therapy can then progress to situations involving specific problems confronting the patient, such as how to respond when people ask why he or she is in a special class. The situation is modeled, the rules, expectations, and aims of the situation are discussed, and alternative ways of behaving are explored. The child is taught to understand that negative feelings, the breaking of social rules, and/or the failure to arrive at the goal of the social interaction all signal a social problem.

In the case of younger children, this process can be called the "social detective game" (Spence 1995). The game has three steps. Step 1 is to *detect,* that is, to stop and identify the problem. Step 2 is to *investigate*—to relax, identify any negative thoughts or feelings, to consider what actions could be taken and what would be likely to happen when each case of the possible actions was taken, and finally to evaluate which option is likely to produce the best result. Step 3 is to *solve*—to make a plan, carry out the plan, evaluate the outcome, and then remember the process. Finally, the therapist and the child work together to determine whether there are other options that might be more effective in the future.

Cognitive Skills Training

The term *cognitive skills training* is used to describe both highly focused interventions that seek to remediate the specific cognitive limitations (for example, in attention or in working memory) that are observed in schizophrenia and more general methods of treatment aimed at helping the patient develop strategies for addressing commonly encountered problems. The more focused programs are currently evolving in work with adults but have not yet been applied to the pediatric population. These programs typically start with the repetitive practice of a particular skill (often with the aid of computer technology) and then attempt to generalize the skill to other situations (for a review, see Rund and Borg 1999). As an example, Hogarty and Flesher (1999a, 1999b) have developed what they call "cognitive enhancement therapy" (CET), which places cognitive remediation in a more developmental context. In CET, specific neurocognitive skills are viewed as the prerequisites for "gistful" interpretations of social situations, which are in turn the prerequisites for good social cognition. The initial steps of CET are to define patients' cognitive impairments (primarily as impoverished, disorganized, or rigid) and to use motivational interviewing to help them develop short- and long-term social cognitive goals. Then, cognitive skills are enhanced by playing problem-solving or computer games that have no social components. As the patients master the cognitive skills employed in the computer games, the skills are transferred to hypothetical social situations that are similar to situations the patient has targeted as a goal. Finally, the skills are extended to social situations outside the clinic.

More general problem-solving therapy closely resembles the CET approach described above. The basic stages of problem solving, which are enumerated in Table 12.5, are explained and demonstrated to the patient and then explicitly applied to simple exercises such as tic-tac-toe. The skills are subsequently

Table 12.5. Stages of problem solving

1. Clearly identify the problem.
2. Generate possible alternative solutions.
3. Evaluate the possible successes, challenges, and outcome of each option.
4. Choose one option.
5. Implement that choice.
6. Evaluate the outcome.
7. If the outcome was not what was desired, choose another option and repeat steps 5 and 6.
8. Congratulate yourself for a job well done.

Source: Based on Tarrier 1992; and Tarrier et al. 1993.

practiced in role-playing that addresses a number of ordinary social situations as well as situations the individual has identified as particularly apt to cause problems. Finally, the skills are applied more broadly in social activities within the community.

School Interventions

Most children and adolescents spend the majority of their day in school, where they are exposed to a large number of cognitive, behavioral, and social demands. Because these demands act as significant stressors, a child's psychotic symptoms are often most apparent in the school setting. It is therefore extremely important to educate teachers and counselors about specific signs that might indicate that a child is experiencing psychotic symptoms. Included among these signs are inattention, disorganized thinking, unpredictable behavior (such as calling out answers in the absence of a direct question or repeatedly getting out of one's seat), noncompliance, and aggression. It is also essential that educators understand the extent to which a child's cognitive abilities may be affected by psychotic illness. Learning to anticipate concerns about stigmatization is a critical part of psychoeducation of this sort. It is also essential to stress the biological basis of the disorder and to explain that although it may be many months before improvement is apparent, there is every reason to be hopeful about the future. In presenting the vulnerability-stress model of symptoms and relapse to education professionals, one should underscore the fact that they may have a unique opportunity to detect the initial signs of a relapse.

Modifications of the child's curriculum and development of an individualized education plan are usually necessary. A child or adolescent suffering from acute psychosis is unlikely to be able to attend regular school for a full day, and so arrangements for homebound services, computer-based teaching, or part-day programs may be necessary. If the child does continue to attend school, he or she should, if possible, be placed in smaller classes. In addition, instructors should use written materials as much as possible as a way of augmenting or reinforcing verbal communication and of organizing the information presented and assignments due. As the child's psychotic symptoms remit, he or she should increasingly participate in school activities. Although there is a tendency to give priority to restarting core classes such as math and language, these may actually prove the most challenging for youth with psychosis. It is generally preferable to have children participate in the classes and activities that they feel are the least threatening and in which they are most likely to experience success. When children have significant negative symptoms, it is often important to facilitate social interactions with peers. This might mean that an adolescent who was not yet ready to participate in an ordinary math class would be encouraged to participate instead in an afterschool activity such as track or photography. Teachers should also be reminded to pay attention to the content of various curriculum materials. For instance, it is inappropriate for a psychotic child to read Kafka's *Metamorphosis* or a persistently suicidal child to read *Romeo and Juliet*. Finally, both clinicians and educators must remain mindful that the ultimate goal is to have the children successfully resume and complete the development tasks they face.

Conclusions

Psychotic illnesses affect all aspects of a child's life. Although psychopharmacological interventions are a mainstay of treatment, it is essential that youths experiencing psychotic symptoms receive comprehensive treatment that includes psychotherapeutic and educational interventions. Despite this critical need, very little specific information is available to guide such work. The suggestions presented above have been based on clinical experience, behavioral work undertaken in connection with other childhood disorders, and behavioral strategies successfully used with psychotic adults. Taken together, these resources suggest a series of interventions that will vary over the course of the affected person's illness. Simplified psychoeducation and steps to reduce environmental stresses, particularly those at school, play a key role during the initial stages of the illness. As the illness begins to respond to treatment, more complex psychoeducation and cognitive behavioral strategies can be introduced to enhance the patient's ability to cope with persistent symptoms and to understand how important it is to adhere to recommended treatments. Throughout this process, motivational interviewing, supportive therapy, and a gradual resumption of normal educational and developmental activities will help the these young patients set attainable goals and maintain a positive outlook on the future.

ACKNOWLEDGMENTS

I am grateful to Drs. David Penn and Diana Perkins and to Kate Kennedy for their helpful comments on the manuscript, as well as to Stephani Brown for her tireless assistance.

REFERENCES

Amador, X. F. (2002). Public awareness and personal insights into psychotic disorders: Patient and family perspectives. Paper presented at the conference "Treatment of Psychotic Disorders: What Is the State of the Art?" New York.

American Academy of Child and Adolescent Psychiatry. (2001). Practice parameter for the assessment and treatment of children and adolescents with schizophrenia. *Journal of the American Academy of Child and Adolescent Psychiatry* 40(7, Suppl.):4S–23S.

Bandura, A. (1977). *Social learning theory.* London: Prentice-Hall.

Beelmann, A., Pfingsten, U., and Lösel, F. (1994). Effects of training social competence in children: A meta-analysis of recent evaluation studies. *Journal of Clinical Child Psychology* 23:260–71.

Bradshaw, W. (2000). Integrating cognitive-behavioral psychotherapy for persons with schizophrenia into a psychiatric rehabilitation program: Results of a three-year trial. *Community Mental Health Journal* 36(5):491–500.

Brenner, H. D., and Pfammatter, M. (2000). Psychological therapy in schizophrenia: What is the evidence? *Acta Psychiatrica Scandinavica* 102(Suppl. 407):74–77.

Bustillo, J., Lauriello, J., Horan, W., and Keith, S. (2001). The psychosocial treatment of schizophrenia: An update. *American Journal of Psychiatry* 158(2):163–75.

Dickerson, F. B. (2000). Cognitive behavioral psychotherapy for schizophrenia: A review of recent empirical studies. *Schizophrenia Research* 43(2–3):71–90.

Drury, V., Birchwood, M., Cochrane, R., and MacMillan, F. (1996a). Cognitive therapy and recovery from acute psychosis: A controlled trial. I. Impact on psychotic symptoms. *British Journal of Psychiatry* 169:593–601.

Drury, V., Birchwood, M., Cochrane, R., and MacMillan, F. (1996b). Cognitive therapy and recovery from acute psychosis: A controlled trial. II. Impact on recovery time. *British Journal of Psychiatry* 169:602–7.

Drury, V., Birchwood, M., and Cochrane, R. (2000). Cognitive therapy and recovery from acute psychosis: A controlled trial, 3: Five-year follow-up. *British Journal of Psychiatry* 177:8–14.

Dush, D. M., Hirt, M. L., and Schroeder, H. E. (1989). Self-statement modification in the treatment of child behavior disorders: A meta-analysis. *Psychological Bulletin* 106:97–106.

Fenton, W. S. (2000). Evolving perspectives on individual psychotherapy for schizophrenia. *Schizophrenia Bulletin* 26(1):47–72.

Garety, P. A., Kuipers, L., Fowler, D., Charmberlain, F., and Dunn, G. (1994). Cognitive behavioral therapy for drug-resistant psychosis. *British Journal of Medical Psychology* 67:259–71.

Gitlin, M., Nuechterlein, K., Subotnik, K. L., Ventura, J., Mintz, J., Fogelson, et al. (2001). Clinical outcome following neuroleptic discontinuation in patients with remitted recent-onset schizophrenia. *American Journal of Psychiatry* 158(11):1835–42.

Gould, R. A., Mueser, K. T., Bolton, E., Mays, V., and Goff, D. (2001). Cognitive therapy for psychosis in schizophrenia: An effect size analysis. *Schizophrenia Research* 48(2–3):335–42.

Gunderson, J. G., Frank, A. F., Katz, H. M., Vannicelli, M. L., Frosch, J. P., and Knapp, P. H. (1984). Effects of psychotherapy in schizophrenia: II. Comparative outcome of two forms of treatment. *Schizophrenia Bulletin* 10(4):564–98.

Hogarty, G. E., Anderson, C. M., Reiss, D. J., Kornblith, S. J., Greenwald, D. P., Javna, C. D., et al. (1986). Family psychoeducation, social skills training, and maintenance chemotherapy in the aftercare treatment of schizophrenia. I. One-year effects of a controlled study on relapse and expressed emotion. *Archives of General Psychiatry* 93(7):633–42.

Hogarty, G. E., and Flesher, S. (1999a). Developmental theory for a cognitive enhancement therapy of schizophrenia. *Schizophrenia Bulletin* 25(4):677–92.

Hogarty, G. E., and Flesher, S. (1999b). Practice principles of cognitive enhancement therapy for schizophrenia. *Schizophrenia Bulletin* 25(4):693–708.

Hogarty, G. E., Greenwald, D., Ulrich, R. F., Kornblith, S. J., DiBarry, A. L., Cooley, S., et al. (1997). Three-year trials of personal therapy among schizophrenic patients living with or independent of family, Pt. 2: Effects on adjustment of patients. *American Journal of Psychiatry* 154(11):1514–24.

Hogarty, G. E., Kornblith, S. J., Greenwald, D., DiBarry, A. L., Cooley, S., Ulrich, R. F., et al. (1997). Three-year trials of personal therapy among schizophrenic patients living with or independent of family, I: Description of study and effects on relapse rates. *American Journal of Psychiatry* 154(11):1504–13.

Jenner, J. A., and van de Willige, G. (2001). HIT hallucination focused integrative treatment as early intervention in psychotic adolescents with auditory hallucinations: A pilot study. *Acta Psychiatrica Scandinavica* 103(2):148–52.

Kissling, W. (1992). Ideal and reality of neuroleptic relapse prevention. *British Journal of Psychiatry* 161:1333–39.

Kuipers, E., Fowler, D., Garety, P., Chrisholm, D., Freeman, D., Dunn, G., et al. (1998). London–East Anglia randomized controlled trial of cognitive-behavioural therapy for psychosis, III: Follow-up and economic revaluation at 18 months. *British Journal of Psychiatry* 173:61–68.

Kuipers, E., Garety, P., Fowler, D., Dunn, G., Bebbington, P., Freeman, D., et al. (1997). London–East Anglia randomized controlled trial of cognitive-behavioural therapy for psychosis, I: Effects of the treatment phase. *British Journal of Psychiatry* 171:319–27.

Kurtz, M. M., Moberg, P. J., Mozley, L. H., Swanson, C. L., Gur, R. C., and Gur, R. E. (2001). Effectiveness of an attention- and memory-training program on neuropsychological deficits in schizophrenia. *Neurorehabilitation and Neural Repair* 15(1):75–80.

Linszen, D., Lenior M., de Haan, L., Dingemans, P., and Gersons, B. (1998). Early intervention, untreated psychosis and the course of early schizophrenia. *British Journal of Psychiatry* 172(Suppl. 33):84–89.

Marder, S. R., Wirshing, W. C., Mintz, J., McKenzie, J., Johnston, K., Eckman, T. A., et al. (1996). Two-year outcome of social skills training and group psychotherapy for outpatients with schizophrenia. *American Journal of Psychiatry* 153(12):1585–92.

McGorry, P. D. (1995). Psychoeducation in first-episode psychosis: A therapeutic process. *Psychiatry* 58(4):313–28.

McGorry, P. D., Chanen, A., McCarthy, E., van Riel, R., McKenzie, D., and Singh, B. S. (1991). Posttraumatic stress disorder following recent-onset psychosis: An unrecognized postpsychotic syndrome. *Journal of Nervous and Mental Disease* 179:253–58.

Milton, F., Patwa, V. K., and Häfner, R. J. (1978). Confrontation vs. belief modification in persistently deluded patients. *British Journal of Medical Psychology* 51(2):127–30.

Mojtabai, R., Nicholson, R. A., and Carpenter, B. N. (1998). Role of psychosocial treatments in management of schizophrenia: A meta-analytic review of controlled outcome studies. *Schizophrenia Bulletin* 24(4):569–87.

Nelson, H. E. (1997). *Cognitive behavioural therapy with schizophrenia: A practice manual.* Cheltenham, Eng.: Stanley Thornes.

Penn, D. L., and Mueser, K. T. (1996). Research update on the psychosocial treatment of schizophrenia. *American Journal of Psychiatry* 153(5):607–17.

Perkins, D. O., Leserman, J., Jarskog, L. F., Graham, K., Kazmer, J., and Lieberman, J. A. (2000). Characterizing and dating the onset of symptoms in psychotic illness: The symptom onset in schizophrenia (SOS) inventory. *Schizophrenia Research* 44(1):1–10.

Pinto, A., La Pia, S., Mennella, R., Giorgio, D., and DeSimone, L. (1999). Cognitive-behavioral therapy and clozapine for clients with treatment-refractory schizophrenia. *Psychiatry Services* 50(7):901–4.

Ratakonda, S., Miller, C. E., Gorman, J. M., and Sharif, Z. A. (1997). Efficacy of a 12-week trial of olanzapine in treatment refractory schizophrenia or schizoaffective disorder. *Schizophrenia Bulletin* 29:151.

Rund, B. R., and Borg, N. E. (1999). Cognitive deficits and cognitive training in schizophrenic patients: A review. *Acta Psychiatrica Scandinavica* 100(2):85–95.

Rund, B. R., Moe, L., Sollien, T., Fjell, A., Borchgrevink, T., Hallert, M., and Naesss, P. O. (1994). The Psychosis Project: Outcome and cost-effectiveness of a psychoeducational treatment programme for schizophrenic adolescents. *Acta Psychiatrica Scandinavica* 89(3):211–18.

Sensky, T., Turkington, D., Kingdon, D., Scott, J. L., Scott, J., Siddle, R., et al. (2000). A randomized controlled trial of cognitive-behavioral therapy for persistent symptoms in schizophrenia resistant to medication. *Archives of General Psychiatry* 57(2):165–72.

Sjostrom, R. (1985). Effects of psychotherapy in schizophrenia: A retrospective study. *Acta Psychiatrica Scandinavica* 71(5):513–22.

Spence, S. H. (1995). Social skills training: Enhancing social competence with children and adolescents. London: nfer-Nelson.

Strauss, J. S., Hafez, H., Lieberman, P., and Harding, C. M. (1985). The course of psychiatric disorder, III: Longitudinal principles. *American Journal of Psychiatry* 142(3):289–96.

Tarrier, N. (1992). Management and modification of residual psychotic symptoms. In M. Birchwood and N. Tarrier (Eds.), *Innovations in the psychological management of schizophrenia*. Chichester: Wiley.

Tarrier, N., Beckett, R., Harwood, S., Baker A., Yusupoff, L., and Ugarteburu, I. (1993). A trial of two cognitive-behavioural methods of treating drug-resistant residual psychotic symptoms in schizophrenic patients: I. Outcome. *British Journal of Psychiatry* 162:524–32.

Tarrier, N., Kinney, C., McCarthy, E., Humphreys, L., Wittkowski, A., and Morris, J. (2000). Two-year follow-up of cognitive-behavioral therapy and supportive counseling in the treatment of persistent symptoms in chronic schizophrenia. *Journal of Consulting and Clinical Psychology* 68(5):917–22.

Tarrier, N., Wittkowski, A., Kinney, C., McCarthy, E., Morris, J. L., and Humphreys, L. (1999). Durability of effects of cognitive-behavioural therapy in the treatment of chronic schizophrenia: 12-month follow-up. *British Journal of Psychiatry* 174:500–504.

Tarrier, N., Yusupoff, L., Kinney, C., McCarthy, E., Gledhill, A., Haddock, G., et al. (1998). Randomised controlled trial of intensive cognitive behaviour therapy for patients with chronic schizophrenia. *British Medical Journal* 317(7154):303–7.

Turkington, D., and Kingdon, D. (2000). Cognitive-behavioural techniques for general psychiatrists in the management of patients with psychoses. *British Journal of Psychiatry* 177:101–4.

Turkington, D., Kingdon, D., Turner, T., and the Insight into Schizophrenia Research Group. (2002). Effectiveness of a brief cognitive-behavioural therapy intervention in the treatment of schizophrenia. *British Journal of Psychiatry* 180:523–27.

Williams-Keeler, L., Milliken, H., and Jones, B. (1994). Psychosis as precipitating trauma for PTSD: A treatment strategy. *American Journal of Orthopsychiatry* 64(3):493–98.

CHAPTER THIRTEEN

Family and Group Psychosocial Interventions for Child- and Adolescent-Onset Schizophrenia

James M. Harle, M.D., and
Jon M. McClellan, M.D.

Schizophrenia is an often debilitating neurodevelopmental disorder that generally appears during adolescence or early adulthood. The prevalence of schizophrenia is estimated at 1 percent of the population as a whole, with the peak ages of onset between 15 and 30 years (American Psychiatric Association 1997). An onset before the age of 18, defined as early-onset schizophrenia (EOS), is thus not uncommon, but cases with a very early onset—before the age of 13—are rare. Because of the frequency and chronic nature of the disorder, schizophrenia with onset in young adulthood is currently one of the most serious and challenging illnesses from the standpoint of public health and policy. There remains a great need for the development and implementation of effective methods of treating this condition.

Psychopharmacology is the primary mode of treatment for schizophrenia. However, although medications have the potential to be life saving, the current pharmacopoeia has a number of shortcomings. As yet, antipsychotic medications treat the symptoms rather than the underlying disorder. Although the atypical agents offer advantages over the traditional neuroleptics, the efficacy of antipsychotics with regard to negative symptoms and overall social functioning leaves ample room for clinical improvement (Bustillo et al. 2001). Adherence to recommended medications remains a major issue, with an estimated 40 percent of adult patients becoming noncompliant during the first year following their discharge from hospital and another 15 percent in the succeeding years (Hogarty 1984; Sarti and Cournos 1990). Although formal studies have not yet been completed, clinical experience suggests that noncompliance is also a major problem among juveniles (American Academy of Child and Adolescent Psychiatry 2001).

Therefore, other intervention strategies are needed to augment the effectiveness of pharmacotherapy, with the goals of further reducing morbidity, decreasing functional impairment, and promoting compliance. Psychosocial interventions are important tools for symptom reduction and for enhancing the patient's overall quality of life. These have taken various forms, most notably family therapy and group-based social skills training. In the discussion to follow, we will review the literature that specifically concerns family and group psychosocial interventions for adult- and early-onset schizophrenia, summarize the current status of the field, and propose ideal psychosocial interventions for early-onset schizophrenia.

Literature Review

The stress-vulnerability model of schizophrenia has been the starting point for the majority of the research literature on psychosocial interventions. This model posits that stressful life events and situations interact with a genetic vulnerability to psychosis to produce exacerbations of the illness, whether as an acute episode or a chronic condition (Falloon et al. 1990). Research has identified two factors that are associated with a relapse into schizophrenia: life events (Birley and Brown 1970; Leff et al. 1973; Leff and Vaughn 1980) and household tension (Brown, Birley, and Wing 1972; Vaughn and Leff 1976; Vaughn et al. 1984). Households in which tension is minimal appear to protect patients against relapse provided they maintain a high degree of contact with the family (Falloon 1986).

The level of expressed emotion, as measured by the Camberwell Family Interview (Vaughn and Leff 1976), is an indication of how relatives spontaneously speak about a patient. High levels of expressed emotion reflect negative and/or hostile attitudes and beliefs, coupled with emotional overinvolvement, and are associated with a tendency toward relapse (Brown et al. 1962; Brown,

Birley, and Wing 1972; Vaughn and Leff 1981; Butzlaff and Hooley 1998). Butzlaff and Hooley (1998) convincingly demonstrated that patients with schizophrenic whose families are characterized by a high degree of expressed emotion relapse more often and that relapse rates usually decrease when the level of expressed emotion declines. Interestingly, the relationship between expressed emotion and relapse was most notable among more chronic patient populations. The influence of expressed emotion specifically in EOS has not yet been sufficiently studied. Communication deficits have, however, been observed in families of children with very early-onset schizophrenia (Asarnow, Goldstein, and Ben-Meir 1988). These likely represent heritable traits rather than responses to the illness. Nevertheless, they are potential targets for intervention.

Family Interventions

In the literature on psychosocial interventions for schizophrenia in adults, family therapy has received the most attention and has proved to have the greatest effect on outcomes (Huxley, Rendall, and Sederer 2000). However, since participation in these studies required family involvement, the findings may not generalize to patients who lack adequate family support. Overall, family therapy has been shown to decrease the likelihood of psychotic relapse, reduce the number of hospitalizations, ameliorate symptoms, and improve social and vocational functioning and adherence to treatment (Huxley, Rendall, and Sederer 2000). Improvements have also been reported in relation to the burden of care in the family, the ability of family members to cope with the effects of the disorder, and the family's knowledge and understanding of schizophrenia as an illness (Falloon et al. 1987; Barrowclough and Tarrier 1992; Zhang et al. 1993; McFarlane et al. 1996). Such improvements appear to constitute distinct advantages over and above the lower rates of relapse (Hogarty et al. 1997; Schooler et al. 1997).

To date, there is only one published study that examines the impact of family interventions in cases of early-onset schizophrenia. Rund and colleagues (1994) analyzed the effectiveness of an experimental treatment model that combines problem-solving sessions, parent seminars, milieu therapy (during hospitalization), neuroleptic medication, and networks—that is, the involvement, education, and training of school personnel. This approach was compared to "treatment as usual," consisting of neuroleptic medication, individual psychotherapy, and milieu therapy. The experimental treatment was tri-phasic. In the first phase, family treatment sessions occurred biweekly, and one parent seminar was held. Occasionally, problem-solving sessions took place as well. In the second, one or more parent seminars were held, and problem-solving sessions occurred monthly in the home. Regular telephone contact also began in this phase. In the third phase, the same interventions were provided, but family treatment sessions occurred only every other month.

The experimental model of psychosocial intervention was based on the work of Leff et al. (1982) and Falloon (1986). The parent seminars were all-day events, held two or three times a year, that had two main objectives: the provision of knowledge about all aspects of the illness and the reduction of social isolation by bringing together families affected by schizophrenia. The problem-solving sessions (based on the approach of Falloon et al. 1987) were highly structured and emphasized the active involvement of all family members. Networks were not described in any detail but generally referred to case management efforts to identify and coordinate special school, residential, and/or social support services.

Study participants were divided into two groups (each with 12 subjects, age range 13–17 years); one group received the experimental intervention, and the other received treatment as usual. Treatment was provided for two years, with the patients typically hospitalized for at least half the period. Control cases were identified retrospectively, which made the accurate assessment of certain factors, including levels of expressed emotion, difficult. Clinical outcomes during the 2-year period, as measured by relapse rates and global functioning, were better for the experimental group than for the control. However, the rate of relapses requiring hospitalization was high in both groups: 58 percent and 75 percent, respectively, during the time remaining in the 2-year period following discharge. The authors interpreted this high rate of relapse as evidence of the poor prognosis associated with early-onset schizophrenia. Improvement in psychosocial functioning correlated with a change in the family's level of expressed emotion in the experimental group. In contrast, none of the families in the control group showed such a reduction in expressed emotion. Interestingly, they noted that the level of expressed emotion in the families who ultimately experienced a decrease had originally been elevated with respect to the frequency of criticism, as opposed to overinvolvement.

One other study, the Family-Centered Program for Adolescents with Mental Illness, is currently in progress at the University of Washington, in Seattle.

The study is designed to evaluate the use of family-centered community-based self-management interventions in teenagers with schizophrenia. Unfortunately, data regarding the effectiveness of such interventions are not yet available. As one might anticipate, however, preliminary descriptive work demonstrates that families in which a relatively larger number of adults are actively involved with the adolescent are better able to moderate the burden of care (Schepp et al. 2001). These findings underscore the need to both assess and promote family support mechanisms and community alliances.

Group Interventions

Group psychosocial interventions for adults with schizophrenia have incorporated a variety of approaches and theoretical orientations. Models based on social skills training (SST) have been the most thoroughly studied and can be generally grouped into three classes: basic SST, social problem-solving approaches (including the Social and Independent Living Skills program at the University of California, Los Angeles), and cognitive rehabilitation and remediation models. In general, these interventions are behavioral in approach and employ the learning-based techniques of direct instruction, modeling, coaching, rehearsal, and homework. Basic SST has been found effective in improving interpersonal social skills, although the gains do not necessarily generalize to broader areas of social functioning. It has not proved beneficial, however, in decreasing symptoms, reducing rates of relapse, or changing a patient's employment status (Huxley, Rendall, and Sederer 2000).

The approaches based on social problem solving have been shown to produce improvements in the specific skills targeted. Furthermore, they have an advantage over basic SST in that these improvements have generalized to overall improved social functioning (Marder et al. 1996; Schaub et al. 1998; Schaub, Behrendt, and Brenner 1998). Unfortunately, other pertinent clinical factors such as symptomatology, rate of relapse, and quality of life have not been significantly affected (Liberman et al. 1998; Schaub et al. 1998; Schaub, Behrendt, and Brenner 1998).

The use of cognitive rehabilitation as a treatment for schizophrenia was originally spurred by findings suggesting that the neuropsychological profiles of patients with schizophrenia were indistinguishable from those with traumatic brain injuries (Penn 1991; Stuve, Erickson, and Spaulding 1991). These findings led to the supposition that an impairment of underlying cognitive processes contributes significantly to poor psychosocial functioning. Cognitive rehabilitation focuses on information-processing skills, including attention, planning, memory, and conceptual abilities (Penn and Mueser 1996). In general, approaches based on cognitive rehabilitation have not been studied as extensively as basic SST or social problem solving, and the findings have been mixed with regard to their efficacy.

Vocational rehabilitation for patients with schizophrenia has traditionally been provided in group settings, with the emphasis typically on teaching patients employment skills they can put into use before attempting to find a job. These skills are often initially practiced in transitional or sheltered workplaces. However, more recently developed methods, such as the Individualized Placement and Support (IPS) models, do not employ group formats. Rather, IPS focuses on immediately helping a patient find employment. An employment specialist, integrated into the patient's primary mental health team, works to set up and maintain the patient's job placement. In the limited number of trials reported to date, the IPS model has proved to be more successful than traditional vocational rehabilitative approaches in assisting patients to secure competitive employment. However, other desirable outcomes, both vocational (such as long-term retention of employment) and nonvocational (such as improvements to self-esteem and overall quality of life as well as the reduction of symptoms and the likelihood of relapse) have not been realized in the research trials (Bustillo et al. 2001).

Cognitive behavioral therapy has some demonstrated efficacy, primarily in regard to decreases in medication-resistant psychotic symptoms. This therapy has been primarily conducted on an individual basis, although Drury et al. (1996) used a group format for some of their cognitive behavioral work. Given that the emphasis here is on individual rather than group treatment, however, we refer the interested reader to the review of Bustillo et al. (2001).

In their review of the literature on the psychosocial treatment of schizophrenia, Huxley and colleagues (2000) noted that numerous group-based psychosocial approaches with orientations other than those mentioned above have been used with schizophrenic patients. These include psychoanalytic techniques, supportive therapy, discussion groups, and gestalt therapy. Although these approaches have been described in a few research reports, none have been studied as rigorously as SST models. Moreover, while some improvements in symptoms and in social functioning have been observed, none of the above orientations has demonstrated significant promise. Likewise, traditional psychodynamic therapies have generally proved unhelpful in treating schizophrenia (Lehman and Steinwachs 1998).

Treatment Interventions

As we have seen, myriad family and group psychosocial interventions have been studied in relation to the treatment of schizophrenia in adults. Although essentially no literature exists on the use of such interventions with juveniles, many of the important constructs and strategies described in the research on adults should apply to early-onset cases as long as developmental considerations are taken into account. Perhaps unique to the EOS population, however, are issues of autonomy. To be effective, treatment must therefore honor and support the youth's decision-making capacity while also balancing the needs of the entire family and remaining on the lookout for the cognitive impairment that frequently accompanies EOS.

In any psychosocial approach to treatment, the therapist should stand at the center of a comprehensive web of services for the adolescent patient, including individual, family, and group therapy, case management, and liaison with other involved professionals and institutions. Case management services, which are crucial, include the identification of and access to educational and occupational support, housing options, and financial support. Especially early on in the illness, families are often not equipped to help a patient negotiate the demands that must be met in order to obtain such services, and the therapist can best serve the patient and family by assisting with these needs.

Psychosocial interventions for EOS should include both family and group elements as part of an individualized, multifaceted approach. Such an approach has been used successfully with other childhood psychiatric disorders—as, for example, in the multisystemic therapy developed by Heneggler et al. (1998) in their work with juvenile offenders suffering from comorbid mental illness.

Ideally, family interventions should consist of the following elements: family engagement strategies, psychoeducation (conducted in single- and/or multiple-family settings), behavioral elements (including the teaching of problem-solving and communication skills), coping strategies, and crisis intervention skills. The common objectives of family-based treatment are the creation and/or stabilization of family structure and resiliency, reduction in the level of negative and/or hostile expressed emotion, and the support of all family members in both minimizing and managing the burdensome effects of schizophrenia on their life (Diamond and Siqueland 2001). Obviously, the nature and degree of family involvement will depend on multiple considerations, including the age of the affected child, the family configuration and culture, and intrafamily dynamics.

On the basis of the adult literature, we propose the following family- and group-related interventional techniques for use with the EOS population.

Psychoeducation

For both the adolescent patient and his or her family, treatment begins with psychoeducational therapies that focus on the illness itself, including the clarification of diagnostic issues and a discussion of symptomatology, prognosis, and treatment options. The goal is to increase the knowledge base of both the patient and family while also engaging them in a therapeutic alliance aimed at promoting future compliance and effective decision making. Rules and expectations relating to the treatment should also be established and explained. Providing consumer-oriented educational materials and visual aids will enhance the effectiveness of the intervention.

Of special importance is the need to create realistic expectations with regard to the morbidity and prognosis of EOS. When a child develops schizophrenia, there is often a very strong desire on the part of the family to believe that the child will quickly return to premorbid levels of functioning. As the adult literature demonstrates, although educational sessions with the patient's relatives do not always increase their level of knowledge to any significant degree, such sessions do foster optimism and increase the family's engagement with clinicians. In addition, an ongoing review of the fundamental information regarding the illness is needed to reinforce what has already been learned as well as to address future issues as they come up. Ultimately, this educational process should also target anyone else in routine contact with the youth, such as school personnel, peers, employers, and any other institutions (e.g., the juvenile justice system) that might be involved.

Skills Training

Problem-solving skills must be taught to both the EOS patient and the family in anticipation of commonplace difficulties, such as preparation for the patient's return to the home after hospitalization or, instead, his or her transition to living independently or semi-independently in the community. The training curricula should take into consideration developmental levels and illness-related cognitive impairments. Helping the family and child negotiate rules and expectations (including those concerning communication), identifying and helping to resolve specific areas of conflict, and organizing family routine and structures to promote cohesion and reduce conflict are other important areas that such training should address. Falloon's (1986) six-step method is geared toward promoting family empowerment and would likely serve the families of EOS youth well.

Social skills training is another valuable component of comprehensive treatment. Basic principles (Liberman et al. 1998) include problem definition, the identification of assets, the establishment of a reinforcing therapeutic alliance, goal setting, behavioral rehearsal, shaping, prompting, modeling, homework, and the practice of skills in concrete life situations. Commonly targeted areas include vocation, recreation, conversation, social problem solving, and personal grooming. Programs such as the UCLA Social and Independent Living Skills program could be applied to adolescent patients, given appropriate modifications to accord with their level of development.

Communication

Rather than attempting to apply a uniform method of intervention to families overall, treatment strategies seeking to address communication issues should be based on the family's degree of expressed emotion and its communicative style. In other words, the treatment must be individually tailored and administered. This includes allowing families who have a low level of negative and/or hostile expressed emotion, as well as families either unwilling or unable to garner the resources and energy necessary to make use of the intervention, to skip therapy sessions designed to reduce expressed emotion. The timing of the intervention should also be flexible, taking into consideration the phase of the child's illness, the family's readiness, and any additional factors such as proximity to the treatment center, competing time commitments, and costs. If the intervention is not well matched to the family's needs, family members may end up feeling in some way inadequate and may perceive the intervention as artificial and arbitrary. This results in families being more difficult to engage and so might actually interfere with the adjustment process.

Children and adolescents with schizophrenia can also be taught skills to help them tolerate the manifestations of expressed emotion, namely, criticism, hostility, and overinvolvement. Potentially useful group-acquired strategies include self-relaxation techniques, narrative therapy, and the teaching of distress tolerance skills.

Support Networks

Families need to be allowed to express grief, a sense of loss, and feelings of frustration in a forum where they feel safe and supported. Formal support groups for parents and other family members are therefore worthwhile therapeutic resources, not the least because access to other families who are similarly affected by EOS clearly fosters a wider social support network. It is also important to build or strengthen informal social support networks. The impact of the illness, as well as other difficulties that often cluster in relatives of individuals with schizophrenia, often work to isolate families from their communities, and yet both the patient and the family must have the chance to spend time apart with their respective peer groups. Family members should therefore be encouraged to bolster or reconnect to their social network. This can, however, be challenging, given the need for parental supervision of the child or adolescent with schizophrenia.

Such support groups can also work within the community to advocate for additional resources and to guide policymaking. At the same time, the relative rarity of this disorder in juveniles limits the feasibility of creating advocacy programs based solely around this population. Thus, support programs will likely need to be broad based, including families of children afflicted with other disorders as well as putting these families in contact with groups such as the National Alliance for the Mentally Ill.

Cognitive Rehabilitation

The development of a modified version of the cognitive rehabilitation strategies designed for adults (Brenner et al. 1994; Spaulding et al. 1999) may be potentially useful for the EOS population. These strategies could be implemented either as group therapy, or as part of special education curricula and could include concept manipulation (e.g., sorting tasks performed in the group), social information processing (e.g., examining and describing pictures of social situations), and verbal communication (e.g., group members listening to each other, repeating the statements made verbatim, and then paraphrasing the same statements). All activities would demand social interaction and would be performed in the group setting, with the complexity of tasks and the degree of interaction required gradually increasing over time. The therapist and/or group leader would attempt to elicit group feedback and discussion, as opposed to direct corrective feedback, and to clarify unclear statements and encourage all members of the group to participate.

In addition to cognitive rehabilitation therapy, special academic programming and services offer resources to children and adolescents that are generally not available to adults. The individual educational plans of youth with schizophrenia should be designed to address relevant skills training and vocational rehabilitation. Moreover, consultations between therapists and teachers with regard to school programs can greatly enhance both the quality of the school program and the impact of treatment.

Conclusions and Future Directions

Family interventions for schizophrenia that emphasize psychoeducational and behavioral approaches have been extensively studied and have demonstrated their efficacy in reducing the rate of relapse, decreasing the need for hospitalization, ameliorating symptomatology, and improving treatment adherence. Although group psychosocial interventions have not been as thoroughly investigated as family treatments, they have proved beneficial in relation to targeted social skills. In view of the current lack of research concerning psychosocial interventions specifically in connection with children or adolescents, their use must be justified entirely on the basis of the adult literature. All the same, given the continuity between early-onset and adult-onset schizophrenia, the inclusion of family and group strategies in comprehensive treatment plans for youth with EOS is clearly recommended.

Many of the goals of psychosocial interventions can be readily applied to youth with schizophrenia and their families. Strategies to improve communication, facilitate problem solving, and provide appropriate psychoeducational information are standard components of any family intervention. However, there are certain issues that need to be addressed in working with EOS patients. The age and developmental level of these patients can vary a great deal and so demand individualized approaches able to accommodate factors such as the cognitive and social maturity of the child, the role of the parents as both caregivers and disciplinarians, and the patient's involvement with social and community agencies, notably schools. Issues of autonomy and independence will also vary depending on the age of the child, again requiring suitable modifications in treatment strategies and goals. For example, for younger children treatment is likely to focus on maintaining the child in the home, whereas in the case of adolescents families will need help in developing long-range transition plans for independent or assisted living. The successful integration of psychosocial therapies with medication management will further enhance the quality of care, promote compliance, and improve outcomes.

On the whole, then, treatment models that draw on psychoeducational techniques, skills training, and behavioral interventions should work well for the pediatric population. However, existing programs will need to be refined so to address the particular developmental, cognitive, and social needs of youth. Moreover, further research is required in order to evaluate how best to tailor specific interventions to the individual characteristics of the patient and/or the family as well as to determine how psychosocial interventions can be made to work most effectively in concert with pharmacological treatment. Finally, additional efforts will be required to design and incorporate therapeutic models of care into special education programs. It remains clear, however, that psychoeducational and family interventions are a critical component of any comprehensive treatment plan and should be considered one of the standards of care for the child and adolescent population.

REFERENCES

American Academy of Child and Adolescent Psychiatry. (2001). Practice parameter for the assessment and treatment of children and adolescents with schizophrenia. *Journal of the American Academy of Child and Adolescent Psychiatry* 40(7, Suppl.):4S–23S.

American Psychiatric Association. (1997). Practice guideline for the treatment of patients with schizophrenia. *American Journal of Psychiatry* 154(4, Suppl.):S1–S63.

Asarnow, J. R., Goldstein, M. J., and Ben-Meir, S. (1988). Parental communication deviance in childhood-onset schizophrenia spectrum and depressive disorders. *Journal of Child Psychology and Psychiatry* 29(6):825–38.

Barrowclough, C., and Tarrier, N. (1992). *Families of schizophrenic patients: Cognitive behavioral intervention*. London: Chapman & Hall.

Birley, J. L., and Brown, G. W. (1970). Crises and life changes preceding the onset or relapse of acute schizophrenia: Clinical aspects. *British Journal of Psychiatry* 116:327–33.

Brenner, H. D., Roder, V., Hodel, B., Kienzle, N., Reed, D., and Liberman, R. P. (1994). *Integrated psychological therapy for schizophrenic patients*. Toronto: Hogrefe and Huber.

Brown, G. W., Birley, J.L.T., and Wing, J. K. (1972). Influence of family life on the course of schizophrenic disorders: A replication. *British Journal of Psychiatry* 121:241–58.

Brown, G. W., Monck, E. M., Carstairs, G. M., and Wing, J. K. (1962). Influence of family life on the course of schizophrenic illness. *British Journal of Preventive and Social Medicine* 16:55–68.

Bustillo, J. R., Lauriello, J., Horan, W. P., and Keith, S. J. (2001). The psychosocial treatment of schizophrenia: An update. *American Journal of Psychiatry* 158:163–75.

Butzlaff, R. L., and Hooley, J. M. (1998). Expressed emotion and psychiatric relapse: A meta-analysis. *Archives of General Psychiatry* 55:547–52.

Diamond, G., and Siqueland, L. (2001). Current status of family intervention science. *Child and Adolescent Psychiatric Clinics of North America*, 10(3):641–61.

Drury, V., Birchwood, M., Cochrane, R., and Macmillan, F. (1996). Cognitive therapy and recovery from acute psychosis: A controlled trial, Pt. 1: Impact on psychotic symptoms. *British Journal of Psychiatry* 169:593–601.

Falloon, I.R.H. (1986). Family stress and schizophrenia: Theory and practice. *Psychiatric Clinics of North America* 9(1):165–82.

Falloon, I.R.H., Boyd, J. L., McGill, C. W., Williamson, M., Razani, J., Moss, H. B., et al. (1985). Family management in the prevention of morbidity of schizophrenia: Clinical outcome over a two-year longitudinal study. *Archives of General Psychiatry* 42:887–96.

Falloon, I.R.H., McGill., C. W., Boyd, J. L., and Pederson, J. (1987). Family management in the prevention of morbidity of schizophrenia: Social outcome of a two-year longitudinal study. *Psychological Medicine* 17:59–66.

Falloon, I.R.H., Shanahan, W., Laporta, M., and Krekorian, H. A. (1990). Integrated family, general practice, and mental health care in the management of schizophrenia. *Journal of the Royal Society of Medicine* 83(4):225–28.

Henggeler, S. W., Schoenwald, S. K., Borduin, C. M., Rowland, M. D., and Cunningham, P. B. (1998). *Multisystemic treatment of antisocial behavior in children and adolescents.* New York: Guilford Press.

Hogarty, G. E. (1984). Depot neuroleptics: The relevance of psychosocial factors. *Journal of Clinical Psychiatry* 45:36–42.

Hogarty, G. E., Kornblith, S. J., Greenwald, D., DiBarry, A. L., Cooley, S., Ulrich, R. F., et al. (1997). Three-year trials of personal therapy among schizophrenic patients living with or independent of family, Pt. 1: Description of study and effects on relapse rates. *American Journal of Psychiatry* 154:1504–13.

Huxley, N. A., Rendall, M., and Sederer, L. (2000). Psychosocial treatments in schizophrenia: a review of the past 20 years. *Journal of Nervous and Mental Disease* 188(4): 187–201.

Leff, J. P., Hirsch, S. R., Gaind, R., Rhode, P. D., and Stevens, B. C. (1973). Life events and maintenance therapy in schizophrenic relapse. *British Journal of Psychiatry* 123:659–60.

Leff, J., Kuipers, L., Berkowitz, R., Eberleine-Vries, R., and Sturgeon, D. (1982). A controlled trial of social intervention in the families of schizophrenic patients. *British Journal of Psychiatry* 141:121–34.

Leff, J., and Vaughn, C. (1980). The interaction of life events and relatives' expressed emotion in schizophrenia and depressive neurosis. *British Journal of Psychiatry* 136:146–53.

Lehman, A., and Steinwachs, D. (1998). Translating research into practice: The schizophrenia Patient Outcomes Research Team (PORT) treatment recommendations. *Schizophrenia Bulletin* 24:1–10.

Liberman, R. P., Wallace, C. J., Blackwell, G., Kopelowicz, A., Vaccaro, J. V., and Mintz, J. (1998). Skills training versus psychological occupational therapy for persons with persistent schizophrenia. *American Journal of Psychiatry* 155:1087–91.

McFarlane, W. R., Dushay, R. A., Stastny, P., Deakins, S. A., and Link, B. (1996). A comparison of two levels of family-aided assertive community treatment. *Psychiatry Services* 47:744–50.

Marder, S. R., Wirshing, W. C., Mintz, J., McKenzie, J., Johnston, K., Eckman, T. A., et al. (1996). Two-year outcome of social skills training and group psychotherapy for outpatients with schizophrenia. *American Journal of Psychiatry* 153:1585–92.

Penn, D. L. (1991). Cognitive rehabilitation of social deficits in schizophrenia: A direction of promise or following a primrose path? *Psychosocial Rehabilitation Journal* 15:27–41.

Penn, D. L., and Mueser, K. T. (1996). Research update on the psychosocial treatment of schizophrenia. *American Journal of Psychiatry* 153:607–17.

Rund, B. R., Moe, L., Sollien, T., Fjell, A., Borchgrevink, T., Hallert, M., et al. (1994). The psychosis project: Outcome and cost-effectiveness of a psychoeducational treatment programme for schizophrenic adolescents. *Acta Psychiatrica Scandinavica* 89:211–18.

Sarti, P., and Cournos, F. (1990). Medication and psychotherapy in the treatment of chronic schizophrenia. *Psychiatric Clinics of North America* 13:215–28.

Schaub, A., Behrendt, B., and Brenner, H. D. (1998). A multi-hospital evaluation of the medication and symptom management modules in Germany and Switzerland. *International Review of Psychiatry* 10:42–46.

Schaub, A., Behrendt, B., Brenner, H. D., Mueser, K. T., and Liberman, R. P. (1998). Training schizophrenic patients to manage their symptoms: Predictors of treatment response to the German version of the Symptom Management Module. *Schizophrenia Research* 31:121–30.

Schepp, K. G., West, M. G., Tsai, J.H.C., and Kim, H. J. (2001). Use of genograms to illustrate family coping with adolescent mental illness. *Communicating Nursing Research* 34:199.

Schooler, N. R., Keith, S. J., Severe, J. B., Matthews, S. M., Bellack, A. S., Glick, I. D., et al. (1997). Relapse and rehospitalization during maintenance treatment of schizophrenia: The effects of dose reduction and family treatment. *Archives of General Psychiatry* 54:453–63.

Spaulding, W. D., Reed, D., Sullivan, M., Richardson, C., and Weiler, M. (1999). Effects of cognitive treatment in psychiatric rehabilitation. *Schizophrenia Bulletin* 25(4):657–76.

Stuve, P., Erickson, R. C., and Spaulding, W. (1991). Cognitive rehabilitation: The next step in psychiatric rehabilitation. *Psychosocial Rehabilitation Journal* 15:9–26.

Vaughn, C. E., and Leff, J. P. (1976). The influence of family and social factors on the course of psychiatric illness: A comparison of schizophrenic and depressed neurotic patients. *British Journal of Psychiatry* 129:125–37.

Vaughn, C. E., and Leff, J. P. (1981). Patterns of emotional response in relatives of schizophrenic patients. *Schizophrenia Bulletin* 7(1):43–44.

Vaughn, C. E., Snyder, K. S., Freeman, V., Jones, S., and Falloon, I.R.H. (1984). Family factors in schizophrenic relapse. *Archives of General Psychiatry* 41:1169–77.

Zhang, M., Yan, H., Chengde, Y., Jianlin, J., Qingfeng, Y., Peijun, C., et al. (1993). Effectiveness of psychoeducation of relatives of schizophrenic patients: A prospective cohort study in five cities of China. *International Journal of Mental Health* 22:47–59.

Index